WALKING WITH A HIMALAYAN MASTER

WALKING WITH A HIMALAYAN MASTER
AN AMERICAN'S ODYSSEY

JUSTIN O'BRIEN

YES INTERNATIONAL PUBLISHERS
SAINT PAUL, MINNESOTA

Yes International Publishers
1317 Summit Avenue, St. Paul, MN 55105-2602
651-645-6808

Library of Congress Cataloging in Publication Data

O'Brien, Justin.
    Walking with a Himalayan master : an American' odyssey /
Justin O'Brien.
        p.   cm.
    Includes bibliographical references.
    ISBN 0-936663-19-7 (cloth)
    1. O'Brien, Justin .   2. Spiritual biography--United States.
    3. Theologians--United States--Biography. 4. Rama, Swami,
    1925-1996. I. Title.
    BL73.027A3   1998
    291.4'092--dc21   97-30876
    [B]   CIP

Printed 1997, 1998

Printed in the United States of America

CONTENTS

PREFACE

In 1984, as I walked in the Himalayas with my spiritual master, he asked, "Justin, will you do something for me? Will you write a book about our life together?"

Traveling to India after Swami Rama dropped his body, that unsurpassed request dominated my attention. It was time to fulfill my promise to my teacher.

I had been with my teacher for twenty-five years. Delving into the abundant notes, diaries, and photos I had kept during that time, I revisited my odyssey with the most incredible yogi of the twentieth century, and the wisest friend and teacher I have ever known.

I felt drawn to share those years of study and learning under his guidance so that others could realize the magnitude of the teacher-disciple relationship, knowing that the wisdom of the sages is alive and powerful and avilable to all those who sincerely seek it.

While composing this book's chapters my teacher's continuing presence was obvious. One day as I was debating with myself the best way to complete an episode about his teaching, I pushed myself back from my computer to pause. The keys began to move of their own accord, and the words "Be Practical!" appeared forty times in the middle of the paragraph I had just written. I resolved to write as practically as I could.

Two weeks later, after another pause, the Edit word on my computer menu bar flashed repeatedly. I reviewed the last few typed pages and realized that the signal was definitely more than a hint.

Another time I averted my eyes from the computer screen as I vividly reminisced a dialogue scene in which my teacher had addressed me. Glancing back at the screen, I saw my name blinking on and off in the very section that I had just been thinking about.

As Theresa worked late one evening editing a chapter, she began to get tired and wondered if she should end her work for the day or continue through her fatigue. Just then, the ceiling light bulb fell out of its socket, crashed on the ground and left her in darkness. She took the signal and went to bed.

There were many more surprises and delights that let me know I was being given help to carry out my promise to the one who brought me into his own mystical tradition.

While no book can ever contain all the experiences and wisdom of my extraordinary master, I present these pages as a bundle of twigs from the forest of his life and teachings, and offer its fruits to the continued work of the Himalayan sages.

Without the enormous help of my guru brothers, Charles Bates, Ladd Koresch, and Maynard Speece, the generous assistance of Harold and Helen King, the professional wizardry of Brad Childs and Ranae Hanson, and the gift of selected photos from kind friends, this auspicious enterprise would be unfinished. Lastly, no words, however beautiful, can ever approach the unselfish support that Theresa furnished throughout this task.

JOB

INTRODUCTION

It is a gift from the gifted. It is the story of archetypal discipleship. It is the story of all those who have ever searched for a guide on the mystic path. The pronoun "I" for Dr. Justin O'Brien in this narrative is only a synecdoche for the rest of us. Someone is chased into the guru's cave by a lion. Someone is claimed from the parents at very birth. Whenever one gets claimed, that indeed is the birth. When Dr. O'Brien speaks of his birth, growth and continuing on an onward and upward climb, we are walking with him. Rather, we all walk with the Himalayan Master.

I could not put this manuscript down. Justin played with my sentiments. In one paragraph I laughed, in the next one I cried, and in the following one laughed again. The Master taught him well how to interchange periods and commas for the best effect. When he blooms, we bloom along; when he is made to burn in the fire of guru's ire, we turn to ashes.

There are some things one cannot say about oneself. The mystics' law of silence forbids speaking of one's innermost experiences. Initiation was always a well-preserved secret. Furthermore, one cannot speak of one's spiritual successes, lest one begin to assume falsely the mantle of a guide while s/he is still a disciple. Justin, with all his generosity in wielding words effectively, has maintained an observance of this law of silence.

I saw Justin for the first time in the then seed headquarters of the Himalayan Institute in Palatine, Illinois, in a motel in whose hall the venerable Master taught, and where often, in order to train us, we were asked to fill in. We would frequently meet in those gatherings.

As the years passed, I was amazed at the changes that took place in Justin's face. The luminosity that was irregular became an even force. The voice grew more effective because of its growing mellowness. An integration of all the forces. He learned to channel the energies towards others. The doubts were obvious, but gradually they vanished. He found that he had begun to experience the ultimate purpose of all the theology and philosophy he had been studying.

Yes, the books, like boats, having done their work of bringing him to this shore, had to be discarded. Time and time again I had read and heard stories of the masters telling the most favorite disciple with the highest learning to drop all his books in the river nearby. It did not happen in some remote time or clime, but right here in Illinois; the age-old story repeats itself.

Of the ten perfections, *paramitas*, required of one before one can reach the Buddhahood, enlightenment, one is called Skill in the Means of Liberating Others, *upaya-kaushala*. Justin's narrative shows the Master's perfection in this skill.

When the Master walked, I was often reminded of the Thai sculptures of the walking Buddha; there are none equal to them. Seeing them for the first time, one could not imagine what it must have been like to walk with that Master twenty six centuries ago, or with Jesus two thousand years ago. But here was a live demonstration.

From doubt to dedication is a long journey, one that I saw Justin undertaking and arriving where he is now—a guide to many, a source of inspiration, still maintaining the rules of discipleship. When one forgets, even briefly, that one is only a disciple, because he is being adored by so many, the downfall begins. I pray that none of us fall prey to the beast of false assumptions of our own stature.

Justin has climbed the physical Himalayas many times, walking on foot to holy shrines where sages have sat. He has sat at the feet of the modern saints at Kumbha Mela and on other occasions. Many times he has been charged with sacred missions by the Master. I recall an incident when both he and I were sent together for the same mission. I kept my own personality trait of softness, and failed. He—having been trained to fear neither dog nor king—succeeded. I earned a reprimand; he earned a pat on the back.

How many times Justin has visited India, how long he has stayed in Nepal, he himself may have lost count. Though he was ordered to discard his books, I notice that intense meditation practice has given him greater clarity of mind than what the erstwhile professor of theology could have achieved without such intense burning of the dross to which a Master subjects his disciples.

Even though the Master has dis-appeared, he remains as the light that he infused into worthy minds, and every true disciple's mind continues to sing: He walks with me, he talks with me, and he tells me I am his own.

I congratulate Dr. Justin O'Brien for having made the grade of being such a disciple who continues to walk with the Himalayan Master. Like other brother disciples, he carries on the mandate with which he has been charged. What a disciple can wish for a brother disciple, I wish for you, Justin. May you be fully enlightened in this very life and the grace conferred on you be ever unceasing.

Swami Veda Bharati
Swami Rama's Ashram
Rishikesh, Himalayas

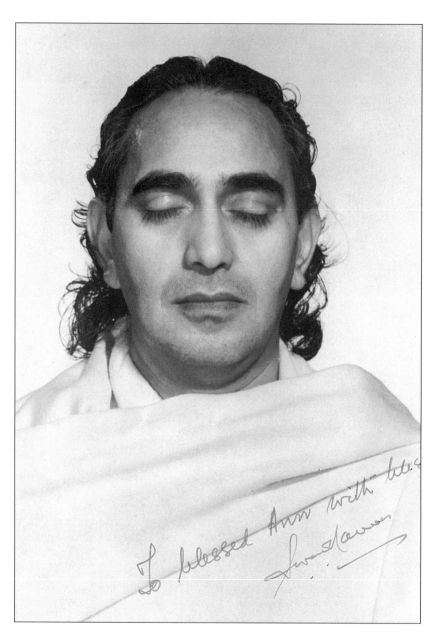

Swami Rama of the Himalayas

CHAPTER 1
DREAMING A FUTURE

I stood in a large pine lodge surrounded by white birch trees on a wooded property near a small lake. I sensed it was somewhere in Wisconsin. I recognized no one among the thirty participants at the seminar I was attending. Everyone seemed pleasantly anticipating the appearance of the speaker. Sitting in the rear, I was curious about the event, waiting to see what would happen next.

THE DREAM ENDED THERE. I would have ignored it, but in that unusually warm early summer of 1972, it felt utterly important as I wrote it down. The next night I had another dream. It picked up from the last dream scene without missing a stride.

I was sitting in the same chair at the back of the seminar room, squirming to see if the speaker had arrived. Suddenly I found myself in the kitchen facing a young blond woman who was wearing glasses and talking about macrobiotic foods. I realized then that I was not particularly interested in the food of the place, but in something else, something far more important.

Again the dream ended abruptly, unfinished, yet its images stayed with me all day. That night I had another dream.

For just a moment I was in the familiar idyllic pine lodge scene. Then I was plunged into total darkness. About twenty yards away, five human-sized, gleaming, elliptical shapes of radiant white light appeared. They were shining with such intensity that I partially shielded my eyes in order to observe them as they slowly descended to the ground in a beam of light. "We have to get Justin

to the healing seminar," one of them earnestly declared.
"Yes, we must have him there," concurred another.
Astonished, I shouted at them, "Hey, I'm over here.
What healing seminar are you talking about ?"
But the light figures payed no attention to me; they
just vanished into the dark. Then huge columns of the
numeral nine zoomed at me, passed overhead in hyper-
speed like flashing numbers on Sesame Street, and
vanished into the darkness. "9 9 9 9 . . ."

I woke up sharply. "What was that about?" I thought.
"Perhaps I shouldn't have eaten that pizza." At that time in my
life, I was keeping a dream diary, so I wrote down the episodes of
the three-night serial dream, chuckling about those neat light-
guys and promptly forgetting about the dreams.

I had other concerns to drive them from my mind. The
income-less summer months weren't passing fast enough. I was
anxious to get back into teaching theology, but my classes at
Loyola University of Chicago did not begin until September. My
wife, Theresa, and I had just returned from two and a half years
in Europe where I had continued my advanced degree work.
Loyola had agreed to a leave of absence for me during that time
but the university administrators had been relieved to know that
they wouldn't have to support me. As a consequence, we had
used up all our savings, spent up several loans, and gone into
hock. Theresa was holding a small secretarial job until her own
teaching would begin in the Fall, but still we were out of money
and bouncing back and forth between credit cards trying to make
ends meet.

Since I didn't have a car yet, July found me wandering
through the Loyola campus, greeting old friends, checking the
bookstore, and strolling around hoping to bump into familiar
faculty. Much had changed in two years. Every now and then I
passed by a bulletin board, either on campus, at an Evanston
health food store near our apartment, or on an elevated train
station, and I scanned for upcoming events and community
announcements. My eyes repeatedly caught a flyer that described
a forthcoming seminar on healing, to be held on September 9, at
Plymouth, Wisconsin, in the woods just north of Milwaukee. The
speaker was to be His Holiness Swami Rama of the Himalayas.
Since I was a brilliant college professor, I never once made the

connection between the announcements and my dreams.

Did you ever have a thought that haunted you despite your dismissal of it? As the weeks rolled into August, I couldn't get the seminar flyer out of my mind. Every time I dismissed it, something would come along to remind me of it. I mentioned the obsession to Theresa and speculated that after more than two years in gray Holland, walking around in the bright Midwest sun must have been taking its toll.

The last week of August, painfully realizing that Citibank was getting richer daily from our credit card interest, I told Theresa that I could not possibly afford to go to the seminar even if I wanted to. I said I didn't even have a car to get there. In her flawless logic, she quietly reminded me of my connections in my home town of Chicago and said that since I was interested in Eastern thought, here was an opportunity to find out about it first hand. No doubt she was tired of hearing me report again how many times I had run into that healing flyer.

After calling around, I reached a colleague in the philosophy department who put me in touch with a businesswoman who would be attending the Wisconsin seminar. Being Chicago Irish, she was glad to have a compatriot who could share the driving.

The morning of departure, I looked over at Theresa, then out the window, then back to Theresa, all the time thinking: "Why am I doing this? It's quite simple, really. I am going to a seminar that I resisted for three months, borrowing money that I can't afford, depending on some stranger to drive me, leaving a spouse (who just contracted the flu) to fend for herself. Yet from her sick bed she bravely whispered encouragement for me to have fun at the healing seminar."

The sleek red Oldsmobile drove up on the 9th day of the 9th month at 9 A.M. The cheery face of Ann Alyward, a hefty, middle-aged, common-sensed woman, greeted me warmly from the driver's seat. I soon learned that she was the first chairperson of The Himalayan Institute of Yoga Science and Philosophy of the U.S.A. recently founded by Swami Rama. A younger voice from the back seat said "Hi," and Ann introduced her favorite niece, Debbie, a student at nearby Northwestern University.

I volunteered to drive, and we scooted north to Plymouth. Ann was excited to share her story and listen to my escapades in Europe. After listening to her brief biography of Swami Rama, I supposed the Swami and I would be meeting as peers and should have a lot to talk about.

We drove off the main highway from Plymouth, turning eastward into a densely wooded area, where white birch trees filled the autumn forest. We finally passed a small lake next to a pine lodge. Of course, nothing rang a bell in my memory.

Because of her arthritic knees, Ann walked with difficulty into the lodge. She hobbled over to greet Swami Rama and beckoned me forward to be introduced. Tall and well-built with long black hair and large, piercing brown eyes, he looked self-contained, powerful, and distinguished in his white silk. I felt he knew who he was. Shaking his hand after his brief acknowledgment, I found him staring into space, saying nothing. "Oh well," I assured myself, "I didn't come up here for friendship; I was hoping to learn something about the topic." I quietly walked away from Ann and the Swami, wondering how Theresa was doing.

Half an hour later, seminar registration began. As I filled out the form, I gritted my teeth: I had misread the cost and needed an additional $50. I felt terrible knowing how much we were in debt. Begrudgingly, I reached into my wallet for my credit card and walked to the desk. Out of the corner of my eye, I saw the Swami leave his guests, bolt across the room, and dash in front of me. He loudly ordered the registrar, "Don't charge this man!" Without looking at me, he then turned and walked away.

"Did he know of my money problems?" I asked myself, stunned and pleased. "Of course not! How could he? Not bad for openers, though."

As the thirty or so participants got situated, the evening lecture began with an invocation from the Swami about "praying to the divine in you." He then spoke about his training, his work at the Menninger Foundation, some of the unusual men and women he had met throughout his life, and the relationship between body, mind, and soul. Most of the audience was Unitarian in outlook and had studied psychic phenomena. They loved his talk; I was not sure about it. With his strong Indian accent, I found some of his words hard to understand, especially when they began with g or s. "His English will improve with practice if he works at it," I thought unkindly. Later I discovered that Hindi has three sounds each for those letters.

The next morning everyone was up early for some Eastern stretches called Hatha Yoga. I stayed in bed.

After breakfast, I engaged in a conversation in the kitchen with the blond daughter of the owner who explained her current interest in macrobiotics. I thought the subject seemed familiar but did not remember why. The morning lecture began and very soon my attention became interspersed with an internal criticism of the swami's lecture, not in any authentic sense but in a harping, relentless critique. This troubling barrage of thoughts then degenerated into caustic observations about his person. Not only was he wasting my time with concepts I already knew, he should be shipped back to his beloved mountains. I tried to stop myself but the hyper-criticism continued. I was grateful for his generosity but annoyed with his words; I was impressed with his knowledge, but had thoughts of competition. I felt like Dr. Jekyll and Mr. Hyde simultaneously.

When the lecture was finally over, we went to lunch and I confidently pointed out to my new acquaintances how trivial the lecture had been. They eyed one another and physically leaned away from me. Realizing how I must sound, I pushed my plate aside and left the room, heading for the woods. For three hours I walked, feeling utterly confused, disgusted with myself, dreading another day. All my money was gone, Theresa was at home ill, and the seminar was a waste of time. If I had had a car, I would have been out of there.

The late afternoon session met in a clearing in the woods; I came upon the group just as it started chanting. That turned me off even more, but the fever of criticism had simmered down into listlessness. I didn't join the group; I just sat watching from the edge of the clearing.

Dinner came and went, and we headed back into the large room for the Saturday night lecture. I felt depleted and ashamed of my internal treatment of the Swami, so I sat unobtrusively off to the side facing his profile. He began his lecture slowly. He seemed more serious than in his previous talks, but it didn't matter; I was just putting in time.

He spoke of an inner quest that we are born with that never ceases to beckon to us. He invited us to reflect on our own quest. He said that in the midst of the most trying and devastating circumstances, or the most exhilarating accomplishments, our quests call to us to keep questioning the value of our current understandings of life. I listened intently.

The Dominican monk, Brother Justin

From Stock Broker to Monk

I began to associate Swami Rama's words with the memory of the restlessness that I still felt even though I had gone to the finest theological graduate school in Europe. Actually, my odyssey had begun in Chicago when I was a stock broker. Working on La Salle Street at Bear Sterns made me feel important since I was on my way to becoming financially independent. I worked hard, knowing my future was set. Three years passed, and one day I walked into the office and surveyed the scene. I noted that one colleague was recuperating from his third heart attack, another was getting his third divorce, six others were using tranquilizers like potato chips, and everyone was heading to the bar daily to forget about their trades. I wondered what malfunction I would acquire over the years. It hit me in a flash that this struggle was not worth it. I resigned the following week and chose the next obviously logical step in my evolution: I joined a monastery.

The path that led me to the monastery had begun when I was drafted into the army in my senior year at Notre Dame University. I joined the 82nd Airborne Infantry and pondered ideas about the perennial philosophy as I jumped out of planes and went on maneuvers. After graduating, I continued to read the classics in mysticism and pursue my philosophical interests. While working as a stock broker I struck up a friendship with a Dominican monk. He was teaching Western Philosophy at nearby De Paul University and had invited me to his evening classes after the stock market closed. His warmth as a person was equal to his brilliance in the classroom. Besides, he practiced his strong Irish baritone in the neighborhood bars we frequented. Meeting him only kindled my thirst to explore the theological and philosophical realms further. Thomas Aquinas, the famous medieval monk, philosopher, theologian, and mystic, became a regular topic of discussion between us. At the same time, the more I read and discussed, the more my appetite grew for experiencing the real thing. I did not want to spend my life window shopping among the writings. If those men and women could do it, why couldn't I? "Get thee to a convent, O'Brien," became a periodic command from deep inside. I knew something was missing in my life but I couldn't articulate it. I told no one.

"All of us," the Swami continued in his lecture, "are on a journey to self-discovery. The events of life, the set-backs as well as the bonuses, are challenging us to know and love truth at ever deeper levels so that we can dispel the ignorance that blights our lives and prevents us from knowing what divine freedom is all about. The body must be kept well, but it is nothing before the greatness of the human spirit, which uses that body. Beginning with your parents, people are your teachers; then as you are led into life's experiences you will meet other teachers."

"Sometimes in the most unlikely ways," I thought, as I finished his sentence in my mind.

When I told my Dominican friend of my resignation from the market trade and my application to his Order of Preachers, he was delighted and told me that he had hoped I would enter but hadn't wanted to influence my decision.

I applied to his Midwest province and was politely turned down. Their policy was not to accept men from a divorced family. From their experience, these applicants proved too emotionally unstable and also could possibly be a cause of embarrassment to pious parishioners who would object to a priest raised from that kind of background. All my childhood, the divorce of my parents had been a terrible burden. My parents had given me up to my grandparents when I was two years old. They had been too young to be successfully married. My Protestant grandmother sent me to Catholic schools in deference to my Catholic grandmother, but the nuns always referred to me as 'that divorced child,' the only one in the entire school.

The Western Province evaluated me differently, and so I headed out to the Dominican Order in Oakland, California. My classmates entered the monastery for multiple reasons: some wanted the priesthood in a monastic format, others were attracted to the medieval tradition itself, many found life in community appealing. The uppermost motive for me? I wanted to become a mystic. I wanted to explore the inner galaxies of consciousness, visit the spirit world, communicate with the saints, bilocate, and challenge evil forces.

Perhaps this curiosity to explore and test new waters had started years earlier. I had run away from home three times before the age of six, not because of abusive treatment; on the contrary,

"I wanted to explore the world," I patiently explained to the policeman who found me near the railroad tracks two miles from home. If his overbearing presence looming above had not scared the daylights out of me, his thundering threat that the next time he would lock me up in a room for years did the trick.

Frustrated in my traveling itinerary, I next discovered Saturday action serials at the neighborhood movie house. From week to week I would fantasize about those invincible defenders of law and order, those men of steel, whose exploits I diligently pursued. Each episode thrilled my imagination as my hero, facing overwhelming odds, escaped each trap the hideous villains laid for him. I stayed up at night gazing at the stars, figuring out ways that my hero could extricate himself from perilous danger. Naturally, I was convinced that I had to follow in his footsteps and do battle with similar villains.

I found a big, old bath towel that I transformed into my bullet-proof cape. My hood was my aunt's discarded rubber bathing cap, which fit my large head so tightly that the blood flow to my temples was impaired. To complete my fearless disguise, I wore her indoor suntan goggles—plastic orbs with tiny light holes—so dark that when I went out the daylight seemed like midnight. No matter! Spy Smasher was here, ever ready to protect society and demolish the international forces of evil. That the weather was often in the high 80s and 90s did not disuade me from my airtight bathing cap and heavy towel cape. When running strategically through the gangways of the neighbors' houses following the pack of spies and their hired thugs, I would sweat profusely and grow dizzy for lack of oxygen to the brain. Due to the limitations of my audacious goggles, I would bang into unseen fences— obviously set up to deter my sleuthing, I reasoned—and stumble over low shrubs while dueling with my treacherous opponents. I proved undaunted, though scarred, and much too clever to fall into their sinister clutches or ever have the public discover my secret identity. I designed at least six different costumes, and chose my daily suit carefully, depending upon which evil made itself known that day. No wonder I later enjoyed wearing a monk's robe with hood; it felt comfortably familiar.

About the third year of my monastic life, my restlessness was still unrequited. In fact, it was now further expanded. I was dissatisfied with the scholastic manuals on philosophy which purported to be written *secundum ad mentum*, "according to the mind" of Aristotle and Thomas Aquinas. I made an endeavor to relearn my Latin in order to read Aquinas's philosophy in its original language. The original was such an eye opener that I was led to challenge my professors in class. They stuck to the commentaries and I stuck to the original. But through it all a nagging thought kept re-emerging, "Where's the mysticism?"

I finally decided that I had had enough of waiting around; it was time to find out about mysticism directly. I made appointments with the senior monks and proposed the same questions: "When does the mysticism start? How do we train? How long does it take to become a mystic?" The replies were consistent. In a very paternalistic way I was told to continue on and one day I would probably teach at a college or be assigned to a parish. That was the answer? Hey, I had already figured on those career assignments, but where was mysticism? I felt cheated. Not only did they know nothing about my burning quest, no one seemed particularly interested. With that dis-appointment, I began to rethink my commitment to monasticism. Pay back time began.

I realized I had been boxed into an intellectual paradigm that had lost its vital juices along the way, congratulating itself on performing textbook autopsies on Aquinas: abstract theology on the greater side and life itself on the lesser side. Rene Descartes couldn't have asked for a better dichotomy. At first, I had the grandiose idea of reforming the spiritual life of the Province. Sure. That fantasy was short-lived since I had not the faintest idea about how to become a mystic. Instead, my mischievous side flourished. I flaunted the house rules at will and made myself a general nuisance. I snuck out to movies at night, I raided the monastery kitchens during the wee hours, I cut my prayer time short. It was time to leave. I could say I resigned—again—but more to the point, I was booted out. At least I had two new degrees in philosophy to show for my four years of finding out what didn't work for me. I now knew that more study was necessary. But without any money and with no prospects, where was I to go with my restlessness?

As I settled into seriously listening to the Swami, my turmoil disappeared. The petty, selfish anxieties about my career didn't seem important any more. His words resonated within me with such illumination that I thought he was speaking only to me. He told of how he had read all the philosophies and could quote long Sanskrit phrases but that, by themselves, these turned out to be dry, lifeless accomplishments compared to the realization of truth embodied in his teachers. My restless vacuum was filling up.

Departing from the monastery, I had returned to Chicago and lived awhile on the kindness of my uncle and his family. A friend heard of my plight of no job, no home, and no money and surreptitiously wrote a letter on my behalf. Soon I received a scholarship to Marquette University Graduate School in Theology. That next year and a half of study became the highlight of my academic career, never to be topped. I found an extraordinary teacher in the person of Bernard Cooke, S.J. He showed how different fields of knowledge could illustrate theological implications, and he also had the ability to ground theological themes in very practical ways.

His class should have held a dozen students, but someone had stolen all the registration checks at the mail depot, throwing away the applications. Near the end of the summer, the theology department found out that dozens of students had applied and, although their checks had been cashed, they had never received acknowledgment of their application. Neither the school nor the students knew who was accepted. I was the last person in a list of about ninety. By the time the problem was discovered, Cooke had decided to open the program to all those who had applied. He divided the curriculum into two concurrent tracks. There were so many nuns and ex-nuns, priests and ex-priests, seminarians and ex-seminarians in my class that we could have started a credit union. They had all left their orders in disappointment after the changes recommended by the Second Vatican Council for religious life failed to be implemented. As I listened to them tell me about their former vocations, it became quite evident that mysticism was not only a rare commodity, but belonged to a past millennium; it was almost a historical anachronism. There were no current takers because there were no skilled practitioners.

The Swami spoke now of his burden, a burden of truth. He had so much to share from the Sages who bequeathed it to him, he said, that he sometimes wept at night. Where were those who would help him?

"Is this a plea for help because he can't do it alone?" I wondered.

"People are lost in their confusion," he went on, "because they don't understand their nature." He explained that we fear the unknown dimensions of our minds. Thinking that the material realm is all that is important, we place our security entirely in externals or we escape to the realm of the mind. Sooner or later we become dissatisfied, disdain life, and find no place to turn. Disappointed with our choices, we undermine ourselves and others. We forget our living center of consciousness which is immortal, which is there to guide us through the flux of life.

"Scriptures can give solace," Swamiji was assuring us, "but they can't enlighten you. You must light your own lamp!"

At this point, for all I knew, there were only two people in the room. His words became mine. The vacuum had been filled to near the brim.

Swami Rama spoke of living an integrated life of body, mind and spirit, not as an intellectual abstraction but in actuality, in daily living. Without this holistic approach he said there was no escape from the wounds of disappointment.

I realized that he was speaking of the missing component in my higher education. I had gone to Holland to study for my doctorate with the finest minds in philosophical-theology, mythology, and religion. Professors like Schillebeeckx, Dupré, and Schonenberg were at the cutting edge and I filled my days with their classes. With the entire university opened to me, I had also sat in on lectures in psychology, anthropology, history, and scientific methodology. I had attended lectures on the same topic from different teachers to get varying perspectives. Among all these dedicated teachers I had had the good fortune to study with, both in America and overseas, I was unconsciously searching for someone to demonstrate a holistic grasp of life, someone who possessed a practical cognizance of the life forces that shaped their whole person. Perhaps I was expecting too much, for brilliant though they were, their lifestyles were shaped by their intellectual vistas. Often my teachers, for all their kindness and acumen, reminded me of many business professionals who, while attaining success in their career, nevertheless are terribly confused about life as a whole and, except for their professionals skills, are unaware of higher dimensions. An educational map for embodied wisdom was not to be found nor even hinted at in academia. University education, including theology, inherited the legacy of Galileo, Descartes, Hobbes, Bacon, Boyle, and Newton, each a genius in their own way but each tragically flawed in understanding human nature and its wondrous possibilities.

What was it the Swami was saying now? "Truth is hard to know; one must prepare for it."

From within me a surge of joy and confirmation arose. I was almost shaking with excitement. It was a long time since I had felt so much enthusiasm. I pictured myself standing by his side saying, "Yes, let's do it. Let's take that truth to the world." I wanted to hug him.

The vacuum had been filled.

When the lecture was over, the audience began to ask questions, but the Swami raised his hand for a pause. He turned left, walked directly to me, and held out his hand. We shook. Firmly, powerfully. I knew that from that moment on my life would be inextricably involved with this man and his vision—my vision. His words made living real. All my crooked meandering over the years, the temporary jobs, the blunders, the desperate searchings, seemed now to be a logical progression to this encounter. Apparently, they made sense, because they had prepared me for now.

And so began my association with Swami Rama of the Himalayas, "Swamiji" as I began to call him affectionately. Two years later we had a good laugh together about this rather tumultuous encounter. "You didn't find me; I found you," he said. "I was waiting for you!" But first he had had to stir up the pot. I had come laden with academic arrogance, prejudice, and general stupidity. He had had to get some of it out of the way so that I could appreciate the moment of meeting my teacher.

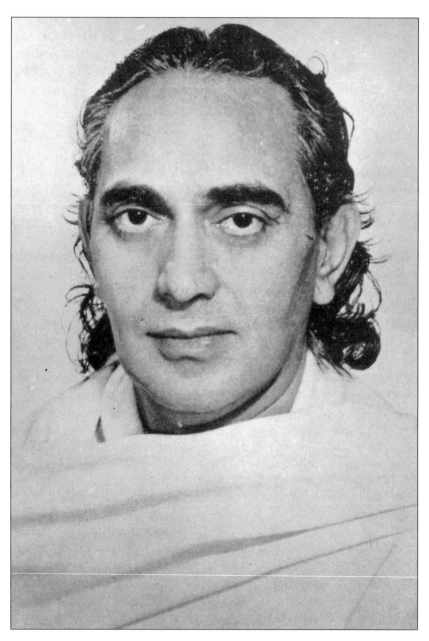

Swami Rama in 1970

CHAPTER 2
WHAT'S A MANTRA?

I rode in an old car from the 1950s with Swamiji at my side. "How are you?" I asked him. "I really missed you!" He replied that he really missed me too, but now that he was here we'd better get going. There was much travelling to do.

ON MONDAY, SEPTEMBER 12, I woke up with the delightful image of a car drive with Swami Rama fresh in my mind. It was the day of my next appointment with him, so I wasted no time in getting there. As I drove to Swamiji's residence near West Chicago I reminisced about the past two years overseas, tracking the episodes that led up to this day. Conversations with the Reverend John Pierce-Higgins, the famous, charming Anglican canon who de-haunted houses in the United Kingdom, broke into my memory. We had shared ideas about mysticism, the nature of God, and the best methods of dealing with poltergeists and explored unique ideas from Eastern philosophy about psychic phenomena. We had laughed together over stories of my psychic grandmother who took me to seances on Sunday afternoons where I watched channelings and healings and listened to discussions among the room full of spirit guides. Grandma definitely had a gift for healing and foretelling the future. John was impressed that she had predicted my college professorship when I was a nine-year-old failing in school, when she told me, "Some day you will travel far and wide, speaking before rooms full of people!"

One evening after dinner, John and I walked in his garden in London, knowing I would soon leave for home. "Justin," he insisted, "because of your interest in consciousness I insist that you read *Autobiography of a Yogi.*"

I was surprised. "You mean the story of the Indian monk, Yogananda, who came to the West in the 1920s?"

"Yes. Read it. You will find many connections to your Christian background that may surprise and delight you. Like you, I have this unquenchable thirst for exploring realms of mystic consciousness and experimenting with Eastern ideas. We Gaelics," he chuckled, "all have that restlessness."

I remembered buying the book in an old shop in Central London on a rainy day in Spring. I had begun reading it in the back of the dusty shop and had to be asked to leave at closing time. I had read it on the underground on my way home. I had devoured it in the next few days before catching the plane to Chicago. In that early edition of the autobiography, Yogananda had prophesied that a great yogi would come to the West and share the science of yoga with researchers and scientists. I had no idea that I was on my way to meet that yogi.

My borrowed car pulled into the driveway of a large, two-story farm house in need of paint in the midst of abandoned fields. A polite American woman wearing a yellow sari opened the door and greeted me. I removed my shoes as requested and waited in the hallway. When she returned, she pointed me upstairs to Swami Rama's room. I knocked on the slightly opened door and entered. The room smelled heavily of incense.

"Oh, that's to purify the air," Swami Rama said, noting my curiosity at the strange aroma. "It's my favorite incense."

I sat down on a chair and watched him watch me. After a few moments, he spoke. "Psychic phenomena won't satisfy you."

I was staggered. This subject had been a real interest to me in recent years both in Holland and England, but I had not mentioned it to anyone but Canon Pierce-Higgins. The psychic search had been my attempt to satisfy my restless yearning for I knew not what.

"You don't have a center," the Swami said. "I will give you one. It's meditation."

"He certainly doesn't believe in beating around the bush," I thought, pleased at his concern for me.

"Come back again and next time I will personally teach you the art of meditation." The Swami ended the appointment.

Then my mind rebelled. "All the way out here just to be told to return? Why couldn't he give it to me now?"

"Make an appointment downstairs" the Swami continued. "But first, you need a mantra!"

I frowned: "What's a mantra?"

Without answering, Swami Rama walked over to me, cupped his hand around my right ear, and chanted a few Sanskrit syllables. I listened intently. He then asked me to join him in repeating the mantra sounds so that he could check my pronunciation.

"What's this all about?" I thought. It made little sense to me, but I began repeating the sounds.

"Oh! You've got the rhythm well," he said, pleased. Then he quickly wrote out on a pad of paper the personal qualities characterized by the mantra, that would develop in me over time. As I read the paper, I was overwhelmed by the possibilities.

"The mantra's vibration will bring forth these qualities in you. It is time now for you to move ahead," the Swami insisted.

He seemed genuinely enthusiastic in putting all this together for me. Since I hardly knew him, I was surprised at his urgency, his care, his solicitousness for my future. I was pleased but dumbfounded to know how to respond. He looked directly at me as his eyes grew large, making me feel that this moment was the most important in my life, and yet he gave me the feeling that I already had all this knowledge, and so I said nothing.

Our second encounter was over. I was to make another appointment and return with a tape recorder next time. Apparently, I was on the fast track, but I appreciated his style: serious without being solemn and spontaneous without being giddy, with just enough surprises to keep me interested. In addition to dreaming my future after the impact of his seminar, I now had a mantra to puzzle out. Downstairs, I asked the woman what to do with a mantra.

She smiled and replied matter-of-factly, "Oh, you'll learn." And I was ushered out the door.

My return visit a few days later was my introduction into the meditative tradition of the sages. The Swami's room was filled with the usual odor of incense. I liked it, so I peeked over at the incense box and noted the words Padmini Dhoop inscribed in red letters. Next to it I saw a packet of cigarettes.

"Do you smoke, sir?" I asked.

"Yes. All the mountain people smoke. Smoking serves many functions for me, one of which is to remind me of the Himalayas. Do you mind?"

I could think of no reason to mind his smoking, so I merely asked if it hurt his health.

"I am a yogi," he replied. "I do cleansing practices to keep my body pure."

That seemed to settle it for me so he asked me to sit down with him, patting the cushion on the floor near him. My mind immediately jumped to embarrassment. "I can't sit on the floor!" I thought. My legs were inflexible, too many years of stiffness since my childhood knee ailment. But the Swami read my thoughts, pointed to a straight-backed chair and explained that folding one's legs is not essential to meditation, nor is the lotus posture that characterizes the statues of the Buddha. In fact, he told me, the lotus posture is not meant for meditation, but is a symbol thereof.

"The key to meditative posture is the spinal column. Keep it erect," he instructed. "In this way, the lungs are free to breathe and the energy of the body can travel uninterruptedly."

He then asked me to close my eyes, seal my lips, and follow his instructions in exactly the manner he elaborated. It must have taken about ten minutes for the entire process, and when his voice stopped, I opened my eyes into the calm, serene atmosphere. I was hooked.

He handed over to me the tape recording of the process and looked me steadily in the eyes, "I am now giving you permission to teach Superconscious Meditation," he said steadily. "You are the first to use this name for the ancient method of our tradition. I have not yet given this permission to anyone else. Go out and lecture in the cities and institutions, teaching this tradition systematically whenever the audience is ready. I have taught you exactly as my master has taught me."

Naturally, I felt flattered, but I also felt unequipped and not quite sure what my adequate response should be for this bestowal.

"During your meditation, you will do 45% of the effort and I'll do 55%," he added, reading my mind.

I sensed by his commitment to me that something of major importance was taking place, but I couldn't even imagine its magnitude. It fascinated me just to anticipate exploring the mind's terrain. His presence gave such credibility to the adventure that I couldn't wait to begin.

"Now that you have your mantra and know the method, I am obliged to you," he said. "Do it twice a day. Let me know the hours you choose, and I will attend you."

"How long should I meditate each day?" I imagined sitting for hours.

"Ten minutes is O.K. Don't force the mind, for it won't be pushed."

"Little does he know," I thought to myself. "Why, I'll be cruising in the higher regions of superconsciousness within days." (So much for my bravado! It took me six months to sit quietly for ten minutes without fidgeting for thirty seconds.)

I wanted to make a donation to Swami Rama, but he refused. Over all the years I've been with him, he has never accepted money from me for any of his teachings.

Again our visit was short and to the point. He invited me to attend his lectures. Driving back home, I realized I had forgotten to ask him my list of questions: everything from dreams, to mantra, to meditation and the responsibility for teaching it. As the years went on, I would always forget all my questions in his presence, yet somehow the answers would always be manifested.

Each day, I practiced meditation morning and evening. Actually, meditation was not new to me. As a monk I had been obliged to meditate at least once a day, but there had been no instructions nor instructors in the art. We were left to our own devices as to how to fill in the time. I had been forced to research meditation on my own and had soon discovered that meditation was considered a "discursive activity," sometimes called "mental prayer." It involved thinking about a scriptural quotation, pondering pious images from the life of Christ or his saints, and arriving at a practical resolution in self-betterment. According to the textbooks, meditation was also considered a beginner's level practice on the spiritual path and was typically reserved only for those in monasteries. The advanced goal of the spiritual path, according to religious authorities, was to get to contemplation, which consisted of a supernatural awareness and union with a divine object of focus. Contemplation, however, could not be obtained by one's own efforts. It was a gratuitous, non-discursive gift of the Holy Spirit.

The entire process of Christian meditation had become strictly

Swamiji teaching in the Midwest

a cognitive activity. The body, the breath, the subtleties of the senses, and the mind's concentration were ignored. Later I found out that my monastery was not unique in its ignorance of meditation; such ignorance prevailed across Christendom. A few old texts found in dusty chambers stirred my imagination to reconsider the way contemporary writers spoke of meditation, but they had been ignored for so many centuries that they were basically unknown. There were no guides.

Now, using Swami Rama's method, I sat down early each morning and began. After a few days, I was surprised that as I sat quietly I could hear the sound of the railroad more than three miles away. I could hear the birds outside, the garbage men working their way down the alley, the creaking of the house. After a while I became annoyed because I kept hearing a loud pounding, finally realizing that it was my heart!

Next I noticed a loud, high-pitched sound in my right ear, which, like the sound of my heartbeat, refused to go away. I broke out in a profuse sweat along my spinal column. I felt warmth expanding up my back. I took off most of my clothes, turned off the apartment heat, opened the window, even though it was late Fall, and still I felt cooked. Bright lights came and went, images popped into my mind, old memories, the usual train of thoughts, but I persisted in remembering my mantra.

These flushes of energy reminded me of a peculiar experience I had had when I was a Dominican monk in 1961. I had been sitting in a small chapel with the rest of the monks as the rector gave his weekly lecture. I had found the talk piously boring and had let my mind wander in all directions, seeking something to interest me. Suddenly, an expanding flush of energy started in my pelvic region and expanded upwards and downwards simultaneously, filling my entire body. I had thought I was going to explode. The feeling of expansion had been accompanied by intense waves of what I had thought were sexual pleasure, yet was not. The intensity had been there, but there had been nothing external about it. I had gasped, reeling from the experience, while my rational mind had tried to analyze it at the same time. It had been a totally unfamiliar phenomenon, lasting a few minutes, but leaving me perplexed, fascinated by the clues to a mystery, wanting to figure it out and not knowing how.

Now that I was experiencing the energy flow in meditation, I realized that my monastic episode had given me a preview of this inner awakening. The mantra drew me deeper into an awareness of these energy changes, and I realized that it was my own self I was experiencing.

Mantra, "that which removes the disturbances of the mind," intrigued me. Mantra is a sacred sound—a vibration—that affects reality. The notion that sound could affect the unconscious part of my mind made me speculate that my nature was constituted by vibrations. In physics I had learned that tangible matter at the sub-atomic level is composed of waves; thus I kept thinking that my body must be a dense field of vibrations. Could my entire mind be finer bands of vibrations? I began to read in the yoga tradition about this obtuse topic and discovered a manuscript that mentioned that sound is the root of all creation and that when it reaches a certain intensity, sound transforms itself into light. I immediately associated this with the opening of St. John's gospel, "In the beginning was the word."

Gradually I learned that the vibration of a mantra affects the energy levels composing one's nature, manifesting the qualities specified by the particular vibrations of the mantra. Genuine mantras are never made up, nor chosen arbitrarily. They were revealed to the ancient sages while they were in deep states of meditation and then tested to ascertain how the vibrations impacted reality. The sages themselves became the proto-experimenters with these mantras and noted their effects on body, mind, and nature. From that analysis, the sages selected mantras for their students to bring out qualities needed for their spiritual well-being. The yoga tradition uses mantras for many different aspects of life: healing, acquiring miraculous powers, awakening intelligence, attracting people and goods, controlling the forces of nature, forestalling death.

HANUMAN REJOINS RAMA

While studying in the Netherlands, I had received a copy of *Fate* magazine from an old buddy of mine. He had known I would be interested in an article about a yogi who could control his mind and body, scientifically ascertained through experiments at the Menninger Clinic. My friend, a top athlete while in school, later told me that he had been in a bookstore browsing through the sports section when the small magazine had fallen on the floor in front of him. He had put it back on the shelf and walked on. Later as he had come down the same aisle, the same book had fallen out at his feet again. This had seemed more than fate, so he had bought the magazine, read it, and dispatched it immediately to me. He had thought it was nonsense; I was thrilled with it.

We two had spent many evenings exploring the night spots of Chicago in our early years. Often we had driven home witnessing the sun rise over Lake Michigan after an entire night of play. He had been as extraordinarily generous with his time, money, and energy as he was generous in girth and humor. I loved him and valued his opinion.

After I met Swamiji, I tried in every way to lure my friend to the farmhouse to meet my new teacher, but he was evasive; he thought I was really off my rocker, and though he tried to humor me, he wanted no part of that "silly Eastern stuff."

Early one evening, my friend drove out to the farmhouse and circled around the area many times. He had already checked out the meaning of the word "swami" and "yogi" in the library but now did not understand why he was there. He walked through the door directly into the presence of Swami Rama.

The swami asked, "Where have you been?" and held out his hand.

The surprised man shook the hand and went into a different space. Visions, colors, sounds erupted in his head and he was overwhelmed by the feeling that he had finally come home. Swami Rama had entered his heart, and he was never the same again.

When I heard next from my friend, all I could think of was the Indian story of Hanuman and the God Rama. Lord Rama's wife, Sita, had been kidnapped by an evil enemy and the Lord asked for help. Hanuman gathered an army of monkeys and rescued Sita, returning her to his Lord. He was offered thanks and gifts in return, but he refused them all; he wanted nothing but the joy of serving his master. To show his love, Hanuman tore open his chest, revealing the shining image of Rama and Sita in the center of his heart.

From the moment my old friend met Swamiji, he immediately became the fearless and diplomatic protector at public Institute events, a duty that never changed over the many years to come.

WHY A TEACHER?

In our American culture it is not unusual to find the idea of mentoring in professional, artistic, and scholarly realms, and in realms of religion, spiritual directors often guide the believers in their personal lives. Those accepted relationships are similar to, but only barely approach, what the guru-chela (master-disciple) relationship means in the context of the ancient spiritual traditions. The Sanskrit word guru actually means, "the dispeller of darkness," the one who leads from darkness to light, from ignorance to knowledge. It is a sacred word, not given lightly.

Too many Christians forget that the master-disciple tradition is central to their scriptures. There are definite expressions of its demands and qualities throughout the Gospel writings. The disciples of Jesus were not academic students but apprentices, as clearly indicated in the writings. Based upon the teaching influence of Jesus, these chosen individuals had their entire lives reshaped in a day-to-day, one-on-one process. That is the reason why Jesus would insist that "He who loves father or mother more than me is not worthy of me."(Matthew 10.37). An unequivocal priority must be established sooner or later. No doubt, the risk/benefit ratio is quite high, but once the apprentice embarks on the path, a profound committment emerges on both sides. It is a difficult relationship to comprehend in our day since there are so few occassions for meeting an Olympian teacher who is capable of taking one to the same heights. This mutual association characterizing Jesus and his disciples was a customary Eastern apprentice model that existed in his day and remains strong to this day for those lucky enough to find it.

To enter into an ancient tradition, to become part of a spiritual lineage, means to link with those preceding masters who have likewise trodden a similar path in their times. Later Swamji would speak of this lineage by citing episodes with his guru as well as his grand-guru. Likewise we speak of fellow initiates of our teacher as our guru brothers and sisters.

I did not want to believe what the accomplished one said; I wanted to experience it. I did not want to be inspired by a talk like the audiences that Jesus had addressed; I wanted to get what Christ gave to his close disciples: the power to heal, the ability to perform miracles, the power to teach. I was aware that that could not take place until some changes were made in myself, but I could not know by myself what those changes needed to be. I needed a master who had done it himself to tell me.

As the days passed, Theresa began to get curious about the yogi whom I kept talking about. I wanted to go back daily to see him. Since she was quite familiar with my exasperating habit of going overboard on new interests, she cautioned me not to let this extracurricular activity interfere with my teaching at Loyola University and my lecturing on theology across the Midwest. She hoped that meditation wouldn't prevent us from going to movies.

The next week Theresa insisted on accompanying me to the farmhouse to meet Swami Rama. She had practiced meditation in a semi-cloistered convent for almost ten years, and her training as a nun had taught her many methods of spirituality. She wanted to learn more and knew the Eastern teacher must be good because I went so often, but she wanted to see for herself.

There was a group of people waiting in the classroom of the farmhouse for Swami Rama to begin the evening lecture, "The Meaning of Life." We stood in the doorway, waiting too, until we heard a door above open and shut.

Swamiji walked slowly down the stairs, turning his head right and left, nodding to students as he descended. On the bottom step he stopped abruptly, took a long look at Theresa, and called me to him.

"Justin," he whispered, "marry that woman!"

"We are married," I said, surprised at his firmness. "We've been married for three years."

"OK then," he answered and asked Theresa to come into the meditation room with him. Twenty minutes later she emerged, her eyes shining, her face full of joy and peace.

"What's a mantra?" she whispered to me. And I could only laugh.

Mama and her son

As I walked along the road, I heard a car come up behind me. I turned to look and saw Swamiji sitting in the back seat. The car stopped, Swamiji rolled down the window and called me over. I bent my head down to see him and he said, "Justin, love everyone. That's the point!"

AUTUMN OF 1972 saw Theresa and me become regulars at all the lectures and meetings of Swami Rama. His teaching attracted small groups of twenty-five to forty people of all ages in every class. The main rooms of the farmhouse were getting too crowded, especially when he led us in yoga postures, breathing exercises, and yogic health techniques. As friends told friends about the treasures they were learning, the classes began to burst the walls of the house.

Years earlier, Swamiji had marched out of a cave inspired by a vision. In his hand he had carried a board on which he had sketched with a stick of charcoal from his fire the name and logo for a new yoga institute: The Himalayan Institute of Yoga Science and Philosophy. He had tied the board with rope and hung it on his back, walking through the streets of India picking up students. The students had come in such numbers that soon the Institute had been officially organized in the city of Kanpur. The first students, (S.N. Agnihotri, Dr. Sunanda Bai, Shiv Nath Tandon, Roshan Lal, among them) remain his disciples today.

When he had first come to the United States on the order of his master in 1969, Swamiji had lectured in New York City. He always laughed when he told us that his entrance into the Big Apple had mixed results. He had just completed his stay in Japan and had begun his U. S. work by speaking first at a Unity Church. He had then given a series of evening lectures at a hotel. His lectures, surprisingly, had had a declining attendance. One evening a member of the audience had come up, introduced himself, and tactfully pointed out that the Swami was not in India where lectures are free. In New York, people expect to pay; they assume that "no charge" means "no value." Swamiji had gotten the picture. This gentleman, who just happened to be in the public relations business, had proposed that with a few modifications, many more people would attend. He had offered to arrange the publicity, set up the venue, and take care of all expenses. If the Swami agreed, they would divide the proceeds at the end of the series. The plan had gone so well that the crowds had filled the hall and the lecture series had to be extended.

After this success, Swamiji came down to the hotel desk to check out, have breakfast with his manager, and divide the proceeds. At the desk, he was handed the bill for his room and board.

"Excuse me, sir, but my manager mentioned that he had taken care of all expenses," Swamiji smilingly assured the clerk.

The clerk smilingly replied, "Your associate checked out two hours ago and said you would be responsible for all the bills."

Swamiji stood there, penniless, stunned, realizing that his new manager had flown the coop with the pot. What should he do? At that moment, a Midwestern couple standing behind him overheard the embarrassing predicament. They motioned Swamiji over to the side.

"Sir, we couldn't help but hear your situation. May we apologize for the unfair way you have been treated in our country? Please have breakfast with us as our guest and let us take care of all your bills.

"We have attended your lecture series and your words have meant a great deal to us. This terrible incident should not have happened, especially to a man of your stature. It would be no hardship for us to make it right."

After that unusual beginning, Swamiji traveled across the country to teach and share knowledge of yoga wherever he was invited. He was among the first waves of Eastern teachers to flow to the shores of North America during the sixties and early seventies. The strange import called yoga was establishing a firm beach head. Each teacher brought his or her own style and tradition. What made Swamiji unique among the various outstanding yogis, roshis, sufis, and lamas was his willingness to submit his vision of life to scientific scrutiny. He walked his talk before scientist and lay person alike. For him, yoga was an intelligible science—more, a sacred knowledge—that comprised down-to-earth principles and practices for enabling people to better the quality of their lives. Yoga wasn't a Hindu cultural piece nor a sectarian dogma. As Swamiji spoke, one got the idea that yoga evinced a universality that touched people's lives because it spoke to their nature, not to their culture. Besides, it made pragmatic sense and that was important to Americans.

One did not need to take yoga on faith and ponder it, wondering whether it was true or not. Instead, each practitioner became his or her own laboratory of experience. It could be put together on one's own terms, gradually, at any pace, and adapted to personal and family needs. In this way, yoga inspired one to trust the life force. One could keep one's religious persuasion and politics and still use yoga as a lifestyle. I relished yoga's sensible, holistic approach, for it strengthened self-reliance and stimulated wonder about what there was yet to discover and enjoy about life. Becoming as physically flexible as some students, whom I suspected had rubber in their bones, was, however, always going to be a challenge for me.

Swamiji insisted that "unless you have a profound understanding of the body, mind, and spirit in their relationship to the world, you will wander in misery. A haphazard search for the truth just leads to more dissipated directions. God has not made you in your negative thoughts. Why do you blame God for your situation? Progress in life only comes when we understand ourselves. You can't learn very much if you just believe my words. We are never truly satisfied with just belief. Christians especially hold themselves back. Why? Faith can never make an intelligent person secure. Borrowed beliefs are not very helpful since they are not tested by experience. I tell you, unexamined faith is not worth having. Faith cannot make up for lack of self-knowledge, and no guru can show you God." Then Swamiji told us a story.

Once he had pressed his master to show God to him. After keeping the young monk at bay for many months, the master had relented, called him over, and announced, "Tomorrow I will show you God."

Excited wasn't the word for Swamiji's mind and heart. He

could not sleep all night; he kept supposing what God would be like, relentlessly analyzing and re-analyzing his anticipations. The hours passed and he was nearly exhausted thinking and rethinking about God's appearance and what he should do in God's presence. He could not decide, but it didn't matter, for now, after months and years of pondering the nature of God, the day had finally arrived for him to obtain his fervent desire.

After showering and fasting, putting on clean clothing and even combing his hair, he came before his master.

"I can't remember you ever looking this clean before," his master teased. "Are you sure you want to see God?" he inquired.

"Absolutely!" came back the energetic reply.

"Are you really sure?" the master looked straight at him.

Tired from the night's ordeal, Swamiji was feeling himself getting a little impatient with this line of stalling. "You promised to show me God so just show me God!"

"All right," said his master. "I promised to show you God. Which God do you want to see?"

I wasn't prepared for the impact of that story. I, too, was stunned, just like I presumed Swamiji to have been. Which God indeed. I took that story home and pondered it. I slowly realized that people claim to believe in God, pray to and rely upon God, seek God's blessings, praise God in ritual, implore God's name in dire circumstances, but no one ever claims that they can show you the God they insist is there. If Swamiji didn't know what God looked like, how would he recognize the divine if he saw it? If his master showed him God, would he accept what was shown as the real thing? I had to think about that some more.

MIDWESTERN VISITS

During a powerful weekend seminar in Colorado, a strange event occurred. While Swamiji was lecturing on meditation, he suddenly paused, turned his head sharply and shouted with anger, "Why are you speaking about me that way? Why are you saying those things?" He then seemed to remember his talk and, although visibly upset, he went on with the topic.

The audience was not aware that as Swamiji was speaking, in another part of the city a well-known female spiritual teacher and psychic was discouraging her audience from going to meet this "phony Eastern fakir." When the woman and her husband entered their residence later that evening, they smelled a terribly offensive odor that pervaded all the rooms of their home. Searching throughout the house but unable to find the odor's origin, they were forced to leave the premises and stay at a hotel. The next day the odor seemed even stronger and more repugnant. Several local janitorial services were dumbfounded trying to find the cause of the odor. A day later it began to dawn upon the couple that perhaps their disparaging remarks against Swami Rama may have a connection to this event. So they contacted Swamiji and formally apologized. Immediately after their conversation, the mysterious odor vanished.

All that Swamiji would say was, "I have *devas* (spirit helpers) who protect me, sometimes in curious ways."

That weekend in Colorado, Swamiji met a businessman named Howard Judt who became his student and invited him to Minneapolis, so Swamiji went there next. Among the first students in Minnesota were Charles Bates, a fine artist, Usharbudh Arya, a professor of Sanskrit at the University of Minnesota, Phil Nuernburger, a psychologist in clinical practice, and Prakash Keshaviah, a research scientist. These four were later instructed by Swamiji in mantra science and were made mantra initiators in the tradition of the Himalayan Sages. Swamiji impressed upon the class that it wasn't individuals, but the tradition itself that powered the mantras. He also inspired Dr. Arya and Charles Bates to open yoga meditation centers to carry on his tradition.

Charles and I met at a weekend seminar in Chicago. As we came to know one another, he told me of his meeting with Swamiji.

"I met Swamiji shortly after he came to the Twin Cities in the autumn of 1969," said Charles. "I was studying in the Minneapolis Institute of Art and learned of his lectures through a television interview. I was skeptical of the value of yoga, thinking yogis were 'milque toast,' even though I had heard of Swamiji's incredible experiments. After I met him, he asked me to be his secretary whenever he came to Minneapolis. By that time in my life, I had tasted the hypocrisy of religion and so-called spiritualities and wanted no part of more, but as I continued listening to and observing this man at close range, I reluctantly realized what was different about him. 'I don't like you,' I told him at the beginning, still suspicious of him, 'but you speak truth.'

"One night Swamiji told me that he would soon meet a professor of Sanskrit who would test him during dinner at his house and then become his student. A short time later, I noticed that a Professor Arya was introducing Swamiji at the lectures, so I presumed the testing was over.

"As time went on, in spite of my doubts, Swamiji led me to see that there are genuine paths to human excellence and I became excited with the possibilities. He asked me if I wanted to be a priest-pandit or a yogi. I replied, 'Both, just like you.'

"He laughed and agreed that it would happen. 'You will become a yogi and teach yoga,' he told me. 'You are a great teacher and I will announce this to everyone and force you to be so.' Four years later it all came true when he introduced me on the stage at the Kanpur Yoga Conference just as he had prophesied.

"I earnestly followed his recommendations, obtaining certificates in Hatha and Raja yoga. When he told me he had done the yoga cleansing called the upper wash for several years, I began doing it daily. After two years, my serious asthma condition was completely healed and I decided that I would practice yoga my entire life.

"In 1971, I went to Chicago for a retreat led by Swamiji. There, Swamiji instructed Dr. Arya, a traditional Hindu pandit and scholar, to perform an ancient ritual for me. He conducted the ceremony during which I was ordained a pandit in the Himalayan tradition and given the name 'Achala,' meaning 'mountain man.' Swamiji added the title 'Yogi.'

Yogi Achala's Twin Cities Yoga Society and Dr. Arya's new Dhyana Mandiram (Meditation Center) continued to draw hundreds of Minnesota students to study the ancient science.

As a result of Swamiji's experiments in Minneapolis, a group of scientists began meeting on a regular basis to explore the significance of his work. Requests for demonstrations before the scientific and medical communities continued, and Swamiji traveled to New York City, Buffalo, Pittsburgh, Dallas, Honolulu, and San Francisco, speaking on all aspects of yoga. Europeans also wanted him back. Initiate groups were flourishing, eagerly awaiting his visits.

Swamiji continued his experiments with the scientific community. Once he swallowed a vial of strychnine before a large professional audience to show the power of mind over matter. Two doctors were so stunned as he downed the poison that they collapsed. When the audience inquired what it tasted like, Swamiji casually answered, "Well, it tastes rather bitter."

In the ensuing months Swamiji strongly considered establishing his headquarters at Minneapolis, but since he was quite sensitive to people's emotions, he discerned that one of the teachers, whom he had accepted as a student, was afraid to lose students to him, so he decided to set up his American headquarters in Chicago instead. Chicago and Minneapolis became his regular loop and his usual residence the Holiday Inns, which saw him so often they issued him a Lifetime Gold Card.

Swamiji's lectures in Chicago were often sponsored by John Schwartz, a successful realtor, in his large office on the north side. Sometimes someone else would make a store front available. Swamiji never complained, even when fewer than twenty people attended. He accepted whatever was sent to him. Chicago was slow to realize who it had in its midst, but Swamiji projected an ebullient energy that took advantages as well as obstacles in stride. When he entered a room, it became filled to overflowing with his presence. Children loved him, running to him for hugs; those not usually affectionate were drawn to touch his hand or put their arms around him. After every talk the room was full; no one wanted to leave. Near him one felt that nothing was impossible; the unimaginable would take merely a moment to achieve. He always kept his students aimed to the future by working in the present. "One day you will have everything you want," he assured us.

The Chicago group kept expanding with new students: Dr. Ladd Koresch, Brunette Eason, Jackie Hornberger, John and Millie Fritschle, Lydia Smith, many college students. Both Protestant and Catholic clergy were also showing a keen interest in Swamiji's ideas. Rudy Ballentine, a frail young physician from the South, had gone to India to meet a teacher and there had heard of Swami Rama. After months of searching, Rudy finally met Swamiji in New Delhi just as Swamiji was returning to America. Rudy then returned home to study with the great yogi he had sought in the East.

A CHICAGO CATHOLIC MEETS HER HIMALAYAN SON

In order to appreciate how yoga got started in Chicago, one needs to know about a remarkable woman. Ann Alyward was in her sixties, unmarried, and Chicago Irish to the core. She was both charming and bluntly down to earth, a hard charger in business with a great temper and equally a boundless source of understanding and compassion when one needed her. She would have swooned had she ever discovered a priest with the slightest paranormal ability, so fascinated with the supernatural was she.

Ann found Swamiji in downtown Chicago. She had heard that a famous yogi, who could control all the involuntary functions of his body and had actually welcomed the Pope to India, was speaking in a Loop hotel. That's all it took. She could no more resist meeting him than she could stop being Roman Catholic. Her long-time friend, Peggy, shared her same interest in the numinous, so they went together.

In his talk that afternoon, Swamiji told many stories of healings. Ann had severe arthritic pain and stiffness in both her knees. So she would be able to pull herself up the stairs to the apartment above her restaurant, her brother had installed banisters on the both sides of the stairway walls. Ann thought, "I wonder if he could heal me?"

After the lecture, Ann and Peggy, like two teenagers wanting a rock star's autograph, nervously approached the Swami. Encouraged by her companion's rib poking, Ann sheepishly asked if he would consider doing some healing on her.

"Of course, I will!" he exclaimed with an impatient "could you think otherwise" look on his face. "How could I refuse my mother anything?"

Against her nature, Ann was reduced to silence. She just looked at him; he looked at her; and for the first time in this life, mother and son embraced.

Peggy wanted a hug too. She was a very short, very fat woman, filled to the brim with good nature. She was so excited that she burbled out, "I'm Peggy and I used to dance with the Beefy Babies dance troop during World War II!" From that moment on, Swamiji affectionately called her "Beefy-baby" much to her giggling delight.

The hours went by. Swamiji told Ann and Beefy-Baby about

his training, his parents' early deaths, his being claimed as a son by Bengali Baba of the Himalayas, and his life in an ancient monastery tucked away in the mountains.

"Do you remember the novel Lost Horizons? I believe it was made into a Hollywood movie. Well, that book is based upon the age-old tales and legends about my monastery," Swamiji said. With a second cup of tea, he began to unfold his mission to the women.

Ann shared some of Swamiji's words with me years later. We discussed them often. Swamiji's master had sent him to the West to share the wisdom of the sages after decades of arduous training. It was his mission to bring their message of hope for humanity across the ocean. He had embarked on a broad, manifold assignment that first targeted the scientific community. His travels to fifty-six countries were to touch and transform the lives of many people, educate hospitals and clinics about holistic treatments, affect research on mind-body communication, introduce breath therapy, and inaugurate an institute to unite Western lifestyles with ancient wisdom. He was to deliver more than two hundred infants and live in dozens of countries to work with students and seekers. He was to be an adviser to many business executives as well as to heads of state. Nearly all of these services were be done quietly, away from the lime light.

No media reporters were allowed at any of his scientific experiments. He did not want the kind of publicity that would generate a cult status. We believed that no one project in America or Europe could hold his energy, for his vision for humanity exceeded any single endeavor, any single continent, any single institution. Whether he was lecturing on higher consciousness to the communists in Moscow or enjoying high tea with the Queen of England, paving a rocky road near Uttarkashi, reading philosophy at Oxford, or acting as a marriage broker for many of his Western students, he kept in mind his master's declaration to him that he was, in truth, a prince of the universe.

During his travels, his master had assured him, he would rediscover many old friends and students from past lives and they would help as well as hinder him to accomplish his world-wide tasks.

When Ann spoke with Swamiji that day in Chicago, she wondered why it had taken her so long to find him. When he asked for her help in starting the Himalayan Institute of the USA, all of Chicago reverberated with the invitation at that moment. She had toiled for years raising four brothers; she had helped them establish a successful restaurant; she had cared for her retarded aunt; she had worked ceaselessly for her Church. This powerhouse was now about to embark on a new mission in life: to help her newly-found son manifest the sages' dreams for America.

That day Ann was named Rani Ma, Queen Mother, soon to be called Mama by thousands of Swamiji's followers.

The weeks went by. Mama introduced Swamiji to her brothers, proudly showed the life-long vegetarian ascetic around the family steak restaurant, and brought him upstairs to her apartment where she lived with her two Chihuahuas and her Aunt Kitty. Kitty, a small, wrinkled, shy retarded woman, spoke to no one and hated meeting anyone. But when Swami Rama entered her home, she flew into his arms and kissed him as she gently stroked his cheeks, tears streaming down her face.

The Swami became a regular at the restaurant. Mama soon learned how to make his favorite drink, tilk, a mixture of boiled milk and Darjeeling tea sweetened with honey. Together in her apartment, the two of them would plan future lectures and ways to get donations to start the American Institute. At each meeting, she worked the conversation gently around to reminding him of his promise to cure her affliction. In an off-handed way, he kept reassuring her not to worry. She told her brothers about the Swami's promise and they, with their street-smart nodding, let her know to take it as a harmless boast, just part of his charm.

One day, a few weeks after meeting Swamiji, Mama was in the restaurant kitchen checking on the seasoning in a large pot of spaghetti sauce. One of the waitresses called to say that the Swami was on her apartment phone. Ann ran through the kitchen, wheeled around the corner and dashed up the stairs, huffing and puffing as she picked up the phone. She and her "son" spoke about some business matters for a few minutes and then said good-bye. As she walked back down the stairs, Ann looked at the banisters with shock. She had not touched them on her way up, nor would she ever need them again.

AUNT KITTY

One evening some of us students were sitting around the lecture hall waiting for Swamiji to finish greeting the newcomers. Mama began a discussion about people born with afflictions. "It seems so unfair that some people come into this world with enormous handicaps," she said. "Others, like Joan's child, born dead, don't even get the chance." None of us could make these occurrances match up with a sense of natural fairness, let alone a just God. Christian theology itself has never offered a sensible response.

"Saying that it's God's will is just an evasion," said Frank.

"Some people get raw deals," agreed John.

Lydia thought out loud, "Perhaps we must just accept the suffering as God's will."

"No, no," she was answered. "The nuns used to say that it was a mystery, which is a euphemism meaning they didn't know and that somehow they had to get God off the hook."

Sitting outside in the car, as usual, was Mama's Aunt Kitty O'Doyle. Tonight she had Ann's two dogs with her, but most of the time she just sat quietly by herself, guarding Ann's purse. Since meeting Swamiji, whom she always called "the boy," she wanted to drive with Ann to any place where he would be. Physicians had diagnosed her as having a child's mind in an adult's body. Since we all knew her, she now became the object of our pronouncements on the injustice of life.

Swamiji had just sent the last audience member away and, walking over, heard our discussion. "You really think Kitty is that bad off?" came his challenging inquiry.

"Certainly, Swamiji, just look at her limitations. She can't be educated, nor live alone, nor get married, nor . . ."

Swamiji interrupted at this point. "As for her basic needs of food, shelter, and clothing, these are amply taken care of by Mama and her brothers. She is not alone, for the whole Alyward family watches over her. As for marriage, what's so indispensable about that association? Kitty is healthy, gets what she needs, and doesn't worry about taxes or old age. How many of you can claim such freedom?"

While we couldn't fault his facts, we still didn't feel

completely at ease with his answer.

"As for her education abilities," he continued, "you all would be surprised at what she knows. Since when is book learning a guarantee of a successful life?"

Then, sweeping us all in by his look, he declared firmly, "Kitty is a realized saint!"

Silence. There was a long pause as we pondered his declaration. I thought, "If she is already a saint, why did she bother coming back?" It didn't make any sense to me.

Then Swamiji added the finishing touch. "Besides, Mama, she didn't come for herself; she came for you. You had to learn to take care of her, not for her sake, but for yours."

By the look on Ann's face, his words had thundered home. She paled, her mouth opened in sudden realization, and her eyes filled with tears. Swamiji had a tough love for this grand woman, and he never flinched from showing it in public. He lifted her by the hand from her chair, put his arm around her shoulder, and walked with her to her car.

One Saturday morning Ann was getting ready for a business meeting with Swamiji at the center. As she was putting on her clothes, she noticed Kitty staring at the picture of Swamiji that hung on the wall. It portrayed Swamiji sitting against a background of mountains. Kitty was amusing herself, tilting her head back and forth while viewing the picture.

Mama, impatient since she was late, exclaimed, "Why are you looking at that picture, Kitty? You've seen Swamiji's picture dozens of times"

Kitty replied, "I'm watching them."

Mama gave a sigh of exasperation, trying to find an article of clothing and keep her mind on the conversation at the same time.

"What do you mean by 'them'? There's only one person there. Sometimes I think you're getting old on me!"

Kitty was not going to let Ann get away with such treatment.

"Ann, there's the boy and the others," Kitty replied assuredly.

Mama had had it with Kitty by now. She set her jaw and marched over to peer at the picture, the same old picture of Swamiji sitting there looking out.

"Kitty," Mama said in her condescending tone," Kitty, I think maybe we should have a doctor examine you."

Retarded or not, Kitty also had had enough with Mama.

Raising her voice, she angrily pointed her finger at the picture and told Ann in no uncertain terms, "There's the boy and there's five others. And that's it, Ann."

Mama went to finish dressing, shook her head, and headed out the door with the parting words, "Kitty, you're crazy."

Arriving forty minutes later, Ann came into Swamiji's room.

"Good morning, Mama," he beamed.

"You won't believe this, Swamiji."

"Believe what? Would you like some tea? Why are you upset, Mama?"

"It's Kitty. I think something's wrong with her. She got me all upset this morning looking at your picture on the wall. Maybe she's getting too old. Maybe she'll do other crazy things."

Swamiji was curiously supportive. "Mama, I can't remember seeing you like this; what is it?"

"Kitty claims to see you and some others in the picture. I think she said five others."

"Those others are my five teachers. I'm never without them."

Ann was stunned and perplexed. "But how can she see them?'

"Because they are in the picture."

Now her Irish was up, and she stared hard at her son: "OK, if they are in the damn picture, how come I can't see them?"

"Because you're not a saint yet! If you were, then you would see them as well."

Mama dropped the subject and went on to business matters.

In the Himalayas

CHAPTER 4
RAISING A SAGE

I sat in a cave with an old yogi, knowing I was in the presence of a holy man. He was older than most yogis I had seen, but he sat upright with a his gray shawl wrapped around him. His words were uttered solemnly, softly, as he looked steadily at me. It is a pity that Swami Rama will be known only for his experiments when he leaves his body."

FOR MANY AMERICANS, there seems to be hardly any time to pursue old dreams, let alone follow the sages' counsel to meditate. Immediate worries about career and family engulf our attention and our imaginations are limited to these concerns. We are unaware of how restricted our lives are because we hide the limitations by heavy-duty entertainment, loud music, constant chatter from TV and radio and phones, ever bigger and better productions. We Americans are strange.

Yet America is where Swami Rama wanted to be. He wanted to infuse the American scene with the wisdom of the sages. If we grasp the country's idea of individual power, the vast educational system, the undisputed wealth, and thus the generous leisure time of most citizens, then one can well understand why he came here. The ground was fertile for the seeds of perennial knowledge; the ideas would grow and spread across the land.

Swamiji was interested in everything and nothing else. His imagination matched the bounty of the universe. His love of life became his playground, his laboratory, his invitation to pursue ultimate questions. Whether he was lecturing in Moscow, healing a child, consulting with a head of state, conducting brain research in Germany, or advising the Mennonites on business investments, he invited all of them to play with the energy of life. Most of them stayed spectators, rendering excuses; a few embarked.

"Take your duties seriously, but take life lightly," he often said.

Organizational structures—the ashrams, clinics, hospitals, colleges, and yoga centers that he founded during his life—were merely some of the vehicles for his unquenchable passion to transform humanity. His mind did not have room for small desires. He was interested only in cosmic vistas.

Swami Rama reminded me of someone who, when given a nickel, would make sure you got a dollar back. There was always a mixture of healthy pride and commitment in anything he undertook. Give him a handful of dandelions and sooner or later you got an armful of roses in return. When someone did him a favor, he couldn't wait to return the same in abundance.

His six foot frame held a joyous response to humankind, but his lyrical vision had not always been like that. In his younger years, he had dealt with plenty of episodes that had revealed an immature, arrogant selfishness, and he confessed it often:

"When I was very young, I was teaching many students about the *Upanishads* and had no experience to back up what I was saying about those scriptures. Actually, I was bothered by this lack and wanted to go back to the mountain to get out of this situation and grow in wisdom, but I was too proud to just close things down.

"One day I noticed a new, older student sitting in my class. I also noted that although everyone was taking notes, he was not. It disturbed me that he would let my precious words get away unrecorded. So I decided that he needed to be taught a lesson. I told my assistant to assign this new student to do the laundry, which he politely did. He then asked for permission to speak with me, but I refused. The days went on in this way and I became more and more upset with the man's quiet presence in the audience. Once again he asked to see me, but I refused. Three times he requested; three times I refused.

"One morning I was squatting down by the river, cleaning my teeth before class. I noticed that the student was walking nearby. 'Where are you going?' I demanded. Since I hadn't finished with his learning, I felt he should not depart.

"The man looked back and said he was returning to the mountain. Well, I couldn't care less which mountain he was going to. As far as I was concerned, he could leave. Good riddance! He obviously wasn't prepared for my knowledge and I was not going to lower myself and persuade him to stay. I shouted that he should definitely go to back to the mountain. Without turning around, he shouted that I should continue scrubbing my teeth. And scrub I did. My students found me two days later, semi-conscious, still scrubbing my swollen gums.

"When I finally got back to our tradition's mountain cave many months later, I saw that same student there and realized that he was one of our own monks, a highly advanced adept. My master told me that after I had prayed for release from teaching, this monk had been sent to take my place. The desire of my heart had been fulfilled, but I had been too conceited to recognize the gift when it arrived."

AN UNEXPECTED BIRTH

Born in the Gahrwal Himalayas, north of Kotdwara, Swamiji often returned to those high hills surrounding the valley of his birthplace, where he composed his writings in the breath-taking vastness, looking north to Nanda Devi mountain, looming in the Himalayan range. In 1984 he took me away from the touring Americans for three weeks to travel with him through these same mountains. As we drove, he pointed out with great pride places of interest. He spoke with laughter about his upbringing.

"I was an unexpected child," he told me. "My mother had passed the time for childbearing, so when my master confronted my parents with the challenge of having a child, they were hesitant and laughed at the idea, but were full of joy. My father could not doubt the master's words in spite of their ages.

"My father knew the power of the Himalayan sages. His own birth had been touched by auspicious circumstances. Just before his birth, his pious parents had traveled, as was the custom, to the maternal village for the birth. While en route, my grandmother had gone into labor. My grandfather had tried to make her as comfortable as possible in the wild, but it was their usual meditation time. What should they do? They had never missed their meditation time. They both decided to go ahead with their practice and leave the rest to God. My grandfather found a nearby rock to sit on and began his practice. While he was meditating, rain started to fall but, deep in meditation, he did not notice. When his practice ended, he felt the rain and immediately ran to his wife. He sadly found that she had quietly died during her meditation time while giving birth to their son. The baby lay on the ground with a huge king cobra, hood fully extended, hovering above the child to protect him from the elements. My grandfather wept over his wife's body, bowed to the cobra, which moved back into the jungle, and took the child to his heart."

Swamiji stopped speaking for a while, and looked out the window at the glorious scenery. The mountains were full of rhododendron and gentians, neem trees and pine. My mind was still assimilating the story, wondering what happened next when Swamiji continued.

"My father grew up to be an acknowledged scholar, astrologer, and writer. Although married, he always wanted to live the life of a solitary spiritual seeker. Once he quietly left his family for many months, attempting to carry out his dream. He wandered eventually to the shrine of Chandi Devi outside Haridwar. After months of practice, he was visited by a powerful yogi, Bengali Baba, who blessed him and initiated him into the tradition. The master sent my father home, reminding him that renunciation is not required for spiritual perfection.

"So when my master told my parents that they would have another child, although already older, they were pleased and promised that their forthcoming child would be his. They knew something remarkable would occur around this baby. Shortly after my birth, my master showed up and demanded his claim. My mother cried, but was reminded of their promise. My master then entrusted them with the care of their child until he would return three years later. My father died a few years later and at his death I was given into the care of my master and taken to live in his cave."

I told Swamiji that this amazing story reminded me in part of a Christian tradition in use during the Middle Ages. Then there existed a similar contractual exchange between many wealthy Christian families and the institutional Church. The parents considered it an honor to have the opportunity to offer their first-born son to the local monastery to be raised by the monks in dedication to God and to the Church's work. For example, Thomas Aquinas, the famous medieval scholar-monk, was sent as a child to a Benedictine monastery for his early schooling in monastic life.

Swamiji nodded his head and drew out a long "Yes," as if he

were remembering.

We stopped for chai, the strong Indian spiced tea, at a small, dilapidated road stand. Swamiji engaged the proprietor in conversation until they both laughed heartily. I wandered to the edge of the road, looking down at the Ganges River.

"Justin," Swamiji shouted, "come get your chai!"

As we sat on the wooden bench of the road stand shop, Swamiji continued his story with warm, gentle eyes, seemingly happy to share his past with me.

"When were you born, Swamiji?" I asked.

He pulled out his passport from the little bag he often carried and flipped it to me. I opened it to find a beautiful photo of my teacher staring up at me. His warm, brown eyes looked serious. Beneath the photo was his birth date: 1925; beneath occupation, the one word: Saint.

I mentally began computing the math. "Let's see now, 1925 would make him . . ."

My thoughts were interrupted by his voice. "The date is not true, Justy. I made it up at the passport office."

"Then how old are you, Swamiji?" I inquired.

"I'm now 67. The age of the body is not important. I've had many bodies."

I did not know what to say next, so I kept quiet. Swamiji continued with his own thoughts. As often, they were about his beloved teacher.

"My master was known as Bengali Baba, or simply Babaji. In the United States, the Self-Realization organization speaks of their lineage as coming from the famous Babaji, but actually, the name is quite common for many elder yogis. In this instance, these two Babajis are related. Both of them were *gurubhais* (brother disciples) of the same teacher, my grandmaster, whom my master sent me to stay with in Tibet many years ago. Each of them completed the training with my grandmaster and went in their own directions."

BRINGING UP A YOGI

We finished off the chai, set down our cups, and told the shopkeeper that it was the best chai ever. Swamiji slapped my back and we walked to the car. He was in a rare mood. Over the twelve years I had been with him, I had learned when to speak and when to be silent, when to question and when to wait for him to speak. I had seen student after student make the mistake of trying to direct the master's agenda; I had watched carefully as they were politely directed to go away. Now I knew that the mountains were playing with the yogi. He was joking and relaxed, ready for fun. I knew I could ask him just about anything.

"Swamiji?"

"Hmm?"

"What kind of a kid were you?"

"Justin, I was such a nuisance! I always wanted attention; I would often pester the meditating monks to play with me. Cave monasteries are not really the best places for children, you see, so I really tried everyone's patience. Once I urinated in the drinking water pot just to show them. I will never forget my master hitting his temples with both fists, muttering 'my karma,' and then picking me up under one arm and the pot under the other and walking the two miles to the stream for fresh water. He, of course, became both parents to me. Justin, I tell you, at night when I cried, he would put on false breasts and bangles to make me feel like he was my mother as I lay next to him. Many times he rocked me to sleep, singing a little lullaby.

"When I grew a little, he assigned a young monk, Swami Sivananda Saraswati, to begin my monastic training. He had the patience to endure my tantrums most of the time. In spite of my need for attention, I gradually became used to living among the monks who affectionally called me Bholi Baba, which means 'innocent sage.'

"When I was eleven, my master decided that I was far too gentle for my own good; the kindness of my brother monks had softened me too much for the hard tasks of life ahead. So I was sent to a mountain monastery near Kalapone for several years to toughen me. I was welcomed into the community and introduced to a young monk near my age. He greeted me by kicking me and knocking me down. Then he showed me where I could sleep. Each day I would bow my head with the greeting that I had been taught and he would respond in his usual aggressive way. As the bruises mounted, so did my tears. I wanted desperately to return to the warmth and cheerfulness of my own monastery. I realized then how much I loved the monks and felt so sorry for the way I had abused them. I thought of escaping one night and running away, but then I said to myself, Enough!

"The next morning as the young monk came for me, I assumed my usual greeting, and as he lifted his foot to kick me, I quickly turned aside and plunged my foot squarely into his ribs, knocking him to the floor. I didn't give him a chance to get to his feet before charging into him with another kick. Just as he was about to get up again, I mounted another assault, but that time got halted from behind by an older monk who said that my action was sufficient.

"The older monk explained that my action was the sign they were waiting for. Now my training could begin. The monks' style was a combination of kung fu mixed with Indian karate, which, by the way, Justin, is a Sanskrit word.

"One of the best teachers in the monastery was completely blind. He always knew where the opponents were. I used to try to sneak up on him, but he could feel as soon as someone moved towards him. He taught us how to strike using our body's electricity."

As Swamiji spoke, I couldn't help but think of the popular TV series that showed the adventures of a Shaolin monk's training in a monastery in China. Some years earlier, as Swamiji, Theresa and I had watched an Indian movie one afternoon, he had pointed out two of the actors and told us they were trained at his kung fu monastery.

"How long did you study there, Swamiji?" I asked.

"I was there seven years. Do you want me to demonstrate?" But I knew better than to say yes. Over the years he had demonstrated to several others besides myself and we had always ended up stunned, lying on the floor. I tried to change the subject.

"Did you go back to the monastery during the kung fu years?"

"Yes. I couldn't be without my master too long. I went back and forth to the many places he sent me, but by my master's side was always best. Since I knew that my master would always back me up should there be any real danger for me, I also became quite obnoxious at times.

"Once I was told that it was time to take my turn in cooking for the monks. I refused. The monks insisted that I take my turn cooking the customary meal. When my day arrived, no one cooked the meal. I still refused, and so no one ate. The next day, I was hungry so I relented, but I was determined to get even for this great imposition. I loaded the pot with rice and beans but also threw in handfuls of hot chilies and a handful of small stones for good measure. I watched the monks very carefully as they chewed the food and saw that they licked their lips and said it was the best ever. 'Perhaps Bholi Baba should cook every day,' they all said.

"I grabbed a dish and put some food in my mouth to find out what had happened to my recipe. Immediately my whole mouth was aflame. I broke a tooth on one of the stones and hurt myself dashing for water to cool my mouth. What I didn't know was that the monks had simply used their solar plexus fire to dissolve my additional ingredients and avoid any discomfort."

We stopped the car to take a stretch along the mountain path. Swamiji told me of his schooling. He had gone to various schools on the plains and managed to keep his résumé for mischief intact. He had been repeatedly dismissed for insubordination. "Justy, I was thrown out of all the schools!" he said with glee. Slightly blushing, he admitted that his master had had to come down from the mountains many times to intercede with the principal to get him back into school. Swamiji had always returned to the mountains with relief after the school semester.

"As I grew older, I accused my master of restricting my growth by eliminating city life, so he gave me some money and told me to explore as much as I liked. I went to the city and walked all around, but as the glamour wore off and I ran out of money, I came back to the monastery. I brought two record players with me and a box of records. I set them up in the monastery and turned the volume as high as it would go. I wanted the valley to enjoy the sounds. The monks complained that it was too hard to do their practices when I operated both players at once. My master called me over and quietly praised my selections of music but suggested that I could appreciate the songs more if I listened to only one at a time. He also thanked me with tongue in cheek for using the rest of my money to upgrade the monastery with the Persian rugs that now covered the cave floors.

"Next I decided that it was time for me to become a big game hunter, not to kill animals, but to catch and raise them. In the jungle, I found a baby elephant and brought it home. My master refused to have it in the cave but gave permission to keep it nearby on the condition that I care for its upbringing. At first, it was fun. The animal learned all sorts of tricks over the months. I took it with me to the village and introduced it to *jalebees* (an Indian candy). Under my encouragement, it developed quite an appetite for them. One day, while I was meditating in the cave, the elephant, now full-grown, wanted his *jalebees*. I was not coming out of the cave, so it went down to the village to get the candy. The candy store owner refused, to his sorrow. My pet was enraged and thrashed about, totally destroying the man's store! The animal soon became a daily burden with its huge requirements for food. My master warned me not to neglect its health: 'Either become a zoo keeper or give the animal to the village people.'

"After I gave away the elephant I got a bear cub. He became so dependent on me that I could not keep him out of my cell. He wanted to go everywhere I went. When he grew up, he became so fierce that, as he prowled in front of the cave, everyone was afraid to come near the entrance. My master said he wanted to take me to some interesting places but he could not do so because my pet would scare people away. So I retired as a zoo keeper and decided that horses were easier to raise.

"I was given a bold Arabian stallion and trained it myself. No one could ever ride this horse because the moment they put their foot in the stirrup the horse would buck and run away. I had secretly trained him to accept the rider only from the right side, not the left. Years later, I played polo in England and always loved the ponies.

"Next I got dogs. My favorite was a German shepherd that I named Jackie. That dog would do anything for me. He once leapt from the roof of a two-story building when I called him."

I stopped him there. "I know all about your dogs, Swamiji." And we both laughed at the memories of the Institute guard dogs he had trained.

Swamiji told me then of his schooling, in 1940, at Shantiniketan, the institute founded by the Nobel laureate Rabindranath Tagore, also a disciple of Bengali Baba. The curriculum embraced the fine arts, including dancing, painting, sculpture, and drama, as well as the basic educational courses. Swamiji loved the arts he learned there. Tagore was beloved in India, not only for his great work in literature, but because, after the British massacre of his countrymen at Amritsar, he renounced the knighthood Queen Victoria had bestowed on him.

"Throughout these years," Swamiji said, "I continued practicing the agenda of training that belongs to our order of monks. I learned all the meditation and breathing techniques and passed the scheduled tests. The first test given to monks in our tradition involves being wrapped in a water-soaked robe. The monk must then raise his body temperature in order to dry the robe. If the test is passed, the monk is allowed to proceed with study because the master knows that he could withstand the mountain temperatures. At times my master would instruct me; at times he would send me to an adept for training, but my master always demanded full attention whenever he taught.

"It occurred to me one morning that I hadn't had a day off in a long time. So when class began, I was missing. My master sent for me. I told him that the rest of the monks needed his class but I was taking a free day. As I turned to walk away, he ordered the other monks to grab me and string me up by my ankles. There I hung, upside down, in the middle of the cave classroom while my master continued his lesson.

"During one class taught by my master on an *Upanishad*, a fellow disciple was bored and began to fool around. My master kicked his wooden clog across the room toward him, but the student ducked and the full force of the clog hit me above my eyebrow. For someone who sat and meditated all day, I realized that he had a good aim.

"I fell backwards, bleeding, and complaining, 'I didn't do anything wrong! Why am I being punished?'

"My master answered, 'Karma by association.' He felt sorry that he had wounded me, and later apologized, but I still have a small scar on my forehead from that episode."

As we drove along towards Gangotri, Swamiji spoke of his days as Shankaracharya, one of the five leading religious leaders in India. He told me about his schooling at Varanarsi and Prayag Universities in India and at Oxford University in England. He told me of his medical degree from Darbhanga Medical College and the research he had done in Utrecht, Hamburg, Frankfurt, and Moscow. He told me of his brother monks who also went to Moscow to participate in parapsychological research. I was surprised to realize that I myself had studied and done research in some of the same schools that Swamiji had once attended. He reminded me that a few years earlier he had tried to send Theresa and me to Shantiniketan and Chandigarh before the politics of India had made that too dangerous. We turned back to the curving view.

"These mountains are so powerful in their beauty, Swamiji."

"Yes. My heart is here. You see, my master took me everywhere in these mountains, meeting his associates. We traveled from Nepal, across the Himalayas, and back into India, staying at all the famous shrines. Once an avalanche started coming down the mountain above us and would have buried us, but my master lifted his arm and the falling rocks and mud stopped in mid air until we passed on the path. When he lowered his arm again, the avalanche continued."

I told Swamiji that it seemed as if most human beings knew nothing. For all our bragging about our technology, we have been using only brain power, neglecting most of the possibilities of which we were capable.

He interjected, "Justin, everything that technology is bringing forth now is not being done for the first time. Whatever an engineer can produce, the mind can do on its own, without matter."

A man of sadhana

CHAPTER 5
MASTER OF SELF

I watched as Swamiji showed a resident a series of small circles, each within the other. "You see?" Swamiji asked the young man, "It is thought that creates the body. The very atoms that make up your cells and tissues are manifestations of your thoughts."

THE DREAM INTERESTED ME; I pondered its meaning and was pleased to find that it was the topic of Swamiji's next lecture. "Conditioning the mind and body is indispensable to right thinking," he taught. After the lecture he passed me in the hallway and said abruptly, "Justy, are you coming over?"

Of course, I would not miss an evening with him for anything. I called Theresa to come from her office, and we followed the master home. Swamiji was in a rare mood. "Tilk? Tilk! Theresa is the best tilk maker. Tree," he said, calling her by his favorite nick name for her, "can we have some tilk?"

As we sat on the floor together drinking the sweet, hot tea/milk that Theresa had served, Swamiji began to reminisce about his training ordeals as a young yogi.

He told us that his master and the other living sages—the many unknown, elder adepts hidden away in Himalayan caves— had strategized together one day and agreed on a most unusual experiment for universal love, an historic first. They would train Swamiji in all the paths of yoga, all the scriptures, all the knowledge of the tradition rather than having him focus on one branch, as was usual.

My mind laid the scene before me. "Let us," the monks proposed, "invite Bengali Baba's young son to be trained in all our accumulated knowledge. Let us expose him to the breath of our specialties and the depth of our embodied wisdom that has come to us through the *shruti* (revealed knowledge) and *smrti* (recollections of knowledge) we have received from Brahman. Let us make sure that no trail of sacred knowledge be an unfamiliar path to him, for he will explore the anatomy of consciousness and become familiar with the landscape of saints. Wherever he finds darkness, let us show him how to expose the light. We will instruct him in the most esoteric sciences born in these Himalayas. He shall be led to self-realization and sanctity. He will know his sonship with the Divine Mother in all her manifestations, so that he will not only grasp the energies of this planet but will be privy to those foundational forces beyond the Milky Way that form all the universes and galaxies, past or yet to come. He will investigate the astrological lore of India, Egypt, and Persia, experiment with the ancient alchemy of the solar science, and entrain with the *bijas* (primal sounds) that constitute the organic processes of human evolution. Mother Nature will take him to her bosom and instruct him in the lore of healing herbs and animal craft. We will also make sure he understands the secular ways of the West as well as the East. He will know the secrets of energy as well as the mysteries between the chakras."

There were no precedents to describe this galactic enterprise in body, mind and spirit. In his journey, the *Yoga Sutras* were to be his departure, not the last frontier. First he would master these scriptures, performing every *siddhi* (miracle) of chapter three; then he would exceed them.

By pre-arrangement with his master, dozens of adepts and sages became Bholi Baba's personal trainers, making him their repository—the sacred mainframe, if you will—of their ancient, revered knowledge. He became their rather reluctant prodigy. In sending his son on this propitious learning adventure, his master advised him to observe four important counsels: "Never lose your temper, maintain calmness; never reply to insults, but try to understand why they come; never get emotionally upset at remarks toward you, but sit down and examine your capacity; never accept material gifts."

Knowing these four counsels is one thing, being aware of the knowing is something else. As the years went by, Swamiji stayed with nearly one-hundred tutors, learning what they were instructed to impart to him. Sometimes an adept would sense his inattention and shout at him, in no uncertain terms, to depart. Others would inexorably point out the contradiction between his immediate behavior and his master's counsels. On occasion, he pitted his physical strength against that of an elder teacher whom he thought belonged in a rest home for the retired. Much to his astonishment, he could not hold up against the other's gentle determination. The adepts battered his petty pride and conceit every chance they could, trapping him red-handed in his failure to follow his master's admonitions, while instilling, unbeknownst to him, their precious knowledge. Swamiji admitted that he managed to fail his master's counsels gloriously.

"Once," he told us, "I came before an adept in deep meditation, so he did not reply to my greeting. He continued to meditate in that state as I continued to implore his attention. Finally, I lost my patience and shouted into his ears, attempting to pry him up with a long tree branch to force him out of his meditative posture. I thought perhaps he was dead, so I stuck a thermometer in his rectum to check. He remained undisturbed. I finally just stood in front of him, shaking with frustrated anger. Suddenly the sage opened his eyes and kicked me in the chest with such force that it sent me toppling head over heels down the hill. I was bruised, covered with rock cuts, sweating, and vengeful. I grabbed a hunk of wood to use as a bludgeon and charged up the hill at him. Just as I reached him with my hand raised high to strike, he opened his eyes and greeted me warmly. He said that since I could not control my emotions, as my master advised, I would be a poor student and thus I should go away. Much, much later I recalled that when his foot hit the center of my chest, I felt something snap. His blow hid a boon; it broke many of my attachments to worldly goods."

Swamiji's sense of failure in attempting to be impeccable made room for his teachers' silent love to slowly transform his recalcitrant temperament. They guided him in astute ways to dismantle his arrogance while preserving his willingness to learn. He was given practices that would have salutary effects simultaneously upon his metabolism, emotions, imagination, and unconscious. He was privy to all the levels of consciousness. Time's confines held no barrier to his pursuits. He was walked through the scriptures, gradually redefining himself in the process.

Departing from cave teacher after cave teacher, Swamiji was convinced only of his ineptitude. The awesome Himalayan scenery hardly assuaged the recurring anger and tears that became his companions, yet in his solitary dejection he always remembered his master's voice telling him that he was on a path of conquest. In spite of everything, he resolved not to quit; he would see the contract through no matter what.

"In our tradition, we don't bend you; we break you!" Swamiji said, turning stern eyes to us. I gulped my chai. There isn't a single serious student whom I know who stayed with him over the years who wouldn't shudder in agreement.

As Swamiji matured, he synthesized the classical *yoga sutras* with his *tantra* practices and *Sri Vidya* experiences. To this wisdom was added his medical studies in Ayurveda and Homeopathy.

When his long, tutorial adventures were finally over, Swamiji returned to his cave feeling utterly dejected. His ego was flattened, and it hurt. He felt that he had not merely failed the opportunities given; he felt that he had disgraced his father.

It was late at night and he had nowhere else to go, so he came home. The monks were in their cells, but his master, who always meditated except when he was teaching, called out to him. Swamiji barely replied. His master beckoned him over again and warmly greeted his disheartened son. Swamiji admitted his failure to his master, but his master only smiled and with great feeling, invited his son to start again. "But this time be gentle."

From that day forward, Swamiji was a different man. He embraced patience. Over the next years, he submitted himself to unparalleled experiments with life's energies, advancing yoga science to a new magnitude of human development that no one in the history of yoga had ever before achieved. This knowledge pushed open the ancient aphorisms of yoga philosophy, codified in the *Yoga-Sutras of Patanjali,* far beyond its customary four chapters. The archive of his cave monastery now holds the fifth chapter, written by Swami Rama.

TRAVELING TO THE WEST

The decades of training accomplished, Swamiji could hardly wait to share his wisdom. His master sent him to the West. Western science, with all its technological progress, cannot see beyond the material level. How curious that psychiatrists and neurologists fervently denounce the reality of mind as a non-dual entity, while actively using it in their denunciations! Swamiji, with his Himalayan perspective, entered this world where consciousness was a marginal stranger and only matter mattered.

I marvel that he could have come to the West. He was such a sophisticated hitchhiker that adequate traveling supplies were hardly his concern. He told me that his master sent him off with only a few dollars in his pocket. Wherever he immigrated, whether in Japan, Europe, or America, a synchronicity emerged from meeting the right people at the proper moment. Each encounter in its way advanced his mission and came in handy later. As he spoke, I was reminded that I also wanted to be aware of opportunities as they arose for my life. Once an admonition had come to me in meditation: "Make yourself aware of what is already there." I now remind myself of it daily.

When members of the medical and scientific community in the Twin Cities of Saint Paul and Minneapolis became interested in Swamiji's awesome powers, Dr. Daniel Ferguson suggested to Dr. Elmer Green at the Menninger Foundation that Swami Rama would be an apt subject for the Foundation's projects. In 1964 Elmer and Alyce Green had co-founded a research program called Biological Feedback for Psychophysiologic Self-Regulation. As the years continued, they founded the Menninger Voluntary Controls Program for biofeedback research, education, and clinical treatment. It was within the auspices of this program that Swami Rama was invited to visit Topeka, Kansas, over Easter weekend, March 28-30, 1970.

In accepting Dr. Green's invitation to the Menninger Foundation, Swamiji became both the subject of study as well as a faculty member, demonstrating and lecturing, consulting and training others. The director of the biofeedback research program offered the scientific ambiance for him to demonstrate his embodied knowledge. An American window of opportunity opened for this master of the science of life to scientifically carry out his spiritual tradition's concerns for the personal, social, and therapeutic well-being of humanity.

Swamiji told me that he had had high hopes for this project. Given the political climate of détente and the rigid interpretations—religious and scientific—regarding the essence and limits of human nature, he had presented a strong contrast, a uniquely astounding version of human possibilities for modern living.

LIFE EXPERIMENTS IN BODY, MIND, AND SPIRIT

Through the Spring and Autumn of 1970, Swamiji conducted an unusual series of experiments related to the range of human consciousness at Menninger. He performed physical and mental feats that had never been done anywhere before. He challenged the prevalent truism in most quarters of medical science that human consciousness—the mind—is restricted in its voluntary control over bodily organs and systems. For some neurologists the mind does not exist; the physical brain alone accounts for it all.

To appreciate the value of his unprecedented contribution, one has to remember that Swami Rama brought a forgotten vision of human nature so free and abundant in its possibilities that it could not fit into the conventional mold upheld by the scientific community. Here was a man who was on profoundly intimate terms with his corporeal existence. Admittedly, the majority of physiological activities—from the rate of cell repair to the acceleration or slowing of the heart—exceeds the pale of rational commands. Our human autonomic nervous system, which directs the internal activities of the body, is not under the immediate sway of ordinary thinking. People don't walk around, for example, controlling their heart beats. These necessary, everyday functions (digestion, heartbeat, cell repair) fall under the domain of the unconscious portion of the mind. Consequently, controlling one's heart beat at will, deliberately slowing down the aging process, or remaining aware of one's environment while asleep seem farfetched, described only in fairy tales or science fiction. Swamiji was quite cognizant of the usual limitations on these anatomical functions, but he also wanted to show the scientific world that their boundaries were hardly the last word.

When I heard of Swamiji's demonstrations at the Menninger Foundation, I was astounded. I had read many mythologies of heroes and wizards, stories of saints and shamans, even amazing episodes of everyday people who, under the pressure of a crisis, had far exceeded their normal physical abilities. Over the years, I had met individuals who could demonstrate genuine psychic abilities, but without much consistency in performance. Their explanations of their gifts often sounded more like science fiction than a coherent theory based on human experience.

While I taught at Loyola University, I had spoken to some

faculty psychiatrists about my favorite ancient tales of super-human endeavors as well as similar contemporary reports. They had regarded them as highly imaginative folklore at best and serious mental aberrations needing medical treatment at worst. My theological confreres, with a large dose of skepticism, had attributed any remarkable stories about saints' miracles to the intervention of the Christian God and had been quick to point out that saints never took credit themselves for their successes.

Consequently, in meeting Swami Rama, I restrained my curiosity about the potential of consciousness by a conditioned skeptical attitude, secure within the rational assessment provided by the scientific community. In short order, he routed all those skeptical limits and provoked new questions in my mind.

Over the years, Swamiji actualized my wildest dreams. He showed me in theory and practice how the miracles attributed to Christian saints and others are less external interventions by a divine force than an innate power belonging to the essence of being human. Miracles were not hit and miss, but had a definite logic to their manifestation. He explained how the mind, being both a "transmitter and receiver," can increase its breath of awareness to become cognizant of the energy formations of things in this world that are not immediately within the perception of the physical senses. The reason that the senses can operate, he taught, is due to the presence of the human spirit—one's unlimited consciousness. The senses are simply corporeal instruments for consciousness to perceive things on that everyday, tangible plane of existence. But the ambiance of the spirit is not curtailed by the channels of the senses.

"Meditation opens the latent power of one's consciousness to go beyond body and mind," he would tirelessly remind his students. "When this expansion takes place," he elaborated, "then the power to interact with material energy awakens."

A NEW PARADIGM

Swamiji more than proved the veracity of his words during his two visits at Menninger. During his spring visit at the Menninger laboratory, Swamiji was wired to the small metal leads of two thermistors, sensitive detecting devices that register temperature changes at the surface of skin in tenths of a degree.

The slender wires were glued onto his right palm, one near his thumb and the other about two inches away near the edge of his hand. He predicted beforehand that he would alter the temperature on each side of his palm. Within a period of fifteen minutes there was a simultaneous warming and cooling of the right hand, causing a discernible pink color on the palm's left side and a gray color on the right side. The temperature difference between the two sides of the hand was recorded at eleven degrees.

At this test period, he began to play with his heart, and in less than a minute slowed his resting heart rate by twenty-one beats. The researchers noted that Swamiji used no muscle tension during this or the hand temperature experiment. Later, while remaining motionless, and upon a given signal, he accelerated his heart by twenty-two beats in less than eight seconds. The recorded subtleties involved in altering his heart beats indicated that he could differentiate control, not just over the cardiac muscles as a whole, but over selected portions of his heart. In a motionless position he also produced a total obliteration of his pulse; no beat could be detected by human measurement nor by instrumentation.

At dinner that evening, Swamiji apologized for not stopping his heart during the experiments. "I know you wanted to see that," he said.

Dr. Green showed enthusiasm at this idea, saying they could set it up for some future date.

Swamiji replied, "No, I'll do it tomorrow."

Alyce Green reminded Swamiji that he had just told them that a three-day fast was required for this heart alteration.

The Greens attempted to dissuade Swamiji from carrying out the experiment, but Swamiji was adamant. "I'll sign papers saying that the Menninger Foundation is not responsible for my death," he said.

Swamiji insisted that he could stop his heart from pumping for three or four minutes without fasting and also do something unique among yogis: carry on a conversation at the same time. "How long a time would be required to demonstrate heart stopping on the machine since I have not fasted?"

"We would be very much impressed if you did it for ten seconds," replied Dr. Green.

The next day, Swamiji sat quietly for two minutes and then

made his steady beat of seventy suddenly jump to 306 beats per minute. In this type of heart beat, a portion of the heart flutters, opening and closing with such rapidity that for all practical purposes, the heart has stopped. Blood cannot get through its chambers, blood pressure drops drastically, producing unconsciousness. It is usually associated with heart attacks and strokes.

This instantaneous change in Swami Rama's heartbeat caught the technicians by surprise. Those waiting for the experiment to begin could not detect when he initiated the alteration of his heart, for he sat utterly motionless. But in the control room, Alyce Green spoke to Swamiji over the intercom as requested, "That's all."

Swamiji made his heart return to a normal beat and smiled. The control room timed the test at 16.2 seconds. He explained that his concern had not been for his gross heart, the physical organ, but for his subtle heart, the energy form that expressed itself as the discernible physical organ. Swamiji then got up from the laboratory chair and walked upstairs to deliver his lecture.

Word was out in the scientific community: an Indian gentleman was challenging the Newtonian world view. For some scientists this was very unsettling. Swamiji, of course, always invited his critics to witness before they made up their mind about the meaning of his experiments.

Another important experiment—the psychokinetic demonstration—involved the movement of material objects by the mind alone. Swamiji demonstrated this ability in the fall of 1970 at Menninger. For this experiment, two fourteen-inch aluminum knitting needles were cross-posted on top of a vertical axis so that they could move laterally in either direction. A 360 degree protractor was mounted beneath so that the arc of movement could be measured. Swamiji was to position himself six feet away, facing the needles. Because the scientists suspected that he would move the needle by moving air currents with his body, a cloth was wrapped around his body to prevent arm movement. They also thought that perhaps he might expel air through his nostrils, thus affecting the needles, so a foam-rubber mask under a Plexiglas cover plate was placed across his nostrils and mouth.

"There was one scientist who, at first, refused to attend the session, Justin," Swamiji said to me. "But I insisted that he be there; otherwise I would not demonstrate. When he reluctantly entered the room, I requested that he call out what direction the needle should move and how far in degrees of arc. The man complied.

"I sat there motionless, with a rubber mask shielding my mouth and nose and a sheet covering my body. Then I began to utter a mantra and gazed upon the needle in front of me."

Swamiji told me that he focused upon the knitting needle mounted horizontally, causing it to gently rotate toward him through ten degrees of arc, exactly as requested. The experiment was repeated with similar results. The skeptical scientist slammed a book on the ground and stalked out of the room announcing, "I saw it, but I won't believe it."

In another experiment Swamiji demonstrated his control over sleep. He announced that he would sleep for exactly twenty-five minutes and then wake up. Brain-wave detecting equipment was connected to his head, thus monitoring and verifying the sleep state. He snored gently while the researchers observed his condition, chatting amongst themselves. Some left the room for coffee during his snooze. Upon awakening at the precise minute, Swamiji repeated the various utterances of every one in the room during his sound sleep, indicating who had departed and what they talked about in the lounge a floor above as well. The researchers were stunned. How could a man register full sleep and still be cognitively aware of his environment? Swamiji explained that he was trained to do sleepless sleep, *yoga nidra*, in which the brain goes to sleep while the mind remains awake, for the mind never needs sleep.

Swamiji told me that he was willing to train anyone at Menninger to do any of his experiments, but there were no takers.

Not always the best circumstances prevailed during his stay at Menninger. "I was also involved," he remarked, "in some electrical experiments to measure how much charge my body could withstand. I was taking more than double the amount that would kill an adult male."

Swamiji was insulated for his safety with rubber clothes and boots to protect against random currents in the room. "One day, when I left the changing room, I discovered that someone had cut the protective rubber boots insulating me. I then dropped further experiments with electricity."

Biofeedback was still a new instrument for researching

psychosomatic changes in living subjects. Swamiji became curious about the range of the biofeedback devices used at Menninger. As he became familiar with the various patterns that were traced on paper while he was wired to the brain-wave equipment, he realized that it was detecting only the basic four bands of electrical waves discharged by his brain—delta, theta, alpha, and beta. These four distinct waves are the typical recordings known in biofeedback self-regulation studies, and nearly everyone can demonstrate them to some extent with sufficient training. The paper tracings indicated the activity of the brain and expressed the brain's frequency waves. Swamiji realized that, however accurate these devices were for recording brain waves, they were not recording his higher mind states. Biofeedback's usefulness was in showing immediately the state of one's brain and confirming the mind/body connection.

Swamiji, however, was exceeding the most sensitive measuring capacity of the equipment. On call, he could easily produce patterns in the customary four bands from zero (delta) to thirteen or more (beta), but his meditative states of consciousness, since he was beyond his body and mind, could not be recorded. These went far beyond zero, and Swamiji asked why the machine could not record them. Dr. Green explained that the equipment was the best on the market, but Swamiji's states were obviously superseding the machines. Swamiji had hoped to work with these researchers in developing more sensitive equipment that could detect these finer levels of consciousness, but it never happened.

One of the interesting developments in the laboratory was when Swamiji demonstrated that mass and weight were not equivalent. While standing on a scale, a reading was taken of his weight. He stepped off and then immediately back on with a weight reading several pounds less. "Mass and weight are not the same," he kept insisting. He could also allow his skin to be cut or punctured with a needle, leaving no bleeding and healing immediately without a trace of injury.

In addition to these laboratory experiments, Swamiji, in a less formal setting, also engaged people in unusual ways. In one casual conversation about tumors with the director of research, he asked the man to place his hand on Swamiji's right buttock muscle. The director felt nothing unusual. "Feel again," said Swamiji. The director now felt a lump under the skin that resembled a moveable cyst. Then, on call, it simply vanished.

He repeated the same congestion of cells at another part of his body which the director ascertained by touch; it also disappeared upon call. Similar cysts that projected slightly upward, resembling warts, were produced on his forearms. These were produced at will within a fraction of a second and disappeared or receded into his body with equal speed upon his will. On one occasion, a biopsy was obtained of two cyst-like formations, one on each forearm. The report of their analysis was as Swamiji predicted: on one forearm, the cyst was benign, on the other, cancerous.

Swamiji told me that the root of cancer is in the mind and that much of the research on cancer was going in the wrong direction. One day, he asked my wife a strange question.

"Tree, why is there so much cancer prevalent today in the West?"

Theresa had no answer, but replied that perhaps it was the chemical pollution of the food and water. "Why do you ask, Swamiji?"

"Cancer is the chosen disease of yogis who wish to leave their bodies and burn students' karma. It was never meant for ordinary people." We were reminded that the great saints Rama Krishna and Ramana Maharshi had died of cancer and we were to remember Swamiji's words years later when they touched our lives in a singular way.

While in California, Swamiji demonstrated for journalist Jon Shirota the ability to withdraw his blood from one foot (the foot turned yellowish-white, like the foot of a corpse) and move it into his other foot (which turned purple-red). Swamiji next slowed his heart rate to twelve beats per minutes, so that his pulse was undetectable. He then created a tumor in two seconds, dissolving it in a flash. When asked about the importance of Alpha brain waves, then quite the rage in the popular consciousness, Swamiji replied: "Alpha and meditation are not the same. Alpha waves simply indicate relaxation; it is not a high state of consciousness. I have hooked up my German shepherd to a biofeedback device and he created Alpha waves 75% of the time."

Sometimes Swamiji did extraordinary things in the most ordinary way. What must the staff person at a research laboratory have pondered when, as he walked down the corridor with the chief subject, he innocently asked Swamiji,

"Can people communicate with nature?"

Almost immediately, without breaking stride, Swamiji turned his head and raised his hand casually as if to wave hello and continued walking down the corridor. Noting the movement, his companion turned likewise and looked through the glass window of the laboratory room they were passing. Every flowering plant in the room was visibly swaying back and forth, returning the morning greeting of this passing saint.

On another occasion, and by the softest touch, Swamiji caused the middle portion of a solid piece of wood, a 12-inch ruler, to fracture into pieces. Similarly, using a metal-edged ruler held at both ends by two volunteers, he merely pointed his index finger in a slow downward motion at the ruler, causing the wood to split apart and the metal edge to twist into a spiral.

He would amaze people by how still he could sit. They were baffled at this ability. Often he sat absolutely motionless for an hour with a feather beneath his nostrils. The feather never wavered. Not the slightest twitch would register on the polygraph device attached to his body. For all practical purposes, he had turned himself into stone. Where did he go?

A clinical psychologist entered Swamiji's office for a visit one day, and he urged her to ask him four questions about any topics of her choice. After getting over the initial surprise of this strange request, she asked him four distinct and totally unrelated questions. Upon the completion of the wording of the fourth question, Swamiji handed her a folded piece of paper. When she opened the paper, the psychologist was stunned to find written on it the exact four questions she had just asked followed by the replies he had just given.

Years later, Swamiji told me that he was frustrated with Menninger because they were not carrying out enough research on what he showed them was possible for human beings to do. He said he had many more things to show about the human mind but he was not able to share them. He poignantly said, with resignation in his face, "They don't know how to interpret what I did."

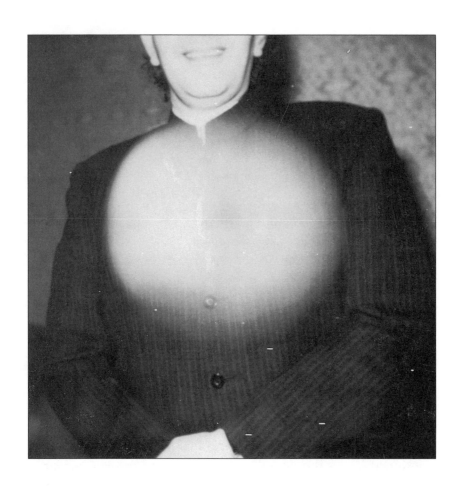

Mama's polaroid photo of Swami Rama's love

CHAPTER 6
DAYS OF JOY, DAYS OF SORROW

The bullock cart stood in our way on the high, steep mountain trail. I was annoyed. "Why do they always stop in the middle of the path and keep everyone waiting? I don't want to be on this mountain all night," I thought. "I'll just creep around the cart and get on my way."

I edged close to the rim of the path and made my way, hand over hand, along the wooden slats of the cart. The wind whipped against my shirt and blew dust in my face. As I neared the large animal, it turned its head to me and snorted, nearly tipping me backwards into the abyss of rocks far below.

"Be careful!" the Swami shouted from behind the cart. "If you fall, I won't be able to get you an American body. And you promised to help me next life."

THE DREAM ENDED ABRUPTLY, waking me up. Like most important dreams, it did not fade during the days ahead, so I mentioned it to Swamiji the next time Theresa and I were alone with him.

"Justin," he said, "that was not a dream, but a memory. It was an event that actually happened in your last life. You will meet many other people from your past life."

"How do you know?" I asked, surprised.

Reclining backwards in his big chair, he cocked his head to one side and replied, "Because I was there with you."

Then, with a mischievous smile he added, "Do you know what my greatest fear is?"

Since we did not associate fear with this man at all, his query stumped us. "No," we both replied together.

"To be born again—and face my foolish students, who keep torturing me!"

With that response, the tone of the evening was set. I knew

that, once again, we would have fun tonight.

"What is so difficult about being born again?" Swamiji asked. "Can one really be perfect like the Father in only one lifetime? Knowledge dawns in disappointment. People live what they think are full lives but are still not satisfied in the end, so they have to come back."

My mind swallowed that and went to the next issue. "Where is the sense of equality before God in view of the lives most people are born into?"

Swamiji answered immediately. "Ultimately, only four questions need to be pursued: Where have I come from? Why have I come? Where am I going? How do I get there?"

Then he surprised me with his immediate follow up. "To answer these questions, one doesn't have to believe in reincarnation, but one must at least not evade the questions. My point is, if you don't question, how can you become perfect? Who's making the tilk?"

Theresa jumped up and headed for the kitchen, and my mind went into overdrive. Wrestling with these four fundamental questions seems to be, sooner or later, part of everyone's issue. I can remember thinking about them even as a kid on the west side of Chicago. No doubt, the exchange with my buddies was hilarious, yet I still recall announcing, at age nine, what college I was going to attend—Notre Dame; where I would live one day—Evanston; and exactly how long would I live. I won't go into that last disclosure, but aside from my childish bravado, Swamiji later confirmed the date. Two out of three have happened as predicted; reports on the third are still to come in.

Swamiji cleared his throat and brought my mind back to the present. "Reincarnation is more fundamental than merely a part of any religious doctrine. By nature, we are travelers toward perfection. What is perfection? To become what you already are! Death is simply a habit of the body, not of the unconscious."

Whoa! He had just said death was a bodily habit. The implication would mean that it's not a permanent endowment. Could we undo the habit? Could we get death out of our bodies? Wasn't Cambridge-educated yogi-philosopher Aurobindo after something like this? My mind chased down all sorts of alleys to pursue these ideas without knowing exactly where I was going. Theresa called me back as she offered me tilk and sat down next to me.

"A seed becomes a tree," Swamiji continued, "which yields another seed. Each stage is responsible for the next stage. Animals are confined to their nature, yet they are evolving to the human level. Pets especially learn from their owners. Death is overrated; it doesn't help anyone. Suspect your theologies on this point. How many Christians or Jews do you know who are fearless before death?"

His ideas were pushing me to rethink my theology of death. I waited for his next words.

"For most people," Swamiji emphasized, "the strongest desire is to live here in this world. So that's what they get; that's their desire. Our actions flow from our desires. It's natural. We can't forego our nature; it's the only way. Your actions, then, are your karmas. Why are people so afraid of karma? It comes from the Sanskrit root meaning "action." Everyone has to do actions or they can't live. The reason we are responsible beings is that we are so close to divinity."

I wish we could have paused for awhile with that last multi-leveled statement, but he kept going even as a few more students tip-toed into the room and sat down quietly.

"If you don't think you have karma, then the next time you are hungry go sit in the kitchen until God feeds you. When we go to the kitchen we don't expect to find books. There is a linked order to things. Every action produces an effect. People bind themselves, not by their karma, but by the fruits, the effects, of their karma, which in turn inspire more karma, and so on. Every action has a reaction. Every reaction produces another action. It all must be balanced; you must balance all your karma in this life or another, but sometimes a great being can help you.

"If you perform your karma just for yourself, then you reap the fruits; if you perform your karma for others, then you have freedom from the fruits. You and Theresa are back together again because that is what you decided. We three are together because we want to be. In your last lives, you two promised to help me in this one. We have work to do; let's do it with God's grace.

"There is, of course, something called grace. You purchase a tree, but the shade from the tree is grace. When you have done your best actions, regardless of their success, grace arrives."

We all reluctantly said good night at 2:00 A.M.

MODERN MIRACLES

As the months of the new year, 1973, went by, Theresa and I taught during the day, she at Evanston's Montessori School and I at Loyola University. We visited Swami Rama at night and on weekends whenever he was not in India. I was pleasantly surprised by the increasing number of students drawn to Institute lectures. More and more people wanted mantra initiation and purchased Swamiji's new books sent from the Himalayan Institute in India. Several decided to stay and live as residents. Swamiji spoke of his dream for America: creating a hub center wherein people of all walks of life could learn the principles and philosophy of the sages. He wanted to make all education free until we reminded him that now he was living in America.

One worry was in my mind. Theresa was experiencing recurring pain in her abdomen which no medication could alleviate. Our physician declared with a constrained face that he thought further tests were needed immediately. "I still want to go to Swamiji's lecture tonight," she insisted.

We stood inside the doorway as the room filled with students. Down the stairs came Swamiji, smiling as he took in the scene. "Hi, Tree!" he said, coming up to her and hitting her in the stomach with his fist.

Theresa gasped; Swamiji walked quickly away and began his teaching. Sometimes one needs a lot of patience with these yogis. I really had to hold on to my temper when I watched that hit, but something told me to keep quiet. After the lecture, he called to me over the crowd, "Justy! Take her to the doctor tomorrow!"

The next day, all the tests at the hospital could find nothing wrong with my wife. She has never experienced stomach pain again after that inexplicable blow from the yogi.

Amazingly, Swamiji rarely called attention to his healing interventions; they were subtle, even though they hid profound phenomena. With other feats, he sometimes wanted people to be aware of the accomplishment.

One day Mama and Beefy-Baby went to attend a public lecture by Swamiji at a Chicago hotel. As he descended the stairs after his talk, Mama yelled out, "Show us your love, Swamiji!" and aimed her camera at him.

Swamiji stood still and smiled at them. When the Polaroid

film developed in front of them, Beefy-Baby looked at it and declared it ruined because it cut off Swamiji's head and was blurred. She was about to throw it away when Swamiji said, "No, no. I gave you a gift as you asked."

Mama looked down at the photograph in her hand and saw that it revealed Swamiji's chest with a radiant disc of light emanating from his heart center.

Swamiji came over and said softly, "Don't you see my heart? It's shining with love for you."

The photo became a precious memory for Mama who kept it in her purse all her life, showing anyone she thought should see it. Later Swamiji explained that he had increased the intensity of his heart energy so that it manifested as light. This made sense to me because all the paintings of saints show them bearing halos and auras about their bodies. Swami also demonstrated this phenomenon before a scientific group during which many similar photos were taken and promptly filed away.

Another unusual event occurred during those early days in Chicago. A minister friend and I discussed philosophical topics together after Swamiji's lectures. I found him as sharply interested as I was in comparing the Christian tradition with yoga. It was a joy to be playing ideas back and forth. He told me of his emotional experience at Swamiji's ashram in India and how ever since he had felt a compulsion to have Swamiji demonstrate his powers. The teacher, of course, kept reassuring him that he would oblige but also politely putting him off. Weeks became months and the minister's patience wore thin. He almost demanded that Swami "put up or shut up," but each time Swamiji would blithely reply, "Soon."

One morning, my friend got the call. He was told to come to Swamiji's apartment right away. He dropped everything. This is what he had been waiting so painfully for! Luckily for him, the Chicago Police must have been looking the other way as he drove the miles in record time.

Swamiji welcomed him and told him to sit in the middle of the living room floor. Removing his large, white shawl from his shoulders, Swamiji draped it over the minister's head.

"Just catch your breath, and do your diaphragmatic breathing," Swamiji said to him. "Do your regular meditation."

Some minutes later Swami asked, "How is it going? Do you

hear anything?"

My friend mentioned that he was being disturbed by what seemed to be people talking in the distance, probably in the next room or the hallway.

Swami immediately told his assistant to check the other room and peek into the hallway. They were empty. "No one in either place," Swami assured the meditator.

"How is it going now?" Swami inquired after a few more minutes.

"Well," replied the minister, "I hear voices discussing ice cream flavors. Why, I recognize two of them! They're women residents! One wants butter pecan ice cream and the other wants chocolate chip."

"All right, that's enough," Swamiji said. "Just continue your breathing, and you can take the shawl off now."

The minister stayed on the floor, overwhelmed and confused, while Swami dialed the center residence. "Hello, this is Swamiji. Where were you a few minutes ago? Who was with you? What flavors did you choose? Thank you."

He hung up and repeated the phone conversation to my friend. "You see? Your mind heard what happened at the ice cream store three miles away."

The full impact of his mind expansion did not register with the minister until later, for he was quite woozy. He was driven home, seeing familiar landmarks in a time warp, as his body involuntarily undulated up and down like a cobra's rhythmic movements. The energy waves then dwindled through the course of the night as his coordination and clarity returned.

Swamiji told us that when the body undergoes a profound expansion of conscious energy, it needs preparation. Otherwise an imbalance will occur when the power opens. Some teachers of yoga allow their students to have a taste of the pure universal force, guiding them through the experience, but usually a student is asked to prepare the body and mind through regular practice.

When yogis reach a certain level of pacification within, the natural sensory powers, such as hearing, are expanded enormously. The range of their acuity far exceeds normal hearing distances. In fact, the yogi can focus his hearing awareness to any location. Distance is no longer a barrier. The human ear in its construction acts as a channel for the normal contact with sound.

But as a structure it also constrains the hearing power to a limited range of perception. The customary human range of hearing, for example, is much less acute then animals. Through meditation, yogis learn to transcend the physical limitation of the ear and utilize the power of hearing directly without limitation.

Swamiji's skill was so consummate that he could affect and monitor the hearing capacity of the minister so that for awhile the minister could enjoy the additional range. Obviously, Swami focused the minister's power to familiar objects in order to confirm the objectivity of the episode. Since the man's body was not fully prepared to receive the expansion of the hearing power, there was a price to pay. The semi-conscious condition that expressed itself in the weaving back and forth of his body was an aftermath of the energy change and the slow re-assimilation back to everyday normalcy. There is a similarity in this instance with what happens when one engages vigorously in physical activity. When the body is not used to the exertion, there is a physical shaking-up that can leave the person somewhat dizzy and feeling physically out of touch for awhile. The body is unused to the intense utilization of energy even though the energy potential is always there.

THE SEARCH FOR NEW HEADQUARTERS

By this time, our Institute needed a new residence. A nearby farm was listed for rent. It was spacious, easy to drive to, and adequate for many students. Almost as soon as we stepped out of the car when we went to see it, Swamiji scowled, turned around and got back in, asking us to drive on. Perplexed that we hadn't given the place a chance, I asked what the problem was. Swamiji answered that he felt upset because that place was filled with the memories of torturous animal death. We later learned that the former owner had used the property as a mink farm. As I wondered how one picks up on the psychic history of place, we continued the search.

Meanwhile, the hatha yoga classes were being primarily conducted by Yogaleena, a hatha yoga teacher in the area who had become a student of Swamiji. She was one of the few who had been personally trained by him in the intricacies of the hatha postures. Some women came down from Minneapolis to train with her and expand the teaching staff. When I first met her, her greeting was cold and indifferent. I felt strong, unresolved tension in the air between us and did not understand it because we had barely met. The rumor was that she was soon to become a swami, and I wondered what she would do with her cute little daughter.

I learned from Swamiji that Yogaleena had been my sister in my previous life in India and that we had fought like cat and dog. He told me that she had remembered our life together when we met and the enmity had arisen spontaneously in her once again. Two years before, on the shores of the sacred Ganges River in India, Swamiji's student, psychologist Allan Weinstock, had taken vows of renunciation and become Swami Ajaya. He had opened a yoga center and bookstore in Madison, Wisconsin, and also had become one of the Institute's teachers. In my typical reverential attitude, I called him The Pumpkin Kid because all his clothes, including his underwear, were ochre, like most renunciates. Now Yogaleena asked Swamiji's permission to also take renunciation vows, but he told her that he did not advise it; it was not her path.

Shortly thereafter Swami went off to India and Yogaleena went to Minneapolis, making vows of renunciation before Pandit Arya and becoming Ma Yogaleena. She bought a house in Prospect Heights for use as the Institute headquarters and we began classes there. Once again we were pleased to have a permanent residence that provided sufficient space for classes and residents.

Swamiji had just completed his new book, *Freedom From Karma*, which was the first book in America to define the philosophy of the ancient concept of human action and consequences. A second book, *Meditation in Christianity*, to which several teachers including myself contributed chapters, began to reach the Christian community and help expand its understanding of spirituality.

THE ALL-INDIA YOGA CONFERENCE

October of 1973 saw a large contingent of Americans head to the Indian industrial city of Kanpur to participate in the All-India Yoga Conference.

This conference was designed in a startling manner: Americans were the featured yogis. Thousands of Indians from government, education, medicine, and business filled a huge tent to listen to Ma Yogaleena and Rudolph Ballentine speak of the ancient yoga tradition of the Himalayas. Yogi Achala demonstrated advanced yoga postures with such proficiency that the audience gave him a standing ovation. Students with lesser expertise fanned out on the stage in various yoga postures, while Swami Ajaya lectured on Western psychology. Dr. Elmer Green and his family from the Menninger Foundation introduced the Indians to the new science of biofeedback, setting up portable biofeedback machines and exposing India to the new brain wave technology.

Our bank balance was not yet ready for the trip, so Theresa and I relied on the reports of our friends to learn about it. At the conference opening, the Americans were astounded to see hundreds of Indians rush forward to touch Swamiji's feet in the Indian gesture of deep respect. They obviously treasured the presence of this revered holy man. Many others, however, found it inconceivable that His Holiness Swami Rama would cross the seas to live and work in America. Dr. L. K. Mishra, Swamiji's student and the conference convener, explained: "Swamiji is the first Siddha Master from the Himalayas to offer himself to the experts of the scientific research laboratories of the West, including the well-known Menninger Foundation of Topeka, the Institute for the Living in Pennsylvania, and Harvard University. Swamiji's chief mission in the United States has been to work with scientists, because science is the guiding principle of today's dominant civilization, yet is in burning need of philosophical direction."

In his keynote address, Swamiji stressed the importance of spiritual practice for the future of humanity. "Divine grace and bliss is overflowing all the time, but we remain sleeping and unprepared to accept it in our daily life. That is the root cause of our bondage and misery."

The audience, full of businessmen, community leaders, and spiritual seekers, asked Swamiji about the necessity of yoga when India already has so many religions. Swamiji replied, "Religion tells you what to do; yoga teaches you how to be."

Questioning continued along these lines until one loud, demanding man stood up to challenge Swamiji vigorously, "Why do you prefer to work in the West? Are you going there just like

the other money-seeking gurus? Don't you know that Mother
India needs you?"

It seemed almost impossible, but the entire audience was
galvanized into silence, awaiting the reply.

Swamiji answered boldly and succinctly. "You people waste
my time. You spend money uselessly building temples of stone
and ignore the temple you are. You come to me and sit at my feet
waiting for me to do everything for you, while you do nothing but
sit. In the United States I find students seriously interested in
practicing yoga."

There were no questions after that.

After the conference, the Americans headed to Swami Rama's
ashram (spiritual residence) at Rishikesh, India. Earlier in the
century this lush area on the curving banks of the Ganges River in
the foothills of the Himalayas had been the preferred winter
residence for many yogis. The name Rishikesh literally means
"matted locks of sages' hair." Each year the sages would retreat
from the snows of the high mountains to continue their practice
along the sacred river as it descended into the plains until the
seasons changed and they could return to their caves. In this
region, many of the mythical stories of the God Shiva took place
and today one can still find mystical, powerful spots where, if in
the right disposition, one will experience an expansion of
consciousness.

Swamiji had spent many of his younger years in Rishikesh
with his master, and there grew in him a longing to establish an
ashram there. In the 1960s he walked along the beach with S. N.
Agnihotri of Kanpur, elaborating his vision. They slept on beds of
sand and rocks on the spot that was soon to become Ram Nagar—
city of Rama.

When Swamiji, a licensed homeopathic physician, had lived
in London some years earlier, he had kept up his medical practice.
He made it a point never to directly charge his patients for any
care; instead he would leave his lower window open at night and
patients could deposit through the opening whatever they
wished. By some coincidence, he was having much more success
in curing people than his neighboring competitors. The word got
out. It crescendoed until British doctors were losing so many
patients to him that a committee came and implored him to retire.
He acceded to their request and used the patients' contributions

for the construction of this ashram.

The American contingent arrived at the three-acre ashram, filling all the rooms, a large tent on the beach, and several rooms in the government tourist bungalow in town. They began a retreat of hatha yoga, meditation, and lectures on spiritual practice in the sacred confines overlooking the river.

One day, for the sake of the American researchers who wanted unusual phenomenon to record, Swamiji instructed one of his young watchmen, a devotee of God as Divine Mother, to perform his yearly ritual near the ashram mango grove. Outlining a square plot in the dirt, the young man built a fire in a pit and set up a small altar there. He stepped into the square and sat quietly before the altar in contemplation throughout the night and into the morning. By mid-morning, Swamiji invited the guests to witness the completion of the ritual. They sat around the edges of the ritual area while the young man remained ramrod still, deep in trance. The ashram cook crossed into the square and fed him with her fingers morsels of food she had prepared. He smiled at her with tears in his eyes, since he viewed her as the holy mother in physical form.

The guests had earlier been strictly warned not to go near the practitioner nor entertain negative or foolish thoughts, but as the young man finished the food he was given, he suddenly turned and yelled in Hindi at Swami Rama for a few minutes. Swamiji continued to watch him calmly, saying nothing. The young man then reached down into the fire pit and brought up some hot ashes, licking them from his hand. Then he grabbed a flat rod of metal about eighteen inches long from out of the burning coals and rubbed it vigorously across his tongue. Once more he reached for ashes and after dropping them into his mouth, he again stroked his tongue with the hot metal rod as the ashes fell from his open mouth. He finally stopped all activity and then sat quietly and calmly before the cooling pit.

Swamiji stood up, signifying that the propitious event was over. He said that the man had yelled, demanding that his teacher make a promise to the Divine Mother but Swamiji would not promise under threat, not even to her. While the group spoke of the "great adept" who did the ritual, Swamiji corrected them.

"He is a watchman," he said, "not a great master." Swamiji pointed out that such acquired talents have little to do with holiness, but with one-pointedness of mind. Expressions of psychism, channeling, seeing auras and other such phenomena comprise a minor level of sensitivity and are not in the least an index of spiritual progress.

MOVING ON

One night while Swami was still in India, my car pulled up to our Prospect Heights center at the same time as Mama's arrived. Mama, Theresa, and I went to the door and rang the bell as usual. No answer. We rang and rang until finally one of the young resident men slowly opened the door and asked what we wanted.

"Have you forgotten that there is a lecture tonight?" I asked.

He shook his head and bluntly said, "There is no lecture here. Please go away."

I was annoyed and persisted in asking about the rest of the lecture series. With a defensive voice, he replied that the series had been canceled and that we shouldn't come back again.

Yogaleena came to the door at that moment, pulled him back inside and angrily told us to leave the premises. Without waiting for a reply, she slammed and locked the front door. We looked at each other dumbfounded. Mama then told us that she had been informed that day that Yogaleena was no longer involved with the Institute and that we should stay away from her house. Mama had driven out in the hope that it was a mistake. Amidst the confusion, my anger began to rise, and I suggested we get into our cars and meet at a local coffee shop.

It all seemed absurd to me. Apparently our hopes and our money had gone into the purchase of a convenient home for a celibate renunciate who had then decided to rejoin her husband and keep the property. But what could we do? It was registered in her name.

Many years later, Swamiji said that when Yogaleena walked out that way, he felt her connection to his heart break apart.

At the coffee house, Mama asked me to help her. She was angry and discouraged; I was angry and perplexed. We talked for hours, supporting one another with hopes and fears, especially the dread that Swamiji might not return to Chicago. We finally decided that this predicament was not going to stop us. We would show Swamiji that we could carry on; our commitment to his vision was certain. The three of us grew much closer that night as we sat in the glaring light of the cafe planning the best way to carry on the ancient tradition.

Thanks to Lydia, a storefront in Evanston opened up for us. We came there one night, looked around, noticed that some students were no longer with us, and talked about building something for the future. Someone asked if Swamiji was ever coming back to us; he had been gone so long. I insisted he would not leave us orphans. David Backstrom was strumming his guitar, and we all began to sing a slow version of the old song, *You Are My Sunshine*. Tears flowed as we sang together, "Please don't take our sunshine away."

I was compelled to turn my sadness into some good use, so a short time later I found us an interim center. Classes would now be held in the large rental space of The Flamingo Motel. There Jackie, Marion, and others taught hatha classes, Ladd and I taught meditation and lectured on yoga philosophy, and to our delighted surprise, the student list continued to grow while we all waited for our Sunshine to return.

Tat Walla Baba and his two visitors

CHAPTER 7
A GATHERING OF SAINTS AND SINNERS

I was lost in the forest and came upon a small hut. I looked inside through the open door. There was a gray-haired Indian man sitting behind a desk. Two younger Indians stood on either side of him. I asked if I could enter because I needed direction. Given permission, I stepped in and bowed to the elder and walked closer into the room. The younger men looked surprised that I was allowed to approach. Then the old man began to tell me things that only a seer could know. I sensed he was blind. "You have a band of fire around you," he said to me. "If you learn to extend it, you will illuminate your path."

IN THE EARLY WEEKS OF THE YEAR, while I dreamt Indian dreams, Swamiji called Dr. Arya from India and told him to organize a spring excursion to the great Indian religious gathering, the Maha Kumbha Mela. Theresa and I and one hundred forty-five other Americans immediately signed up. During that Chicago winter of 1974 the winds and snow blew long and hard, and we were glad to head to the warm homeland of our teacher, curious to see what we would find there.

Our first arrival in India was like landing on another planet—a hot one. We left Chicago near zero and arrived in India at one-hundred degrees. The place fascinated us. We had never expected such an entourage of sights—noisy traffic jams of strange vehicles and animals, people with shiny black hair and Sikh turbans and colorful saris, great varieties of unknown food served with spicy tea, flowers of every color and scent and shape. On the roads, the cows demanded as much deference as a Mercedes. Because the roads have no center line and horns constantly blare, roads are one of India's undeclared combat zones. I imagined that the game of Chicken must have originated on these streets.

We overnighted in New Delhi at the infamous Lodi Hotel,

complete with mouse-sized roaches, leaky toilets, no air conditioning, questionably clean linens, and a courtyard full of noisy families cooking and washing and tending their children. All the inconveniences were forgiven because there I first encountered what became my favorite cooling drink—sweet lassie, made from yogurt, sugar rose water and ice, and topped with almonds.

At 5:00 AM, we boarded our tour bus for a weaving, wearying eight-hour trip north. When we finally turned into a long tree-filled lane, we found ourselves in Swamiji's ashram, in Ram Nagar—estate of Rama—our sunny headquarters. We walked about looking at three white, stucco lodges facing northwest, just outside the town of Rishikesh, right on the bank of the Ganges, with the dense jungle swimming-distance across the holy river. Off in the compelling mist the snow-covered peaks of the Himalayas loomed against the bluest sky. There was even an elephant path, heavily used during the yearly elephant migration, a hundred meters from the ashram entrance.

None of us could have imagined the intensity of the next three weeks. The stupendous events of the Maha Kumbha Mela occurred about twelve miles away in the small city of Haridwar. Alternating every three years during a twelve-year cycle, Kumbha Melas are cosmic spiritual gatherings held in one of the four holy cities—Allahabad, Ujjain, Haridwar, and Nasik. The auspicious time for these sacred fairs is determined by the planet Jupiter passing through the zodiac. The Maha Kumbha Mela, however, is a most extraordinary celebration, the conjoining of Jupiter and Aquarius, celebrated once every sixty years.

The Kumbha Melas have the distinction of being the largest religious gatherings in the world, attracting millions of believers. From ten- to forty-five million people—from the holy saints in the mountains to the poorest believers in the outskirts of Calcutta—come on foot, by tractor, by trolley, on rickshaw, by train and by plane across the sub-continent to converge on the banks of the holy river.

Haridwar, normally a city of 50,000 inhabitants, was filled with three-and-a-half million seekers the day we were bused there. The city was now a *tirtha*, a holy place of pilgrimage. Miles and miles of tents had been erected by the government along the shores of the Ganges River to house the pilgrims. One would think that the planet itself was sponsoring a global bazaar. If one blended the excitement and splash of a presidential election with the pomp and circumstance of a royal coronation, and then combined those with the endless rows of goods in the largest imaginable garage sale and with hundreds of booths for private religious guidance, and finally doused the scene with a plethora of exotic aromas from the ceaseless cooking and representatives of the entire Yellow Pages of India, one would start to grasp the atmosphere. Here were winding dirt paths and swirling corridors of tents and bamboo shacks that displayed for discerning seekers ancient magical ritualists, yoga demonstrators, ascetics in extreme, authoritative pandits, and even religious feminists marching with banners and flags. The stellar attraction, however, was the parliament of *sadhus,* hundreds of reputed God-men and women from the various spiritual traditions, the mystics who hold their *darsans* and *satsangs*—gatherings of saints—during those auspicious days.

Queuing up is unknown to Indians. Consequently, people collided in waves across our paths, tugging and pulling with their momentum, always with the sun hovering intensely above. It was impossible to stand still. All night long the chanting wafted down the river. Thousands of small bonfires speckled the shores as pilgrims cooked their evening meals. The crowds swelled to fifteen million.

During that first week, I realized that we stood on sacred soil where the divine makes its presence known in multifarious forms: boulders, mountains, stones, rivers, lakes, trees, plants, animals, and, lastly, human beings. Divinity is celebrated in nature-created and man-made sculptures and images, through hymns and festive songs. What is a modern electric battery, I thought, but an invested container of charged energy? Likewise, in this ancient land of saints and sages, *sadhus* and *sanyasins,* even the lowest rock could and has become a living idol, an accumulator and conductor of spiritual energy. The Mela, like a vast continental ritual, permitted each of its millions of devotees to glimpse the divine in that person's preferred form and thus allowed each person to be inspired to move closer to his or her ultimate destiny.

At the opening ceremony, Swami Rama, standing high on the balcony in the main temple, blessed the entire crowd with the opening prayer. We Americans sat on the bridge spanning the river and watched the ceremony unfold. Yogis and ascetics—the naked warrior yogis first—marched with their particular group in a kaleidoscopic procession of elephants and thrones, silks and homespun cloth, begging bowls and golden weapons to the Ganga, "the river of heaven," to submerge themselves while the others awaited their turns. As the final ascetic group emerged dripping from the holy water, mayhem ensued. Thousands, following the *sadhus*, dashed into the river for the cosmic bath which washed away the stains from their previous births.

Every Mela has its tragedies; some people are trampled in the stampede to the water. The faithful are undisturbed by this catastrophe; it is a sure key to a propitious new life. If there were deaths at this huge Mela, however, the Americans were not informed of them.

The day after the great bathing ritual, we were received as guests of the Police Commissioner responsible for the order and safety of the entire Kumbha Mela. His family and staff generously prepared a resplendent Indian buffet for the American entourage at his home. Swamiji entertained us with stories of our host, his student, who ordered one exotic dish after another for us. We basked in the garden, and its quiet atmosphere rejuvenated us, giving us energy to return to the Mela.

SAINTS AND SURPRISES

Every culture especially reveres a few men and women in the hearts of its people. At Swamiji's request, our group was invited to meet one of them: the saint, Anandamayi Ma. Stories were passed among us of this woman's relationship with the divine since her childhood. She had the reputation of assisting anyone who came to her for help; miracles were ordinary occurrences around her. Swamiji and Ma had known each other in their youth, and each greatly respected the holiness of the other.

A private audience was scheduled for us. As we headed through the massive crowds, I was irked by one of the pandits who kept commanding the group to maintain his particular order. His demands, coupled with the relentless heat, were too much for me. Rapidly losing my patience with his incessant harping ("walk this way," "hold your arms that way," "men keep separate from women," "don't speak"), I was about to turn around and confront him—verbally or physically. I wanted that confrontation, but just as I turned to him, we arrived at Ma's large tent. I still wanted the showdown, but as we entered I began to feel upset with myself over the less than charitable thoughts in my head. We were about to meet a saintly woman.

The men rushed in first and quickly searched for front row seating; they were politely informed by Ma's disciples that only women should sit up front. I was momentarily amused that all the men had to shift to the rear of the tent, but my head was still buzzing with anger and guilt. Then as the group chanted songs to the Divine Mother, Anandamayi Ma came out and sat before us.

Looking at her, I forgot what had just been preoccupying my mind. What was it I had been thinking about? I couldn't remember; it was a total blank. I was drawn to Ma's remarkable, peaceful presence as she spoke about spiritual practice, reminding us that in order to progress we must do whatever our teacher requested.

Theresa, selected to represent the group, offered a flower garland by placing it on Ma's feet. The saint smiled at her, lifted the garland and placed it around Theresa's neck saying, "Take this home with you as my blessing."

I was so impressed with the quiet dignity of this saint that I was full of joy, but as the crowd departed from her tent, my mind picked up agitation exactly where it had left off when I entered. How strange! In her presence I was absorbed only in her serene mood. It was an undisturbed interlude between the chaos of my thoughts. As soon as I got beyond the range of her presence, however, my mind returned to its previous agitated condition. I was intrigued that a person could exude such power to distract me. The wonder of it all made my argument with the pandit absolutely trivial.

The next morning at five o'clock, I was invited to join a small group that was leaving on a journey to meet selected *sadhus*. After a quick cup of tea, we walked through the city streets for an hour before entering a small hut where a hefty, gregarious swami welcomed the ten of us. He expressed his pleasure that Americans were attending the Kumbha Mela and made sure that each of us was comfortably seated while he spoke on the meaning of spiritual practices. Since he walked gracefully about, it took me some time before I realized that he was blind. Although his eyes remained closed, there was not the slightest hesitation in his bodily movements nor in his attention to his guests. It puzzled me that he could maneuver himself without even a hint of his impairment.

Swamiji later told us that, although the man did not possess his physical eyesight, he saw the world with his "third eye." Apparently, continuous meditation on the space between the two eyebrows stimulates the pineal gland to deposit a sandy secretion that forms a circular pattern beneath the skin resembling the shape of an eye. When the biological secretion has reached a certain consolidation, the power of sight can be manifested there without the customary physical eyes. When this third eye or *divya chaksu* is used, a wide range of energy levels can be perceived. Some months later, Swamiji showed me how it was done. He asked me to write something on a sheet of paper, and then to blindfold him with a towel. He moved his hand above my paper, felt the energy of the message, and then proceeded to perfectly write the sentence on another sheet.

After visiting the blind *sadhu*, our little group walked for another hour on the hot sands to an isolated spot where women were not allowed. Here we found a strange camaraderie that thoroughly intrigued us—the *naga sadhus*. Dozens of men, their naked bodies smeared with ashes to keep them cool, performed strange physical penances, from standing on one foot for many years to holding one arm aloft until it withered. I noticed one man with a clasped fist above his head, the nails growing through the hand to emerge on the other side. I was told he had held his hand up this way for twelve years as penance for the world's sins. Many ascetics were in *mouna*, silence, spending their days, months and years without any conversation. All these men chose a rigorous path, disdaining the world and hoping to achieve enlightenment through severe penances. With their permission I took some photos, but I didn't know what to make of them. I reflected that if their regime was truly yoga, it certainly wasn't the middle path.

It was near noon when we left the settlement, and we still walked on without food. I wanted a cool glass of lemonade and a shower. One of the guides came running to us, excitedly saying that we were invited to meet another holy man. "Big deal," I thought ungratefully. "Just what I want, another *sadhu* on a hot afternoon." At first I thought of excusing myself and returning to the tent for rest, but I realized I could never find my way back. When we were told this *sadhu* lived in a pine hut resting on stilts above the beach, I realized that meant we would be trudging over blazing sand. I very reluctantly tagged along.

After a grueling march, we were ushered up to the yogi's hut, which was surrounded by a few hundred devotees. I leaned against one of the upright stilts supporting the floor of the hut while the guide shouted to the yogi inside that we were students of Swami Rama. At those words, a stirring began in the hut. Suddenly, a wrinkled, dark-skinned, bony arm appeared on the ledge three feet over my head, followed by a small, bearded face crowned with disheveled, matted hair. The saint peered down, looking directly at me. We stared at each other for about twenty seconds until I bowed my head to him.

"There's something familiar about you," I puzzled. I snapped his picture, while he surveyed the rest of the group and gave us a mini-lecture. His words emphasized that *sadhana* (spiritual practice) was essential to purify us for God, and that we should learn to love meditation from the core of our hearts. We were then asked to sit down and chant a mantra—Sita Ram—with him. On the sun-baked ground with its reflected heat bouncing into my face, I was brought to new levels of impatience by my weariness. I couldn't wait until the singing would be over; all I could concentrate on was my sweaty misery.

Then, as the saint returned to his hut and I stood up, all my fatigue, hunger, irascibility, and boredom dropped from me like sweat into the sands below. I stood erect and felt such refreshment and strength and clarity of mind that I started jogging back to our tent, a mile away. I had heard about Englishmen and mad dogs in the noonday sun, but I could not hold back my exuberant energy. No one in the group seemed to share my feelings, but when I told Swamiji what had happened, he smiled and said that Devraha Baba, reputed to be 280 years old, remembered me from the past and had given a blessing to his old friend.

As I went back to my room, I quietly pondered about a saint who calmed emotion, a sightless swami who could see, men who revered pain, and a centuries-old yogi who blessed a former acquaintance with vitality.

Swamiji gathered the entire group together one night at our

camp and, after answering questions on what we saw in the Mela, spoke to us from his heart.

"There are two laws of life: contraction and expansion. The contraction of your personality makes you selfish; you cannot grow. You just want to fulfill your wishes, regardless of how they affect others. Loneliness and sadness follow upon contraction. Thinking only of the little self becomes a serious problem in life. Expansion allows your awareness to increase its knowledge of reality. You have to be prepared for expansion. Your thinking processes won't lead you to this realm; you must purify yourself so that your innermost consciousness can speak to you from its silence.

"There is nothing to fear. Fear doesn't lurk outside you, ready to pounce. It's your own creation. Some only see the horizon through a small window; no matter how much they move around in the room the same window view remains. The angle of vision is more important than the object in order to know truth. Men and women think about the same things but their angles are different. Unless this is appreciated, communication can fail and lead to misunderstandings.

"Ego loves to say 'No.' It makes itself feel superior. Just watch a child resist the entreaties of the parent. Learn not to show your ego nor condemn yourself. An appreciation of all of life is important on the path. When you realize that the divine is within everyone, then the law of love becomes spontaneous and easy."

The Indian sun broiled on. Haridwar became oppressive with crowds and heat. One afternoon Swamiji looked at us, melting in the sunshine, and ordered us to the bus. *"Chelo, chelo!"* he cried as we shuffled across the compound and climbed up the soft rubber steps of the bus. The Hindi word meant "Let's go!" but for years afterward Theresa swore it meant "Get on the bus."

We drove to the outskirts of town, passed the lines of tents, and turned into a patch of vacant beach. Here relief welcomed us—the Ganges River. We all jumped out of our clothes and into our swim suits and splashed into the water. The river cooled and refreshed us. We became giddy as we played in the water.

"All right, kids, move over," came that familiar, stentorian voice.

There he was in full swim regalia, maroon swim trunks and a

denim hat, recently swiped from my head. Clowning, Swamiji strode with long strides into the water, greeting everyone.

"Why didn't you people come here earlier?" he shouted. "I was waiting for you to do this."

The noisy Americans laughed and splashed, submerging their bodies in the brown water to escape the oppressive sun. On the opposite side of the river a small herd of dusty elephants relaxed after their Mela duties. They sprayed water from upraised trunks and swam in circles around their handler. In the middle of the river, between both groups, the son of the Himalayas frolicked in the current.

Some of the American faces and whispers revealed a strange reaction. "Is that Swamiji swimming? Actually playing? Who would think that was allowed?"

I had to laugh, for they reminded me of the clinical psychologist who fainted when she heard that the Swami went to the bathroom.

Why do we humans make rules for our great ones? We form idols of them in our minds, placing them on such high pedestals that we delete all their human characteristics. We ignore the people who exist before us, substituting an abstract notion of what we want and expect them to be. Why do we find it so hard to combine humanness and holiness?

"Hey, what happened? Who took them?" We heard the shouts from the middle of the river and watched Swamiji looking about, as if he were searching for something.

We were all curious. Did I see apprehension on his face?

"I've lost my bathing suit," he yelled to us. Can you men help me?" Apparently his borrowed trunks were too large and had slipped off with his swimming.

I couldn't resist. "Hey, Swamiji, wouldn't you like to sunbathe? I know just the spot."

He glared at me for only a moment and began shouting again for help.

Two male students rushed into the waters carrying a pile of towels. A few minutes later Swamiji marched out from the waters, wearing my hat and bands of colorful wet towels around his waist and chest and shoulders, majestically striding as if he had just parted the Red Sea.

A few days later, Swamiji arranged for a handful of us to visit some local sadhus in the foothills near his ashram. On the way, we visited the Divine Light Society of Swami Sivananda and the large Swarg Ashram. These were just like the medieval hospices in Europe that gave shelter, food, and medical care to pilgrims. At this moment there were about a dozen wandering sadhus occupying the shelter while the staff of swamis and renunciates cared for the poor and the sick.

We crossed the river at Lakshmanjhula, walked into the forest and climbed a few thousand feet to the clearing in front of a cave. Within a radius of about fifty yards, we passed through an invisible curtain into an idyllic setting of such tangible serenity that normal anxieties and daily cares disappeared. Our thinking remained sharp but its pace slowed. Theresa and I entered the cave with our guide. Tat Walla Baba, "The Saint Who Wears Burlap," welcomed us with a smile as he sat in the dark coolness. It was evident how the serene aura of this spot had come about. This *sadhu* had been a householder who, after raising three children and seeing that his family was well taken care of, had renounced the world and come to this cave forty years earlier. His continual meditation had charged the atmosphere, drawing birds and butterflies into the forest conservatory. He was the confessor, counselor, and guardian of the mountain people who lived nearby. They came for advice and blessings and brought food for the saint and his disciple.

The Baba noticed our discomfort after the steep climb and offered us some cool mountain water. I remembered that it was Easter Sunday, so my mind prompted questions about Jesus' resurrection from the dead as we drank.

The saint pondered awhile and then replied, "One must go further than raising oneself from the dead. Jesus was a great sage, but resurrection was not his main work."

Well, that certainly was a novel answer to share with the Jesuits back at Loyola University, I thought.

"You need only follow the words of your guru (spiritual teacher) in order to obtain all your desires," Tat Walla Baba continued. "Your guru holds the shortcuts."

Noticing my camera, he politely asked if I wanted pictures. We stepped outside into the sunlight, and I couldn't help but notice that his body was virtually wrinkle free and his skin glowed. He scampered up the rocks as if he were a youngster, though the baba, we were told, was in his late seventies. Although we were reluctant to leave, our guide hinted that the Baba's time for meditation was near, and so we thanked him for his blessings and departed.

Coming down from the cave, we met the rest of our group who had gone to meet a young swami living in the forest. Together we walked along the river bank to a heavy, middle-aged swami living on the sand in a large open tent. Our guide told him about us and asked for an interview. We waited and waited for the swami's invitation to approach, but it never came. We observed him being fed fruit by women disciples as others massaged his hands and others fanned him with large peacock feathers. He kept us at a distance but sent some *prasad*, a sweet candy. His presence disturbed me, even at a distance, but I couldn't say why. All I knew is that I wanted to get away and have nothing to do with him. We soon departed and, along the way, stopped for a cup of chai. I mentioned embarrassingly to the group how I had felt and discovered that I wasn't alone in my negative feelings about the swami; all had felt the same.

A few years later, a phone rang in our Glenview center and told us of an attempt on Swamiji's life. A paid thug had climbed over the wall to our ashram and crept up the steps to Swamiji's private room with his rifle ready. He had been suddenly assailed by one of the ashram's Nepalese Gurka guards who began choking the breath out of him. Swamiji had had to get two servants to pull the guard off so that the man would live. Then the truth came out. The intruder was one of a gang who were roving the valley assassinating all the *sadhus* on orders from their ringleader, the very swami in whose presence we had felt upset during the Kumbha Mela. The gang had murdered Tat Walla Baba and three other famous *sadhus;* Swami Rama had been the next on the list. Apparently, the ringleader had wanted the whole Rishikesh valley to himself. He later went before a judge, was found guilty of murder, and was sentenced to life in prison. The judge said publicly that he waived the death sentence out of respect for the order of swamis.

When Swamiji returned to America that year, we spoke about the situation. He said that in his experience the most tempting phase of spiritual development occurs when some of the latent powers of consciousness, the *siddhis,* or what Christian theology refers to as charismatic gifts or miracles, emerge in a yogi. He told us stories of yogis he knew who had gotten trapped by the success of their practices and had begun to abuse their powers for egocentric goals. It was only a matter of time before they had tripped themselves up and paid the price. As we reminisced over the Kumbha Mela incident, I reflected how our little group had immediately sensed the negativity around that swami although we had not known how to reconcile our feelings.

Back at the ashram, we were entertained by the laughing Swami, Aum Prakashanandji Giri, "The One Who Sings the Joy of Aum." Witty, gregarious, and full of teasing humor for any audience who would listen, he loved to poke fun at himself. He easily won our hearts. After the seriousness of the Kumbha Mela and the discomforts of the trip, his laughter relaxed us. Any stereotype of swamihood I may have entertained was now irretrievably shattered.

Later, as I sat in the courtyard talking excitedly with Rajan, a local journalist covering the Mela, Swamiji entertained some guests on the porch of the next building.

He spied me across the yard and energetically shouted, "You owe a lot to this woman, Justin."

I glanced at the woman my teacher was pointing to, knowing I had never seen her before. So I nodded politely and smiled.

"Yes, she did a lot for you," he continued, "You were her favorite brother."

I was intrigued and walked toward them. My teacher introduced me to a tall, dark woman, a physician from New Delhi. Swamiji escorted the group inside his room saying over his shoulder, "I'll see you later, Justin."

So Rajan and I continued our conversation on Indian saints. "I have a story to tell you, Justin," he said.

When I showed keen interest, as always when stories were to be shared, Rajan began. "Once I had an assignment from my editor to find any genuine saints living in the Rishikesh valley. I visited all the local ashrams and temples looking for holy beings, and while many people told me of this person or that, I was not convinced of their accomplishments. After lunch one afternoon I took a walk to the Swarg Ashram and sat down in the garden to relax. A sweeper came by with his broom of twigs, bent over, wearing the typical white cotton pajamas that the villagers wear, and cleaned the garden walk. I watched the old man work, but I was feeling only discouragement.

"Eventually the sweeper worked his way down the path to me. He looked up and asked, 'What is disturbing you, son?'

"I told him about my failure in finding saints for my article and added, 'I think there are no more saints.'

"The sweeper urged me not to give up my pursuit and recommended that I go into the nearby jungle to search. So I took his advice and walked through the jungle, but I found nothing. I returned about a week later to the ashram garden and once again the sweeper was there working.

"I went to him and told him about my trip to the jungle and said that I would write an article about the end of the era of saints in India. As I stood up to depart, the sweeper stopped me and said, 'You have tried so sincerely that you deserve a gift.'

"The old man held out his empty right hand to me, smiled, and suddenly, before my very eyes, a beautiful red apple suddenly appeared in his palm. I realized in a flash that I had been meeting saints all along but did not have the eyes to see them!"

A few days after we left India, Swamiji mentioned to me that in addition to meeting my former sister, I had met my brother. Rajan had come weeping to Swamiji one evening asking, "Why doesn't Justin recognize me?"

"Worry can't solve any problems," our teacher said in a lecture one evening during the Mela. "It's very unhealthy. Rather engage your mind in that which eliminates worry: meditation. Here you allow the mind to let go of worries. Thought is more powerful than you imagine. Your actions are nothing before thought. In fact, you are nothing but thought—so have one predominate thought guide your life. Thoughts bring people together or apart. You strengthen your thought by thinking about it. We constantly think that we are separate from others. We constantly reinforce this thought. Diversity is in our awareness but unity is not. You definitely influence others with your thoughts. The power of thought is underestimated, especially with children. Children in their sleep can pick up on your conversations about them or your arguments with your spouse, and they can become harmed by what you say.

"We live among three interspersed worlds. The world of equality where the sun shines upon all regardless of character is an equality given by nature. The second world is one of tranquillity which is unknown to most. The third, the world of disparity, the most familiar, is built by us in preference to the former. We create it for our convenience, out of all the boundaries we place around ourselves. Our thoughts erect them. We need to live without forgetting the first world.

"When you feel jealous of anyone, note why your jealousy arises. It can easily dry up love. It is important to remember that pliable imagination can create anything, but its forms don't always resemble the truth. What you create for yourself affects you more than others' thoughts do. No one knows your real self, no one knows everything about you, so never be tossed about by others' remarks; they cannot define you.

"When we foster thoughts about the first world, then our nature will lead us to experience the second. We learn on our own that peace and tranquillity are not found in externals, not in the body, mind or speculations, however important they may be to one's career. Peace is from within. First, get familiar with your breath; develop breath awareness. The moment you switch your attention to the breath any disturbance begins to lose its hold on you. Then enter meditation—the threshold of eternity—which frees your mind from its conditionings of time. After meditation come back and deal with everyday life."

Later that evening, a silent visitor arrived. Mahatma Shyam Charan Dasji, whose name means "The Servant at the Feet of the Mother Divine," quietly joined us. He was a handsome young man in robust health, about thirty-five years old, wearing long, black hair and a small deerskin wrapped around his waist. Fresh out of college, this man had entered a sales career. He had tried with all his heart, but just could not seem to make it. More and more discouraged, he had been ready to kill himself. Then as he walked along the river, looking for a holy man to help him, he had staggered into an ancient temple ruin. Without food or consolation he had decided to stay there and die. Instead, he had fallen asleep and the next thing he knew, an old *sadhu* was kicking his leg to wake him up.

"I will show you the answer to your quest," the man had said. "Come with me."

Questions about the meaning of life had begun to stir in the young man's mind as he was led up the mountain to a Himalayan cave at Gangotri. There he had been taught the path of devotion to the Divine Mother. There, at ten thousand feet, he had continued to live with a vow of absolute silence.

Like many mountain yogis, he had answered the telepathic messages and came down to the plains for the Maha Kumbha Mela. At the river's edge he found Swamiji, touched his feet, and was embraced by my teacher.

"My son," Swamiji said to him, "will you break your silence for my students from America?"

We watched the young yogi smile, position himself on the ashram dais and sing praises to God as Mother. There was a magnetic presence about him, full of self-confidence and mystery. Out of reverence for Swamiji, he had broken twelve years of silence to share his feelings for the divine with us. When his singing was complete, he knelt before Swamiji to receive his blessing and then walked quietly back to the mountains.

Swamiji gardening at the Glenview Center

Chapter 8
The Glenview Center

I sat at my desk working on some writing and looked up to see Swamiji standing in the doorway. "Have you done your work, Justin?" he asked. Before I could think of what to say he spoke again with a smile, "You can't get rid of me in this life!"

MANY GREAT TEACHERS in the Eastern tradition test their students, setting up circumstances to force them to choose between their old habits and their commitment to their spiritual path. The shock of the test turns out to be a wake-up call. Every few years Swami Rama woke us up. He took advantage of complex factors—the students' jobs, relationships, meditation practices, the season, national and local politics, global disasters, food prices, and finally the depth of the students' desires to grow—and made them converge into a crisis that edged the students closer to the very reason for the teacher's existence in their lives: awakening. The dominant theme of the *Upanishads*, the writings of the Himalayan sages, is awakening. In retrospect, a student might begin to grasp the process, painful as it was, and appreciate what the master had orchestrated. Often the student did not, but chose to leave the teacher, sometimes with treachery. Long-time students referred to this process as "Swamiji shaking the tree" to see who would fall off and who would cling like ripening fruit. Other students called the process "The Cosmic Toilet Flush."

After the Maha Kumbha Mela of 1974, Swamiji returned to Chicago as if nothing had happened there. He was pleased with all the arrangements we had made, said nothing about the missing students. Then the yogi ascetic of the Himalayas, the spiritual guide to kings and queens, the Shankaracharya of Karvirpitham, the research subject and teacher at the Menninger Foundation took up residence in Room 25 of the Flamingo Motel on Milwaukee Avenue in Palatine, Illinois.

As his American reputation grew after the publication of his demonstrations at Menninger in *The World Book Science Annual* of the *Encyclopedia Britannica,* more and more people came to see him. He lectured across the country, before groups at universities and clinics and conferences, appeared on TV and spoke on the radio. Each event resulted in more and more followers.

One day during a weekend retreat, Theresa and I were called to Swamiji's tiny room at the Flamingo. He was elated, smiled broadly, and said, "Sit down, sit down. I spoke to the sages about you. They were pleased and wanted to present a gift to you, a symbol of their love."

We were astounded; we did not know what to do, what to say. Before I could think of my response, Swamiji continued. "Go into the bathroom and wash your five limbs—your feet, hands, and face. Touch nothing after that, but return here."

Theresa and I did as requested and then stood before him. He told us to look at him, note his clothing, his hands. He wore white silk pajamas, the sleeves rolled up to his elbows in the hot summer air. "Is there anything in my hands? Anything near me?"

We admitted that there was nothing near, so Swamiji began a soft Sanskrit chant, moving his arms in wide circles around us. Then he told us to open our palms, touching them to form a bowl. His palms were laid in ours and the chant continued. Suddenly, from out of the air, a huge, beautifully-colored, ripened peach dropped into his hands. He opened his hands and let the fruit drop into ours.

Swamiji clapped his hands together and smiled. "Ha! Isn't it a wonderful gift? Go sit together and eat it. Eat it all, but do not throw away the pit. Keep that for the rest of your lives as a symbol of the traditions's love."

We walked out of his room in a daze, giggling with the huge piece of fruit, almost afraid to taste it. Finding a quiet corner of the hall, we broke the peach in half, enjoyed its juicy meat, and slipped the peach pit into my pocket for safekeeping. We treasure it to this day.

BUILDING GLENVIEW

All this time, the students were looking for a permanent

center. Mama and Marion Moranetz searched; Brunette Eason and Marian Peterson asked their contacts; John Schwartz made phone calls. But nothing seemed just right. Finally, John Fritschle remembered an abandoned property in Glenview, just off Greenwood Road. It was a former rest home for the elderly. It had been empty for years and ignored by the realtors because it was falling apart. We all went to inspect it. Behind the trees on three and a half acres stood a rambling building with single rooms for offices and a large room that could be turned into an auditorium, a ranch house, and another small building. Everything was, indeed, in a dilapidated condition: the grounds overran with huge weeds, the windows were all broken, the roof was full of holes. Swamiji declared it perfect.

Shortly after we purchased the property, we were taken to court by our neighbor, the Glenview Navel Air Station, who complained that we were in the way of their flying routes. We explained to the presiding judge that since we had no plans to build towers to interfere with air flights, and since people had lived there for years before this complaint, we did not understand how we loomed as an obstacle to the Navy. The judge concurred and we were in business.

There was another hitch. Because the former owner had fallen afoul of the law, our new property was condemned by the county. With that dark history in the minds of the local and county inspectors, and because some of the neighbors feared we may be a bizarre cult, we faced unrelenting scrutiny. An army of building inspectors—electrical, heating, plumbing, building, health— appeared, together with the tax assessor and the fire marshal. They would pop in unannounced so often that I began to think they were Institute residents until I noticed their clip boards.

Swamiji rounded up an unusual group of helpers to get the buildings into shape. Students from around the country served as carpenters and plumbers. Four British plasterers arrived daily in formal business suits, each carrying a pail of tools. Cary Caraway, a pupil of Frank Lloyd Wright, designed the renovation plans.

It was time for Swamiji to make his regular winter trip to India, but before he left, he asked one of his students, a Methodist minister, to take on the job of Institute administrator. Mama was pleased to have help with the growing duties, and the request answered the minister's fondest dreams. He had wanted the job badly; he told me that he couldn't wait to run the Institute and take it to new heights.

Over the years, I have witnessed Swamiji give people exactly what they wanted to fulfill their ambitions. Then the fun would begin as we watched what they would do with their newly acquired desires. Not surprisingly, the minister was soon in a quandary. Coincidental with the offer to run our Institute, another plum was offered: would he like to be the student chaplain at the university? At first, he thought he could do both. The church board that controlled the prestigious chaplaincy quietly let him know that, in view of the highly competitive nature of the pastoral post, he might want to reconsider his association with that Eastern yoga organization. He got the message.

Coming home from Loyola one afternoon in late fall, I received a frantic call from Mama. Amid tears, she told me that the minister had resigned. Building renovation had just begun, she had to run the family restaurant, she could not be in both places at once, and Swamiji was in India. She was beside herself! Would I consider being the Institute administrator? I was teaching full time at the north campus of Loyola University, had a full lecture schedule in Chicago and Wisconsin, but I could not refuse to help. Theresa volunteered to be my secretary provided I promised to take her to a movie on weekends whenever possible. There was, of course, no money for salaries. In all our years with Swamiji, we never drew a salary of any kind except when we lived and worked full-time on the campus. Then we had been given a small monthly stipend to cover necessary personal items. We all worked for the joy of being with the master and the knowledge that we were doing something worthwhile for the world.

Little did I know what was waiting for me in Glenview. An early winter hit the city with blustering snow and ice. The Glenview main building, where most of the internal reconstruction was going on, was without heat and plumbing. The wind blasted through the rooms, blowing sawdust everywhere. We wore gloves, mufflers, and scarves and worked in front of small heaters throughout the day. Institute bills, three months old, lay in piles around the floor. Mama explained that we had to keep within a budget each month, regardless of the bills. The chief contractor, Ray Barnette, had to be paid without exception since he did most of the work and subcontracted the rest. The phone rang constantly, demanding payment. I soon discovered I had a talent for stalling creditors, blaming it on my inept secretary, who should have sent the checks. Of course, I promised I would reissue orders that she reexamine her accounting as soon as she returned from her two week vacation, which she kept extending due to family illness. My objective was to spread the bills over a few months, keep the contractor content, and get some heat in the place. Every extra hour I spent at Glenview. Four days a week I was there from seven in the morning till midnight and the other three days I was there all evening after classes. Theresa quit her teaching job and worked from the time I dropped her off at 7 A.M. until I returned from Loyola at 3 P.M. Then we would dash madly to the town library to use the bathroom facilities, grab a meal, and drive back to work at the Institute until midnight.

Mama would visit often with marvelous bakery goods (to sustain our cholesterol, we joked) and reminded us of how she couldn't prevail without us. John Schwartz brought pastries from his wife. The young men who lived together in the small green building on the property were absolutely indispensable. They put in long hours of hard work in the cold. I remember particularly Gopala, Kevin, Drona, and Ram Prasad with his friendly German shepherd. Another permanent resident arrived in a crate—Raja, a Doberman Pincher pup with huge brown paws. He was a gift for Swamiji from a grateful student. The pup stayed in the ranch house garage each day, moaning for his new master.

In his early Chicago lectures, Swami had kept returning to the same theme:

"Modern life is self-created turmoil; human beings do not understand their nature. Often people in their distress deny their real nature. Scientists are the worst. Their concept of truth is so narrow that they become near-sighted and miss the grandeur of truth throughout the universe. When you deny your nature, the outcome is profound loneliness. In truth, you are a nucleus and the universe is your expansion."

Now with all the work going on, my mind returned to these thoughts. His lectures made me feel like I was standing on a precipice viewing the many trails and valleys through the mountains of life. As the philosophical explanations of consciousness were buzzing though my mind, I stumbled upon a series of writings dictated by a master yogi named Ramana Maharshi.

Many mornings while waiting for my Loyola University theology students to arrive, I read from *Talks with Ramana Maharshi*. His incisive replies to all questions captivated me. I was absolutely fascinated by his sense of reality. He was relentless in having people pursue the question, "Who am I?"

One Sunday afternoon while Theresa and I were taking a rest before going back to work at the Institute, I lay on the floor reading and musing over Ramana's philosophy. I fell asleep. The next thing I knew, the sage was sitting in front of me. I was so shocked by his presence that my mind kept reeling with the question, "Is this for real or am I dreaming?" His head was slightly tilted, his white hair and beard shining, and his dark eyes piercing me. He was naked except for a white loin cloth. Here was the man who avoided academic questions, forcing one to deal with real issues. We looked steadily at each other without speaking. His calming presence was a purification, yet my tears flowed, as in my anguish over the magnitude of my desire, I implored him with the burning question I had long been carrying, "Will I ever become enlightened?"

He smilingly replied, "How can you miss with a guru like yours?"

I woke up with a start, finding the open book on my chest. The interchange had been so movingly vivid that the encounter continued to affect me for days. I read everything I could get my hands on about this yogi. He confirmed that Swamiji was the true guru, the "dispeller of darkness" for my heart.

Years later I asked Swamiji about Ramana Maharshi. He told me that his master had sent him to study with Maharshi for several months in Arunachala. "Ramana was the highest yogi I ever met on the plains. He was the reincarnation of Shankara, the great eighth century philosopher-yogi. He also belongs to our tradition."

The snows continued as we worked over the winter and early spring to build our center. Once again there were rumors that Swami would not return to the States. Dr. Arya, up in

Minneapolis, grew concerned about the talk and thought that he should look in on the Chicago group. He called to propose a visit, but John Schwartz and other directors thought otherwise, insisting that we didn't need any "inspection." Tempers mounted, sides were taken, strategies were planned. In the midst of the turmoil, Swami telephoned from India and told me to allow the visit but to stay out of the interaction.

The high summit meeting occurred one cold winter evening. After welcoming the players and their restrained tempers to Swamiji's little ranch house, I said nothing. Dr. Arya wisely had brought his newborn son to the assemblage, softening all tensions as the directors passed the beautiful baby around the room. The energy changed to a sense of struggle for a common goal; suspicions dwindled.

At ten o'clock I thought of Swamiji, wondering if he knew what was transpiring. Instantly, there was a loud knock at the door. The discussion stopped for a moment but then continued around the question at hand. I quietly opened the door, knowing full well that no one would be there. No one stood at the door, but the atmosphere in the room had suddenly turned to lightness. The evening ended amicably soon after with a warm agreement to keep each other posted on any developments or problems and thus help bring the centers closer.

Swami called that same night to ask how things went. I told him that he should knock louder next time. He replied, "Listen better."

BLESSED TILK

Neither Theresa nor I could have made it through that winter without Joe Lubinec's thermos. This irrepressible electrician must have felt a divine mandate to illuminate the world. He wanted the center to be devastatingly bright. I think his role model was the sun. More than once, I had to persuade him that we didn't need another fluorescent light in the hallway since the effulgence in the place could already support brain surgery. Begrudgingly, he agreed—until the next room.

Theresa began to show the environmental toll first. Near Christmas, she began coughing repeatedly while typing on the dust-coated IBM, wearing gloves with cut-out finger tips. She was

Swamiji lecturing in Chicago

allergic to the big dog that curled up by her feet as well as to the dust, so she worked in her coat and woolen hat with a red bandanna tied across her nose and mouth. I was worried about her health, and her plight did not escape Joe's perception either. One day he brought her his thermos, poured out steaming liquid into a cup and told her to down it. She couldn't believe how much better she felt after the drink. Her energy resuscitated, her coughing ceasing, she charged back into the dustbin. Joe insisted that she take a cup from his thermos as a daily constitutional.

A few weeks later, I started to look weary. Again, Joe brought over his thermos with the same generosity. He poured me out a cup full of what looked like tilk, the favorite drink on campus, but I had never tasted tilk like this before.

"Is it goat's milk?" I asked. Joe put on a silent smile, which told me he wasn't about to reveal the recipe. I perked up. Placebo effect or not, we eagerly awaited our daily fix and cruised through the chilly months.

One day I poured out the last drops from the thermos. "Oh, what if Joe needed some more?" I thought. There was nothing I could do, so I just set the thermos on the designated 2 x 4 and returned to the office down the hallway. Later that day I was walking near the shelf and saw Joe pouring himself a drink. I stared in disbelief; I had emptied it a short time ago and knew he had only one flask. "Hmmm, this bears investigating," I thought.

A few days later the situation occurred again. At midday I poured the last ounces of tilk from Joe's thermos into my cup. Someone yelled that I had a phone call, so I carefully screwed the top on and stealthily packed sawdust around the thermos base so that if it was moved I would know. I dashed to the office, noting the passage of time. Putting the phone down, I rushed back to the flask. Eighty seconds had passed by; the flask was undisturbed. I was about to walk away when I thought, "Let's take a peek." Unscrewing the thermos top, I was almost burned by the steam of the hot tilk.

"Joe, I need to talk to you," I called.

He came over sheepishly.

"We are old friends, Joe. You are not going home until you tell me what's going on with your thermos."

The story unfolded. Joe told me that when Swamiji had departed for India, he had walked Joe through the building and handed him a thermos. Joe was to drink a cup of the contents daily. He could offer a cup to anyone who might feel tired or ill during the renovation. He was instructed to bring the thermos home and leave it overnight on the kitchen table.

"It fills itself up," said Joe.

April was now around the corner, and the renovation was nearly complete. One day, as I poured out the last few ounces of tilk, the thermos slipped from my hand to the concrete floor, shattering the glass lining. Joe and I looked at each other, stunned. Swamiji must be coming home!

The next day, just after our Sunday group meditation, the phone in the office rang and Theresa ran in to answer it. As she spoke, she heard someone come into the office behind her. Before she could end the call to investigate, she was slapped so hard on the back that she sprawled forward across the desk. Turning her head in anger, she met the smiling face of Swami Rama, newly arrived, wearing a little beard and mustache.

"Hi, kids!" he yelled. "Let's have pizza!"

Grand Opening

With Swamiji home, restoration was finished in remarkable time. The work crew, with many new volunteers, moved outdoors next, turning the property into what began to resemble a national headquarters. With his usual high enthusiasm, Swamiji was everywhere: planting trees, buying jeans for the residents, setting up Rudy Ballantine's medical office and biofeedback clinic, ordering homeopathic remedies, holding occasional spiritual gatherings, staking night lights along the sidewalks, designing the large sign over the entrance, cooking special meals for the hungry workers, supervising the planting of flowers, and putting up a fence around his house so his dog could run. This man did not sit in his office giving orders; his style of management meant hands-on involvement. One never got the idea that he would not do what he requested of others. Because of his expertise in road building, he closely inspected the rock-bed in our parking lot; he had Samskrti, fresh from Minneapolis, organize a room for his office; he made sure the kitchen had enough pots and dishes and food supplies; he requested Theresa to set up the typesetting and layout room; he and Gopala picked out the placement of our first printing press, thus eliminating any possible car space in his garage. When new recruits came, he manifested a knack for discerning people's talents, even when they didn't know they possessed them. A steel manufacturer came to his lectures, and the next thing we knew a huge steel girder reinforced the auditorium.

Swamiji's student from Kampur, Pandit L.K. Mishra, arrived at the Center and was given the job as administrator in my place. At first I was surprised by Mama's decision; then I got angry. "What right had she to dismiss me so cavalierly, to replace me with some guy wearing white pajamas? Where was he when she pleaded for someone last autumn?" My ego was hurt. Hadn't I done a good job? Where was my thanks? Didn't anyone notice how hard I had worked and how much was accomplished? Now that the hard part was over, she wanted to give the cream of the job to an Indian? My mind churned with these thoughts until I was ready to explode.

I marched up to Mama, who was drinking tea in Swamiji's house, and told her she was making a mistake. She informed me icily that she was chairwoman of the organization and could make decisions without my help. Before me now sat the hard-headed businesswoman I had heard so much about. I knew by the tone of her voice and the choice of her words that my retirement was a *fait accompli*. I glanced over at Swamiji, who lounged quietly in his recliner, casually observing the two of us. He said nothing but obviously listened as I argued in vain. Finally, I realized that Mama was adamant, so I just shook my head and left the house. "I still think you're making a mistake, Mama," I said to get the last word in, but was thinking, "Who needs that job? There was no pay anyway!"

The next day, Swamiji met me in the hallway. "Justin," he said, "you argued well with Mama, but you should not have lost your temper. That only made her more adamant." He walked on down the corridor, leaving me with the remarks to chew on.

Reflecting over the confrontation a few days later, I recognized my relief at being back teaching without having to worry about all the details of running an institute. That was not my life work, and I would have been stuck in administration when I should be doing something else. Smilingly, I now reviewed the little power struggle between us. Mama knew how to run things; I knew how to teach. She had her Mishra; I had my classes. We both had what we wanted, and I also had the freedom to come and go.

Once I made that decision, I was called into Swamiji's office. "Justin," he said right off the bat, "Do you want to be an administrator or a teacher in the tradition? They are not the same."

Recoiling from his no-nonsense question, I didn't have to think; the answer was obvious. "Teaching is my main interest. I want to teach like you and become a sage like you." Swamiji put his arm around my shoulder, and we walked down the hallway together, getting back to work. That night Mama and I spent ten minutes giving each other hugs and kisses.

Announcements about the grand opening of the Himalayan Institute in the United States soon were sent around the country. We planned a whole day for the press, various Chicago dignitaries, spiritual teachers, and students to come to honor Swamiji's new work.

Spring was late that year in the Midwest. It had rained for weeks, but few flowers were visible yet. We made up for the lack of garden growth by hanging flower baskets and setting out potted palms. We prayed for sunshine and tried to temper our excitement in the fact that we had our very own Chicago center.

"You just wait," Swamiji said the night before the opening. "My master is preparing a gift for you tomorrow."

The next morning, before anyone arrived, Martin Grider motioned me into the auditorium. Behind the rostrum was a nearly floor-to-ceiling window almost five yards wide. Growing outside, and perfectly centered in the window, was a large, old magnolia tree. Its buds had weathered the long winter but had been still tightly green yesterday. Martin walked me to the center of the auditorium and pointed out the window. The old magnolia was a cloud of huge white and pink flowers. Who would believe that the tree could blossom overnight? I walked outside to check on the other trees. The trees on either side of the magnolia still showed only tiny buds; everything else was hibernating. The magnolia alone stood out in the sunshine, its huge pink petals opened wide to catch the light of this special day.

In fact, the day overflowed with joyfulness as the grounds filled with students, admirers, and curiousity-seekers. Ministers and priests, neighbors and students from across the country, teachers of yoga and those wishing to learn all came to the new property. The biofeedback rooms were open for inspection; Yogi Achala demonstrated hatha yoga expertise; David filled the air with music. Ray the contractor was there with his family, Joe the electrician peered around corridors to see if there was enough light, and our four spiffy plasterers looked like the British delegation from the Home Office. Chicago TV filmed the crowd; the press took interviews. The homemade donations of food from many kitchens, including tray after tray of Mrs. Schwartz's sweets, outdid any event in Glenview for a long time to come.

Mama chuckled, "From a store front to four acres in just four years. Chicago never had it so good."

Swamiji leading a retreat in 1975

CHAPTER 9
EVENINGS IN GLENVIEW

I sat with Swamiji in a large, bright room. "You know what's going on when you are out of your body, don't you?" I asked him. "Yes," he answered, "I do." A new thought then came to me. "I can't understand why you want to come back into a body when you can have so much fun being out of it." Swamiji just smiled at me.

THE PRIDE AND HOPE FOR THE FUTURE that permeated the grand opening of Glenview buoyed me up for days. The Institute had opened its doors fully: a combined therapy program integrated treatment and training in total wellness; a residential program offered young men and women the chance to devote themselves to personal training in all aspects of yoga; a biofeedback clinic specialized in teaching self-regulation techniques for mind-body integration; a teachers association taught classes and certified teachers in the art and science of hatha yoga.

Theresa and I moved from Evanston into a small rented house on five acres two miles from the Glenview Institute. It was fun to have a real house for the first time, so we spent a bit of energy painting cabinets, varnishing floors, planting flowers, and buying furniture to make the rooms cozy. Theresa spent the days sewing drapes and cushions and setting up kitchen and bath in Swamiji's house and then came home to spend the night hours doing the same for ours. Soon we were home only to sleep, so many hours were spent working and studying down the road.

Samskrti became Swamiji's secretary and organized the center office, moving from Minneapolis to join the other resident women in an apartment just walking distance from the Institute. Swamiji asked Theresa to become his personal assistant. The little green house on campus, which had served as the men's residence during the remodeling, was filled with young men anxious to do something worthy. Many young people came to the Institute in those days, seeking an identity. They floated in from across the country, after having tried drugs and free sex, having no place to go. Swamiji introduced them to a life of discipline and study. They rose early; practiced hatha yoga postures, breathing, and meditation; ate natural, healthy foods; worked on the grounds; attended lectures; and went early to bed. Most came and learned, got control over their lives, and then moved on. A few stayed to learn more.

Rudy Ballentine was now our resident physician. Swamiji taught him homeopathy during evening sessions in his living room and began teaching Eastern psychology to him and Swami Ajaya. Later their work with Swamiji, including the book, *Yoga and Psychotherapy*, would help change the country's ideas about medicine and psychotherapy.

Swamiji's living room became the nerve center on the campus. During the day he counseled students, advised professionals, saw patients, and entertained important guests in his small office at the end of the corridor. Hardly a night would go by without at least a few people in his house well past midnight. He then sat for several hours of meditation and breathing. His schedule would begin again at six o'clock the next morning when Theresa arrived to bring him tea, usually finding him already walking the campus. We used to wonder if he ever slept. We already knew that he hardly ate enough for his large body: orange juice and one slice of toast for breakfast, a dish of rice, beans, and vegetables for dinner, and a bowl of soup with another slice of bread for supper. He often skipped meals during heavy work or when doing a special practice, and frequently gave the food off his plate in the traditional Indian gesture of affection to students who sat nearby.

Phil and Charles often drove down from Minneapolis to study with Swamiji. Through those lengthy hours with their teacher, Phil conceived an entirely new approach to working with the number one modern malady: stress. He took the basic yogic practices of breath control and transformed them into a practical model that enabled Westerners to grasp the self-training methods of the yogis. Swamiji took Charles further down the road of advanced counseling and esoteric practices. "You both must continue my work, the legacy of the sages, each in a different way," Swamiji would say to them.

I also spent many evenings with my teacher, sitting on the floor next to his large black recliner, or with him on Indian cushions on the floor. Always there was tilk.

One night he asked us questions about the remodeling work when he was in India. We entertained him with stories of all the errors we had made, the army of inspectors, the fear that he would not return.

"I tell you, Justin, when I went to India at that time of difficulties, my master said I didn't have to return to America if I didn't want to. I seriously considered staying in my beloved mountains. But then I looked and saw some students struggling to make a living and yet giving of their time and energy to help sustain my work. That's why I came back—for all of you."

Often Swamiji dictated books to Theresa, to Samskrti, to several others. He was so prolific that he could keep three scribes struggling to keep up. The Himalayan Publishers began in earnest; books would now be produced in our own country for Americans. Theresa, frequently called "Tessa Typeset" by Swamiji, was assigned the job of "typesetter," which to him meant taking the book down in dictation, typing it up, reading it back to him for corrections, editing it, designing the interior, working with the cover artist, typesetting the manuscript, selecting the type and paper and artwork, selecting possible photos, seeing the book through printing and production, and finally bringing the first copy to him for either praise or blame. Gopala was in charge of printing; he set up the first press in Swamiji's garage (after building a substitute doghouse for Raja), and like the typesetter, learned his new trade as he worked. Nothing was too difficult for us in those days.

After Theresa brought him the first draft of the first book from the new press, he handed her a piece of fruit, smiled and said, "Our publishing will be one of the lifelines of the Institute."

We were, of course, a holistic center. Thus, along with the serious innovations in pioneering yoga spirituality, holistic health, and career development, Swamiji sponsored a rousing volleyball game on the campus. Residents, neighbors, visiting guests, or anyone he could get his hands on became eligible players—except Theresa who was always ordered to be scorekeeper so she would not injure her invaluable typing fingers. The game was a

A volleyball game on the Kuruksetra battlefield

battlefield—the Kuruksetra of the *Bhagavad Gita*—always hot and controversial, a major vehicle for spiritual combat. Swamiji would carefully select the two teams, taking the best players on his team and making sure that whomever he was working on at the moment opposed him. One of his creative rules was that he assigned himself the job of player-referee. He also corrected the score whenever the scorekeeper had obviously made a mistake. His side seemed always to be the only one with cheerleaders.

As the game progressed week by week, the rules changed to favor his side. This incited such anger in the opposite team that occasionally players stomped off the field. It took a while for some of us to realize that he was simply having fun, teasing us, and yet teaching powerful life lessons at the same time. Standing up for oneself, speaking the truth, learning how to assist, taking oneself less seriously, and adapting one's ego were some of the insights gleaned on the battlefield of the volleyball court in Glenview. Swamiji's side always won, but the losers always went home with a treasure.

With Dr. Mishra taking over the administrative duties, I could settle more into my classes at Loyola University and Mundelein College. Since my initiation, I had taught a course on the dynamics of spirituality, infused with the philosophy of the yoga tradition. The classes were always filled, and I was pleased with my work, but a nagging began again in my mind: "Something is missing," it kept insisting.

Between classes I often went to the most vacant area on campus—the chapel—to meditate. One afternoon as I sat in the cool darkened room, my activities over the last year streamed through my mind. September would mark my ninth year at Loyola teaching basically the same courses. There was a limit to how much Eastern thought I could adapt to the Christian content. I felt that once again I was outgrowing what I already knew.

During the school year, Swamiji had spoken to me one night. "If you stay at Loyola, you won't grow," he said softly.

More and more, when he wanted to impress me personally, he would simply make a summary statement and leave me alone with it. I appreciated things on those terms, since I resented being ordered to do anything by anyone. Now the months of reflection were over and I realized that Loyola simply was not the proving ground for my future. As I sat in the quiet chapel on the lakefront campus, I saw what I had to do.

The following Tuesday afternoon, I walked into Father Mark Hurtubese's office. Former chairman of the theology department, Mark was a warm friend and a special colleague. After teasing him about his fifth diet program of the year, I told him I wanted to resign.

"Mark, if anyone would have told me four years ago that I would be saying these words to you, I would have said that they were crazy. Bear with me, old friend, for I want to share something with you. Ever since I was a teenager, I have been fascinated with mysticism. The interest would come and go, but it always returned, regardless of my wild and woolly lifestyle. Even when I was in the army paratroopers, I would read about the medieval mystics. This whole business of experiencing levels of awareness beyond the rational, of verifying what the myths and legends of sages and saints purported, enthralls me. The opportunity to finally embark on this adventure to mysticism has been opened to me. I want this to be my last year on campus."

Mark looked astonished. His Jesuit common sense rose up.

"Justin, I appreciate your telling me this, but think about what you're giving up. You are one of the most popular teachers on campus. Everyone here respects you. You've accomplished something that I always wanted to do—study in Europe. Your career here is moving along without a hitch. And you want to walk away? I don't really understand your decision."

Slowly, I began, "Mark, if Jesus reappeared and walked into your office one evening, telling you all your personal and scholarly ambitions, answering all your questions to convince you of his validity, and saying that he would teach you whatever you needed to learn, would you give up your career and follow him?"

He looked at me for awhile without saying anything. Then he smiled. "I'm going to miss you," he said in his husky voice, "but I wish you all the luck in the world. God bless your endeavor."

MEETING THE MIND IN MEDITATION

When Swamiji began lecturing on meditation in Chicago, my teaching and public lecturing schedule luckily allowed attendance. I devoured his every word on the art and science of meditation. Over the next twenty years, I attended his courses on meditation seventeen times. They offered the most provocative concepts I had ever encountered in understanding the total dynamics of mind. Oliver Wendell Homes once said, "Every now and then a man's mind is stretched by a new idea or sensation and never shrinks back to its former dimensions." So it was that Swamiji stretched my mind.

He demonstrated the knack of combining theory and practice in a compelling manner. Frequently, during his lectures, he would make a few statements that seemed completely disjointed from the theme. They were. He didn't drift, however; his words were deliberate. Once in a while someone would mention to me after the lecture that Swamiji "gave me the exact solution that I was looking for, and yet I know that it had nothing to do with the topic." Other times people would comment how the lecture seemed to be designed exactly for their issues. Others said that he seemed to be reading their minds during the lecture. As I learned to pay close attention to the logic of his topic, hardly a lecture would go by without these bonuses being given to the audience. Teaching for him was multi-leveled. He touched your soul as well as your mind.

Meditation was his favorite topic. "Everything that I have attained I owe to meditation," he would say frequently. Accepting his complete sincerity about this matter was not a problem; the problem was believing that one day we could actually come near his attainments.

"Your problem is that you don't meditate in time. You procrastinate. You run hot then cold. What do you expect to reap from meditation if you are not consistent in practice?" Swamiji scolded a student one evening.

I was standing within earshot. "What a reprimand," I thought to myself. I pitied the recipient until I noticed he looked too bewildered to be the guilty one. "Oh, no! He's talking about me," I realized.

It took a few years before I caught on that Swamiji would often ream someone in front of one or two people, and the entire diatribe was for someone else in the room who heard it all. It was always quite instructive, if not entertaining, to watch the perplexed individual walk away wondering what he or she did to deserve this dressing down, yet the real target didn't always grasp the correction or know it was for him.

But the guru had other ways of shaking one up.

During my sleep one early morning that unmistakable voice ripped across my cozy repose, "Where are you?" it demanded.

I flew out of bed, late again for my practice.

That night at the meditation course, he scolded those who had ears to hear but didn't listen. "The key to progress is doing your practice on time. If you tell me when you will meditate, I am obliged to attend you. I often tune in to my student, and he is not there to be found. This is not fair to me."

Half the crowd must have slumped lower in their seats upon hearing that incriminating salvo.

One night Swamiji brought up a topic about meditation that we hadn't heard before. "Grace comes continuously, but without preparation you can't hold it. You want to see things without preparation, but actually you want to see things according to your wants and not according to your nature. Instead of harmonizing your wants with your nature, you allow your wants to hurt you."

A whole series of incidents got clarified in that statement. I realized, for example, how often I chose food, not for its nutritional value, but because it was sweetly there. I had a whole litany of desires that had nothing to do with a coherent lifestyle with mediation as the centerpiece. I was intrigued with this notion of grace and not being able to hold it.

"Only through meditation," Swamiji continued, "can the human personality fully unfold, for then one meets his or her real self. It is a journey without movement. Along the way you cast aside all the opinions and appraisals with which others have labeled you. Behavior is the effect of thought, and thought stimulates emotion. Your journey inward must travel past everything that moves in the thought realm. Meditation means you are becoming independent of this world.

"People get stuck with their pious images. Does anyone really know what Christ or Buddha looked like? What difference would that make? You can't be enlightened by an image. You have to travel beyond the borders of the imagination and the discursive mind. People, however, are afraid to venture forth into the unknown. The territory of the unconscious looms as a frightening question mark. For the meditator there is no escaping: you have to deal with your unconscious. Through meditation you will meet your unfilled desires. They will flare up in your mind as you struggle to sit still. Old memories with emotion will arise to haunt you. The Buddha and St. Anthony of the desert had the same alluring encounters in their early attempts at meditation. No sage ever made it to the other shore without getting shipwrecked. You are no different.

"If you refuse to cross the ocean, then you have to put up with the limits you have imposed on yourself. What good is it to have faith in God if you evade knowing yourself? You may say you love others and seek the truth, but the question is deeper. Are you fearless? Unless you have conquered fear, even your love is tainted, and truth gets compromised. People take all sorts of precautions just so they don't have to face the unknown."

I realized then and there that this man spoke from his own experience. That was what made his words ring with such resonance in my heart. Before me stood the most fearless man I had ever encountered. He had gone through incredible life adventures and had stood firm in the face of fear. Here was someone I would follow.

An episode in Swamiji's early life came to mind. For the culmination of his training, he had been called to take the final test of his monastery. Like many monks before him, he had entered a special cave which was then sealed, eliminating all light except for a tiny pin-point opening slightly above his forehead. In an area about five by five feet, where standing was impossible, he was to perdure. Alone in the darkness, all his learning was at his disposal, but all his fears were poised to entangle. He was fed once a day with a meal slipped quietly through a darkened slot. He was on his own: no distractions, no obligations, just silence. How could he stay sane and healthy? How could he face himself in that darkness? All things that had ever been on his mind became his companions—desires, memories, fears, hopes. His tools for survival were meditation and breathing. To stay strong and supple, he did the hatha postures that the small space could accommodate. To stay clean he performed an advanced breathing practice called "the waterless bath." To stay concentrated, he focused on the pinpoint of light. He could ask to be released if the practice proved to be too much. He stayed the full eleven months until the test was over.

"The principle endeavor in meditation is to arrive at stillness," Swamiji continued. "Entering into the silence of your soul is the only passageway to all its treasures. If your body isn't relaxed, then its stress holds you back. That is why one should practice in a systematic way, bringing the external limbs, the lungs, and the nervous system under a rhythmic control. First take care of the body so that it doesn't demand attention later. Address all the levels of your body from the outside inward. Suggestions to yourself and affirmations are not the best way; words can't entirely eliminate the mind from its afflictions. It's only by deliberately engaging your life force as it flows on various levels that you can insure progress in meditation. Everyone wants to talk about their progress; everybody wants to know how close they are to *samadhi*, the experience of superconsciousness where all your questions will be answered, but how many are really prepared for it?

"It doesn't matter how many degrees you possess," Swamiji added, looking pointedly at someone in the audience, "because the mind can only derive a little knowledge from the world. Everything it knows in the world changes. So then where is your security? People take refuge in their imaginations, visiting old memories for safety. Meditation helps you to inspect your mind to find the motivation for avoiding the unknown. Meditation burns, not the world, but your attachment to it. With meditation your hunger grows for more than just the world. A new awareness emerges for what is beyond the world. It needs daily nourishment; meditation supplies the diet.

"The yardstick of meditation is how it affects your daily life, especially your relationships. How do you think about and treat your peers? How are you taking care of your health? Are you becoming stronger in your self-reliance or are you making yourself more dependent on others? What thoughts do you have when you are alone?

"When you bring the fruits of your meditation—the concentration and tranquillity—into your workaday world, then you have something to measure. Your thoughts, speech, and behavior are what count in the outer world. How is meditation influencing those forces? Don't think that length of practice means much. Most of you sit and chase your thoughts, dreaming about the past or entertaining plans for when meditation is over. If you could sit quietly focused, undeterred, for ten minutes, the highest secrets of the universe would be yours.

"Remember that you carry a dual citizenship. With meditation you can built a bridge between your two worlds: the world within and the world without. When you successfully manage both worlds, then the fruits of meditation will bloom.

"Everyone has trouble meditating. I know all the excuses since I, myself, have thoroughly gone through them. One day my Master called me to him but I didn't answer. He called louder. I paused and told him that I was meditating. The next thing I knew was his foot vigorously intruding upon my bottom. 'Don't try to fake it with me,' he exclaimed, 'Either do your meditation honestly or don't waste your time trying to impress me.'

"Spouses like to impress each other with their practice. Some of my teachers, too, like to show off to their students."

I looked over at Phil and we knowingly smiled at each other. Had we tried the old impression trick?

"Examine your motivation for meditating," Swamiji was saying. "The mind is slippery and tries to fool us into believing we are a flawless, spiritual person that even the angels envy.

"We forget our real nature because we identify with our thoughts. When we meditate, the unconscious identifications rise to the surface of our awareness. Your job is not to interfere and hold on to things. Let meditation clean house. It's not what you think that prevents your growth; it's your ego's attitude toward your thoughts. All spiritual traditions teach detachment in some form. Very early in the *Yoga Sutras*, the importance of *vairagya*—detachment—is mentioned. Some students think that spiritual detachment means indifference or showing no emotion. The scriptures don't insist that you renounce your nature in order to achieve enlightenment. You are here to perform your duties, to love life, to shrewdly allow the things of this world to become a means to your ultimate goal. In our tradition, the world with all its charms and crises—*maya*—is not a threat to liberation. On the contrary, *maya* is a companion. She is alert to assist those who sincerely follow their path.

"The *Yoga Sutras* connect *vairagya* with *abhyasa*—sincere practice. The practice of meditation enables the aspirant to purify his or her intentions so that things can be seen in their proper light. One acts towards the world in a dispassionate way, with discretion, which means respecting the nature of things. This is why sincere practice prepares for right thinking about life. The ardor and enthusiasm for living should never be derided in the name of detachment. They should boost the aspirant to act courageously without selfish attachment to the fruits of his or her actions. Then one is free. Did not Krishna urge Arguna in the *Bhagavad Gita* to have esprit in rising to the challenge of his times? Having a zest for living unselfishly makes room for enlightenment, which means fulfillment.

"You already proclaim and protect the fact that you are an individual. But your individuality is all appearance since you are only defending a personality. What was your personality as a child, as a teenager, as a young adult, as middle aged? You have undergone changes, but you haven't met your real self yet. Through meditation you will get down to the source of living which supports all your personalities. Then your journey will be almost over. Then you can converse with sages and lose forever all your fears. The cosmos will be your playground. But still there is something more. Just because you are at home with the sages doesn't mean you stop meditating. Meditation has further plans for you. It wants to lead you to the realization that you are more than your individual, sublime self. You are meant for no less than the Self of all. Your union is with the omnipresent, infinite divine."

There were no questions. The audience just sat there, stunned. Then we meditated for a while with the master.

MIRACLE AT CANA

One evening as Theresa and I walked in the garden of our rented house, we found a large vine of concord grapes just ready for harvesting. They were big, fat, deep purple grapes. Theresa thought that they should be used to make grape juice for Swamiji. So the next morning she went to take care of her teacher as usual but this time brought along a bucket of just-picked grapes, some cheese cloth, and a sieve. Since I did not teach that morning, I went along.

Swamiji was curious about all the paraphernalia as Theresa brought into the kitchen. Learning that he was to receive a surprise, he smiled at her and went back to sit in his lounge chair. There was often a stack of mail sitting nearby, ready for him to read. He would flip through the pile and pull out one or two particular pieces and place them on the arm of his chair to be answered immediately, leaving the rest for another day. I presumed he must have seen the return address to know they were important, but sometimes the envelopes were backwards in the pile or upside down, yet he would still pull several out without looking at them. Then he would dictate an appropriate reply to whoever was helping that day, often without ever opening the envelope.

This particular morning he put the entire pile on the floor, saying that they could wait, and sat with his eyes closed. Not wanting to disturb him, I sat on the sofa across the room, just enjoying his presence.

Theresa worked in the kitchen. First she washed all the bunches of fruit several times. Then she began to pull the grapes off the stems, discarding those that were not perfect. The perfect fruit was then checked again and put in a cloth to be pressed through a sieve into a bowl. That took some time because everything was done by hand. She then poured the juice through another cheesecloth to make sure no bits of fruit had fallen through into the juice. Finally she poured the pure juice into a tall, clear glass that she had brought from home.

At that point I heard a sad sigh emitting from the kitchen, but before I could get up to investigate, Theresa came out of the kitchen carrying a half-glass of juice on a little glass tray. She knelt down next to Swamiji's chair and held out the gift with many apologies, saying she didn't think such a large a pile of grapes would yield so little juice. She had hoped to present him with a glass full of fresh grape juice, but this was all she had to offer.

Swamiji looked at her for awhile and then raised his finger to his lips indicating secrecy and saying, "Sssh!" He placed his right hand above the glass that Theresa held and moved his left hand along the side from bottom to top. The juice immediately rose up and filled the glass to the brim.

Theresa was stunned. "Swamiji" she exclaimed, "how wonderful!"

"Because you made it with such love," he replied, "you should have your desire."

We all shared the juice, and Theresa and I rejoiced in the miracle we had just witnessed.

On the banks of the Ganges in Rishikesh

CHAPTER 10
LIVING WITH YOGIS

Swamiji stood before me, a smile on his face. "You have much work yet to do with me."

THE PUP THAT HAD WHINED during the center's renovation was now full grown. Formidable in appearance, yet with a sweet disposition, Raja, who by now was a hulking hundred pound Doberman, became the watchdog for Swami Rama's house. He was a beautiful mahogany color with an enormously developed chest. The animal was truly for protection, for some people took it upon themselves to barge into the house unannounced late at night.

Whenever a guest, formal or otherwise, visited our teacher in the yellow ranch house, Swamiji would take the opportunity to deepen his visitor's knowledge of dog lore. With somber attention, the visitor would listen carefully as the yoga master explained that the cast of a Doberman's jaw was so uniquely constructed that when he bit an assailant, the jaws interlocked with such viselike compactness that they were nearly impossible to release. The guest's knowledge of dog bites had now been expanded. He was duly impressed. Then, if in a playful mood, Swamiji would demonstrate the canine's ferocious power, insisting that his dog could handle elephants and tigers, prevalent as they were in the Chicago area.

Now properly disposed, the guest was allowed to witness an ever-unfolding drama. Showing how ferocious Raja was on defense, Swamiji would order, "Justin, attack me!"

I would then rush in madly, swinging my arms, and punch at my teacher, being careful to miss him as he sat in his recliner desperately calling out, "Raja, Raja, save me."

If Raja was a little slow on the response, having had to endure this game many times before, then Swamiji's voice would up the volume, yelling louder, "Raja get him, get him!"

In a flash, this four-legged, pectoral block of barking muscle would hurl himself toward me, as I quickly circled around the chair. The two of us would whirl around the recliner, Raja leaping to get his mouth on my forearm to prevent my striking the chair an inch from Swamiji's shoulders, Swamiji cheering Raja on with pleas to chew up the attacker, and the attacker making snarling noises befitting the pounding. By now, the visitor was on the brink of horror, biting his nails, not knowing what to do to prevent the impending bloodshed.

At that point Swamiji usually could not help himself; he would begin to roar with gleeful laughter. That would come at just the right moment because by then I would be running out of breath. Raja always whined along with his barking, knowing it was all stage play but unable to understand why two people he liked so much were playing this ridiculous game. In desperation to be obedient, he would finally pounce on my forearm with his distinctive viselike, unreleasable bite and proceed to mouth me to the ground. Laughter would fill the room. The visitor would be utterly non-plussed while Theresa would get a towel to wipe dog saliva off my arm.

This drama was performed dozens of times over the three years we all spent in Glenview. Raja was probably the worse for it. How can one follow the master's orders, knowing full well that one is fond of the attacker? The dog finally had his day, though, when he accidentally discovered that a slight pinch on my Achilles' tendon would force me to yelp out in distress. I swear that from then on he had a glint in his eyes as he came after me. I could see his thinking: "I can't get my boss, but I'm going to give a little pay back to my friend for working me up all the time." Never once, however, did his vise grip puncture my skin.

One day some people were petting Raja through the fence. According to Swamiji, the dog should have known better than to permit his ferocious reputation to be compromised in public. As Swamiji came out of the house and saw what was going on, he yelled at the top of his voice to Raja, scolding him at length. The people got the point and walked away. Raja sat with his head down, shuddering under the riot act being read to him by his master. Swamiji then ordered him to walk by his side. The dog immediately put on his fiercest look, lifted his huge chest upright, and marched, ominously peering from right to left. This animal meant business. No one had better come near. I stood by the side of the road, having witnessed the entire scene from petting to scolding. As they walked together past me, Raja's tongue suddenly lashed out to lick my hand without breaking stride or ferocious appearance. Swamiji did not notice, and the two of them continued on down the road to the main building. "What finesse," I thought. My fondness for that dog soared.

Raja died when he was seven years old. Swamiji had other dogs after him—Lucy and Ringo and Gucci—but none were so loved. One night our teacher revealed that this most devoted student had been with him before, and for his own spiritual growth had come again to serve his master in this unique way.

Theresa mentioned one day that she never had the slightest allergic reaction to Raja's presence, even when she stayed only a few feet from him for hours. Strange, for all she had to do was look at a dog and her body would let her know in no uncertain terms that it was time to exit. I told her that I was never irritated by Swamiji's smoking either, even though I am sensitive to cigarette smoke. We pondered that for awhile until the evening Swamiji called us to his house.

Raja greeted us at the door and was ready to play, but the master's voice ordered him back to the living room next to the recliner where he usually stayed.

"Tree, when did you become allergic to animals?" he asked. "Did something happen to you?"

"When I was a child," she answered, "a big, black dog charged at my sister Judy and me. We screamed and ran as fast as we could with the dog behind us until the owner called the dog back home. I was so frightened! Just a few years ago I noticed that I cannot breathe around dogs and cats," she replied.

"Would you like to get rid of your allergy?" he asked gently.

"Yes," came the quick reply.

I wondered what the remedy would involve.

"You have to get a dog," he insisted.

The ashen look emerging on Theresa's face told all: "Let's forget about this topic; it must be time to go home," it said.

"If you really want to get rid of the allergy, then you must get a dog and learn to love it." He looked at her with both fondness and sternness.

"Now what?" I thought. Swamiji and I looked at each other

and I understood. We lived in a rented house with a 150 acre backyard. The dog would have room and would be a watchdog whenever I was on the road lecturing. The idea passed with me; Theresa was not so sure.

Swamiji added the kicker, "You can't just get any dog; you must get a big dog. When you love it, I guarantee you'll be better."

Theresa gulped, her eyes large and full of fright.

Swamiji turned to me and asked, "What is the biggest dog?"

My mind pulled up Irish wolfhounds and Great Danes. Both met with his approval.

A few days later we selected a manageable animal—a Great Dane puppy. The litter had nine. Which one should we choose? Theresa and I knelt down before the kennel fence and waited. Soon one of them separated from the pack near its mother and waddled over to us. "That's the one," we decided.

The first three weeks were hell for my wife. Interludes of gasping for breath, dizziness, and general discomfort emerged when she stayed too close to the animal. Little Dublin's affection for her drew her fondness toward him. In spite of her discomfort, she fed and played with him daily. In exact proportion, as the two bonded, the allergy diminished.

A few months later I took Dublin for a walk in the field behind our house and noticed that he had only one gonad. "Oh, poor dog," I thought, feeling sad. Without saying anything, Swamiji noticed that there was something on my mind at the Institute that day.

"What's troubling you?" he inquired.

I told him that there must be something wrong with my dog and explained what I noticed.

"Hmmm," he said and walked on down the hallway.

The next day as Theresa and I romped with the puppy, I stared in surprise. Dublin now had two gonads. I felt much better.

MIDNIGHT COOKING CLASSES

Just after midnight the telephone rang but I knew who it was. No one but my teacher would call at that hour, and for him it was normal. Swamiji's night hours were his public hours—the brightest, and, for us the most dangerous. One never knew what his imagination held in store as the next project.

"What are you doing?" he asked cheerfully as if he didn't already know.

"We were just going to sleep," I assured him definitively.

"What for?" came the response.

Now I knew something was up. "We're tired?"

"You don't want to be tired; besides you should come over and we'll have a party. I know you can never turn down a party."

We dressed and drove the few blocks to his home. Swamiji was ebullient, pulling pots and spices and utensils out of the kitchen cupboards. There stood Rudy and Samskriti looking just as excited as I.

"Tonight we are having a party; I will do the cooking and you people will be my assistant chefs," Swamiji announced.

He passed out the assignments, and I got the prestigious task of slicing onions. He kept reminding me to pay attention to my duty and make the slices thinner. He rolled up his sleeves and took over the front burners, cooking with a huge iron pan, adding spices to the clarified butter. As he worked, giving orders about the sequence of vegetables to add to the pan, telling me to pay attention to my task, the kitchen filled with delicious aromas.

"No, not the broccoli, first the peppers," he declared. "More water, more water in the rice."

While the basmati rice, vegetables, and lentils were cooking along, he went right to work on the desert, halva with walnuts. We chopped and cleaned; he stirred and instructed.

It was after 1:00 A.M. when we all sat down on cushions on the living room floor. He led us in a prayer and waited for us to begin eating.

"How is it?" he asked.

We could not believe how tasty everything was. It was a meal fit for royalty, exotic and simple at the same time.

"We should do this more often; you people should learn how to cook Himalayan style," Swamiji insisted. These words foretold a prophesy.

That evening thrust into the kitchen proved to open a new vista for my appreciation of how this coach worked his students. The rambunctious fun that filled those late hours alerted me to the way he would mix humor and natural surroundings to instill truths for our development. This prosaic scene, from coaxing us from sleep to preparing a midnight meal, became a metaphor for life. From that point on, I watched carefully to see how he would invite students into a cluster of circumstances that allowed them to find out about those aspects of themselves that they had been evading. He never had to force anyone. The opportunities were always showing up, but it was up to the student to capitalize on them. Occassionally I would grumble to myself about his insistence to get things done in time. To my regret, it took me too long before I realized he was under life-ebbing deadlines to complete his missions with us. I did learn that tasks did not get easier the closer they came to completion.

The astonishing cooking episode repeated itself almost nightly for six months whenever Swamiji was in town. Rudy and Theresa stood by the stove taking down the recipes between chopping. Swamiji hardly answered any questions, forcing us to observe keenly how he maneuvered about the kitchen. If we missed a maneuver, that was our problem. We didn't go backwards, we moved ahead. Never once did he refer to a cook book, and every few days there was a different dish.

"Read me what you have written," he asked Theresa one evening.

She began to read, "Heat six tablespoons of clarified butter in the pan, add small spoons of turmeric, cumin, and coriander, stir with large wooden spoon, bang edge of pan three times, scold Justin for not paying attention . . ."

Swamiji laughed as hard as the rest of us, and we were off to a good start on the cookbook. I learned slowly, and my promotion from onions to other vegetables did not occur for at least a month. The others explored the range of variations on *subzi* (vegetables), rice, and *dahl* (lentils), with side dishes of chutney, *raita* (yogurt salad), and wonderful desserts. The recipes were later organized and tested with American measurements by Rudy's mother, becoming *The Himalayan Mountain Cookbook.*

One night five of us worked in the kitchen together, and just about the time when the meal was to be served, a group of unannounced Indian guests, nine in all, burst in. They smelled the meal, their tongues licking their lips. Some were initiates living nearby, and others were their friends. By now I knew it was Swamiji's habit not to waste food; I had noticed that he always cooked exactly the right amount to feed those who were present. It was too late to commence cooking another dish, and besides, we were out of ingredients.

Swamiji invited the intruders to sit down, and we set places for them around the table. Theresa and Samskrti began serving the food while Rudy and I watched with big eyes to see what would happen. As they dished up the plates, the pot seemed to remain full. The food that had been prepared for five plates now easily filled fourteen. There was even a little left over because Indians always are served second helpings. I never learned that recipe, but my heart swelled with gratitude for the added ingredient.

A few days later, Swamiji and I began a long conversation about starting a Graduate School in Eastern Philosophy and Psychology. "Look into it, Justin, and find out if we can do it in Illinois."

I answered that I would be pleased to do so. In fact, I had just been part of an academic team that had completed the re-evaluation accreditation for Loyola University and was familiar with the processes. That settled, he looked at me carefully and said, "There's something bothering you. What is it?"

I told him that I lost my wedding ring and could not figure out where it could be.

He just said, "Hmmm," and we went on to other business.

A few days later I came home for lunch while Theresa worked at the center. I made myself a plate of spaghetti and read the newspaper at our tiny kitchen table. Wanting a little more, I went to the stove to get the pot, putting the remainder of the spaghetti on my plate. As I did so, I noticed that my plate was tilted up from the table on one side. Why was that? I didn't remember the plate being lop-sided, as if there was something under it. Setting down the pan again, I lifted my plate to find my wedding ring, shining like new, laying there.

I was stunned and very moved by this act of love from my teacher. As quickly as I could manage, I drove back to Swamiji's house and walked in.

"Swamiji, thank you so much! You found my ring!"

"Yes, son," he answered. "But you don't know where I had to go to find it. It was down in the sewers!" he said, his eyes big with passion. "Don't take it off in the bathroom again."

THE OPEN DOOR

One day a visitor came to the Institute and asked about our work. Because he was a medical doctor, he was given an especially warm welcome by the Combined Therapy Program staff. This program was unique in the country. It was the first major holistic therapy, utilizing meditation as an essential component along with homeopathy and ayurveda. We explained to the patients (as well as to each guest) how they could "put all the pieces together"—incorporate cleansings, exercise, diet, relaxation, meditation and rest into a practical, healthy lifestyle. No doubt Dean Ornish departed with a head full of ideas.

Like the doctor, many people came to "pick Swamiji's brain," to ask questions and advice, and then move on. Movie stars, politicians, scientists, religious leaders, journalists, business entrepreneurs—all sought this man's wisdom. I was sometimes annoyed that they did not bother to come back, or send a thank you note, or leave an offering. Reading my mind after another guest had just left, Swamiji called me over.

"Not all my work is in the Institute, Justin," Swamiji said. "Do you think the work of my master can be held by four walls?"

Sometimes scientific researchers came to see Swamiji. John White, Stanislov Grov, and Professor Otto Schmitt were just a few of the many who visited. One researcher in particular was of special interest to me. I was asked to sit in on his interview with Swamiji and take notes. The man wanted Swamiji to confirm that this planet was in imminent danger of vast natural disasters. He inquired about volcanoes, earthquakes, fires, severe weather, food shortages, a whole panorama of catastrophes. Swamiji went into a trance state and spoke from the future to answer the questions the guest put to him. After the man left Swamiji sadly told me of his disappointment. "Justin," he said, "that man never once asked how people could prevent these events."

Another visitor drove from his home just north of the state line to Glenview to see the yogi he had heard so much about. Blithely entering the Institute, he requested a visit with the Swami. The receptionist inquired if he had an appointment.

"Nope. Just thought I'd drive down for a visit," he replied casually, smiling brightly and presuming that all would be available.

The woman was not in a mood to suffer fools that night. She proceeded to firmly inform him that one did not just barge in, expecting His Holiness to drop everything and talk to him. At that moment, Swamiji came around the corner and saw the man. "Good evening. Where have you come from? What is your name?"

The man was taken within the long arm of the master's embrace and walked down the corridor. There he was initiated with a mantra and asked to attend the evening lecture.

They separated, Swamiji to the front of the lecture hall, Peter to the back. After the lecture, Peter departed quietly for Wisconsin. As he was driving along, Peter thought, "Gee, that wasn't even three minutes with him."

Then he heard the distinctive voice of Swamiji speaking to him, "I know about your scientific work and I will assist you," the voice said. It told Peter about his research and its future directions. It encouraged him to keep working in the subtle energies of sound and instructed him to experiment with the technology that can interface between consciousness and matter. Swamiji's voice assured Peter that one day his inventions would help all of humanity. The words continued for nearly the entire trip home.

Over the years Peter has seen the master only twice for a total of twelve minutes, but each time he was given a precious gift of knowledge from the tradition.

SPIRITUAL PRACTICE

One day in late Spring, Swamiji called Theresa and me to his room and asked us to undertake a special spiritual practice, a *Gayatri Purash-charana*. "Piece of cake," I thought.

"Good," he said. "You must sit quietly in the same space every day, do a cleansing ritual before a burning fire, and repeat 124,000 *Gayatri* mantras within 40 days."

Swamiji made us a tape with the mantra sounds and rhythm; we burned it into memory. These ancient sounds are described in one of the oldest scriptures on record, the *Yajur Veda*. Swamiji explained that this practice was an essential part of our tradition, and that he himself once did serial practices of the same mantra for sixteen months.

"What good does it do?" I asked.

The solemn reply came back: "It purifies. In fact, you may act a little disoriented during the practice."

"That I can handle," I decided, once again overestimating myself.

I had no idea of the power of this initiation that my master had given us until I read the profound article on the Gayatri Mantra by my brother disciple, Pandit Usharbudh Arya. He describes a mythological tale that tells how the *devas*, the shining ones, were intent upon discovering the secrets of the universe. In seeking the consultation of God the Progenitor, they were eventually bequeathed the *Gayatri* mantra which sums up the power of the scriptures and offers protection with its powerful energy. In remembering these sounds, one draws upon the creative essence of the entire universe, which will, of course, affect one's total personality. The repetition of the sacred sounds stirs a purification within the practitioner .

This purification, and the eventual dissolution of ignorance, is not pathological; on the contrary, it leads to a reorganization of the underlying energies which guide thought, will, and behavior. With a new grounding in body/mind integrity, wisdom asserts its presence in the practitioner. The ancient sounds resonate with the vibrations of one's biology and psychology, aligning them with the original intent of one's divine template. Self-knowledge grows. One then participates in the music of creation, hearing the new sounds of self-becoming.

I later learned that Swamiji had shocked the religious establishment of India and upset convention by initiating women into the *Gayatri* mantra, traditionally forbidden to them by orthodox pandits. Swamiji insisted that this important mantra be used by all.

Theresa and I were pleased to do anything to further our spiritual growth, so we began the *Gayatri* practice at once. We set up our home office with the necessary ingredients: fire and water and flowers and incense. We settled ourselves unto cushions on the floor, determined that we would not allow any disturbance during the days of our solemn practice.

After a week of daily practice—ten hours a day in the same position—the phone rang late at night. "Would you house a visiting yogi for awhile?" came the request from our teacher. We were honored to have an Indian yogi live in our home and so we assured Swamiji that we would take good care of the guest. We would fit him somehow into our schedule, even though at this point my mind had difficulty focusing on anything around me other than the mantra.

Yogiraj Swami Bua, an elderly yogi with extraordinary flexibility and stamina, entered our house with a flurry of irrepressible cheeriness. "Happy?" was his perpetual greeting to all. Crippled at birth and not expected to live beyond childhood, he came under the tutelage of a wandering saint, Sri Yogeswar Ji Maharaj, who nursed him with herbs and a routine of yoga postures for seven years. He told the child to follow the path of hatha yoga for the rest of his life to fulfill his destiny. The next day the saint vanished, never to be seen again. Swami Bua followed his teacher's words and became a leading exponent of hatha yoga in India. He now was traveling in the West, instructing students and setting up his own center in New York.

"I will cook for you," Swami Bua said enthusiastically after we established his place in our home. We were pleased that he wanted to gift us with meals, not realizing the work for us it involved. Every pot and pan and dish in the entire kitchen was used for his cookery; the ceiling and walls got a new speckled design from the sizzle of burning butter; all the towels turned yellow from wiping up turmeric powder mixed with grease. For Swami Bua, cooking was a passion. We thought we should buy stock in a local dairy, as he loved to make vats of clarified butter for his many dishes. Every day we drove him to the supermarket where he filled the cart with vegetables, rice, ice cream, milk, and, of course, pounds and pounds of butter.

Theresa and I gave him a wide birth for his spontaneous proclivities, but our dog, Dublin, who never got over being very suspicious of this stranger in his house, gave not an inch. As far as Dublin was concerned, this unwanted five-foot guest was perfect bite-size. The suspicion was mutual. We had to keep the yogi and the dog apart.

Swami Bua soon grew tired of forcing us to eat more, so we packed our car with boxes of meals for the Institute residents, who were pleased that the visiting Swami thought of cooking just for them. Theresa's time was taken up with cleaning the kitchen after his cooking excursions, washing and ironing his clothes, and cleaning his room, making practice time difficult.

Next Swami Bua was invited to teach special classes at the Institute. One class was *dhoti*, the swallowing of strips of the thin cotton cloth usually worn by Indian men as a waist-to-ankle wrap. The practice cleaned out the mucous in the abdominal region. For days we drove all over the city looking for the cloth to no avail. Either it was not pure, or it was not fine enough, or it shredded too easily, or it released threads which might injure a student. Exhausted with the search, Theresa finally asked our teacher what to do. He sent her into his closet to cut apart his finest *dhotis* into strips of practice cloth for the class.

The following morning the classroom was filled with students gagging and weeping and struggling to swallow several yards of cloth as true yogis. With tears coming down their cheeks, a few managed to swallow two or three inches while Swami Bua walked through the group cheering them on.

"You eat haaam-burgers, you eat ice-sa-cream, why do you not eat *dhoti?*"

In spite of innumerable interruptions, keeping our dog from eating our guest, answering the interminable phones for the yogi, I finally completed my spiritual practice because Theresa locked me in the practice room, insisting that at least one of us should finish while she took care of the yogi.

When we gave our report to Swamiji, he laughed and told us that he, too, was assigned the same practice by his master, except his number of repetitions was in the millions. Twice, as he was near completion, he broke the practice and was told by his master to start all over again. That made me feel a little better, except I felt guilty that only one of us had gotten the benefit of the full experience.

"Don't worry. You don't know who she is; she will have the benefit of everything," he said with a loving look at Theresa.

A few days later, the phone rang again in the middle of the night. "Would you mind giving up your house?" came the next request from our teacher.

A Minnesota couple had come to town and could not find a place to rent because they were not yet married. No realtor would bend the village rules for them. So we sublet our house to them and found an apartment down the road. Sadly, moving meant giving up Dublin. That was hard for us. The dog never viewed himself as a canine; he thought he was a person. Consequently, he proceeded to eat anything he noticed us putting in our mouths, as well as pursue any activity he saw us indulging. We gave our dog away to a couple on a farm with four kids, and Dublin distinguished himself the first night by consuming the owner's dentures.

"Would you mind housing another yogi?" came the third succeeding request within a few weeks. Swamiji must have read the cautious look on my face, for he immediately added, "It's only for a short while."

The contrast of our new guest to our previous resident could not have been anticipated. Lambika Yogi Ramananda, 67 years old, stood hesitantly in the doorway. His five foot, slender frame and gentle, modest demeanor belied the enormous super-strength and physiological control that this yogi possessed. Quiet and self-contained, he stayed in his corner of the apartment where he had set up a sleeping mat and a small pile of clothing and books; we hardly knew he was there. Married, with three grown children, he had devoted his life for decades to the yogic pursuit of control of bodily processess.

While Yogi Ramananda was in America, my friend, Otto Schmitt, Professor of Physics at the University of Minnesota, examined him in the laboratory. The yogi was wrapped with a 3/8 inch-thick iron chain, usually used to corral elephants, and used his breath control to shatter it, exploding the links in all directions and shocking the witnesses.

He liked to practice with leaves, rolling them like a cigar, and cutting the roll between his index and middle fingers. The force of his pressure would snap the leaves, sending the parts flying across the room. In India he had submitted himself to underground burial, without oxygen, for thirty days. His internal systems and metabolism were carefully monitored throughout the project, showing that, like Swami Rama, this yogi could also directly slow down those parts of his biology—heart rate, air consumption and sleep—that are not normally within the realm of will power.

One morning I came out of my bedroom just as Yogi Ramananda was beginning his daily pushups. "May I join you, yogiji?" I asked.

"Yes, of course, Mr. Justin. Lie down next to me and we'll

begin together."

After about thirty pushups, I decided to retire, noticing that my companion went merrily on his way. I got tired just counting his movements; he completed one thousand and then stood up, smiling.

"Hmm. Now I am warmed up. What shall we do next?" the yogi asked.

I made up an important meeting and left scratching my head in wonder. How could this 108 pound elder contain so much strength?

One day I came home from teaching and found the yogi missing. When I saw the sliding glass patio doors standing open, I grew worried, knowing that he was not at all familiar with the neighborhood. Just then the doorbell rang. I opened the door to find Yogi Ramananda standing sheepishly between two tall Glenview policemen.

"Does he belong to you?" they asked. "Are you Mr. Justin?"

I assured them that the yogi was my house guest from India and was officially asked not to allow my visitor to saunter outside on his own. Apparently, the police had spotted him, bare chested, his flimsy, cotton skirt trailing wind-blown behind his body. He had looked like a ghostly apparition as he marched against the traffic of Lake Street, trying to cross the highway. When the police had stopped him in the midst of a traffic jam of confused drivers, the yogi had had no identification, no shoes, no shirt, and had not known his address. He had had to lead the police to our apartment door.

"I needed some leaves, Mr. Justin," he replied. "I used all the ones near your house."

There was a simplicity about him that made one want to protect him. Once Theresa saw a small package in the refrigerator when she came home late one night from the Institute. Opening the white paper she found a little pile of mud inside. Seeing her puzzled face, Yogi Ramananda came over to explain that he had washed out the track of the patio doors and brought her all the dirt. Each evening Theresa would find the yogi's dishes in the bathroom tub. He carefully stacked them and washed them with the shower head, not realizing that anyone would have to scrub the walls clean from food. Theresa showed him how to use the kitchen sink and the dishwasher, but Ramananda wanted to save water by washing his body and his dishes all at once.

A month after Yogi Ramananda returned to India, we moved the living room sofa to vacuum and found bits of leaf rolls and another little pile of mud, leftovers from our dear guest.

A CONFERENCE OF TEACHERS

Three thousand people walked into the Himalayan Institute's First International Yoga and Meditation Conference at the Palmer House and filled the auditorium with excitement and anticipation.

Under its old-world roof serious committed students and curious investigators of this new age came together to appreciate spiritual leaders and masters from around the world. Students and seekers from North America gathered for four days to learn and celebrate the meaning of spirituality and holistic health.

We had worked for months on this conference, meeting night after night to set up speakers, organize schedules, and move staff downtown, learning the importance of team work and discovering even more skills hidden just below the surface of our teacher. He drew upon his authority and reputation as one of India's most revered yogis to invite some of the very best spiritual leaders, artists, and demonstrators to share their knowledge.

Yogi Ramananda, entering Chicago's Palmer House Hotel for the first time, looked around in amazement at the spacious ambiance, the high ceilings, and the abundant furniture and declared wide-eyed, "Swami Rama, what a big house you have!"

On June 17, 1976, Swamiji went to the podium and lavished his obvious delight on the remarkable collection of men and women gathered together for the first time in this Age of Aquarius.

Swami Satchidananda welcomed everyone in his keynote address. Here was one yogi who always radiated a relaxed warmth, a wry wit, and a sparkling enthusiasm for life; we could not have been better blessed then with his inaugural presence. The Ambassador of India to the United States, T.N. Kaul, then spoke of the range of commonalities between America and India, with an emphasis on the contributions of the various yoga traditions.

Fifty speakers from many countries brought their knowledge,

Swamiji, Swami Satchidananda and Justin in 1976

humor, and inspiration to the participants. Topics ranged from the latest scientific investigations into body, mind, and spirit to the esoteric meanings of major spiritual traditions. Teachers like Yogi Bhajan, spiritual head of the 3HO Foundation and chief authority of Sikh Dharma in the Western Hemisphere, held the audience with his analysis of the philosophy of kundalini. Dr. Barbara Brown, a pioneer in biofeedback, took the audience for a tour of mind/body research. Roy Eugene Davis, disciple of the great saint, Paramahansa Yogananda, shared his reflections on the art of meditation. Sister Francis Borgia Rothluebber, President of the School Sisters of St. Francis, and theologian Dr. Anthony Padovano spoke of Christian meditation. Pir Vilayat Inayat Khan shared his philosophy of Sufism. Katagiri Roshi introduced Zen, Geshe Wangyal described Tibetan Buddhism, Dr. Felix Mar-Quand shared the riches of Chinese meditation. There were demonstrations of yoga postures by Swami Bua and their therapeutic value explained by Yogi Achala. There was the entertainment of Indian music and dance, thousands of years old. Thus began an annual event, much copied by others over the years, during which the scientific and the spiritual interacted.

Mid-afternoon I began to feel weary and felt I just needed to get away from all the excitement. I went to my room, unnoticed, and lay down on the bed. It felt so good to relax and let my mind wander away from conference concerns. But then I began to think that everybody else must feel the same way, for they had been working just as long and as hard as I. I had to get up then; it wasn't fair. Leaving my hotel room and closing the door behind me, I turned to see a figure standing at the end of the corridor. It was Swami Rama smiling at me. I nodded to him and went down the stairs, wondering "Why was he there? That was not his floor. Was he pleased that I decided to work instead of sleep?" I pondered these questions as I rejoined the busy staff.

The last afternoon of the conference I entered the hotel lobby and saw my friend, Yogi Ramananda, standing cautiously ten feet in front of the escalator. He had never before seen moving stairs. His face showed the question on his mind: How do I mount them? He studied the situation a while longer, and as I came near to assist, the yogi suddenly ran the distance toward his latest challenge and leaped up to the sixth step. He stood proudly on the ascending stairway until he was nearly to the top. Then, crouching down carefully, he leaped off cleanly at the top.

WHERE THERE IS A PERIOD, I CAN PUT A COMMA

Back again in Glenview, we returned to work as usual. Swamiji's new book, *Life Here and Hereafter* was published, and classes were steadily full. Our teacher traveled across the country giving lectures and retreats, encouraging students to begin yoga centers to continue the teachings.

I was busy drafting the class content for our eventual graduate school and starting the necessary library. Book donations were few and far between, and I worried that we would not be able to afford the volumes we needed. Swamiji paid a visit to our home one afternoon, smiling as he sat drinking a cup of tea.

"Justin," he said wryly with a twinkle in his eye, "you have too many books here."

I knew this meant trouble; my books were my pride and joy, my stability in a life of ignorance, my riches buried in the quiet of my office. Theresa, sitting at Swamiji's side, turned ashen as her mind anticipated the next command. It came quickly.

"I will give you one day to cry over your books," the teacher said, "then I will send a truck to pick them up."

Sure enough, the next afternoon a large blue truck appeared in our driveway, disgorging several resident men with piles of cardboard boxes. By day's end, the room set aside for the Institute library was filled with two thousand of my former books in philosophy and theology, all ready to begin the graduate school.

A frequent visitor to the yoga center was Mama's niece, Debbie, who was matriculating at Northwestern University. One weekend, just after the new library was filled, she and her friends decided to rent a cabin near the Wisconsin border to rest and talk about their boyfriends and have fun. It was Friday afternoon when she called Mama at the restaurant apartment to say she would be leaving soon. While Mama spoke to her niece at one end of the apartment, the booming voice of Swami Rama rang out from the room at the other end.

"Tell her not to go," he insisted in no uncertain terms.

Debbie heard Swamiji's voice and immediately resisted his instructions, but her aunt turned on her finest Irish diplomacy and persuaded her to reconsider. Uncle Swami, of course, gave no justification for his abrupt words.

"I know he has your best interests at heart," implored Mama, "just do what he says. I'm sure you'll find something else to do."

Debbie wasn't convinced. Besides not liking men telling her what to do, all she knew for sure was that her friends were going to have a neat weekend without her while she had arranged for the cabin rental. It was not fair. But when the car horn beeped outside, Debbie yelled for them to go on, pleading that she had last minutes things to take care of that couldn't wait. She was too embarrassed to tell them about her 'instructions.'

What should she do? She decided to take her frustration out in the kitchen by making a batch of cookies. As she lit the match to preheat the oven, a loud explosion filled the room, knocking her backwards. Flames flashed into her face for a searing moment and then subsided. Debbie turned off the stove and ran to the mirror finding that her eyebrows had vanished and first degree burns had turned her forehead and cheeks red. More embarrassed than pained, she immediately called Mama and protested.

"It's all his fault. Here I stay home to suit his arbitrary will, and look what it gets me."

Mama did not know what to say.

"I could have been having fun with my friends," Debbie wailed, "but now I can't even face them looking this way."

Swamiji had already departed for Glenview; it was a long night for Mama.

The next morning she raced over to see Swamiji with only one thing on her mind. "How could Debbie get hurt like that following your advice?"

"Mama," Swamiji answered sternly, "she was supposed to burn to death; it was time for her to die. All our actions, our karma, produce effects, fruits. These, in turn produce more karma that shapes our destiny. There is a cause and effect relationship. Death's time is never arbitrary; we are not born without karma from our past. "

Mama's glasses almost fell off her face. Swamiji continued, "If she had gone to the cabin, she would have died. I cannot stop the entire karma but I can tone it down. Wherever there is a period, I can place a comma in the book of life."

Master of Ceremonies in Glenview

I stood in the garden on the Institute grounds wishing that someone would come by to assist me in raking and picking up debris. I thought the work would go much faster with help. From out of nowhere a group of boys appeared and immediately pitched in. I was puzzled to have helpers without even asking. I stared at them doing their work and Swamiji appeared. "All you have to do is think," he said. I looked at him incredulously, realizing in a flash that he had arranged for this response to my wish. "I live through you bluntly," he said. Totally surprised by his words, I reached out and spontaneously hugged him, laying my head on his chest.

IN MY FINAL YEAR at Loyola University I lived a double life. The conventional world of the scholarly campus occupied my days; in the evenings I entered a vast, mysterious realm in which ancient echoes of mythological figures, and explorers of consciousness filled my mind. Sitting before my teacher late at night I imagined myself to be the sorcerer's apprentice listening to the wizard, imagining what powers I could bring forth. I felt more excited than I had when I had attended the Saturday movie serials of my childhood.

Whenever we weren't attending classes, I learned about the subtleties of life through Swamiji's stories. His formal lectures, along with the midnight gatherings, widened my appreciation for the true nature of human consciousness. From my studies in Greek, Medieval, and Modern philosophy, I had realized that the academic approach, however valuable, pleased the rational mind but left out the dynamic interplay between mind and body, as well as those dimensions beyond reason's borders. My campus colleagues, for all their brilliance, thought about the mind strictly as an object of rational study, fascinated with its unending concepts and theories. Their lifestyles followed suit. This approach was akin to a medical student boasting about knowledge of the human body after studying Gray's anatomy and dissecting a cadaver.

One visitor to our ashram, Pir Vilayat Khan, influenced my thinking greatly by showing how modern physics was getting closer to some of the ancient teachings about the universe. I had enjoyed his presence immensely, especially on one occasion when Theresa and I were asked to accompany him to the airport, and we all spent four hours waiting for a delayed plane. The great Sufi had enraptured us with stories of his father, the sage Hazrat Inayat Khan, and of his fascinating hobby of raising eagles.

Over the years I have been given a rare privilege in observing how Swamiji interacted with many of the great world teachers. I stood near him when he spoke with and embraced Anandamoyi Ma, Pir Vilayat Khan, Sri Swami Satchidananda, Yogi Bhajan, Ashley Montagu, Watru Ohashi, Rabbi Gelberman, Rabbi Zalman Schachter, Vijayendra Pratap, Hiroshi Motoyama, Roy Eugene Davis, Virginia Satir, Irina Tweedie, Jagdish Dave, Munishree Chitrabhanu, Buckminster Fuller, Dainin Katagiri Roshi, Geyshe Wangyal, Vasant Lad, Andre van Lysebeth, Goswami Kriyananda and others. Always his eyes filled with joy, his heart emitted great love, and the excitement of the exchange of energy was palpable. Hearts and minds met on two planes. Afterwards I would ask Swamiji about the meeting. Usually he would say with a broad, warm smile, "Yes, such a great soul!"

One evening Swamiji launched a marvelous lecture on the nature of the mind. "The mind is a battlefield of conflicts and diverse forces," he began. "It likes to externalize itself, run to the sense world. The mind can't help but take in a barrage of various impressions, all of which demand equal time for attention. As a result, average people are under mental and emotional stresses that hurt their health. They brood over these mental skirmishes, giving these thoughts more strength. Then they condemn themselves. The fact that uncomfortable thoughts roam through the mind is not justification for punishing self. Religions have condemned people too much in this regard."

He was saying things that I could certainly resonate with from my personal life experiences. "If the mind can't help but entertain uncomfortable thoughts," I ruminated, "how can a person ever know freedom?"

Swamiji was saying, "Your mind is both a path and a block to your destiny. People train their bodies for sports but where do they learn to train their minds? If you don't train your mind, how can you expect to have much control over its many whims and fancies? You are good but it's your untrained mind that gets you into trouble."

It sounded strange to me to connect "train" with "mind." All my education had been concerned with using my mind on a field of study. A student was judged by his or her comprehension of external subject matter. Education involved using one's mind for ideas. In contrast, my teacher pointed out that the mind itself can be its own subject matter, it's own field of study. How novel!

He next began a story about his own life. "One evening after my brother disciple and I had walked thirty miles in the mountains, we stopped to rest two miles past Badrinath. I was very tired and soon fell asleep, but my sleep was restless because of my extreme fatigue. It was cold and I had no blanket to wrap around me, so I put my hands around my neck to keep warm. I rarely dream, but that night I dreamt that the devil was choking my throat with strong hands. I felt as though I were suffocating. When my brother disciple noticed my breath rhythm change and realized that I was experiencing considerable discomfort, he came to me and woke me up. I said, 'Somebody was choking me!' Then he told me that my own hands were choking my own throat.

"That which you call the devil is part of you, and the myth of the devil and of evil is imposed on us by our own ignorance. The human mind is a great wonder and also a great magician. It can assume the form of both the devil and a divine being any time it wishes. It can become a great enemy or a great friend, creating either hell or heaven for us.

"A trained mind is more powerful than any explosive. Here in the West, we are very concerned about outward appearances and outward goals. That's fine. Yet people get so caught up with external things that their minds disdain doing anything else. The world is a busy place that can't afford to give you the peace you are looking for because peace is not one of its products. If you continue to externalize your mind, then you will reap its diminishing returns.

"The human mind conditions itself with time, space, and

causality. We live in a society that is ruled by time. It's like an intoxication. If people don't allow themselves to let go of the past and stop planning the future—in other words, live in the now—then society will become sicker than it already is. The East has its problems with passivity, while in the West you make speed king. You live so fast that you can't discern something sacred within you that needs to be acknowledged, that is beyond the three conditions of space, time, and causality. Because of that you can never know true peace. You need to establish friendship between yourself and your mind."

This last statement at first sounded silly. Become friends with my mind? Then Swamiji's idea hit me full force. Of course! People always complain that they can't stand the chattering in their heads, that their thoughts harass them, reminding them, whenever things go wrong, of what a failure they are.

As if reading my mind, Swamiji continued. "Establish friendship with your mind; don't fight it. Don't hide from any thought that appears. Love changes a personality, so love your mind and learn to see the soul in others."

He then spoke about the unobserved part of the mind. "Outside the border of your everyday consciousness is a vast territory—the unconscious—that holds all latent desires, memories, and promptings for the future. And beyond that realm is the superconscious. Many are under the sway of the unconscious portion of their mind much more than they realize. You need to establish friendship with this dimension, too. Otherwise it can intimidate your conscious life. Within your unconscious is your memory—a mixed bag of merits and demerits. The rational mind can't force the unconscious to open its contents, so another tact must be deployed: invite your unconscious into your awareness through meditation. Meditation's invitation can't be resisted for long, especially when you combine it with rhythmic breathing."

Swamiji ended his lecture, promising to teach more on breathing the next time. He invited a few of us to his house as usual. There we told stories about the day's events, listened to chapters from his forthcoming book, and drank tilk. As the night grew longer, I inadvertently glanced down at Raja, exuding sounds in his dreaming sleep. This slight deviation didn't get lost on the teacher; he suggested it was time for us all to depart.

YOGA COMES TO LOYOLA

The following week at the university a long experiment began. With the *Yoga-Sutras* in one hand and those midnight excursions in the other, I began to challenge my students with questions that widened their eyes. If theology in a university setting is supposed to be the study of ultimate reality, then we have to become critical of our assumptions, our expectations, and our methodology. Unless we include these three elements in our study, how can we hope to call theology a science? Moreover, I proposed, if you leave out this critical apparatus, then you no longer have a university course but a catechism class, which would be no different than attending a seminary. I wanted my students to wrestle with how the mind creates a sectarian theology, how the mind could explore theology from scratch, and where that all would lead. By now I had their rapt attention.

I told them that our task was not to force different theologies to compete with each other so that we would have winners and losers, but that we wanted instead to examine the theological models proposed by various Western traditions and note the outcomes they produce in their followers. Every student admitted in class that no teacher had ever approached theology in this way. With that admission their first weekend assignment was to wrestle with the question: How does one start a theology and what are its components? They were to bring a one-page paper on the topic to the next class.

The semesters flew by. I kept enticing students to examine the grounds for their theological statements, to ask how they established credibility for their assertions, and, especially, what role their consciousness played in constructing their theology. Some of the best papers in my teaching career crossed my desk that year, including one from Linda Johnsen, who would distinguish herself in the future both for her devotion to yoga and her writing about it.

Concomitant with these unorthodox lectures, I had more and more students asking to see me for counseling.

"You want me to jog around the track each day?" a student asked dumbfounded.

"Yes, not hard, but slow and long enough to work up a sweat each time," I insisted.

"I don't understand how that helps my depression, sir."

A week later when I asked him how he had fared with the new regime, he said, surprisingly, "What mood? Was I depressed?"

Another student embarrassingly admitted that she felt she did not deserve good grades, even though she was a keen student. "I have a sort of voice that tells me I am not good enough," she admitted.

After telling her that the voice was only a created sound from her past and that she probably had forgotten when she heard it for the first time, I gave her another sound to replace the bothersome one. "Calm your breath and begin to listen to this sound," I told her, giving her a mantra to repeat mentally.

As the weeks went on, the student reported that the negative voice got fainter and fainter. I was pleased when she burst into the classroom one day proudly showing me her honor grades.

From my learning in yoga I knew that exercise stimulates the flow of prana which supports activity. It's very hard to feel sad when one feels energetic. So jogging and skating and tennis became part of the theology curriculum. "Keep the sport up throughout the semester and you will get a bonus in your academic life," I told my class. Equally important was the practice of meditation, which I added to the curriculum so that they had the experiential foundation for understanding how theology went beyond the borders of the rational mind.

Examination time traditionally gives everyone permission to panic. Once my students learned how to practice yogic breathing, however, they could control their nervousness before their tests. Many students struggle to study because their diet is atrocious. But out went the pizzas, colas, chocolate, and sugar snacks in O'Brien's students and in came more vegetables, fruits, rice, and water. In less then a week, they had calmer energy and more endurance to sustain their studies.

More and more I shuttled learnings in counseling into my formal lectures to integrate a holistic concept. Theology had to involve the total person as part of its subject matter. Every sectarian theology assumed a definition of human nature and proscribed its limits and potentials for development. Where did the definition come from? Who were its architects? What data did they claim? How did they arrive at their conclusions? What ascertainable criteria had they used to make sure they had their conclusions accurate? These were the questions that criss-crossed my work throughout the semester. My goals were twofold: I wanted students to grow beyond passive acceptance of religious concepts and become critical of their beliefs. Secondly, I wanted them to realize that unless they could go beyond the rational mind in their pursuit of theology, then their theology would be nothing more than allegations and would have no business calling itself a study of the divine.

One of our more interesting times came with a little 'lab' experiment. The subject matter of mystics and the phenomena of healing, bilocation, levitating, reading minds, and other miracles associated with saints intrigued their imaginations. The hardest part for the students was putting aside their religious conditioning in order to examine the mystical data for what it was without dogmatic overtones. They began to suspect that the chief component in this study was consciousness and its range of applicability, at least from the individual mystic's side. I suggested that we do an experiment in class that could shed light on the dynamics of mysticism.

On the following Monday I introduced them to a thermistor. To tease the students, I proposed that anyone who could raise his or her skin temperature five degrees would get an A for the course. They almost trampled me to line up. One after another challenged the thermistor and each time their skin temperature cooled, which, unknown to them, indicated that they were straining. In none of my classes did I ever have to assign an A for this experiment.

Afterwards I explained to them that when a person gets nervous or anxious, their capillaries tended to constrict, cooling the hands. "In your determination to gain that A, you were trying to bully your body into relaxing," I said, "and it won't work that way. Your body was carrying out exactly what you wanted it to do; you thought that you could force your internal systems to comply." Naturally, they challenged me. To make it interesting I came back with a counter offer. If I couldn't raise my skin temperature ten degrees for them, then everybody would get an A. If I reached ten degrees, however, they would all get dropped one grade. A long pause ensued; they did not know whether to bet with me or against me. So I laughed and said, "All bets off; let's just see what happens!"

I attached the wires to my hands and began to lecture to the excited class on body/mind communication. The thermistor faced out toward the class so that they could observe any movement in the dial hands. Twelve minutes later, after starting from a surface temperature of 78°, the dial had increased to 95.°

I have always found it curious that Dr. Herbert Benson of Harvard University, after receiving a grant worth thousands of dollars, went to Tibet to find individuals who could raise their skin temperature. Apparently he found a few that could increase it by nine degrees. Why did he have to travel so far when any decent meditator in the U.S.A. could have served just as well, if not better?

SPECIAL TEACHINGS

One by one those who became teachers at Swamiji's many centers were given gifts of wisdom and knowledge as they served their teacher.

Occasionally my spiritual brother, Ladd, came down from Lake Geneva for special appointments with the master. Swamiji instructed him in an ancient *vidya,* a sacred knowledge, on vision. "Son," Swamiji told him, "when you practice what I am giving you, you will touch the lives of many people. Give these teachings as part of my work."

Ladd was enthralled with this new knowledge, which he gradually incorporated into his professional practice of optometry. Over the years, I have attended his seminars on vision training many times at the center and the annual Congress. He always conveyed to the audience the wonder and excitement that he no doubt experienced at the marvel of the yogic understanding of the nature of sight—both internal and external—and how to improve the vitality of vision. He made me aware of the relationship between clarity of vision and calmness of mind. An intriguing point in his presentation was the difference between staring at things, which provokes stress, and learning the subtle art of gazing, which expands the depth of awareness. I have practiced this *vidya* much to my own benefit over the years.

One Friday evening, some of us drove to a beautiful lakefront auditorium on the south side of Chicago where another student,

Brunette Eason, had arranged for Swamiji to speak. The huge room was packed. An enrapt audience listened as he explained the laws of karma and reincarnation. The lively crowd converged with Swamiji's energy; questions and answers peppered the hall. The teacher was in his element. He always appreciated when people took a serious interest in the subject matter, and he always knew where they were by the types of questions asked.

A member of the audience, after listening to the lecture, raised his hand. "I'm not sure I believe in reincarnation at all," he said.

Swamiji answered with a serious face, "It does not matter if you believe or don't believe; it is a fact."

Another student raised the question of whether or not meditation could reduce karma and was told that meditation, along with selfless action, were the two best ways to counter the effects of karma.

"My daughter has wonderful students," he said as Brunette smiled. "I want to take you all to India with me."

Upon the words of one questioner, however, the entire atmosphere focused intensely upon the speaker.

"Sir," the young man stood to ask, "it has been said that you are an incarnation of the apostle Peter."

Time seemed to stop, patiently waiting for the reply. I held my breath, as I too had heard this rumor and wanted to know the answer.

Swamiji looked at the young man, saw his sincerity, and answered softly, "If I say yes, I will be bragging; if I say no, I will be lying."

The silence continued for a moment as the reply reached the hearts of the listeners. Then the hall erupted. People spoke to the stranger next to them; the answer was passed out the windows and doors to those in the hallway; the noise level grew as the excitement mounted. The feeling of celebration was tangible as Swamiji turned to Brunette, asked her to end the evening, and quietly left the stage.

On the ride home, my curiosity could not be held. "Swamiji," I asked as respectfully as I could, "during the time of Christ and St. Peter, was I around?"

Swamiji looked long at me, deciding how much to share. "Justy," he said carefully, "you were one of those crucified a little later." The topic was officially closed.

"I pray to the divinity in you."

MORE TRAVELS

Swamiji's lectures ranged wider as months went on. Every aspect of body/mind wellness, including the psychology of life and the secrets of sleep, were available now. He was also lecturing in and out of the country. At a conference on consciousness in Puerto Rico, Swamiji was a huge success, but the psychics became upset that he was drawing most of the participants. Journalists were frequent visitors, resulting in long articles about "the scientific yogi" in national newspapers and magazines.

Once, when Swamiji had just completed a lecture at a major downtown hotel, he strolled out unto a busy Chicago street. It was evening, but there was still light in the sky. He decided to stretch his legs with a short walk. Turning the corner, he saw a tall, muscular man holding a knife to the chest of an older woman, demanding her purse. Swamiji yelled immediately at the man, "Stop what you are doing!"

As the assailant turned to see who dared yell at him, Swamiji stepped forward, and with one swinging motion, whipped his large white shawl off his own shoulders, threw it over the man, pulled him down to the concrete, and stepped on his throat. "Call the police, madam," he said to the woman, who ran to the corner and returned with one of Chicago's finest, gun drawn.

The shawl was removed, the assailant was hauled up to his feet, eyes big with shock and admiration, and the woman was calmed. "Sir," said the attacker, "how did you do that? No one has ever done anything like that to me before. Can you show me? Will you be my teacher?"

Swamiji looked deep into the eyes of this individual and apparently saw something there. "Officer, this man is my student," he said unexpectantly. "I will take responsibility for him."

Since the woman was content to walk away with her bag safely under her arm, the policeman gave the attacker a lecture and left him in the care of the man with the shawl. Swamiji told us that the man followed him around for days, asking questions, receiving guidance and scoldings, and eventually straightening out his life. Occasionally Swamiji would get a letter or telephone call from him, reporting on the success of his destiny.

Another incident provoked my consideration for my teacher's sense of fair play and justice. In college, I had became fascinated with the virtue and concept of justice. It didn't take me long to understand that the so-called justice system in our democracy is, in reality, a far cry from justice. It is usually nothing more than conflict management. I have never thought of justice as something rigidly insensitive, devoid of compassion. On the contrary, I have always viewed it as a search for balance and restoration, a bringing home of what is properly due. A just person in my mind is someone who has a keen eye for the natures of things and isn't afraid to defend them.

One afternoon I got into an argument with one of the women in the institute and overwhelmed her with my articulation of the facts at issue, reducing her argument to a shambles. When she turned and walked away on the verge of tears, I felt a swaggering sense of triumph and domination. No sooner had I strolled ten feet than Swamiji turned the corner and loomed before me. He stood right in my face and his was not friendly. He thundered at me in the hallway. "Why did you treat her that way? Right or wrong, you had no business talking to her like that and taking advantage of the situation. Have you no feelings?"

I could tell from his irrefutable words that he knew how smug I had felt. He walked away in disgust; I walked away in shame. In those brief moments, my teacher made me see the injustice with such repulsion that I have never forgotten the episode and, thankfully, have never repeated it.

Some time later, Swamiji asked me to drive him to a neighboring state where he was to meet with several businessmen. Occasionally he quietly counseled business leaders, if requested, because they recognized his incredible grasp of world politics, the global market, and probable major events. In addition, he had an uncanny ability to know their own propensities to make mistakes. He could read the future rather easily and did not hesitate to give that information to others if it would assist their business to help humanity in some way. Sometimes the grateful recipient would offer a monetary gift, in which case Swamiji would place it in his huge charity budget; other times nothing was given in return, in which case the business would have to deal with its own karma.

Swamiji and I stayed in a small motel on the outskirts of town, using the night hours for quiet talk with cups of tea and hours of meditation. In the morning, two maids came in just before we left for the day. The women were very excited to meet Swami Rama because they had heard much about him. They shyly asked a few questions to ascertain his identity, and then, growing in confidence, asked more.

"Will you tell me what to take for my arthritis?" "What should I do with my son, Swami? He's always in trouble." "Do you think God will punish me for some of the things I did in my past?" "Will you show me some yoga for my back?" "Do you think I should marry the man I am going with?" The questions went on and on as Swamiji quietly answered each.

Finally he held up his hand a moment and said, "I will be leaving now. Will you wash my pajamas?"

The women looked shocked. "Oh no! I don't wash anyone's clothes," they both insisted.

With a poignant smile my teacher nodded, picked up his attaché case, and headed toward the door. "You won't wash my clothes," he said sadly, "but you want me to wash your souls." The motel door closed quietly behind him.

Cultivating roses in the early ashram garden

CHAPTER 12
IN WOODS OF SELF-REALIZATION

I was in a dark cave undergoing an initiation. The dream was vivid with the sound of water dripping down the damp walls, the musty odor of mushrooms growing in the crevices, and a numinous air of guidance. The teacher sat in front of me and invoked my mantra, which resounded intensely through my mind.

LATE ONE FRIDAY AFTERNOON, as I drove Swamiji to a retreat sponsored by our Milwaukee Center, I could not resist the opportunity to question him about the powerful dream I had had a few days earlier. "Justin," Swamiji said, "your dream was right. That's when I initiated you in your last life."

His words opened a floodgate of peace in my heart and I wanted to know more. On my mind since the Kumbha Mela experience was Swamiji's association with a delightfully audacious philosopher-saint, Swami Rama Tirtha. Most Americans had heard of Swami Vivekananda, who had electrified Chicago by his words and charismatic presence at the 1893 World's Parliament of Religions, but few had heard about this equally important yogi, beloved in India.

"Swamiji, I find it interesting that so far you have spoken in many of the places that Rama Tirtha visited at the turn of the century—New York, Buffalo, San Francisco, Portland, Denver, Minneapolis, Chicago, Boston, Philadelphia, Washington, D.C. You seem to be retracing his itinerary."

"Tirtha's message is my message, Justin. He did not identify with any religion but had an international vision for humankind. He enjoyed America very much and carried the teachings of the philosophy of Vedanta, the ultimate unity of life, throughout the States as well as Europe and Japan. He called his teaching Practical Vedanta."

"I read that he was the first person to climb Mt. Shasta in Northern California," I said, "and that he lived in a tent on the Sacramento River for many months."

"Yes."

Trying to be respectful, I attempted to put another question to him, not knowing exactly how to phrase it. "Swamiji," I began, "were you that person?"

"Yes."

"Well then, was it you as Rama Tirtha who initiated me in my last life?"

"Yes."

"Wow."

"He did much for yoga in the West, you know," Swamiji said. "He loved scholarship, he loved to write—many letters, poems, books. Have you seen any?"

"I read a volume called *In Woods of God Realization*, Swamiji, but I haven't read many of them yet. Are you returning to the same places he visited?"

"Yes," he said slowly, "I am meeting my old students who have come back again."

"Swamiji, was he married?"

"Yes. He was promised in marriage at the age of ten, as was the custom."

"He left his wife to go to the Himalayas?" I asked again.

"His wife left him. She found his lifestyle too difficult."

"Why did he come to America?"

"Because he wanted to encourage a vision that held the human spirit free to explore life and the mysteries of freedom and enlightenment."

Swamiji then closed his eyes, and I felt I should not question him further. Since that drive, however, I have learned to love the great man in the body of Rama Tirtha. He inspired his countrymen to reclaim their own rich spiritual history, exhausting himself in world-wide endeavors to awaken citizens of every country to their divine identity. He finally jumped into the holy River Ganges, assumed a yoga posture, and departed from his tired and sick body at the age of thirty-three.

In a short while we drove into the wooded compound where the retreat was being held. Nina Johnson welcomed Swamiji, setting him up in a log cabin. We all went to the main lodge where the first lecture was about to begin.

"I pray to the divinity in you," Swamiji began as usual. "The *Upanishads* remind us that knowledge is never ending. Life means learning. Be careful, for the day you think you know something is the day you have closed the door of your mind to knowledge and learning.

"Many think that hatha yoga is a small subject. With knowledge of a few postures, students think they have mastered yoga. To appreciate hatha yoga, you have to understand the philosophy and psychology upon which it is based.

"The ancient school of Samkhya philosophy comes from the sage, Kapila. This word *samkhya* means that which explains the whole; that is, it explains the body, mind, and spirit, as well as your relationships with the teacher. When we speak of philosophy, the Sanskrit term is *darshan,* and that means that through which you know reality. It is more than just love for wisdom or knowledge, as the word philosophy in the West denotes.

"Samkhya was made practical by the yoga codifier, Patanjali. He took this complete philosophy and gave it a practical shape; when you study the *Yoga Sutras,* you are discovering a whole life process. The *Yoga Sutras* are samkhya philosophy in practical form and samkhya philosophy is the source of yoga psychology.

"In explaining the path to enlightenment, which is the goal of samkhya and yoga, Patanjali first focuses on one's mental life. He is reminding the student that if the body moves and the mind is absent, then life becomes very inefficient. We know that when we are absent-minded, we are likely to make mistakes.

"To conduct your duties properly, and fulfill the purpose of your life, you must first learn to organize and control all the thought forms that arise in the lake of your mind."

Swamiji went on to talk a bit about breath, the link to the body and the mind, but was distracted by many questions from the audience. They kept him asking him about yoga postures and philosophy.

That evening Charles arrived from Minneapolis to visit Swamiji. I walked in just as they sat down to tea.

"Justin, come in. I was wondering where my other silly gunk was! How's Tree?"

"Oh Swamiji," I answered with an exaggerated solemnity to my voice, "I just phoned her, and she is very upset with us. You told her to stay behind to work while I spend the weekend with you. I don't know if she'll ever forgive us; in fact, she might even seek other employment."

Now fully into the spirit of fun, he replied, "Really? Then I won't give her a recommendation! What do you think, Charlie?"

As always, my brother remained attentively quiet. He just smiled, saying nothing.

"You might consider raising her benefits, Swamiji," I said. "Give her two cups of tilk a day instead of one."

When we stopped laughing, Swamiji turned to Charles and continued the consulting I had interrupted when I entered.

"Listen to me, sonny," he said as he leaned forward into Charles' face. "If there is a mistake to be made, I have made it. Some things I will tell you to do, and you should question until you are satisfied. Then stop questioning. Other things you should do as I say because I know what is for your spiritual growth.

"Many years ago my master told me, 'People will want you to change yourself to please them. You should polish your ego, but be yourself.' I give the same to you."

We began talking of Charles's center, Dr. Arya's center, and the Milwaukee center. "Americans associate yoga only with postures," Swamiji said. "Part of the reason is that your culture is too much at the body-conscious level of its spiritual development. The body is not an end in itself; this is what Americans forget. It is a preparation for higher investigations. When most Americans teach hatha yoga, they leave out the breath, the mind, the unconscious, the superconscious of yoga."

"Why is breath so important?" I asked.

"Breathing," he eagerly replied, "is the link between your body and your mind. The latter two are different levels within your nature, subject to different laws. Your breathing connects them."

"What do you mean by the link?"

"Everything that you do or think is reflected in your breath."

That declaration was a first for me. Trying to wrap my mind around that brief statement took a while. Neither science nor everyday language ever put those two together.

"When you get emotionally upset, your breath shows that

mood. Watch the way people breathe when they are emotionally agitated. When they are disturbed, their breathing pattern becomes very irregular. Breathing and the mind are like twin companions. Unfortunately, modern science doesn't pay enough attention to this association. Many things can be corrected in the body through medicine, but if the patient's breathing is not regularized, then health can't be sustained. If the patient practices proper breathing, however, then many ailments can be avoided as well as healed."

Charles wanted to know more about this link aspect.

"The functioning of your organs is connected to the way you breathe, son. When you regulate the exchange in an even manner, then the right vagus nerve, which affects your autonomic nervous system, gradually comes under your voluntary control. In this way, your entire system gets purified."

He immediately went to the practical import.

"The finest object for meditation is the breath. The mind can take to it very easily. You don't need anything else. Focusing on your breath is concrete and simple. This is called breath awareness. Equal exhalation and equal inhalation lead the mind to a state of tranquillity. Now body, breath, and mind are aligned. Before this alignment can happen, you must attend your breath and inspect the flow."

It didn't seem to me that there had to be anything special about the way one breathed, as long as one were actually breathing. I wanted to know why the alignment was so important.

"People have habits of irregular breathing due to the demands and stresses of life. Unless these habits are corrected, you will be held back from going to tranquillity. In inspecting the flow of your breath, first note if the exchange is jerky, or shallow, or noisy, or interrupted by long pauses during the flow. Then make the flow smooth, deep, silent, and close down any gaps between the exchange. By smoothing out the flow, your mind will soon note how gentle and fine the breathing becomes. Both mind and breath will become subtle. Those moments lead to peace."

Charles and I were massaging Swamiji's feet as he spoke. This was one service he occasionally allowed close students to perform for him. A foot massage is something done for parents and relatives in India, always considered a loving and respected way to offer something to the teacher as well. Now he looked down at

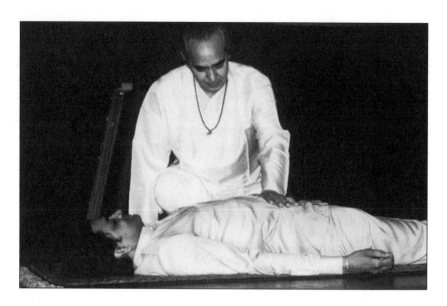

Swamiji teaching diaphragmatic breathing

us and said, "OK, I think that's enough for tonight. You go."

"Can we continue tomorrow?" I asked.

"When have I ever turned you away, Justy?"

We went away to our bunk beds, practicing breathing with new conviction.

The next night, after a full day of lecture and appointments, we thought Swamiji would be tired, but when we knocked at his door, his voice loudly welcomed us.

Someone had brought goodies. The spiced tea and cookies were exceptional, and off we soared with our questions on breath.

"Breath is a great ally," our teacher began. "It is constantly cleansing the city of life. Yale University research indicated what the yogis already knew, that the flow of electrical potentials differs in each nostril. The right nostril is warmer than the left. The ancients referred to the right side of the body as the sun side, pingala, and the left, ida, the lunar side."

At that moment, I recalled that the first nerve generated in the human embryo is the olfactory nerve. The olfactory cluster is found in the roof of the nostrils and goes directly to the brain. During the act of breathing, the air stimulates the brain even before oxygen gets pumped up there.

"Breathing serves a five-fold bridge," Swamiji continued, "the body, the nervous system, the emotions, the rational mind, and the unconscious mind. When you do the breathing practice of *kapalbhati*, for example, you channel the breath with the help of vigorous diaphragmatic movement to clean the blood of toxins and tone the nerves. When you practice alternate nostril breathing, *nadi shodanam*, you gradually gain control over your emotions. Calm, even, diaphragmatic breathing supports the clarity of your rational mind. And when your breathing becomes finer and finer, as in meditation, then you open the door to the study of the unconscious and beyond."

We could have stopped right there with all that to reflect upon but Charles asked, "What's beyond?"

"The aim of life," Swamiji replied.

"When you proceed step by step" he continued, "it is much easier and less confusing than if you attempt to jump to get to the subtler truths."

He was reading my mind again, for while listening to him I

was trying to figure out how to expedite the process.

"Right now your breath is too much under unconscious influence. It needs to be brought into the range of the conscious mind. Then, under conscious choice, you can get at the reservoir of merits and demerits."

He smiled as I asked, "What's the best way to bring it under?" I could barely wait for the answer.

"Breath is to mind and emotions as a string is to a flying kite."

Ah! My mind zinged.

He smiled and continued.

"Typically, the mind scatters its energy, shifting from mood to mood, and you keep blaming yourself for this unsettling predicament. Charles, put him into the crocodile pose."

I was stretched out on the floor on my stomach, with my legs apart, feet turned out, arms folded under my forehead.

"Now pay attention to the motion of your lungs," Swamiji told me. "After awhile mentally assume that you are exhaling from your crown downwards to your feet and out. Then inhale back up and out through the crown. Continue this down and up to gain a sense of rhythm in your breath. Whatever distractions come before you, let them come. Your job is to get in touch with coordinating your breath with your awareness. The only precaution is to make sure that you foster the smoothness of your breathing by gradually eliminating any jerkiness, noise, pausing, or shallowness."

I felt increasingly calm and at the same time had a pleasant sense of being energized.

"OK. Get up now," Swamiji said. "This is how you make new students aware of their breathing. Only five minutes daily.

"Your next level is to lie on your back in the corpse posture and perfect diaphragmatic, even breathing. This balanced breathing relaxes you on three levels: muscle tissues, nervous system, and mind. As you get used to using your diaphragm, make its motion your norm. Walking, sitting, working in the garden, at your office, remind yourself how you want to breathe. If you have to, pretend you are breathing through your navel. Later, this becomes habitual.

"As you gain confidence, then expand to two to one breathing. Allow your exhalation to be longer than your inhalation. This will give your entire body profound relaxation.

Just as you eat three times a day, feed your lungs with these exercises three times daily. You will see an improvement in your concentration as well as a reduction in sleep time.

"If you work with elderly people who have lost touch with their breathing, place a five to ten pound sand bag over their midsections. The exertion to raise and lower the bag will stimulate their awareness of proper breathing. In this way, they will be able to regain the deliberate use of their diaphragmatic muscles."

As our teacher stopped speaking, he became very quiet. His eyes gazed into the distance. We just sat quietly, watching him. By this time in our relationship with our teacher, we knew not to disturb his silences; he was no longer in the room. After five more minutes, Charles and I tiptoed out the door, preserving the quiet as we walked through the pine needles to our own room.

The next morning's lecture took us by surprise. It was a continuation of our evening talk. Swamiji began with such exuberant eagerness that we felt he could not wait to share the information.

"Learning to breathe—the study of *vayu*—is only an important beginning in yoga. After that you all need to grasp *prana vidya*. *Prana* is the life force. The oxygen you breathe does not keep you alive. If it did then we could revive a corpse by pumping air into it. *Prana* gives you life. *Prana* utilizes the gross chemical elements of the air in order to enter your body. The scriptures speak of air as a horse having a rider. That mysterious rider is *prana*.

"You get *prana* from food and sunlight, but the atmosphere is the chief source for the life force. More than any other source of *prana*, the act of breathing recharges the body and mind. Breathing is the most fundamental factor in metabolism. Under stress, breathing is restricted and the cells starve.

"Proper breathing can cure coronary heart disease as well as many other ailments. Learning how to manipulate the two nostrils through control of the breath—*pranayama*—gives a tremendous control over moods."

Swamiji walked closer to the students. "Let me tell you something. Once I was invited to sit in as a team of physicians listened to a woman's migraine history. In front of her they discussed various remedies from sexual therapy and oral suppressants to brain surgery. As they were concluding that the latter was best, I asked if I could make a suggestion. I mentioned that the woman's right nostril had been closed for a long period of time. If surgery could be postponed for forty-eight hours, she could try the nasal wash twice and the practice of alternate breathing thrice. The doctors reluctantly permitted this intrusion. Upon following my suggestions, the woman's headaches vanished and did not return. Of course, one of the doctors accused me of conspiring with the woman beforehand.

"The ancients discovered that there is an energy polarity in the human body exactly like the positive and negative potentials, the attraction and repulsion, found in electricity. The two sentinels—your nostrils—of the city of life guard the passage of the life force as it flows in and out of the body. Human beings pass through moods throughout the day. In a normal, healthy person the flow of breath switches its nostril dominance approximately every two hours. All animals, being creatures of Mother Nature, have seasonal changes. Human beings also have daily changes in which the polarity of their body alters its prominence. Without these changes, the full range of human personality would never be expressed."

As I listened to him expound on the intricacies of the life force in its functional association with the human body, my appreciation of the beauty and wisdom of human nature kept widening.

"*Prana* is that subtle energy by which your mind functions," Swamiji went on. "It is impossible to die unless *prana* leaves the body. In the Jewish scriptures also, the act of life and death is discerned as the influx of breath and its departure.

"Breathing and thinking are twin companions. Have an anxious thought, and your breathing rate accelerates, with the result being that your blood pressure rises. Reverse your breath rate to a slow, gentle, smooth cycle, and your blood pressure lowers. Unfortunately, medical therapy does not take advantage of this natural law.

"Sometimes parents who smoke retain too much carbon dioxide and do not realize that they can pass the carbons through the semen and the woman's blood; thus the newborn child carries that toxin and has respiratory ailments. The body/mind reacts to excess CO_2 by becoming restless and insensitive.

"When you regulate the motion of the lungs, you gain

supervision over the functioning of the 10th cranial or vagus nerve, and with that ascendancy comes the voluntary control over your entire nervous systems.

"Many years ago I needed a quiet, undisturbed place to do a certain meditation practice that required leaving my body for a few days. A physician friend of mine gave me an empty room in his hospital to use. 'Make sure no one enters this room,' the doctor told the floor nurse. So I folded my legs and sat in my meditation posture on the bed, closed my eyes, and began my practice.

"After about a week, the doctor was called away on an emergency and left the hospital. He forgot about me in his rush to leave. Meanwhile, the head nurse was looking for an empty room for a new patient and, hearing that no one had come in or out of my room in a week, unlocked the door. She was surprised to see me sitting there on the bed, and not finding a heart beat or any sign of breathing, decided I was dead.

"Orderlies took me down to the hospital morgue. They could not get my legs unfolded, so they simply covered me with a sheet and left me there. It was cold in the morgue; I began to come back into my body because of the temperature change.

"Into the morgue that evening came a simple sweeper, cleaning the floor. He swept his broom close by the table where I was placed just as I pulled the sheet off my face and asked, 'Where am I?' The poor man was so frightened that he screamed, threw down his broom, and ran out of the hospital. He was never heard from again."

When the audience stopped laughing and heard Swamiji's assurance that the strange event had really happened, he continued the lecture.

"There is nothing complicated about gaining comprehensive control of the breath. All one has to do is observe the moving capacity of the lungs. Internalize your awareness and you can feel it. By focusing your attention on the motion of your lungs, its control becomes a conscious ability. Your awareness alone brings control.

"Medical science did not think it possible to control the involuntary aspects of the body; most of the body functions on this involuntary basis. Yet the yogis, through patient observation, gradually acquired the facility to bring all their involuntary functions under conscious direction. That is why they could heal themselves, determine their deaths, and become aware of higher powers of cognition. The more you work with your breath, the more you can become sensitive to the treasures of *prana.*

"This study of *prana* is called *swara swarodhyam.* When one of your nostrils is blocked, you notice your breathing, but to seriously study breath behavior you need to have both nostrils open simultaneously. Then you can study the conditions of the mind and even the realms of intuition and pre-cognition."

From that day on, as I jogged along my regular exercise route, my mind kept turning over my teacher's statements about breath. I was much more aware of my lung motion and how I felt during my workouts. I began to notice the association between the exertion of my body and the pattern of my breathing. The idea to run, not by a predetermined plan, but by using my breath as a guide and monitor, spontaneously arose in my mind. I found it fun to explore this bodily adventure and took notes as I worked on the practice.

Back home again in Glenview, a strange conference was going on. Mama, who always had some mischief brewing, had a new plan. Over the years she had sometimes used a few rather unsavory slang words, and when asked for their meaning by Swamiji, assured him that they were "just Americanisms." He would then gingerly try one out on Theresa, Samskrti, or some of his other close women students. If they blanched and gasped, or stood with their mouths open and their eyes filling with tears, he knew he had a winner and would use it again whenever the mood suited.

One such word was "bitch." Theresa particularly hated that word, and so, of course, was presented with a colorful tee-shirt from her teacher emblazoned with the hateful word across the front. After crying and throwing the shirt in the garbage, she retrieved it and wore it to welcome him home from a lecture tour, much to his embarrassment.

That day Mama sat in the Institute office with Samskrti, Veda, and Theresa. They were making plans and writing notes, laughing uproariously, their giggles spilling all the way down the long corridor. When Swamiji entered the room, Mama was ready for him.

"Swamiji, we feel rejected and so are starting a new order of renunciates. I am the spiritual leader and these are my disciples."

"Really?" he asked her, his eyes big and dark, his lips breaking into a grin. "What sort of order is it?"

"It is called the Bitchananda Order, and no men are allowed to join. We will wear special clothing with aprons so our clothes stay clean, and we will carry a begging bowl just like mountain yogis. Our bowls, however, will be fine porcelain, and we will carry them in our purses."

On and on the order grew amid laughter and howling. The joke took on a life of its own eventually, and over the years the women used it as a kind of refuge whenever life with Swamiji became too hard. They would look at each other and quietly say, "But when we join Mama's order, things will be better!"

Home in the Himalayas

CHAPTER 13
FINDING BRIGADOON

I stood on the top of a hill next to Swamiji, who sat atop a powerful stallion. Suddenly he began riding pell mell down the steep, grassy slope. I had the feeling that he had urgent business down in the broad valley below. I turned to my left and found a slender, old woman with long, black hair standing next to me. She reached out her hand and touched my shoulder saying, "Be prepared; something wonderful is going to happen to you."

"CAN YOU FIND ANOTHER PLACE for us, Justin?" I looked up, surprised, wondering what Swamiji was joking about, but his face told me he was serious. We had been living and teaching in Glenview for just about a year, and I thought we were set for life. Swamiji had other ideas. So I began to scout around the Midwest, searching for a larger piece of real estate. Other students did likewise. We were all pleased that our Glenview center had fulfilled its promise of rooting Swamiji's teachings in American culture, but our teacher had more dreams ready to materialize. He spoke of a multi-dimensional center with acres of land to renew students and offer space for building expansion. It should be a place where men and women could live on campus as residents and have enough room for a graduate school, an expansive combined-therapy program, a psycho-physiological laboratory, guest suites, space for a large press—a full-range educational institute that would nourish in body, mind, and spirit.

Swamiji announced in his lectures that while we would retain the Glenview center, it was imperative to expand the horizon of activities and find a much larger campus. We were lucky, in one sense, because it was a time when many convents, seminaries, high schools, and boarding schools were put on the block for sale.

My search took me to nearly a dozen Catholic residential properties; inspection of each lasted from three to five hours.

It was curious that never once did the proprietor, usually a nun or priest, offer a cup of coffee or a glass of water to their prospective buyers. (Perhaps they should have read the Rule of St. Benedict, which insists the visitor be treated as Christ.) The exhausting hunt for property continued for a year.

Meanwhile, Swamiji's busy teaching schedule continued. A Chicago policeman, Frank, also a student of our teacher, lived only a few miles from our apartment. He was often asked to drive Swamiji to the airport, especially when things were running a little late. A friend of Frank, who lived in Wheaton, called Frank to announce that he and his wife had been pleased to learn that Swami Rama would be speaking at their church the next Friday evening. They all decided to sit together to listen to the yogi.

A few days later, Frank got a call from the Institute office asking if he would drive Swamiji to the airport early Friday evening because Swamiji would give a weekend seminar in New York. "I guess the Wheaton Church lecture is canceled," thought Frank. On Friday he picked up his favorite passenger and drove Swamiji to O'Hare Airport. He walked his teacher down to the gate, carrying his bag. Swamiji thanked him warmly and boarded the plane.

The next morning, Frank's phone rang. "Where were you last night?" his friend asked. "We held a seat for you."

Puzzled, Frank said, "What do you mean? Swamiji didn't lecture at the church last night."

"Of course he did!" insisted the friend. "Everyone loved his talk. He promised to come back again next spring."

Frank gave regrets to his friend, hung up, and sat staring at the phone for a few minutes. Then he called me and we talked of yogic miracles for the rest of the night.

MIDNIGHT WITH THE MASTER

Back at the Glenview center again, Swamiji conducted his Super-conscious Meditation course. I attended as usual, but I kept notes differently this time. Instead of taking down only my teacher's words, I watched what they evoked in my mind and recorded them as well. After the talk, people filed out as Swamiji walked through the crowd, greeting newcomers and encouraging people to see him if they wanted. If you were his student, the door was open and free. He finally got into the hallway, saw Theresa and me standing there and said "Let's go."

We headed over to his house and Theresa went into the kitchen to prepare the tilk. He asked how his English had been that night, and I told him that his annunciation was certainly better than last year. As the years went on, if I was present for a lecture, he would always walk by when it was over and whisper, "How was it?"

As we got comfortable in his cozy living room, our teacher launched right into a story. "Once on a flight from Delhi to Frankfurt, a passenger became annoyed with me. He associated my snoring with the fact that one of the engines on the right wing had failed. He woke me up to tell me what was on his agitated mind. 'Sir, your snoring has knocked out the right engine!'

"I looked at the worry and fear in the man's eyes and replied, 'The other engines are still running due to my sleeping and calmness.' Then I went back to sleep."

We all laughed heartily at the incident, and when tilk arrived, Swamiji continued in the same train of thought.

"No worry is ever genuine." He looked pointedly at Theresa, the worrier deluxe, and continued, "We worry for the future instead of enjoying the present. Whenever you begin to worry, apply this principle: All the things of this world are to be used but not possessed. You need to acknowledge this insight as a law of life. Without it, society can give you hard shocks. Don't go through life the way therapists do in mental hospitals—picking up the disease by identifying with their patients."

I sipped my tilk and asked, "Why are emotions so hard to manage?"

The answer came right back, "Emotion creates problems because its object is outside you, and thus it makes you feel helpless. You have to change the way you relate to the object. Without this understanding, you will have pain and shock. The latter is a danger to your health."

At that point, I associated his words with a tragic episode in the local newspaper and shared it with the little group. The media had reported that an elderly father, upon hearing an unofficial radio announcement that his Air Force son had been shot down, fell over with heart failure. Later the news was proved to be slightly inaccurate; the pilot had been a different man.

"With understanding you may have pain," Swamiji continued, "but no shock. It's the shocks that cause the worse damage, and there is no medical treatment for them. Only with control can one have freedom."

My mind began surveying past moments when I had gotten shocked, as it were, by disappointments brought on by myself or unexpectedly from others. I could remember how my neighbors were totally distraught by a sudden death in the family, or a spouse walking out, or a relative diagnosed with a dreaded disease. I took another sip of tilk as Swamiji continued more animated than before, which tipped me off that he was really going to explore the topic at hand.

"People get discouraged with life because they rely on their imaginations and speculations instead of on experience. Something painful happens to them and they cry out in their shock, 'How could this happen to me?'

"Or else they go about relating to life inside out. They want external things to be different. Some of my students come to me and say, 'Oh, Swamiji, I know I could meditate better if only I had more money, or a better job, or nicer neighbors, or more popularity.' They assume that their problems will miraculously disappear once they have what their imagination tells them is required to feel better about themselves."

I interjected that I found nothing wrong with wanting these things and that it would be difficult to get on in society without them. At that moment Raja yawned, checked out the scene, and promptly went back to doggie-dreamland. Perhaps his yawn was a sigh saying, "What's wrong, Justin, don't you get it yet?"

Swamiji took a quick gulp, put his cup down, squirmed around in his recliner, and charged on. "Many conventions are necessary for society to run well, but how many of them lead you to enlightenment?"

"Nuts!" I thought, "he had me again." For some reason I glanced over at Raja. Was he suddenly smiling in his sleep?

"The majority of circumstances around you can't be controlled by you," my teacher continued. "The trouble starts when you assume you can control them. If you think the purpose of life is to fulfill society's conventions, then you will never get off the treadmill and will one day wind up exhausted. If you agree, however, that the aim of life is to become aware of eternal truth, then you will order your life goals differently, yet without ignoring society. You have heard me say repeatedly, 'Don't disturb people and don't let people disturb you.' To act that way, you have to understand the good as well as the bad. People go through life with too many fears—my students are no exception—and then, as they get older, these fears will pounce on them relentlessly and ruin their health."

I felt ambivalent. I wished we could stop there and just rehash those words as my mind saw so many connections to my own life. Yet I also wanted more. Listening to his words increased my appetite for more on the spot. He wasn't ready to quit. Wonderful!

"Study yourself up close and from afar. Study life as it is, but here's the challenge. How can your study be effective when the data from the external world is incomplete and often misleading? To resolve this challenge, you have to resort to preparation. You must prepare your mind, which is the instrument that does the study. The mistake people make is that they expect the external world to calm down in order for their minds to make their study. This will never happen; even God can't make it happen.

"You are going in the wrong direction with your study. The world can't calm down, but you can. Being calm is a power not found in the external world; it is only found in you. Don't be concerned about calming the world at large, for change is its nature. If you want to become a student of the book of life you have to start with and maintain a calm mind. For that you need to build strength within yourself."

Swamiji looked over at the young resident who had come in quietly to join us. "I don't mean using drugs. Drugs produce fantasies, which you take to get the real thing; they deteriorate the nervous system. Enlightenment is never the product of a chemical pill. I've even experimented with many drugs in the laboratory but all I got for my trouble was a headache. Your mind has the power to be unaffected by the events of the world unless you permit it, so always study life from a calm perspective."

"Excuse me, Swamiji," I said; I couldn't wait. "In the ordinary course of a day at work and home, it's too difficult to maintain a calm outlook. Demands are pushed on one, one's peers are uncooperative when needed, sometimes the kids get in the way, one runs out of money. The list is endless."

Swamiji spoke slowly, deliberately, "If the world is getting in your way, that's a sign that you don't understand the world."

That shocked me. In one stroke he knocked out from me my woeful arrogance. "No excuses anymore, buddy," I thought to myself. Before I could finish my own train of thought, he jumped back in.

"One can attain enlightenment in this world as it is. Just as you don't feel pain during sleep, you can develop sufficient strength to withstand anything the world dishes out. Adjust yourself so that the world can't annoy you no matter what happens."

I had to admit my ignorance. "How?" I asked.

"Tree," he looked up suddenly and said, "will you get Mama on the phone?"

It felt good to let up on the concentration. Truth can wear you out. But after the short call to say good-night, the learning went forward anyway.

"To understand life, don't start by analyzing your thoughts; you couldn't live long enough to complete that endless task. Study the process of the mind. Then get practical.

"First, be on friendly terms with your problems. Second, study how you use time; explore ways to improve your use of it. Next, never suppress thoughts and feelings; instead learn to control them for your enjoyment. Always be fully in the world and yet remain above it all. How? Experiment! The middle path is the path of experiments. Begin gently—that's very important—otherwise, you expect too much from yourself too soon. Be truly in the present with your senses. Give them your full attention. For example, really taste your food. In this way, the coordination between your objective mind and the external world improves. This kind of growth is for anyone at any age."

Strange, but I felt calmer than usual. His words quietly filled my mind so that I lingered with the illumination of the insights.

Swamiji looked off into the distance and then tilted his head back toward me calmly saying, "We know all truth already. So why are we here? To unlearn! We must put aside all the things that clutter up our awareness. Your perfection is a matter of awareness within you. We radiate that awareness by becoming human. Eternal reality can be realized by constant awareness."

Just then there was a knock at the door. I looked at Theresa and shifted my head for a moment toward the door, thinking,

"Who would come to visit in the middle of night?" We both shrugged our shoulders, wondering.

"You'd better go now; I'm being reminded to get to my practice," the guru said quietly.

Driving home on empty streets after finding no one at the door, I turned toward Theresa and said, "I wonder if whoever it was would be willing to knock at night to remind me to practice."

BACK TO WORK

Swamiji now began work on his written masterpiece. He wanted to share the stories of the Himalayan saints and sages with his students so we could benefit from his training. Swami Ajaya was asked to go through his teacher's old Indian diaries; Swamiji dictated other remembrances night and day to Theresa; Dr. Agnihotri came from India to work on the glossary and Sanskrit terms; others were asked to assist in correcting grammar, typing corrections into the chapters, and reading the results.

"I feel this need in my heart to honor my master and the sages; everything I have done, I owe to their wisdom," Swamiji poignantly said in the midst of all the activity. "People in the West don't understand that a path of spirituality is not the same as professing a religion. One is built on experience, the other is accepted on faith."

When I heard from my wife about the dictation sessions, I could hardly wait for their completion. From my experience of living in monasteries, I knew that most Christian religious people viewed the spirituality of mysticism as hopeful aspiration—one either received the grace of mysticism or not. That there were definite systematic practices that could produce evidential results was a concept totally foreign to the Christian culture. I hoped that Swamiji would touch on those aspects of practice and outcome in his book.

As the manuscript grew, Swamiji began the process of reading parts of it to students and friends. Each evening he would invite a few of us into his room and have the day's work read to us. He would telephone Mama, Dr. Arya, Phil, Ladd, Charles and others to listen in as well. Sometimes he called people in the news or important political or spiritual figures that I did not know he knew. "What do you think?" he would ask excitedly. As I listened to the reading of his spiritual experiences, I knew that my fondest wish was coming true.

Early one morning, about two o'clock, I started to doze involuntarily as Theresa and a few others read newly edited portions of the manuscript back to Swamiji for correction. "Justin," he said, "you are getting tired. You should go home." I was chagrined, but I knew that this manuscript was so precious to him that he would not tolerate inattention. I left with regret. Little did I know that something wonderful would soon happen. Within a few minutes, the door to the office slowly opened. Swamiji looked up at the space in the doorway, bowed his head, and smiled without speaking. The door then closed and work continued. One of the women asked, "What was that, Swamiji? How did the door open and close on its own?"

He replied softly, "My master came in to bless the work."

Theresa told me that this happened several times as the book was being compiled, sometimes accompanied by a polite knock at the door. She said that on many an early morning when she brought Swamiji's tea to him after a long night of dictation, he would tell her, "We need to change a few lines" or "Tree, my master gave me permission to include this" or "I can add another story but must change the yogi's name." Photos were selected for the book, including several I took of *sadhus* in India; dates were checked; maps of the Himalayas were drawn.

The manuscript appeared now to be complete and ready for production. Swamiji called Theresa in to see him and quietly asked her to make a vow to eat only fruit and wear only white clothes during the time she did the final edit, design, and typesetting of the book. After the vow was taken, just before midnight on a Thursday evening, she was asked to rush to her office and begin work on the book at once before the auspicious day—dedicated to the guru—would end.

I didn't see her much during that time. She worked in her small office behind the kitchen, called the mole-hole, stopping only to sleep for three or four hours nightly, sometimes on the floor next to her desk. The work took much longer than expected, but my wife kept her vow, even when Swamiji, worried for her health, invited her to eat meals with him. After three and a half weeks, she brought the camera-ready manuscript to him. Swamiji raised the pages in both hands, closed his eyes, and offered the text of *Living with the Himalayan Masters* to his teacher. Theresa sent it immediately off to be printed. A celebration dinner was held that evening in what was called the onion room, the small room adjacent to the kitchen, with Swamiji himself making the special dessert. When everyone left the party and Tessa Typeset was saying good night to Swamiji, he removed the prayer beads he always wore, kissed her on the cheek, and placed his beads around her neck.

That weekend, Howard and I, continuing the property search, went to a fifty-acre prep school north of Rockford, Illinois, just across the state line. It seemed to have everything we needed on its trim grounds and well-managed buildings. I thought we had at last found a real possibility for our expanded center. As we were leaving, the caretaker casually mentioned that the State of Wisconsin was in the process of passing legislation to guarantee that the property would belong only to the state.

For the first time in the year of searching, I felt discouraged. That was a rare mood for me, so on the way home Howard and I decided to stop to visit our friends, Behram and Katy Guard, who lived in Rockford. Not only were they excellent cooks, but I needed to see a cheerful face. We enjoyed a sumptuous Parsee meal, and, because they were also students of our teacher, we all spoke of the needed property. Behram brought out some real estate listings that he had collected. As he shuffled through the pile, he threw away a listing for a property on the east coast ("Too cold," he said), and concentrated on Arkansas. We collected his selections to bring back to Swamiji and said our good-byes. As we neared the door to head back, however, I had a compulsive urge to retrieve the listing thrown away earlier. So I made an excuse to go upstairs for a moment and fished the crumpled clipping out of the waste basket. There was something about that place. I stuck the balled-up paper quickly into my pocket and returned to the car.

Two hours later we were back on the Glenview campus in the onion room, where a small group of students was listening to Swamiji telling stories. He welcomed us in and asked how the search had gone. We reported our disappointment over losing the Wisconsin property and showed him the new listings. As Swamiji studied the brochures, I found myself pulling the crumpled paper out of my pocket saying, "But I prefer this one, the seminary in

Pennsylvania."

Swami almost leaped off the sofa as he pointed to the phone. "Get it, Justin!" I called the priests who owned the property and told them we wanted to visit the grounds immediately. They accepted our visit, eager to sell. The next day, three of us hired a small plane and flew to Scranton, Pennsylvania where we were met by a priest from the order that owned the seminary and chauffeured to the property.

I will never forget the ride from the center of Honesdale into the Kilroe Seminary in the northern Pocono mountains. It was a cool, brightly lit October afternoon, my birthday, in fact. We exchanged stories in the car and were told some of the history of the place during the drive until the car turned into the property. I could not hear the conversation anymore; I was dazzled. I felt like I was entering the legendary village of Brigadoon. The long, steep entrance overlooked 425 acres spread out before us. Like sentinels, tall pine trees circled the grounds, the leaves of the ash and beech trees flared in crimson and magenta, while the phosphorous gold of the maples shimmered in the wind. Scarlets, purples, and ochers mixed around the spreading brick building, and tall, yellow-green grass waved across the rolling hills. It was the scene from my hilltop dream exactly. Was the autumn day celebrating our arrival or my birthday?

Our tour of the buildings and grounds left me nearly ecstatic as I envisaged the incredible potential. Uncharted paths in the woods were waiting exploration; a small pond for swimming lay a short distance from a two-story house for staff. The barn was big enough to house a helicopter; it could easily be converted into a press. Two more buildings stood next to the barn, another down the path. The main building was stately and protective, with a new east wing which contained a large auditorium capable of holding hundreds of students. The property was within easy driving distance from an airport as well as from the cities of Binghamton, New York, and Philadelphia. To me it was a dream come true; my colleagues were not impressed. They thought it was too far away. "Obviously both are comatose," I could only think at their response.

When we returned to Glenview the next day, Swamiji hardly waited for our verdicts; he put in his bid via the telephone, giving the priests ten days to consider our offer, much less than the asking price. Acceptance arrived within forty-eight hours.

Ten days later, Swamiji sent a resident student and myself to the new property. We assessed the building's damage from neglect and weather and began advanced PR work. The town of Honesdale had fewer than six thousand inhabitants, but rumors of an invasion of Moonies filled the streets. I went from one end of Main Street to the other, walking into every major store and business, introducing myself and explaining the work of our Institute. Not knowing a soul in the place, I remembered that the priests had told me of twin sisters in town who were better than today's Internet at disseminating the latest news. I phoned them next, requesting their assistance in inviting the most important people in town to come to the seminary the following night. Our common bond of Notre Dame paid off: the twins arranged for more than eighty of Honesdale's prominent citizens to join me at the seminary for cider and donuts while I told them of Swamiji's work for humanity and our vision for an educational and scientific facility.

A few days later Swamiji flew to Honesdale. We drove around town and through the outlying area, reconnoitering the territory. He spent the evening hours on the phone, asking for donations from his students and admirers. I helped with his phone marathon, from Maine down through New England, through the south to the Keys of Florida, across the Midwest, westward to California, up into Canada and across to New York. He asked hundreds to help defray the expenses for the property. "It is not my Institute," he insisted. "This is all for you and your children."

I held his personal phone book and called out the numbers as he dialed and then I kept score on the promised donations. In all my years with Swamiji, tallying math was about the only talent, except for my so-called 'canine hunger,' that put me ahead of him. There were moments, however, in listening to the conversations, when I wished he wasn't forced to involve himself this way for the sake of our Institute. Some supporters tried to put him off, tried, I say, but he managed, in the nicest way, to solicit deferred pledges. I listened to mini-lectures by phone, as he teased the listeners, reminding them of the benefits that awaited their visit to the grounds. At times, it was so amusing that I clinched my teeth to prevent background laughter during the calls. Many financial promises turned out to be empty. Some people backed out; some reversed their support when a check was due.

"I want this deed free of encumbrances," he said as he looked over at me, with his hand over the receiver. "I don't want you people saddled with a big mortgage."

So Swami Rama, salesman extraordinaire, called in his markers from all around the world. I could not believe that I was assisting the illustrious yogi from the Himalayas in such a mundane, worldly task, but I grew out of my naiveté and realized his immense love for his students. Theresa and I felt badly that we had nothing to offer, so I cashed in my university retirement fund and added it to the tally.

Many little checks from large hearts and a few very generous checks paved the way for the enormous accomplishment of the Honesdale Institute. It was another important star in a constellation of accomplishments that Swamiji would manifest during his years abroad and leave as a living legacy when he returned to his beloved mountains.

One evening, when it was too late to phone any more, Swamiji turned to me and said, "Justin, Theresa is supposed to die tomorrow."

I was stunned. My mind panicked, thoughts jumping from one idea to another. Finally I blurted out, "What should I do?"

Swamiji looked at me intently. "Do nothing. I will place a comma."

The next morning Theresa called. She sounded astonishingly calm as she told me that earlier that morning, when she arose for her three o'clock meditation, she had tried to light a candle on her altar and had dropped the match in her lap, setting herself on fire. Her clothes burned quickly, shooting flames up and down her arms and legs. She stood up, looked in the mirror, and watched all the flames. She wasn't afraid, she said, realizing that it would be all right to die. Then she remembered the people in the apartment complex; she didn't want anyone else to be hurt. With that thought, the fear came. She peered through the flames around her face to Swamiji's picture and asked for his help. She beat at the blaze with her hands, attempting to smother the flames, when suddenly they all went out. Her clothes were a pile of black shreds at her feet on the burned circle of carpet; her skin and hair, even her hands, were untouched. She then sat down in the smoke-filled room to do her meditation practice.

When she called me several hours later, she also asked to talk to Swamiji. He took the phone and said, "Hi, Tessa. You did not die today; I have too much work for you to do yet."

"My life is yours, Swamiji," she replied with emotion. And then our teacher told her to get going on the typesetting of his next book.

Justin caring for the pine grove in Honesdale

CHAPTER 14
LIVING IN HONESDALE

I stood with Swamiji and said to him, "After all these years with you, have I made any advances?" He replied, "Definitely. One-tenth of one inch." Somehow that did not make me feel uncomfortable.

ON DECEMBER 11, 1977, a tired caravan pulled into Honesdale in the gale of a snow storm after leaving Chicago amidst hugs and tears and good-byes to Mama and the staff who would be staying behind. Swamiji, who had arrived at the new center with some male residents a few days earlier, greeted us at the door. Since we had driven for sixteen hours, he put Theresa and me to work scrubbing the kitchen stoves, long covered with grease and rancid meat scraps. As we worked, he sat on a stool in the corner, telling us about the caretaker hired by the priests who had used the kitchen as a butcher shop for hunters' deer. In a tired, surly mood, I cursed under my breath with every stroke of the soapy steel wool, every splash of water. "I'll clean this damn contraption if it kills me," I thought. "I don't care how tired I am; he won't see a single scrap of meat scum!" A half hour later, Swamiji quietly told the two of us that we had done enough and should retire. We climbed exhausted into sleeping bags on the linoleum floor of one of the less dirty rooms. When we awoke, Swamiji asked Theresa to pack his suitcases. He had waited for us, he said, but now it was time for him to depart for India.

Cassie, Howard's wife and a kind, competent business-woman, helped get things moving in Honesdale. We were soon scrubbing the place down, making it habitable. Although Theresa and I had donated all the furnishings of our house (furniture and dishes, linens and silver, appliances and rugs) to the new Institute, it was obviously insufficient to fill the huge building. I found an advertisement in the local newspaper about a New York college auction of all its furniture and classroom equipment—the timing was perfect. Cassie rented some trucks and we all dashed up state to purchase everything we could—chairs, dining hall tables, dishes and silverware, pots and pans, mattresses, desks and lamps.

Next we began painting. We turned the wildly decorated "rainbow lounge" of the young seminarians who had lived there years before, into the white-walled meditation room and turned the dining room into a place conducive to eating. We vacuumed up thousands of flies, removed several huge hornet nests, hauled away rusty farm equipment and bags of soiled baby diapers and empty cans, and overhauled the immense heating plant. Roofs were inspected, drain pipes were patched, carpeting was installed, the long, wild fields of grass were cut. It was hard work, but we loved it. The open air reminded us that we were creating a future for ourselves and others.

Swamiji did not stay long in India that year; he soon returned to Honesdale, boosting our energies even further. What surprised me throughout these refurbishing and growing days was his ability to inspire and instill a commitment in others without being frantic or oppressive about it. One may not have always agreed with him and certainly could raise opposing viewpoints, which he always considered carefully, but he usually offered the best advice. While his exuberance in ordering us about to get things done may have offended the ears of some sensitive souls, it never occurred to me that he was taking advantage of his position nor that he was doing any project to showcase himself. Blunt, candid, yes—it was part of his temperament. But domineering, overbearing, never—he had too much respect for human nature. He would let one know his mind on the issue at hand, but he wasn't in the business of intimidating anyone with fear. If I was to catalogue his mistakes, they would be: too much enthusiasm for people's declared intentions and too much patience with others' laziness, as I personally well know, in responding to his vision. Over the years, I wondered if he would ever violate these impressions; he never did.

Theresa and I moved into the first suite in the men's dormitory in the east wing. Small wasn't the word for it; it had two pantry-sized rooms, just large enough for two chairs, my desk, some books, and our clothes. We had given our futon to a new resident physician, and so we slept on the linoleum floor on a blanket that we kept folded in the closet. What made it livable for Theresa, and even fabulous in her eyes, was the small bathroom that held the only tub on the floor. After seven years of living there, Swamiji jokingly referred to us as his two half-swamis, having nothing, wanting nothing, getting nothing.

The women residents lived on the second floor; the third floor held the biofeedback rooms and a large room used for chanting morning and evening prayers and group meditation. On the opposite side, the west wing housed the therapy department with its private rooms for patients, Swamiji's office and apartment, and a row of guest rooms. Rooms on the second floor were prepared for seminar participants and classrooms.

Whenever possible I went outside. I scouted everywhere on the property, the woods, the fields opening to thousands of acres of state land, the rock formations, the pond, and the waterfall. One of my favorite spots was a hill beyond the pine trees that offered views of the entire valley. I could see for thirty miles from that spot and felt pleased to do my practice there.

In a mischievous mood shortly after our arrival, I decided to try an experiment in truth that I had always wondered about. I came into the dining room and sat down with some of the young residents. "I just had a wonderful break at that famous spot on our property," I told them.

"What famous spot?" they asked, all excited by the possibility.

"You know, the place where the Hollywood studio filmed the opening scene for the movie, *The Sound of Music.* Julie Andrews sang her song to the hills there," I said without a hint of a smile.

Everyone looked puzzled, a little skeptical, but wanting to believe me and to have something special in their day to pass along to others.

I added the clincher, "Go on top of the hill behind the pines and see for yourself."

The next day at least three different people told me the same story, slightly expanded. The place has been called The Sound of Music Hill from that day, and I learned something important about rumor.

That cool March of 1978, we opened our doors to the first therapy patients, quickly followed by students from New York, eager to learn at the new facility. We were thrilled to welcome the public to America's newest enterprise in holistic living.

With the spring upon us, Swamiji often walked energetically about the grounds with some of the permanent residents, calling over anyone else in earshot. We didn't need much convincing to go on tour with him. We all loved to be in his presence, even if it meant more work. Visitors didn't stand a chance of getting away from his polite but compelling invitation to accompany him on a walk. Always entertaining, perking up people as he pointed out what needed to be fixed, cleaned, removed, or grown, so that the building expansion could take place, he basked in the open country environment, telling us how it reminded him of the landscape of his beloved Himalayan foothills.

"We have to raise our own organic vegetables," he said with a sharp gleam in his eye. Later, he got angry when he discovered that some of us went into town to eat at the famous Bullet Train Diner on Main Street. He did not understand the American pastime of dining out. "I provide all this land for your nourishment and you prefer to eat in town?" came his accusation.

Our staff began to reach out to our neighbors. The local Rotary club requested me to join their organization and asked if I would give some talks on yoga at their luncheons. Knowing everyone loved flowers, Theresa and her friend, Murti, decided to beautify the front entrance, digging up the grass to plant a huge ring of perennials around the driveway. After weeks of private early-morning classes with Swamiji, Theresa began teaching yoga at the local YMCA, and a few married students arrived from around the country to buy property and work in the towns nearby.

One afternoon Swamiji and I walked up the hill past the big barn, talking of future plans. "We will build a playground and eventually a school for all the children of the resident families," he said slowly, visualizing his plans.

"Swamiji, we will have children here?" I asked, amazed at the thought. "I thought this was an ashram!"

He turned to me, put his hands on my shoulders and said, "Son, be practical. How can this place grow unless we allow people to marry and have families? We aren't training renunciates here; we are creating a holistic community from all walks of life. I want to see this place flourish. We should allow people to live a full life and then go out into the world and share the teachings with others."

"Of course," I thought to myself. "This is not an Indian ashram. Swamiji is creating something new, bringing East and West together in a different kind of synthesis." This reinforced my belief that he was indeed a rare type of yogi.

As we walked along the road, he pointed to a double row of tall pine trees. "Look how dry and barren they're becoming," he lamented. "They've been neglected. All they need is some TLC." He spoke for anyone to hear; one had to be deaf to miss the message. "Nature is very sensitive to human presence," he added. Over the next few weeks I found great satisfaction and pleasure in trimming the entire lane from a high ladder. The trees and I became friends as I worked, and when I was done I could feel the difference in their energy, as if they were thanking me.

BARKING DEER AND OTHER ANOMALIES

White-tailed deer soon returned to our grounds, knowing that this was now a safe haven, especially during hunting season when they would flock onto the property. One late afternoon, I was jogging past the main building and heard what sounded like a chorus of snorting. Curious, I moved slowly among the trees by the side of the road to check. Peeking through the scrubbery, I saw a small herd of deer about twenty yards away preparing to bed down in the tall grass. They were vigorously exhaling with such force that it sounded like barking. Fascinated, I watched for a half hour hidden in the bushes. Was this animal pranayama? Their snorting resembled a breathing exercise I had practiced for years. The strong expelling of carbon dioxide by contracting the diaphragmatic muscles as Swamiji taught us was an excellent blood cleanser. Now I couldn't wait to tell Swamiji about my find. But first I wanted to ascertain whether this phenomenon was a one night performance or a daily regimen. For a week I went running at that hour; sure enough each twilight the deer gathered to perform their ritual.

"Of course, the animals teach us many things," Swamiji said. "Where do you suppose hatha yoga got its names for the postures? The yogis carefully observed animals and then practiced their movements and discovered the energy changes within themselves. Let me show you how to do deer barking. You should begin every morning with this practice."

And I did.

Getting ready for classes to begin at the new center was much work. I wrote schedules and class descriptions while Theresa typeset brochures and newsletters, and the office staff mailed them out to a growing data base. Being one of the few faculty members on campus for a long time, I was usually asked to handle the writing projects. I struggled with the new membership brochure, trying to think up something a little different. "The Himalayan Institute is its Members" I wrote, and Theresa set it into type. When she brought the sample brochure to Swamiji for approval, he did not seem pleased.

"What is this? Who wrote this nonsense? How can the Institute be its members? Who will understand such a silly statement? I ask you to work and you bring this?" came the response.

"I'm sorry, Swamiji," Theresa replied. "I'll have it rewritten right away."

"No, leave it," he said with a sly smile, and ended the conversation.

Not wanting to hurt my feelings, Theresa did not tell me about the encounter for many years. In the meantime, the line had been used hundreds of times, and continues to be used, as one of the most effective statements in our literature. I never figured out my teacher's response. Perhaps he gave it a back-handed blessing?

The publication office was now on the first floor near the central entrance. Theresa and artists Bala and Randy shared the office space. One day she had an unexpected intruder in the midst of hurried last-minute work. Swamiji cheerfully marched in and asked how things were going. Hardly waiting for an answer, he glanced down at her beloved violet plant sitting on her desk, and asked, "What's this ugly plant doing here?" He began to cough and then cleared his throat as Theresa frantically searched in her drawer for a box of Kleenex to offer.

Without waiting for the tissue, Swamiji proceeded to spit a mouthful on the plant.

"Swamiji!" Theresa, of course, was utterly non-plussed. That a holy man would spit on flowers somehow just didn't compute, especially when it was her favorite office plant.

He turned and walked out, leaving the room. The next

morning the plant burgeoned with beautiful purple flowers; in less than a week, it had tripled in size and had to be separated into three pots. Over the years they continued to be the largest, fullest violet plants in Honesdale. Some yogis just love to tease.

A BITE OF THE BIG APPLE

Swamiji next said it was time to sell books in busy New York. "Let's open a bookstore," he declared. Once again Howard and I were told to examine some real estate and then case the rest of the city for possible property. We drove around Soho, The Village, and the West Side, but the best selection showed up at Fifth Avenue and Fourteenth Street. We rented several floors of an old building for our new East-West Bookstore. I wrote course descriptions and brochures for this center and began a long series of weekly excursions to the Big Apple to teach. With myself, Phil, Swami Ajaya, Rudy, students, and occasionally Swamiji as well, we offered a full menu of programs: meditation, stress management, philosophy, psychology, homeopathic medical care, hatha yoga, counseling, and more to the interesting citizens of New York.

Late one afternoon, after the bookstore had been open for a few months, Swamiji was downstairs in the basement classroom finishing a business conversation with the manager. He suddenly blurted out, "What else is there to do? I might as well sell some books."

I heard these words less as a request for help than as a self-admonition. A few of us heard it as a hopefully-fulfilled prophesy. Walking upstairs, I followed closely behind him, sensing something was up. When one was with him long enough, one developed a sense of anticipation, either from the words he used or the tone of his voice, or from his gestures, facial movements, or combinations, or from that sure feeling inside that knew something would happen. This was one of those moments. Swamiji marched to the front of the store, threw his big white shawl over his shoulder and inquired of the two men behind the counter how things were going.

"Sorry, Swamiji," they answered. "It's a very slow day; we've hardly sold anything."

"Hmmmph!" came the familiar reply.

Swamiji turned around, eyed the store up and down, and concluded his visual survey by bowing his head and closing his eyes. In less than a minute, he looked up, yelled at me to join him in a half hour and walked out of the store.

"He has his moods," I thought. "Why didn't he take me with him now?" I knew where he was going uptown, but I couldn't justify any good reason for leaving me temporarily behind. I should have known better. While I was busy rehearsing my self pity, other forces were forming.

Soon it was dangerous for me to stand near the doorway. Customers jostled me as they rushed into the store. The front area swarmed with people; even the corridors filled with men and women carrying armfuls of books to purchase. Did we have a sudden fire sale? Another worker was brought upstairs to help at the cash register. I twisted and turned and shoved just to get out the door a half hour later.

The next day the store manager told me that they did more business in those two hours on Sunday than they had done all month. My mind reeled. How did that yogi attract customers when he wasn't even there? A memory stirred in my head as I pondered.

As a young man, Swamiji had been sent to teach and study in Tibet. Invited to be an honorary examiner at a Tibetan monastery, he had sat with the other judges on an ancient dais looking down at two monks seated in the center of the floor. The signal had been given. One of the candidates had closed his eyes and remained motionless while everyone watched.

"Soon I heard bees," Swamiji said as he told the story. "The room became full of large black bees flying through the air. Unnoticed, I reached out with my shawl to snatch one and crushed it against my thigh. I quickly looked down to make sure it was a real bee, for I wanted to ascertain whether I was being hypnotized or whether this was really happening. The judges gave their termination sign; the bees then vanished as quickly as they had come.

"Now came the other candidate's turn. He likewise closed his eyes while some minutes passed. Suddenly, the jungle was at the front door. Snakes, monkeys, butterflies, and numerous small creatures all approached the open door to the hall. Just as they were about to cross the threshold, the judges signaled for termination. The animal entourage turned around and headed back to the jungle. Both monks passed their exam.

"Justin, the power of concentration is unlimited," he emphasized to me one night, "few people ever explore even a small part of its potential. I, myself, was negligent in this regard for many years until my master made me aware of how many treasures I was missing." He recalled those days in Tibet when he had experienced the training routines of the Asian monks. There, in that mysterious land, he had also visited with his grandmaster, an exceedingly cheerful and powerful yogi, who had lived hidden away in the Eastern Himalayas. His story inspired in me not only a desire to meet his master and grandmaster, but the desire to work miracles of my own.

With all the work and my weekly three-hour drive into New York to teach, the months rolled by. One weekend in summer, a large contingent arrived by bus from Manhattan and upper state New York. They registered at the front desk, got their room assignments, and mingled happily in the lounge before retiring. Usually before going to bed, I would stroll down the halls, carrying out my rounds of night security. The last part of my walk took me to the attic, which ran the entire length of the building. So solidly erected was this structure, with reinforced concrete and steel girders, that it served as an atomic bomb shelter for the town. We could have run hundred yard dashes with six lanes across the attic floor, so large was the space.

Opening the door that night, I peered down the length of the attic. All seemed well. But as I turned to go downstairs, I thought I saw a wisp of smoke about fifty yards away at the other end of the room. What was it? I couldn't tell for sure, so I walked slowly towards that spot, sniffing the air, and listening for any sound. The closer I got, the thicker the wisps of smoke became. Now they were accompanied by a definite odor of incense. On my right, an unusual scene opened before me. A series of cardboard boxes were arranged one atop another to a height of six feet, forming walls. Smoke wafted over the top. The entire structure resembled a rectilinear igloo without a roof. I walked around the cardboard corner and found a surprise. Sitting on a card table was a pot of burning incense, an ashtray, and an open book on Buddhist philosophy. A small collection of books was neatly arranged along one edge of the table. Carpet pieces, collected from various corners of the attic, formed a colorful wall-to-wall covering upon which sat a husky young man with a red face. He stared up at me.

"Were you assigned this room, sir?" I inquired, tongue firmly in cheek.

The young man coughed and sputtered and blushed. He was so apologetic that his words fell over each other trying to explain: he did not want to bother his roommate with night reading, he wanted to smoke a few cigarettes, he thought that up here no one would be disturbed, he hoped no one would mind if he moved a few boxes and pieces of carpet. It took all my restraint to act and look the serious security guard as the hilarity of the situation ran through me.

I quickly recommended that he find a more congenial area for his study and barely got down the stairs before laughing out loud. The next day I reported my evening chore to my teacher, and we both laughed heartily. Swamiji then arranged an appointment to meet the Attic Yogi. As the years went on, this gentleman, an incredible humanitarian, became one of my closest friends. Among his talents of law and philosophy, he could create the most irresistible spaghetti sauce in the entire state of New York. Both he and his wife demonstrated such commitment to Swamiji and his vision that no task was ever too much for them, regardless of the cost.

One late evening between programs, a few of us sat with Swamiji on his dining room floor, talking about the master-disciple relationship. We told our teacher that he must have thousands of disciples, but his pause, followed by the slowly answered words unnerved us. "I have five, maybe six, disciples," he said.

"But Swamiji, there are thousands who come to see you, write to you, ask for teachings," one of us sputtered out in surprise.

"They are admirers," he replied, "not disciples. I have just a handful of real disciples."

Immediately the minds of all in the room began to think, "Who are they? Am I one of the disciples?"

Swamiji rose slowly from the floor and began to say good-night to us. It was time for his meditation practice, and time for us to go to sleep.

Theresa was concerned about her teacher's words for many

days. "How could anyone be with him and not want to be a thoroughly-committed follower?" she asked me several times.

I had no answer for her, wondering if part of her concern was the worry that perhaps she was unfit to be called a disciple. A few days later Swamiji completed his small book *Marriage, Parenthood and Enlightenment.* As he dictated the last pages to Theresa, he told her to take down the acknowledgments. Therein he wrote, "The Institute expresses its appreciation. . . to Mrs. Justin O'Brien, also a disciple, who typeset the manuscript."

MORE COMMAS

The late fall of our first year, Swamiji left as usual for India. He always picked the damp, cold winter months to work with his projects and students there, leaving us to carry on as usual. As he said good-bye to all the resident staff before entering his car, one student whispered in his ear. "Yes," he told her, "you will soon have your wish." We bowed and waved and wished him a good trip while his car sped away.

About ten days later, two residents drove into town on roads shimmering with ice from the night's storm. About a mile away from our entrance lay a gradually sloping stretch of road that forced preoccupied drivers to pick up speed. Having driven it dozens of times, I knew how easy it was to accelerate unawares. At the bottom of this incline lay a flat area, often iced over.

That morning the office received a call from the hospital. The police had found the students' car jammed into the large oak tree by the side of the icy patch. One of the women was dead, the other was severely injured, but would recover.

When Swamiji returned from India a few months later, he showed me a long letter written by the deceased detailing the reasons why she no longer cared to be alive on this earth. She had done everything she wanted, she was ready to go on, she implored for an early death.

Now everything made sense to me. Many months before, one of the staff women who had come out east to work with Swamiji had bought a new car. As she drove past his window one day, he ran out the back door into the parking lot and shouted at her to get out of the car. Startled, she did what he said but was puzzled by his insistence. "Sell that car!" he demanded vehemently. The woman laughed and said there was no way she was going to sell her new car. Livid now, he insisted that she listen to him. "I am ordering you as your teacher to sell that car. I forbid you ever to use it again."

The woman herself was not without a temper. Furious at his seemingly unprovoked and discourteous manner, she yelled back, "How can you speak to me like that?" But Swamiji just turned on his heel and reentered the building, leaving her there stewing in her fury.

The woman drove home in the car but slowly began to reconsider her actions as the days went by, knowing that Swamiji always wanted the best for her. The next week she asked him if she could sell her car to one of the women residents who had seen the "For Sale" sign. Permission was granted. The woman who bought the car was the one who died in it.

Swamiji seemed to know death well. Over the years, I also met many students whose lives were saved by him. One student told me how the doctors had not been optimistic about his heart operation, for the tissues were too worn out to mend properly. Their prognosis had been discouraging. As he lay in the hospital wondering about his family, heaving irregularly for breath, Swamiji appeared at the foot of his bed. Without saying a word, the master placed his palm on the patient's chest and pushed down so intensely over the heart that the student yelled out in pain. Swamiji smiled, turned, walked toward the window and disappeared. Much to the surprise of the hospital staff, the man fully recovered.

Another student's baby had been sick and weak so often that his father asked Swamiji's advice. "Have his heart X-rayed," the teacher told him. "He has a hole in his heart." Tests confirmed that the child had a hole in a heart chamber but the doctors recommended postponing the operation, because the child was too young. When the child reached operable age, it was found that the aperture had mysteriously healed.

Sometimes Swamiji gave warnings that portended serious danger but were still ignored. One night he called in a New York student and poured out on him such concerned attention for his welfare that I was deeply touched. Swamiji wished the young man a wonderful vacation and markedly told him not to travel on a certain date. The young man had spent the holidays with his fiancé in Wisconsin and had delayed his return, starting out on the forewarned day. He could not afford a plane, so he had convinced himself that if he drove carefully and took along another friend to help with the driving, all would be well. Within five hundred miles of his destination, he fell asleep at the wheel, crashed into a concrete embankment and died instantly. His companion was injured but survived.

I felt the loss of that friendship keenly and was disconcerted about the entire drama for weeks. My friend had known better than to ignore the warning, yet he traveled anyway. I felt hurt. Days later, I went jogging at dusk one autumn day; I have always liked the coolness of that hour. As I ran, I began to realize that to sojourn through life with our teacher was to glimpse what it might be like to join a benevolent feudal knight, courageous and clairvoyant to a fault, adventuring through the kingdom. He was ever ready to help anyone in need, exposing himself to their affection as well as their ridicule, and, regardless of those, never holding ill will, never forcing himself on anyone, knowing full well the consequences of their choices. Ever so gently yet extremely meaningfully he summed it up for me, "I don't care what people do to me. I do my work. Why should I allow their words or actions to make me do otherwise?"

God, I was glad to have him as a friend!

A child claiming a hug from Baba

CHAPTER 15
SPIRITUAL PRACTICE IN HONESDALE

In the bright sunlight, I walked down the hillside with my teacher. He was dressed in pure white, his shining black hair framed his smiling face. We stopped for a moment and turned toward each other. He put his right hand on my shoulder and spoke to me with blazing eyes, "Your dream will come, if you don't let ego get in the way. Just follow my instructions and everything will come."

I AWOKE AT THE SOUND OF MY ALARM. Dreams like that were coming fast and furious those days when our thoughts focused on expansion and teaching some of the ancient treasures to the world. I thought that the dream referred to the pending contract for our graduate school. That morning I was to have a luncheon meeting with the administrative officials at Scranton University to confirm all the academic arrangements.

"How did the meeting go?" Swamiji asked at my return.

"Well, I think. I met with the president and the dean, both of whom were very gracious and favor the arrangement; all we have to do is complete the curriculum and send it to them for their catalogue," I was pleased to report. Swamiji jumped up from his chair and shook my hand vigorously.

"I told you it would all happen. Just be very objective in all your dealings," he smilingly urged me. "Stay close to everything, since you have been involved from the beginning and understand their approach."

After my initial visits to the university, we were involved for many months with their entire range of academic officers to propose a joint collaboration for a new master's degree. My personal goal was to eventually make us autonomous with our own state charter, and I had already begun meetings with the State's director of higher education. With the five year academic experiment in an existing university, however, our credentials would improve those chances in the eyes of the State examiners.

The room we stood in proved too small for Swamiji's excitement. "Let's go tell everyone," he exclaimed as he whizzed out the door and down the corridor, his quick steps carrying him to the dining hall, where he burst in and announced to the quiet eaters that we would soon have a graduate school on campus; it was just a matter of months. Everyone started talking at once. By that night every one of our centers around the country knew what had transpired. The five-year contract would soon be ready, allowing students to attend Institute courses accredited through Pennsylvania's Jesuit University.

One day, several months later, I sat in my second floor office reading some reports. Theresa rushed in and asked me to hurry down to Swamiji's apartment for the New Year's Day gathering. We had been invited to dinner. I found a small, intimate group assembled in the little dining room. Most of the residents had gone home for the Christmas holidays, so Swamiji, with the help of Theresa and Samskriti, had prepared a special meal to celebrate the first day of the new year with those on campus.

After a wonderful Indian dinner with much laughter, the TV was turned on, and since the American pastime was a rare event at the Institute, everyone's eyes were soon glued to the college bowl game featuring one of my alma maters, Notre Dame. As we all got cozy with mugs of sweet tilk, Swamiji told us of his exploits with "real" football, (soccer, as we referred to it) until we couldn't ignore the shouts from the television set.

Watching TV with the yogi was quite an experience. He turned on the set to keep us amused while his mind traveled elsewhere. We watched this departure scene repeated many times over the ensuing years. For Swamiji, television was more than a screen for entertainment; it kept budding yogis distracted while the real work went on. Usually his absence would last but a few minutes; sometimes it lasted the length of the feature. I was often called on to be the official commentator, to bring him back into the action after one of his departures.

"What going on, Justin?" he soon called out.

I told him that it was the last quarter of the game and things looked bad for Notre Dame. As I spoke about the import of the two teams playing that day, I watched his mind go away again for about three minutes.

"Who's winning?" he asked as he turned his eyes back to the flickering set.

"It isn't Notre Dame, unfortunately," I replied.

"Hummph," he answered and turned his glance back to the far wall. While our eyes watched the action of the game, his slowly glazed over. He had gone somewhere else, probably to check up on the condition of another student somewhere across the globe.

He suddenly opened his eyes wide and said sharply, "Sam, get my phone book." Samskrti ran into the office and returned with the phone and his small book, dialed a number in a state hundreds of miles away, and handed him the phone.

"Hello, this is Swami Rama. Don't worry, the operation is the right choice. There's nothing to worry about; you just wait. I will pray for the boy; he will be all right. God bless you." He handed the phone back and sent his mind somewhere else. As we students watched the teams' linesmen collide on the football field, he surreptitiously reordered destiny.

Over the years I watched many movies in his presence, usually with a room full of guests. I eventually realized that he used awful movies as definite solitude interludes; any visitors that sat before the set were sure to think of a reason to leave or else to fall asleep. I think his favorite movie of all time, however, was *The Doberman Gang*. In between his mental travels, he laughed and laughed at this staple of late night TV, since the movie was like a memorial to his great dog, Raja. He always insisted that his dog would have been a better actor than the dogs on the screen, and added that Raja also would never have been caught. The movie that drove me to sheer boredom, however, was the Japanese production of *Godzilla Versus the Smog Monster*. We must have watched that one at least six times, and I could never understand his preference for it until I remembered that he had spent quite a bit of time in Japan. He also liked to relax with old American Westerns because the good guys always won. With Westerns I had the job of explaining the plot and its connections over and over as he zipped in and out of this dimension as the movie unfolded.

"What's going on now?" He had returned now and wanted to know what had happend. "Why did he kick the ball then instead of running with it?" he asked as he peered at the action on screen.

I began explaining 'punting' to him, knowing that there was less than one minute in the game and that Notre Dame with the ball was still behind. Swamiji chose that precise moment to walk into the kitchen, declaring, "Notre Dame is going to lose," with a snicker in his voice that did not go unnoticed by a certain woman in the audience.

For Swamiji the game was over, but Theresa immediately erupted, "They won't lose! They're going to win."

"Oh, you want to bet?" came the challenge from the inspector of the future, stirring his rice pudding in the next room.

Defiantly, Theresa threw down the gauntlet to her teacher, "I'll bet you a thousand dollars."

With only seconds left in the game, I got very nervous. "Where are we going to get a thousand dollars?" I thought, "I'll have to get a night job in Honesdale."

But the game wasn't over. We all held our breaths as Notre Dame's last chance was put in the hands of its quarterback, Joe Montana, who threw a long arching pass across the goal line into the arms of his waiting receiver. Unbelievably, Notre Dame pulled the game out with seconds to go—a classic finish. Pandemonium broke out both in the stadium and in Swamiji's apartment. We shouted in jubilation.

"Theresa just won a thousand dollars, Swamiji; Notre Dame won," Gopala reported, egging him on.

"I didn't see it," came the blasé retort.

Unable to hold it in, I broke out in laughter over his aplomb.

"You owe me a thousand dollars," Theresa insisted.

Just as he was about to defend himself, the television commentator replayed the final scene and everyone, including Swamiji, saw the proof of the touchdown again.

"OK," Swamiji uttered with a slight grimace on his face, "I owe you a thousand dollars."

I cheered in my heart and beamed my delight to Theresa, thinking, very reverentially, of course, "The old man lost for once." To the best of my knowledge, Swamiji never bet with Theresa again (and Theresa never collected her money). Perhaps he was cautioned by the sages that this woman was exceptionally lucky playing against yogis.

With the winter slowing down, the reconstruction of the barn took place in time for another first. The huge four-color Heidelberg press arrived and became Gopala's new toy in his arsenal of tools for service to his teacher. He amazed me with the dedication and late hours that he and his crew spent turning out our many publications. Whenever anyone came by the press, he had time for them, and he loved explaining the intricacies of the machines. I always let him continue his fascinating explanations, even though he usually lost me about five paragraphs back.

One cold evening, Swamiji told us that he hoped one day we would own all the properties between our campus and Bethany, the nearby village a few miles away toward Honesdale.

"We'll build a city for people to live and learn. We'll expand our organic farming and raise all our own food and maybe have cottage industries. Why not have a few cows and goats? We will have milk and cheese, and the staff can have their own homes and cabins," he enthused. Earlier he had mentioned that we should have an inn at the top of the hill by the entrance to the property. "Guests could stay there with their families," he thought out loud, "and we could have shops for their needs also."

"With that wild dream," I pondered, "the next few years are going to be something else." Strangely, it all made sense. Once I played a game in my mind, imagining that I was in Swamiji's shoes. With this vast property and the recognition of our holistic contributions to society, wouldn't I shoot for the moon? We certainly had the drive and the commitment. More and more people wanted to become a part of the work, professionals sought staff positions, families asked to be admitted, the graduate school neared acceptance, students fresh out of college came to stay. A Chicago attorney, Steve Jurco, and his gracious wife, Dee, enabled us to qualify for a generous grant from the Dana Foundation. With Mrs. Dana smiling broadly, the new Eleanor Dana Psycho-physiological Laboratory was ceremoniously dedicated. Swamiji had seen that the Institute's future was now solvent and secure.

While awaiting that dream to touch ground, a big change on campus slowly took shape; it was the readjustment of the residential social statistics. Theresa and I had always been a little suspected by the younger residents. After all, we were 'householders,' as they would put it; we were a married couple. They weren't quite sure that we truly qualified as 100% yogis because of it. Within a few years of the Institute's opening, however, celibate life seemed to dim in the consciousness of the residents as the master encouraged his students to marry. Everywhere one turned, one could find another wedding announcement, and soon the campus was full of married couples living in newly-built apartments. Apparently, the O'Briens were full yogis after all. Nature, of course, continued to have her irresistible way and the corridors soon echoed with the sound of tiny voices, not always harmonious. Potential little yogis tottered in abundance. Next, it occurred to some of the residents that the O'Brien spiritual status was again in jeopardy; we couldn't be fully yogi-householders since we didn't have children!

In the midst of all this change, a new faculty member from India energetically joined us. Pandit Rajmani Tigunait, who had met Swamiji a few years before and was told that he would one day work with him, arrived to carry out his destiny. He stayed with Dr. Arya in the Midwest for some time and then arrived in Honesdale, ready to begin. From the first time we met, I was impressed with his enthusiasm, intelligence, and spontaneous sense of humor. I knew that with his energy and good will he would make enormous contributions. Theresa took care of his personal needs, sometimes helping him to understand the intricacies of American English and the ever-increasing projects of the center. Some months later, much to his surprise and delight, the pandit also became a householder.

Theresa's duties grew as mine did. Along with her work as the irrepressible Tessa Typeset, she was busy sewing and cleaning and cooking for Swamiji, taking dictation, writing letters, and planting the flower garden. I was traveling and teaching in New York and our many other centers springing up all over the country. We usually saw each other between travels in our teacher's room, where we caught each other up on news and then fell to sleep, exhausted, on our blanket on the floor of our room.

While in New York City, I went jogging one afternoon. As I watched the New Yorkers huffing and puffing around the lagoon in Central Park with unrelenting stress written all over their grimacing faces, it occurred to me that the application of yoga breathing methods would take the sting out and put the sensual pleasure back in. I began researching a book on running. It would be fun, I thought, to experiment with my favorite sport. So in January I came out of retirement. Over a nine-month period, I gradually introduced the central concept of regulated breathing into my running workouts. Theresa made me a running suit that fit like a wet suit for scuba diving. She thought it was too tight; I thought it was perfect for the wintry weather.

By the following October, I tested my running theory before three examiners who clocked me for one hour of running at about seven minutes thirty seconds per mile. During the entire running time I kept my mouth closed, breathing at a two-to-one ratio through my nostrils in synchronization with my steps. The witnesses were amazed because when I came to a stop before them, they noted that my breathing was as calm as theirs. There was no indication of any strain or visible sign of having run for an hour. With their assurance, I wrote my method into the book, *Running and Breathing*.

It seemed to me then that the foundation for just about everything was in place. We students had the space, the location, the equipment and, most important of all, the full house of willing people from all walks of life and professions to fulfill our dream. A dream, of course, can yield many different interpretations, not all of them complementary. Little did I know that other tendencies would soon compete with the positive direction that had so gloriously begun.

A CHILD OF AGNI

Snow was never an enduring challenge in our portion of Pennsylvania. Consequently, spring always arrived on time. Once he sensed the warmer seasonal change coming over the mountains, Swamiji would rally the troops and call for the annual day of grounds cleaning. We donned old clothes, hats, and gloves, put the phones on hold, and set the kitchen staff making picnic food. Everyone enjoyed the outing, for it was a pleasant change of pace from the indoor work. Of course, the master himself always pitched in, enthusiastically barking out assignments and organizing crews. On cleanup day he was in a rare mood, pleased to have so many students working in the outdoor beauty, loving the sun and the wind and the challenge of such a huge space. He teased as he walked around, humorously inspecting everyone's work and strongly recommending their consideration for new careers.

Our focus was the immediate grounds within a rolling mile radius of the main building. Bramble bushes with thorns were waiting to be cut out; dead branches pleaded to be trimmed; weeds and rocks and debris all found new homes. In the cool air of the bright sunny sky, we scattered in all directions, grabbing tools and snapping to work with orders to chop and pick up and rake and tear out.

I volunteered to take care of the fires. I pursued the endeavor alone, finding dead branches and uprooted scrubs strewn on the paths from the autumn and winter toll, collecting the piles the other workers left for pickup. Once I stacked the piles of branches eight to twelve feet tall, I lit a match and moved to the next likely pile. I kept a canteen of water at my side and ate fruits most the day. The aromas of the fires, the textures of the branches, the struggle of lifting and stacking the twisted limbs, and then lighting the flame and feeling the heat made the hours slip by. I enjoyed working alone, hearing the others scrambling in the woods and fields about two hundred meters away. Swamiji, in the meantime, came by and swiped my hat, and not to be outdone by me, set a few fires of his own among the grass fields behind the building to encourage new growth. By five o'clock, we usually had about thirteen fires burning.

One late cleanup afternoon, some of the students who lived in town arrived with their children to join us for an outdoor supper. Looking like a bunch of displaced immigrants with thorn cuts and bruises, we laughed at our dirty attire and reminded Swamiji of how much he owed us in wages. He replied that we owed him, not only because we undoubtedly destroyed many of his plants in our careless clean up, but also for the opportunity to gain experience in possible new caretaking careers.

People were tired, but felt good, and after supper they headed for the showers. The sun dropped behind the hills, and the first stars began to blink. Swamiji called Theresa and me for a walk through the grounds to survey the day's efforts. My clothes reeked from burned wood and sweat, and my face was charcoaled with soot, but no one seemed to mind. My earlier fires were smoldering safely; the last one, which had a huge log in it, was still ablaze. We sat on rocks before it and watched the flames.

Swamiji didn't say anything for some time, just sat pensively looking at the fire. He wasn't staring like most people would; rather his peering seemed to discern something about the fire, as if the fire was revealing to him that which no one else could perceive. Without turning his head, he poked the flames with a thin branch and spoke to us.

"Agni is my friend."

His admission didn't surprise me, for I had noticed over the years that fire, called *agni*, beckoned with fascination for him.

"When I was a boy," he continued, "my uncle wanted my inheritance, so he hired some thugs to kill me, in order to make himself the sole beneficiary. Once my master and I were walking in the mountains when suddenly he said that we should camp. We gathered some wood and built a fire. We continued to throw logs on the flames until it was a blazing bonfire. Then my master lifted me up and placed me in the center of the fire. Just then the killers came into our camp and demanded to know where I was.

" 'As you can see,' replied my master, 'there is no boy here.'

"The men peered about saying 'The boy must be dead, for no child can survive these mountains at night.' They said the same to my uncle who accepted their report and stopped looking for me.

"After their departure, my master reached in to the fire and took me out. I did not burn; the flames were harmless before him.

"Never be afraid of fire. Agni, the God of fire, promised me that you would always be protected."

Our teacher looked at us across the ebbing flames and reiterated the words of his master to us.

THE AUSPICIOUS PERFORMANCE OF THE VEDIC DANCERS

Beauty always enchanted Swamiji. He cultivated his tastes in classical music and dance and painting and sculpture during the months he spent at the world famous Indian academy, Shantiniketan. There, under the tutelage of its famous founder, Rabindranath Tagore, the Nobel laureate in literature, Swamiji participated in an education that emphasized the integration of the fine arts with history, politics, and science.

"I enjoyed my stay even though I was mischievous and got thrown out three times," he laughed to us as he spoke. "But I learned to love what is beautiful."

When guests entered Swamiji's spacious living room in the main building at Honesdale, they walked on rare Oriental carpets and sat amidst striking paintings, ancient carvings, wood and ivory inlaid tables, delicate Indian chairs, tall plants in brass pots, and jade and porcelain art pieces. His own chair, a black recliner set in one corner of the room, was covered with a Nepalese spotted deer skin—the traditional symbol of a man of self-mastery. Beauty was everywhere; attachment was not. Students and admirers from many countries sent gifts to him. Sometimes they were placed here in the large room to add to the rich environment for visitors while Swamiji himself slept on blankets on the dining room floor or sat to do his practice on the mattress of the seldom-used bedroom.

He himself composed and sang songs in his youth in India, even on the radio, much to the delight of an ever-growing enthusiastic audience. His master assured him that he could not only be good, but his playing and singing could climb to the top of popularity and dominate the Indian music field. The only hitch, his master explained when Swamiji returned to him after his initial acclaim, was that his outstanding success would slowly distance him from his real mission in life. So Swamiji decided to put his music career on hold.

Swamiji had also studied painting and produced many beautiful still lifes, yet try as he would and to his quiet disappointment, the Americans did not seem interested in designing art programs at any of the Institutes he founded. He always encouraged the arts, and over the years at least one session of dance and music crowned each of the Institute's annual Congresses at his request.

The autumn cookout during our early years in Honesdale was always a special time. We would build a huge fire, eat wonderful food, relax from the busy summer work, share camaraderie, sing spiritual chants, listen to some inspiration from Swamiji, and meditate together around the fire.

One year I thought that something else should be added to the program. After the sun went down, and the big tree limbs were added to the flames, I announced that this evening we would be entertained by a renowned pair, "The Vedic Dancers." Excitement passed through the crowd of students and guests as Theresa, Randy, and I slipped into the nearby hallway. Theresa helped us dress in two of her Irish kilts, one quite long and one very short, acquired from European travel. Being much taller, I donned the short kilt; my friend wrapped himself in the long one, hanging down to his ankles. We both folded long, fringed plaid scarves around our necks and glued huge handlebar mustaches on our upper lips.

Under the stars of the cool evening we let the expectation grow in the crowd until we sensed their whispers full of anticipation. Then we suddenly turned on our ancient music. The night air was filled with a sprightly Irish jig, and Randy and I dashed out before the group. With the strong beat of flutes and drums around us, we leaped before our audience in front of the soaring flames of the bonfire. We danced a mad jig in a whirl of bounding energy, our kilts flapping, our scarves choking us as we danced. We skipped, hopped, and shuffled across the grass. Back, forth, slipping and skidding we went, prancing with our knees rising up and down, rotating wildly to the strains of the Gaelic melody. We loped round and round and swung each other about in a unique rendition of the traditional dances.

As we continued in almost a delirium of bouncing twists and turns, Randy's mustache began to sag and droop, looking like hands on a clock reading 4:30. He tried to twist his head to encourage his mustache to return to its previous state, but this effort made him lose his balance and fall into me. I bounced off in the wrong direction, trying to pick up the steps of our routine in vain. My rolled-up pants began to slip down one leg, beneath my short kilt. I tried to keep in step while shoving my falling pants back up my leg but they refused to remain there. My partner, undaunted, continued with the routine as I struggled along. All at once, my shoe flew off my foot into the fire and Randy's kilt began a descent from his hips to his feet. I tried to rescue my shoe and continue the dance steps simultaneously but we were dizzy from jumping and circling and I almost fell into the fire myself. The crowd, with tears rolling down their cheeks, was ecstatic with laughter. Swamiji doubled over again and again, throwing up his hands and pointing out to those around him the latest dismantling of the dancers' costumes. Finally, gratefully, the music faded and we two unprecedented Vedic dancers withdrew never to be seen again, as the sounds of a standing ovation of laughter and clapping filled the night air.

Although I'm sure the Vedic dancers shall never come out of retirement, I will treasure that auspicious night like no other.

AN UNEXPECTED VISITOR

One July full moon, when Swamiji was in Japan, we celebrated the yearly tradition of Guru Purnima. This is a day of re-dedication to one's spiritual path and a remembrance of gratitude to the teacher, the guru, the one who leads from darkness to light.

It is customary for the student in our tradition to bring a small bundle of dry sticks and present them to the teacher. These sticks represent the karma that the student wishes burned by the compassion and wisdom of the teacher and the tradition. The auspicious fire becomes the symbolic instrument that the teacher uses to free the student from his or her bondage to the unwanted karmic consequences.

As usual for Guru Purnima, Theresa and I had collected small bundles of sticks for our teacher that year and mailed them to the address in Japan that he would grace at the full moon. A friend who had accompanied Swamiji told me that on the special day Swamiji and several students trekked up a mountain outside Tokyo and built a sacred fire. Swamiji then told them to gather bundles of dry sticks. As they all sat around the fire, he chanted in a low voice, telling the students to call out the names of students as they cast each twig into the fire.

As the ritual continued, a stick sprang from out the fire and landed in the dirt. One student picked it up and threw it back into the fire. The stick jumped out again. Three or four other sticks did the same.

The astounded students looked at Swamiji for an explanation. He shrugged his shoulders and announced, "Some people don't want their karma burned."

At the Honesdale center on the same day, a bonfire blazed behind the barn, trays of halva and pots of chai waited on the tables to be enjoyed, and benches and pillows sat facing the fire, ready for the program. It was early evening when everyone gathered and began chanting. Because Swamiji was overseas, we listened to a recording of our teacher speaking on the purpose of meditation, and then began chanting spiritual songs.

I sat on a bench between Theresa and Swami Ajaya, who had spoken earlier on the significance of the day. Looking up ahead, I noticed a moving figure off to the right on the road in front of the long line of pine trees about thirty-five yards away. At first, because the shrubbery by the side of the road hid his full form as he walked slowly westward, I thought it was a therapy patient strolling by. Then the figure stopped and turned to face the crowd. Standing in his familiar white pajamas with the edges of his gray shawl flapping in the wind, Swamiji gazed at us.

Overwhelmed, I watched him. He stood there poised with a faint smile on his face for about thirty seconds before turning and walking twenty feet more. The eyes of my heart followed him until he vanished among the trees.

Many minutes passed as I peered at the woods. Then I turned to Theresa. It was obvious by the warmth of her look that she, too, had seen him. That we were blessed seems the proper but inadequate word, for I felt so strongly confirmed in my life force by his presence. Then I remembered his words, "When you are on the path, you will never be lonely."

Sitting there, the simple feeling of being consciously alive, jubilant in my life force, perceiving and acknowledging all that was going on in the woods and about me without being dependent upon any of it in the least, filled me with joy. It wouldn't have mattered if tonight everything I owned was taken from me. I was at peace.

As we rose to join the students at the dessert table, it became obvious that the crowd showed no knowledge of that holy visitor who had passed by the horizon. Their unawareness only made Swamiji's momentary visit all the more touching. We joined the rest of the celebration; all was complete.

A special event on the Honesdale campus

CHAPTER 16
DARK NIGHT OF MY SOUL

I could hardly take my eyes from the view of the valley. Milarepa and I were building the small house for his guru. Back and forth we trudged carrying heavy rocks to erect the walls. My hands hurt from the sharp edge of the rocks, and my skin burned in the broiling Sun. Then, for some reason unknown to me, we were taking the walls down, much to my consternation. But I knew that we were going to build the house again.

I WOKE UP WITH A START. "Now I'm dreaming about him!" I laughed to myself. The dream, quite vivid, left me with a bad feeling. I had been reading about Milarepa, the Tibetan yogi, for months. I shared the dream with Theresa, who asked to know more of his life.

"Milarepa, who lived in the eleventh century, was somewhat of a rascal and got himself into a lot of trouble by practicing sorcery."

In her down-to-earth manner, she asked, "Why are you dreaming about him?"

"Maybe because he was after the same things I am—the sacred truths of liberation," I smilingly assured her. "He's been on my mind a lot."

With her inescapable logic, she parried, "Then why were you helping him build rock houses?"

For the next twenty minutes, I explained my coveted interest in this yogi's life story, touching the high points. He had wanted to change his life and embrace a path to enlightenment. He implored a revered teacher, a great Lama, to accept him as a student, fervently proclaiming that he would undergo any discipline for the eternal truths. The teacher had accepted him at face value. First, however, Milarepa was to prove himself worthy of this treasure. So his teacher assigned the student the task of building a crescent-shaped house for the teacher's son. If he built the house correctly, then Milarepa would be given the ancient truths from India and provided with the necessary sustenance to complete his study.

"Beginning in earnest," I went on, "he completed about half the house when his guru came by and halted the project, telling him to dismantle the structure and return the stones and clay whence they had come. The Lama admitted that he had been a bit tipsy when he had uttered the former orders, but now, clearly sober, he realized that a correction in the architecture was necessary. Milarepa should erect a triangular building, more fitting to the dwelling of a tantric mystic. The teacher assured his student that it would not be demolished.

"Once again the student lugged the heavy stones to the site and began his daily labor. After he had completed a third of the walls, his teacher came by again and denounced the project, ordering its demolition and the return of the heavy materials to their original location at once. If the student disagreed with his teacher's assessment, he could leave and forfeit the promised teachings.

"Frustrated and near exhaustion, Milarepa tearfully pulled the structure down again. By now, his severely strained back muscles showed a sore lump near his upper spine, which, along with other wounds, would soon suppurate. For his part, he was still willing to endure these perplexing and exhausting labors as the cost of the promised truths, but all he could acquire for his concentrated efforts were injuries, insults, weariness, tearful plights of discouragement, and the gnawing temptation to flee the absurdity of his task.

"This painful scenario between teacher and student repeated itself twice more. Two more commanded structures, one quadrangular, the other circular, obtained for Milarepa's excruciatingly painful efforts the usual rejection notices. Amazingly, throughout his humiliating ordeal, he sustained an abiding trust in his teacher.

"Finally, the ordeal was over. His teacher called Milarepa and sat him down to explain the tribulations. The Lama's coarse and indifferent manner of treatment was designed to bring the student to ignominy and sorrow, verging on despair. Milarepa, after all, had practiced sorcery and callously afflicted suffering on many people. Each geometrical structure symbolized the workings of a chakra—the body's energy centers—through which his action was done. Milarepa's past karma needed to be balanced by working with the chakras before he could be given the higher teachings. His endurance, despite his inner trials of faith, and because of his trust in the teacher, won over the Lama's compassion. His teacher bestowed the boon Milarepa sought."

That, I told Theresa, was the essence of the spiritual ordeal. The story swayed my imagination for months. When I first read about this incredible yogi, my reaction had been that he was a fool to put up with his meaningless tasks, but I had read the story again and again until it began to make sense in the context of the spiritual journey. My wife listened to my ramblings about Milarepa's courage and growth in personal self-control and knew I admired his relentless determination, in spite of irrational and painful obstacles, to cope with whatever challenges his teacher could hurl at him. Comparisons with other heroes of history and mythology emerged in our minds. His story reminded us of medieval knights searching for the Grail, combating all kinds of trials, facing humiliation and even death for the glorious trophy.

Some months later, Theresa and I went to Swamiji one night and expressed our fervent desire to obtain self-realization; we wanted to know truth; we asked for the enlightenment that the sages enjoyed. We requested him to take us through whatever was necessary for this accomplishment. Like Milarepa, we entrusted the project to our teacher's capable hands. He accepted.

We thought we could do anything for our enlightenment. If we were asked to build and tear down, we would do it. If we were told to do strange and insignificant work, we would do it. If we were instructed to travel anywhere on earth, we would go. We left our teacher's presence that night convinced that we were ready for anything. When the trial finally came, we didn't recognize it; we weren't ready.

Two unforeseen events unfolded. Swamiji suddenly removed Theresa from all his personal work, completely distanced himself from her, and told her not to come into his presence any more. She was devastated. I was then called into his office where he looked at me with concern on his face. It was the way he used his eyes and voice that got my immediate attention. "I have protected you from many things," he said now, "but there are some things you will have to go through. You will be persecuted."

A short time later, I was called to meet with some of the officials of the Institute's Board, of which I was a member. They questioned the veracity of my fifth university degree, the Doctoraal, from Nijmegen University in the Netherlands under Professor Dr. Schillebeeckx. When I asked what provoked their interest at this time, no answer was forthcoming, but they challenged its existence as a bona fide degree, as well as its equivalency to the American doctorate. While there were probably fewer than six American citizens who had obtained the degree, it had long been accepted by major American universities as a doctorate. Professors at all Dutch universities taught and obtained tenure with it. Before I had the chance to establish these facts, I became *persona non grata.* I was not permitted to use the degree's letters after my name on any Institute publication, since in their eyes the latter was an invalid degree.

This became a cause célèbre, lasting many months, like some kind of contagious mania. Each week something was taken away from me. I was replaced as director of the graduate school; my name was eliminated from the faculty boar; I was removed from the Institute board of directors. A stern group of residents knocked at my office door one morning to inform me that I could no longer occupy this nor any other office in the building. The faculty scurried into my entire academic history: all my degrees were scrutinized, my years of teaching required corroboration, all my published articles were checked for authenticity. Institute centers around the country were told of the scandal and informed to cancel my lectures. When the final papers were signed for our masters program in Eastern Studies and Comparative Psychology; I was not allowed at the signing nor given any credit for my years of work on the project.

Rumors spread that O'Brien had falsified his education, that he would be kicked out, that he should resign, that he should come clean and apologize for embarrassing the Institute, that he had lied to his teacher. Some suggested that I be reassigned from teaching to cleaning duties in the main building. People avoided me, turned their eyes away as I passed in the hallway.

The last straw came when board members and residents began harassing Theresa. Snide remarks were spoken behind her back and sometimes to her face when I was off campus. No one would sit with her during meals. She was asked to retype all publications bearing my name and remove all degrees from them. Ganging up on her was not my idea of fairness.

When all this began I was getting ready to take some actions against my accusers and demand due process for myself when Swamiji called me in. He went right to the point. "You have to go through this, Justin, and you are not to defend yourself in any way." I didn't like those words at all. My anger rose to the surface and I walked abruptly out without another word. Swamiji then removed himself from the situation.

Watching my own demise was not to my liking. Burning resentment grew in my imagination toward my enemies. The Institute building felt oppressive; without my office, my tiny bedroom felt like a jail cell. I wanted to confront my accusers one on one, no holds barred, and tell them where they could go. When my mind wasn't preoccupied with some task, it would revert back to scenario after scenario of confrontation. I was caught in my own mania for settling the issues. My one release was jogging, which took the edge off my tension and helped me regain some perspective each day. To my surprise, even running got challenged. The Institute president, who had had my running book manuscript for months, called me in. He wanted me to write into the pages some additional thoughts from the chairman and then add his name as co-author. The chairman had written no book and needed one for his resume. I couldn't believe his gall. "I'll think about it," was my reply. That same night, Swamiji surprisingly called to me as I was walking by his office. He motioned for me to sit. After a few polite remarks about the garden, he suggested that I accept the book suggestions. Anger exploded in me. Instantly, I jumped up to face him straight on, and with surging energy, told him firmly, "Over my dead body will his words get into my book; I'm not here to make his reputation." I stood fearless before my teacher. I felt very self-contained and clear during those moments; my rancor was with the absurd request and not with the man in front of me.

Swamiji stepped back and immediately deferred, "O.K., you don't have to agree. It's entirely your choice." We parted.

"Damn right," I thought to myself walking away. It felt good to take a stand on something and express it, even if it was to him. A few moments later I went out for a walk under the stars.

Suddenly it hit me: shades of Milarepa! Like him, my whole world was crumbling around me. "They have done an exemplary job," I thought. "I'm without name, rank, or serial number. All the houses that I built are demolished—degree, position, reputation, office, directorship, career. There is no recourse to appeal; I can't even protect my wife."

One evening a faculty member, who knew me well, came and suggested that I go and apologize to the officials. Then everything would be fine, he thought. I told him where he could go with his suggestion; I had done nothing for which to apologize. My book on running was then rejected by the publication committee.

Among my destroyed houses there were two that were closest to my heart. First, my love for teaching was being denied and, second, my sense of justice was being trampled. I lived to teach and coach. I felt at home involved with others in the pursuit of knowledge, whether in arts, science, or simply sheer speculation. To the best of my recollection, I had never abused this privilege of teaching. So why was this happening?

Crucial to me also was a sense of justice. Among all the setbacks and benefits I have had in life, deservedly or not, there was a rock bottom conviction that stayed me through every incident: the universe was fundamentally sound and just. Now for the first time in my life, I felt an ugly insight emerge involuntarily: my core principle was wrong.

I thought to myself, "At the heart of all things there was only a semblance of justice. When challenged, it collapsed, just like my world did." In view of the facts of these past months, how could it be otherwise?

"If that principle was wrong, then life has no ultimate meaning," I shuddered. The truth was simple: there was no rhyme nor reason to my colleagues' frenzy. In a world absent of genuine order, what difference would it make to have a little more frenzy? Facing that admission drained the energy from my will to live, much less care about anything. I felt let down deep inside. My technicolor world faded to grays. "There are no houses left to demolish," I thought one night, "all are down. Move over, Yogi Milarepa, you have company."

During those months, almost ironically, I was finishing another thesis for the Netherlands' highest academic degree. Europe had academic traditions different from America's. Its

Doctoraat degree was a post-doctoral award granted after exceptionally original research had been completed on a focused subject and an extensive thesis published. The thesis was to be printed in the hundreds, for it had to be placed in all the university libraries on the continent. The awarding of this degree demanded that one stand to defend one's field of study before the entire community. Scholars, students, and the general public were invited to challenge the defendant in a public forum.

I had been doing research for this honor for eight years. Only the approval of the final chapter of my research publication was still required. In late spring, I was notified of final acceptance by my promoter in Europe and told that I must appear in person in the aula of City Hall in Nijmegen, Netherlands, to defend my work before sixteen faculty members from the university as well as before the general audience.

Shortly before I departed for Europe, a member of the Institute faculty knocked at my door to inquire how things were going. He asked what I was doing, and aware of my promise to Swamiji, I told him about the advanced degree defense, first getting his word not to mention it to anyone. He was surprised, but pleased for me; I reminded him again to keep my disclosure to himself. As he walked out the door, I thanked him for coming, and feeling an unusual urge to remind him of his promise of silence, received his third assurance that he would keep his word.

The following morning as I walked out of the dining room, Swamiji passed me in the corridor and, with a quick flick of his wrist, handed me an envelope which I spontaneously grabbed. Without a pause, both of us continued down the hall in opposite directions. Opening the envelope, I read a letter to Swamiji from one of the faculty. It stated that a faculty member had visited me and found out that I would soon defend an advanced degree in Europe.

Theresa and I traveled to the Netherlands a few weeks later. As I meditated the night before my defense, a strange calmness overcame me and remained throughout the next day.

My formal examination lasted sixty minutes as per tradition. Dressed in medieval garb, the examiners and administrators marched slowly into the large hall, filling up the tiered wooden pews circling the podium. The public sat in rows before the podium and filled the balcony. The time keeper walked in with an enormous wooden pillar and pounded the floor thrice, signaling the commencement of the official inquiry. In replying to the questions, I found words flowing from me; I could hardly keep up with the deluge of ideas and actually felt impatient with the slow process of questioning. I savored this opportunity to defend my work, which deployed Swamiji's scientific experiments as establishing a new basis and methodology for religious consciousness. As I built my case, I looked around at my examiners—both pro and con—and knew that the examination belonged to me. The hour ended too soon with the triple banging of the time-keeper's pillar. The examiners retreated to their chambers to decide my standing, and after twenty minutes returned in procession with my promoter, Professor Dr. Wilhelm Dupré, carrying the large, red cylinder that held the special degree. At the reception following the awarding of my degree, my thesis director said that I did not so much defend my work as teach it to the examiners.

Theresa and I were welcomed home with warm embraces from Swamiji. When I handed him the cylinder, he took it in both hands, raised it in the air, and offered it to his master. He then surprised me by saying that his master had helped me write it.

"We are pleased with your work, Justin," he said. "You will continue to serve others this life." Then he added with a twinkle in his eyes and a nod to the outside door, "Now you may compile a defense for the board."

Theresa and I began to search for and compile the necessary formal papers and depositions that established the credibility of my Dutch degrees. When I asked the assistance of the Dutch Consulate, the Consul General was outraged that anyone would dispute a formal state degree and urged litigation. Yale University, Notre Dame University and Nijmegen University sent letters explaining the U.S./Dutch degree equivalency as I had explained it. The American referee on higher education offered a positive analysis and questioned the competency and integrity of those denying the foreign academic degree. It took months but we gathered a huge dossier of evidence.

I went to the chairman and placed the report on his desk. He immediately recognized the nature of the contents, looked up impatiently at me, and asked, "Are you still at this?"

"Not any more," I answered. "It's now complete and it's all

yours." I walked out of the office pleased with myself. I then sent copies to all my accusers.

For me, the case was now closed. For those who had coveted my position, my new degree only added a new problem. It took the administration six months to place my name back on the faculty board, but several degrees were eliminated from my biography on it. Letters re-establishing my credentials were never sent to the centers. I never got my old job back. As the future unfolded, I found it curious that every colleague that had been involved in my degree investigation departed from the Institute and left their teacher.

The next evening, Theresa and I were guests of Swamiji again in his room. "I wanted you to know who your friends were," Swamiji said knowingly. "Innocence is not enough; you must also be worldly wise."

I was instantly reminded of Matthew's Gospel in which Jesus told his apostles, "Be wise as serpents and innocent as doves."

"It's always the people you love that hurt you the most," Swamiji continued sadly. "The world is like that."

"Next time I'm going to a different planet," I assured him, "You're welcome to come along." When we both laughed, I realized why my favorite beliefs in life had to be demolished. The house of my faith had to be torn down so I could replace it with a castle of experience.

Theresa sat quietly throughout the conversation. Finally she looked up at our teacher with tears in her eyes and said, "Swamiji, you killed us!"

"Yes," he answered with his face beaming, "but look what came out of the grave!"

Walking with the master on the ten day retreat

CHAPTER 17
RUMBLINGS IN PARADISE

Swamiji stood on a scaffold, painting over the crumbling and dirty walls of a house; he held a bucket of white paint and a large paintbrush. Three-quarters of the house was already painted white.

THE DREAM ENDED ABRUPTLY. When I woke up, I remembered it clearly all day, realizing that I was surprised to see my teacher in the position of a house painter, feeling a strong desire to rush in and help him paint, and also wondering about the crumbling structure that he was trying to repair.

I did not have enough time to think about it sufficiently because this was the day I would begin my yearly retreat. Each year from 1978 through 1981, Swamiji guided four unusual retreats. Before the first retreat, he selected the major members of his faculty, those he had initiated himself, and telephoned them one by one, inviting them to a retreat, asking that they tell no one about it and prepare to stay ten days. To take care of our needs, he asked Theresa to be "den mother," giving her instructions on what to cook, clean, and arrange.

I, like the others, was excited to receive the invitation. We were assigned to rooms in the brick bungalow, formerly the nuns' convent, behind the main building of the Honesdale Institute. A general announcement was given to staff and residents to the effect that we were in total silence, not to be disturbed for any reason. All calls were held, all mail stopped, all the community stayed far away. An atmosphere of calm and quiet enveloped us as we entered our own modern "cave" for the retreat, surprised and pleased that we would be on retreat with our friends and fellow teachers.

We started at dusk. Swamiji called us together then in the main room of the house to give us an orientation.

"Keep a diary, if you wish," he said. "Remember that these ten days will give you ten more years of life. You people are tired; sleep all you want."

He gave us only three simple rules: no speaking, no reading, do your practices. Ten days? It sounded like an easy, wonderful adventure to me, even though I had to store away the huge pile of books I had intended to read.

"Begin now," our teacher said solemnly, and walked out of the building, leaving us in silence.

We looked at each other, noting the accumulated stress and fatigue on each face. Then all twelve of us left the common space and headed to our private rooms.

That first night, most of us went outdoors and scattered along the various paths and roads on the campus. The sunset was gorgeous in its panoply of golden reds against a deepening blue sky. I stayed out for an hour, went back to my room for a glass of water, and laid out my personal items. That didn't take long. I was now bored and wondered what to do next, so again I went out. It was night, the campus was quiet; only a few students still walked about. I walked in the darkness for awhile, went back inside, did my meditation practice, and went to sleep.

The food during those four years, as far as I was concerned, was superb. Theresa and Swamiji planned the best menu for health and calmness. There was nothing to distract us, nothing to stimulate us, nothing to cause fatigue, indigestion, or sleepiness. There were no stimulants—no chilies, pepper, caffeine, or sugar; very little salt; and, of course, everything was pure vegetarian. Our den mother approached the cooking and serving as part of her own spiritual practice and raised meal preparation to the level of focused prayer. She bathed before preparing each meal, changing into clean clothes. She squeezed fresh fruit and vegetables into pitchers of juice for us and served cut fruit on silver trays. Fresh-baked bread and homemade cheese spread with little bowls of nuts were served for supper; Indian meals of vegetables, rice, and lentils arrived at dinner. Some days we received yogurt smoothies with fresh fruit or mint. We ate together in silence, sitting cross-legged around the tablecloth spread on the floor of the main room. Surrounded by quiet, the sensuous essence of the food revealed itself. I became totally absorbed in the activity of eating, slowing down, noting the subtle sensations of odor and shape, texture and flavor as the chewing continued. Each meal pleasured me, and I learned the subtle differences in food that the yogis have long spoken about.

Little did we know what else was waiting for us after the first few days. We all knew and taught both Vedanta's and the *Yoga-Sutra's* analysis of the mind; we knew that the mind's receptivity, *chitta*, had all her thought forms, *vrittis*, and memory forms, *samskaras*, tucked away. Reading texts that explained that, however, was one thing, but having to face the raw reality for ten days was something else. Our shadow awaited us. It sprung into our awareness in the most unlikely, and even fearsome, ways. Coping with the eruptions of our unconscious minds showed up in the most unique ways, some of them hilarious. One retreatant spoke loud and clear in his sleep every night. After a few days of being awakened by his monologues, I soon lay there quietly listening for the next interesting installment. Another sneezed incessantly throughout the day. Another was constipated. One snorted loudly, constantly clearing his throat. Another wrote notes to people outside, leaving them for Theresa to deliver. In my sleep I wrestled amorously with seductive women who turned into hideous serpents in my arms.

With all our daily defenses and distractions stripped away, we could no longer dodge what we avoided in ourselves. We would watch each other at meals and when on walks, noting changes in complexion, the speed at which we ate, who took how much of what. Some members filled their plates and took them back to their rooms; some wrote notes, asking for exceptions to be made in their food; some wanted to get really "holy" and miss a few meals.

"Don't fast or miss any meals; you need the nourishment," Swamiji said to us one night, during his instruction time. "Showing off won't get you very far." He was on to us. Some nights he came to address us; some nights we expected him, sitting around the main room quietly waiting, and he didn't come. He shared with us new knowledge, longed-for practices, interesting yoga techniques. He taught us some concentration methods that were Yogi Aurobindo's favorites. At other times, he showed us how to systematically prepare for higher experiences.

The retreat format each of the four years remained the same, but the content changed and, to put it mildly, so did the experiences. Each year the first few days were an ordeal, settling the mind down to go deeply within. There was a strange fatigue that overcame me each year for the first five days. All I wanted to do was sleep. One year I had a 24-hour fever during which my entire life came before me. Throughout the day I watched it unfold, year by year, all the way back to my birth. When the itinerary of my life was complete, the fever vanished.

"Get outside. Don't stay indoors during the day. Walk in nature, she will heal you," Swamiji always urged.

He didn't have to tell me twice. I treasured the walks in the woods, listening to the various sounds, feeling the wind and hearing its movement around me.

"Sleep more than usual. Take all the naps you want. Don't fight your body's need for rest, for stress has taken its toll on all of you, " he reminded us. That was fine with me. He explained that by withdrawing from our usual routine we were giving the body an opportunity to restore and rejuvenate itself. In the last half of each retreat, vitality resurged in me so strongly that by the ninth day, I felt more than fully charged and discarded sleep entirely.

As the retreat days moved on, I always noticed a major change in the acuity of my senses. Every year this expansion of innate ability occurred. The forest colors grew brighter, almost phosphorous at times. My range of perceptive depth increased as the retreat progressed. Specific features of nature dominated my hearing; I could pick out birds and small animals from great distances, knew where the swirling wind turned the grasses, heard when a small fish broke through the water to air. My skin increased its ability to feel; temperature and wind direction and humidity were all strongly apparent. My sense of smell was intense. The pines called from the hill, small plants became obvious by their scent, water held several different smells. I could open my mouth and experience in the air varying tastes on my tongue. It was like seeing and hearing and feeling and smelling and tasting in 3-D. As I walked the forest with its multi-shaped, vein-filled composition of leaves, the moss textures and hues of tree bark, the crowded motions and scents of tiny animals traveling through the undergrowth, the cry of the birds, the enlivening feeling of the wind, all were part of the ambiance of my awareness. Nature assumed a fascination that I played with for hours on end. I took more time with relaxed running, enjoying the paced synchronization between breathing and leg movement.

At night I would walk under the stars breathing deeply in the cool air, listening to the nocturnal sounds. I grew in gratefulness for my bodily senses.

During the days of being totally alone, I became very comfortable going inside. It seemed more like home than my outside existence. My meditation practice was a joy, extending in length and intensity day by day. One afternoon, I sat on the north side of the Sound of Music Hill to meditate, spying a small cluster of deer farther down in the valley before I closed my eyes. After awhile I heard a slight movement in the grass. Slowly opening my eyes, I found six deer grazing within twelve feet of me.

In the evenings, or sometimes early in the morning, Swamiji would come to the brick house to teach us. He sat in a large chair in the main room with all of us huddled around him.

"The first principle that should be understood," he said one evening, "is that your body is a shrine. What's more, there is an inner dweller within, the Self, or cosmic consciousness. In our tradition, the student is first made aware that he or she has been under the notion that he is a soul separated from reality or truth. Given that admission, the student is then led from this departure to see that the former admission is not true.

"The second principle is that you are a nucleus and the universe is your expansion. Theological manuals state that one is a soul created by God. These books also state that one has to assent to this proposition. I assure you that is why believers are prevented from knowing God or absolute truth. Let us propose this question: Why are people in spiritual authority doing this? The answer is that they do not know any better.

"Yoga science already declares that one is prevented from knowing the fullness of reality because one identifies with one's thought patterns. Let us now approach the topic differently. Ordinary everyday living means that one is not aware of the second principle, the nucleus. What part of you is the nucleus? It is your consciousness, the primal force within you. Your awareness of your body, your rate of breathing, your various thoughts still overlook the primal force that connects you with your unconscious and your soul. Your spiritual awakening is not possible unless you connect with this vital force. All your prayers, degrees, and searching travels are in vain unless this power is awakened from its hidden depths. And it resides in every one of you."

Phil and Justin during the annual campus cleanup

Swamiji told us that his teaching was the science of self-realization. His words were based upon two non-religious books written by the eighth-century sage, Shankara: *Wave of Beauty* and *Wave of Bliss*. I had long wanted to explore the highly esoteric character of these texts, and now my teacher opened them to us.

"The third principle" continued Swamiji, "states that this primal power needs awakening and there is a system for doing so. To appreciate the system, one needs to recognize that in this universe all things happen as they do in a human home. There the family is the result of the father and mother principles. We can call the father principle Siva and the mother principle Shakti. Without the mother principle, Siva is only *shava,* a corpse. That which is responsible for manifestation in this universe is the mother principle. Without knowing her consciousness, nothing is possible. There are many analogs throughout nature revealing these two principles—male and female, sun and moon, day and night. Your body's electricity has positive and negative nerve currents. In yoga anatomy, there is *pingala* and *ida*.

"The inner dweller within the shrine of your body is self-illuminating. It is this force that accounts for the state of enlightenment. There are thousands of believers in God, but they are not enlightened. For them God is out there. They are satisfied with a few puny emotions and thoughts, and so need God's mercy. Who says God and the universe are this way? Your mind does. You are always measuring your highest potential with your smallest criteria."

"Know who is within you first. Your body is only a covering; underneath is a power, a primal force, or what is called the *kundalini,* the very force through which you live. This force transfuses through you in three ways. Your life force expresses itself through your intelligence, your will, and your actions. If you desire that these three help you in this world, then you must get at the root—the primal mother force, the *maha shakti* or, as it applies to individuals, the *devatma shakti,* the *kundalini*."

He had spoken before about the *kundalini* force, but not in the context of the existence of the universe.

"The origin of this word, *kunda,* has many meanings—a bowl of fire, a cave. And *lini* is that which dwells in the cave. In your body is a bowl of fire constantly burning, but you are ignorant of it. You suffer in life because you don't know how to arouse and lead this fire, this mother force which transfuses your three channels of expression. Your life force resides in a sleeping state, resting like a coiled serpent. Only a slight amount of that power stirs now, enabling you to be alive with limited thoughts, desires and behavior. An elixir is dripping within you from the heaven above and you can't receive it properly since it is being consumed by the fire in the bowl. The sleeping serpent, the primal force, sips the liquid and remains in an intoxicated stupor. That's why your thoughts and actions are so small and you worry for your future. Your real power is dormant. Your individual soul starves and thus you are restless in life, trying this and that, reading books, taking self-improvement seminars. You are searching for the meaning of life since you are not getting that elixir, the *amrita*, the water of eternity."

He cast the spiritual journey into a mythology of creative consciousness that brought my understanding to the ultimate principles for anything to exist. I took more notes, fascinated with his ideas.

"The *devi*, or bright being within everyone is waiting in her shrine. She awaits because she is intoxicated from the elixir. You have to stop her from imbibing. Instead of keeping yourself restless for want of the elixir, you must prevent her from consuming it. She will then awaken and search for her real love, the honey of her life. When she embraces her Lord, then you are enlightened. All this happens in the shrine of your body."

His words stirred me; I could resonate with them because of my own search with the meanings of this mythology. As an academic student, I had found metaphysics, the science of being, the most enthralling portion of study. Over the years I had studied every metaphysical agenda that I could get my hands on. It was Plato and Aristotle along with the Medieval philosophers that most held my interest, but there was something missing—the connection between the microcosm and the macrocosm. Who would ever think that my search would end in the woods of Pennsylvania?

"There is much wisdom in the *Upanishads* that leads to self-realization. They contain universal methods valid for everyone. But how does one enjoy the dripping of the honey of life and enter the center of self-consciousness, the very source of life and light? One needs to practice a definite method; I'm introducing you to the finest of all knowledge: Sri Vidya."

Swamiji then reached over and opened a thick red book and turned to the diagram of interlaced triangles and circles called the Sri Yantra. He began to teach us the fine points of the wisdom portrayed in the visual summary of the tradition.

"In this method," he said, "our concern is not how the universe came into existence. First, you must learn about yourself. For this knowledge, two additional principles must be understood. You have an ascending force, the *kundalini*, the primal force, the mother of human potentialities; and you have a descending force, the divine within, the fountainhead of light and life. When you have completely exhausted your resources and made sincere efforts toward enlightenment, then another force, called grace, dawns in you. When you build a firm desire, not for mundane attainments but for the higher aspiration of the center of consciousness, then grace crowns your attempts, for you have made deserving efforts. You will have learned to use your mortality to attain immortality.

"You need to create the conditions within yourself for truth to reveal its treasures," Swamiji said another evening. "Truth hides itself until one is ready for it."

"Spirituality is not sectarian," he explained another night. "You prepare yourself for high spiritual states by understanding two realities: your own nature and the nature of the world. Truth flows from understanding your nature from within and knowing how it relates to your world. If we neglect the world within, then we get too preoccupied with the world without. Eventually, you will see that the world cannot satisfy you entirely. Relative truth is not enough for your soul. This should not be a cause for pessimism, but rather a positive insight that you are made for more than this world alone. People go to work and come home dreary; they don't love their work. So how can it possibly make them feel good about themselves? A sense of freedom is only possible when you learn to love your duties.

"If you are bothered by emotional problems" he answered practically, "if you keep rehearsing problems in your mind, then practice alternate nostril breathing. If you are preoccupied with physical problems, involving food or sex, then do even breathing. In this way you gain control over the life force instead of having it thrash you.

"Don't disconnect thought from feeling. Allow your strongest thought to be supported by your strongest feeling. If you need control, then choose breath as your object upon which to meditate. Remember that the equal exchange of exhalation-inhalation always leads you to tranquillity."

I remember one evening of the last retreat as if it were photographed on my mind's film. Swamiji began in an unusually solemn manner, which was unlike his customary enthusiastic demeanor. His quiet words were a revelation of things to come. He told us of troubles the Institute would have to endure. He unveiled his betrayal by some who were quite near to him. He described our futures, saying that he had chosen us to bear the Himalayan tradition to the world, each in our own unique manner.

He explained that although the Institute was only a small fraction of his mission and work, we should stay loosely associated with it while working elsewhere in the world, continuing to "teach the teachings." He stunned us as he spoke of his pending death, explaining that his master had given him fifteen years from his own life span so that Swamiji could live to complete his work. He told us that Babaji had said, "One of us must die, and since you are more important to the world than I am, I will die that you may live."

There were no dry eyes in the room by the time he finished. We walked our beloved teacher to the doorway in silence, received his blessing, and watched him walk alone into the night.

Never again did Swamiji concentrate his attention so fully on the group of those he selected to teach in the tradition. The forty days with the sage were one of the high points of my life. It also led to a strange sadness. I could not understand how anyone could turn away from both the retreat and the retreat master, but it happened.

Of the original twelve, whom I thought were disciples, a few did not return, finding the exercise a "waste of time." Some just lost interest in yoga and the teachings. One thought he could do it better "on my own." Some made it all the way through and years later turned against their teacher. Those who completed the forty days of training and continued as disciples of the master are Usharbudh Arya (Swami Veda), Charles Bates, Ladd Koresch, Phil Nuernberger, myself, and, of course, the mother who took care of "her boys."

A TIME FOR CONSOLIDATION

After the retreat we all went our separate ways. I returned to work, teaching, traveling, and spending as much time with my teacher as possible. There was a different demeanor about him now that was hard to describe. He spoke more cryptically; he no longer demonstrated yogic powers publicly, he seemed to be trying to wind up his administrative duties, giving more and more work to staff members to continue. During one late night visit, he said to Theresa, "Our time together is now very short. I don't have much more time." Another night he told a few of us, "Something shocking is coming to the Institute; be prepared. I will send you away so you are not hurt."

Naturally, we came up with all sorts of excuses for these words, never taking them literally, but we weren't sure from which context to interpret them. We gave them our best spin, never supposing that our teacher was serious about leaving. We thought that perhaps it was a passing mood from overwork. At the same time there seemed to be a new urgency about him. We took this as a sign that everything was humming along. But Swamiji leave? Never.

The apparently dislocated utterances from our teacher were accompanied by other uncomfortable signs. Rumblings started in the most innocent way and exacerbated into tense conflicts. New residents would arrive and after few weeks insist that they knew better than the staff the direction that the Institute should take. Everybody wanted to "correct" the Institute's future.

From the beginning of the '80s, knowing he would be leaving soon, Swamiji began to intensify his consolidation of administrative authority to others. He wanted Americans to run the American centers. What disheartened me, however, was that in the process, the newly appointed took it as an opportunity for pushing Swamiji to the sidelines. He was consulted less and less about Institute matters; his requests for new staff members were ignored; his stipends were cut; his scholarships for students were curtailed. I was disappointed that power made people crazy with their own agendas.

Most distressing to a few of us was the publishing arm. Several new people asked for positions in the Institute. Swamiji asked where they wanted to work; almost invariably they asked for the publications department. Soon they wanted to change the priority list of books to be published. They believed that Swamiji's books should be allowed to go out of print and that we should publish health and psychology books exclusively. Older staff insisted that books on spiritual topics hold top priority. A meeting was called to clarify issues and come to a decision on this important topic. Tempers flared, unkind words were flung about the room. We could not agree on anything.

Suddenly Swamiji burst into the meeting. "Why are you speaking this way?" he demanded, standing there confronting the entire room full of people. His whole being was in pain. My breathing almost stopped from the intensity of his accusation.

"What are you doing to each other; what kind of meeting is this?" he went on without letting up. "Why can't you love? Why are you hurting each other?"

Then he said a sentence that I have never forgotten.

"Don't you know that I have a body?"

Silence prevailed as heads bent down uncomfortably. "Oh, my God," I thought as recognition flashed, "he feels everything we say, everything that goes on. He feels our negativity in his body." As I peered at him, sensing the pain beneath his words, my frustration at not being able to relieve him pushed aside my remorse. "What are we doing to this man?" I asked myself. "Let's stop everything, first acknowledge who he is, and start all over again. He is so much with us, he is aware as we live each moment." I couldn't pretend to comprehend the compassion of our teacher for all his students. I will never know how many others in the room perceived what he was going through, and I wondered if anyone else knew the implications of his words. He was calling us to task, less for the matter that we had talked about than for the manner in which we were conducting ourselves. Our production and sales might be climbing, but we were failing each other.

"Settle the matter, decide your preferences," Swamiji said slowly and sadly, "and agree on what you want to print. There is no need to fight. You can talk without indulging your egos. You can disagree, but you don't have to hurt one another in the process. I have no interest in staying here if this is the way my people treat one another. I will leave this place if this fighting continues. Why am I here if not for you people? What do I gain if you do not progress? I want you to bloom," he said with physical pain showing. With that, he walked out of the room.

We finally worked our way to a compromise, and the rest of the afternoon I reflected on the confrontations and other conflicts that had emerged. I wondered what Swamiji must be feeling. I realized that we thought of him as an invincible super-yogi, the stainless steel sage, master of all emotions, serenely impervious to the squabbles of daily life. Those appellations were quite true, but he also unquestionably loved his people. That made him vulnerable. Swamiji wanted us to work things out without feeling any pressure from him, and so he did not become involved, but he looked pained at the way we were going.

"I have a terrible flaw," he once told me. "I get disappointed. I try my best with people, and they eventually turn on me. That still hurts me."

Now I realized how ignorant we were. Could any of us love to the degree this man loved us? Angry with myself, I walked in the woods at dusk asking myself why I didn't see this earlier. How could I stop the fighting? "No more," I thought to myself, "I'm through with all pettiness." This drop of insight fell mercifully into my awareness as an answer to my silent prayer.

Later that night in his apartment, Swamiji mused over the day, turned to me and asked, "Where have I failed, Justin? My people won't work together; they won't forgive each other." He repeated his plea, "Where have I failed?" But his question was only the beginning, a prototype of forthcoming events.

Many years earlier, a famous saint in India pondered an exasperating predicament: he had too many students. They weren't bad students; they were just lazy. They would attend his lectures, sit before him, come to him to have their needs met, praise his name, but rarely do any practice on themselves. The saint came to our teacher to ask his advice. Swamiji mentioned an unusual option, which the saint willingly adapted.

As the saint's followers strolled down the street to the city ashram one day, a shocking sight met their eyes. Their holy master sat in an open carriage waving to them with a bottle of whiskey in one hand and a well-known prostitute in the other. Word about the unbelievable fall of the great saint went like lightening around the city. Not surprisingly, the saint's original problem was quickly resolved. With such indisputable evidence, most students abandoned him as an evil man. For some devotees, reputation makes the swami.

A similar episode occurred across our northern borders with Swami Radha, the first Western woman to be initiated as a swami by the saint, Swami Sivananda. Radha announced that she would no longer wear Indian dress, and one day appeared in simple Western clothes. Within a short time, enormous numbers of her seemingly devoted students showed their disapproval by leaving her. For some devotees, clothes make the swami.

Some students of our teacher were appalled when they discovered he was fond of smoking, owned a car, or traveled first class in the thousands of hours he flew. For some devotees, third class travel makes the swami.

In our culture, no great being is ever free from the stigma of rumor. We build up our leaders only to tear them down with innuendo and false interpretation. We want our saints to be like us, but when they show the slightest human element, we stay away. We want our saints to be other-worldly, but when they are too much above us, they are condemned. Are we any different from the people of two thousand years ago? They took everything the Nazarene had to offer and then turned on him. Of the ten lepers cured, only one gave thanks. When a woman poured perfume on his feet to show love and respect, his students fought over the cost. One of his disciples betrayed him for thirty pieces of silver; only one remained at his ignominious death. When the people he had served were given the choice between the healer-teacher or a notorious prisoner, they chose Barabbas. Secular and religious authorities wanted Jesus put out of business; the same has happened to great mystics and seers throughout the ages.

Every few years fresh rumors about Swamiji competed for attention. Truth or falsity did not matter; only the element of shock carried weight. Does he really own a chateau in Switzerland? Does he have private stock in Japanese businesses? Is it true that he never sleeps? That he drinks wine? That he has dozens of children? That he smokes cigarettes? That he never bathes? Does he have hypnotic power over people?

The shock litany went on and on. Some took their allegations to court; some wrote scathing letters and articles. Swamiji remained himself, loving and self-contained in the midst of it all.

I remember a student who had been entrusted with the responsibility of managing one of the Institute's public projects. We found out that he kept double books and siphoned off the unreported money into his own pocket. Swamiji, being told of the fraud and recognizing that the man handled the job competently, even if unethically, offered the man the opportunity to buy the project at a competitive price and continue on his own with the work he obviously liked. The man turned down the proposal and then tried to sue Swamiji for bringing his embarrassment to light.

Another prominent student implored Swamiji to select a spouse for her. In the meantime, she found someone on her own and brought the intended to meet the master. Privately and gently cautioned by Swamiji to reconsider her current choice, the woman went ahead anyway, insisting that she knew what she was doing. The marriage became an almost intolerable burden and the student told her friends that Swamiji had given her insufficient warning. It was Swamiji's fault that she had made a poor choice.

One student damaged his leg severely. Nightly, regardless of his schedule, Swamiji drove to the student's home to clean and dress the wound. In all my years, I never saw him lavish more discernible care upon anyone. Later, however, the man attempted to publicly demean Swamiji for an imagined slight.

Not infrequently, people would fantasize about their association with the great yogi and notify him and others of their interpreted "facts." One woman's letter praised his ingenuity in visiting her frequently by slipping through the vents in her apartment's air conditioner. Another student broke a limb and interpreted its slow healing to Swamiji's lack of prayers for his recovery. One woman came for his blessing on her unborn child and when told by Swamiji that she was not pregnant, she became outraged. How dare he deny a blessing to the child in her extended abdomen? She cursed the teacher and charged out of his office only to be diagnosed six weeks later with a false pregnancy generated by intense desire. One wealthy woman's family nearly went to court to prevent Swamiji's health recommendations because they wanted to get her "out of his hands" so she would die and they could inherit. One woman would periodically march defiantly into our teacher's office and loudly accuse him of everything from communicating with UFOs to undermining the Federal Reserve. Those weekly confrontations went on for several months until the staff wanted to curtail her visits. "It's therapy for her," Swamiji would exclaim with open hands and hunched shoulders "Let her be."

It became obvious that many people held him to a standard that he never required of others and then derogated him when he didn't meet their expectations. Many wanted attention at all costs, and when not satisfied, turned their energy to attack instead. They viewed Swamiji as a God-man but often denied him the latter status. How to explain it? To some extent, it goes with the territory and the culture. Rumors in our society easily accelerate into accusations like a modern-day Salem witch trial.

Western societies, for all their rugged individualism, want to be saved from their fears and pains, but in a democratic context, and usually on their own terms. We want to be rescued but don't want to make any changes in our lives. That's why it is so hard for us to comprehend the significance of a genuine guru. We don't truly understand the importance of an individual who has attained Olympian heights in soul development. When the hero doesn't comply with the wishes of the masses on their time schedule, then he's castigated. We ask for assistance but want only comfortable assurances. We demand the teacher's full commitment, but relate to him or her as though ours was a part-time job. Then, of course, we all want salvation and liberation if it doesn't cost too much either in time, money, or effort.

"I have three kinds of students," Swamiji said. "Some come only for periodic family blessings; some admire me, attend my lectures, and line up for advice on their issues with life; only a few are genuine students, who will take anything I give them."

I once asked him if he would mind telling me the reason why some individuals who received so much could walk out and turn against him.

"That's as far as they can go in this life," he spoke softly.

For me that meant they had reached their spiritual 'Peter Principle.' Besides, there's always litigation, which has become a hobby in America. Since we live in a cultural climate where there is a tendency to blame someone else for our misfortunes, the easiest way to duck responsibility is to target the individual who is always ready to assist one's endeavors. Whenever property and money is seen as a possible gain, the probability for accusation is higher.

The Institute and its real estate is immediately impressive, but as the years went on I realized how few people knew about the extraordinary efforts it took this man to maintain the dream for us. I was chagrined to watch the dreary work our teacher did day after day in order to obtain sufficient funds for the preservation of the American centers. When I softly complained to him that he shouldn't have to perform such drudgery, he brought me up quickly. "Who's going to do it, then? I have to deal with people as they are; what else can I do?"

Looking at him, I also realized that he had saved me from embarrassment then and there by not reminding me what I would do in the same situation. My naiveté was rightly shot down. At that moment, I was proud to know a few students who had quietly shared a depth of awareness in these matters and had indicated some measure of comprehension of the ordeals he put himself through for our benefit. There were many individuals—some old-timers from Chicago days, some recent ones around the country—who remain unsung for their magnanimous generosity, who have never entertained a thought of abusing the teacher's graciousness, or tried to wheedle an advantageous position with a hefty donation. But there are many others who have. I cannot even pretend to know the extent to which our teacher went to help his students, but based on my experience with him, I know he did.

One evening as I was feeling particularly low over the daily machinations for power and prestige in our spiritual community, Swamiji said to me, "Everything going on in life is going on right here at the Institute. Just watch and learn. In two years we will hand over this place to others to run and go to the Himalayas."

Swamiji on the tennis court

CHAPTER 18
GOOD-BYE TO AMERICA

Swamiji stood in the background with Mama. The light around them was warm sepia, other-worldly, and I was concerned about their health. Mama handed me her two personal diaries which covered the years with her teacher and son.

S WAMIJI WAS NOT WELL. My dream told me so, even though it was a sadness I already knew. For all my years with him, I had always been accustomed to interacting with my teacher at a fast and steady pace, noting that his health kept up with his projects' growth and the work he had to do. Now that he was finishing his work in America, it seemed that his health was in a serious decline. Whenever I asked if there was anything I could do, he would answer that he had been here longer than he should have been.

Many years earlier, Swamiji told us of the time he had been traveling in Tibet and had been caught in a sudden snowstorm before he could find shelter. He was pulled nearly frozen out of a snowy grave by mountain villagers who placed him in a pit and surrounded him with hot coals for more than a month, coaxing his metabolism to rejuvenate his body. That strong body recovered except for the teeth. Dentists in New Delhi did repair work, telling him that he would have to undergo mouth surgery in the future. In the early '80s the foretelling proved exact. Swamiji scheduled dental surgery carefully, because he had promised his master that he would never lose consciousness through anesthesia or anything else. In the midst of the painful rebuilding of his jaws, he carried on his spiritual work, but when we saw pain in his face, we noticed that he had slowed down.

A few close students spent extra time with the teacher, getting ice, making tea, reading his mail to him, and filling the hours with ridiculous card games of his choosing. Samskrti and Theresa were regulars, fitting their work schedule around the call of the card table; a fourth was chosen from those who walked in the door at the given moment. Sometimes, I'm pleased to say, my feet took me there.

Swamiji was a good player; Samskrti even better. After a week or so of normal playing and losing, our teacher decided to amuse himself by cheating. He asked Theresa to be his partner in crime and they quietly worked out a series of signals so that she would know which card to throw down to augment his hand. The Swamiji/Theresa pair won every single hand. Samskriti and I grew disgruntled, suspicious, and tongue-in-cheek, accused them of cheating.

"What?" our teacher asked innocently with a slight smile and blinking eyes, "Would we do that?" And when we could come up with no appropriate response, he'd shift the ice pack on his jaw, hand over the pile of cards to someone to shuffle and say, "Let's play another hand."

About that time, new staff members arrived at the Institute, wanting to offer their lives, too, to the ongoing work for humanity. A young woman whom Swamiji named Kamal arrived and was immediately put to work learning to become his next secretary; a new physician came to learn homeopathy and combined therapies and offered to work in exchange; an older couple asked to join the work crew doing whatever the master wanted them to do.

The couple drove to up to the Institute from South Carolina, taking their time and enjoying the ride. The wife was an ardent student of Swamiji's but her husband, a retired furnace engineer, had never met her teacher. When their car crossed the state line into Pennsylvania, Bill immediately smelled an unusual scent in their camper, not offensive, but a strong aroma that he could not identify.

"Honey, what's that odor in the air?" he inquired.

She sniffed. "What odor?" she replied, smelling nothing.

The scent grew stronger as they continued their northerly advance through the wooded highway. When they finally arrived at the Institute, they were shown to their new apartment where they sat down to enjoy a cup of tea after the long journey.

Suddenly, Bill jumped up exclaiming, "That's it. That's it!" There across the room on the lamp table, a small tray held a burning stick of Padmini Dhoop incense, the scent our teacher loved to keep near himself.

One evening, after Swamiji's mouth surgery was completed, he called my wife and me into his apartment. He always sat with students around the small dining table or on the floor in front of it. This night we drank tea with lemon on the floor. "How is the Institute doing?" he asked. I reported as best I could from my perspectives, Theresa, working in other areas, answered from hers. Our teacher uttered his usual "Hmmm" and looked away. We spent the time massaging his feet, waiting for his mind to come back to us. When it did, we were not ready for the words he spoke. "I am very attached to you both and must do something about it." It didn't sound like a threat since it was spoken in an almost light-hearted manner, so I wondered what was in store for us next.

A few days later, Swamiji sent Theresa a letter saying that she should teach several other people how to do her publication work so they could take over her job. She should merely continue to work with the flower gardens outside, manage the special guest rooms, and work in the library. She was devastated. She could not understand why she should not work as hard as she always did. Had she made a mistake? Was her teacher disappointed with her service? She carefully enumerated the thirty-five books she had produced for the Institute, thought about the countless newsletters, magazines, catalogs, programs, department forms she had published, the hundreds of letters she had answered for her teacher and tried to find a flaw in her work. She worried as the weeks went on with Swamiji seemingly ignoring her. Her energy declined. Everyone but she seemed to have a project. She felt there was nothing for her to do anymore at the Institute nor, worse, for her teacher. The next morning as she walked down the hallway, Swamiji suddenly came out of one of the offices and asked her to get him a letter from his desk. Happy to be of service again, she retrieved the paper and returned in a flash. He smiled, took it from her, and gave her a big hug, saying softly, "You presume too much. Remember that I love you."

With little to do, Theresa asked if she might attend some family graduation celebrations. She had not seen any family member since we had left for Pennsylvania years before and now felt that she would not be needed during an absence. Swamiji gave her his blessing as well as money to pay for the journey. I drove her to Syracuse and saw her off on the night train to Chicago. On my drive back to Honesdale, I rehearsed all my grievances about my wife's treatment, letting them build with my ire, and decided that I would confront our teacher with them the next day.

All the staff was outdoors, cleaning the property before the Annual Congress, now held on campus, when I walked up to Swamiji. "Is she safely off?" he asked.

"Yes, she is. She'll arrive this afternoon. You know," I said to him, "I don't like what's happening to Theresa; I think you are too hard on her."

"Stay out of it, Justin," he answered slowly. "She is my student, just like you. I'm working on her and you are getting in the way. Defending her before me is useless."

"OK, sir," I answered, not believing him. I went on raking and steaming as he walked away to supervise some planting.

Later that afternoon, Swamiji came over to me and asked me to sit with him. He began with the topic on my mind. "Theresa is the hardest worker I have ever met; she works harder than I do!"

I relaxed a bit, trying to listen with my heart as well as my head. "She is strong but needs to learn how to deal with others, just like everyone else," he continued. "She is a genius; she speaks to others from the confidence she has within herself, not realizing that others know they can't compete with her. Jealousy is the most difficult obstacle on the spiritual path. My master reminded me of that fact often. Theresa is not aware of others' jealousy and can be hurt. I am teaching her, but you are not helping her nor yourself by your interfering ways. Learn to be more objective. I'm not unfair to her; I respect her far more than you do. She is very close to me. Let me do my work!"

The next evening I was invited to Swamiji's new log cabin on the property. It was the sixth house he had lived in since we knew him. Each time he would select a house, completely rebuild and refurbish it, live in it for some months, and then give it to one of the couples. Then he'd come back from a trip and say he had nowhere to live, and we'd begin building him another house. In this one also I saw the handiwork of my wife as usual and was reminded of my self-righteous attitude of the morning. It made me face reality, remembering that Swamiji took work from those he loved, and was hardest on those he loved the most.

"Justin," he began this evening, "when I was fourteen years old, some relatives wanted to kill me for my inheritance. I was very sad and went to my master for solace. 'Why be sad' he said to me, 'when you have God's protection? But you must also protect yourself. The way to do that is to cultivate the best protection in the world—not violence in return, but friendship. Friendship, however, should be earned; it's not easily given.' This land is for growth and peace," Swamiji said, full of thought, "but those here do not make the best use of it. They ceaselessly bother me from morning till midnight and beyond, fighting for their egos and their private agendas."

I listened carefully to his words, realizing that what he said made sense. Without friendship on campus, there would be no community, just bickering. My ear caught his voice again and brought my mind back to his words.

"I scold students like Theresa deliberately. I even say things about her to others that are not true for the purpose of getting her to complain to me so that I can have the chance to help her. I cannot hate. I scold to help, for it's an expression of my concern. I want people to blossom. Others scold and lie and cause problems because they wish to glorify themselves. They use the Institute as a way to personal glory and power."

I felt chagrined; I should not have complained to my teacher about my wife. Of all people, I knew he cared for her. Perhaps it was a husband's ego?

"Look at Theresa's eyes," Swamiji was saying. "Anyone can tell that she is a meditator from the Himalayas. Can't you tell? She lived in the mountains as a nun, as a yogi, doing practice. You lived there also, Justy. Don't you feel it?"

"You told me I was with you in other lives, Swamiji. Was Theresa with you also?"

"Of course she was," he answered with love in his eyes. "She was with me many times. I've told her that before. She was a nun in several lives, beginning in Europe four hundred years ago. Her name was Theresa then also, and she established convents all over the country."

My mind raced. "I'll never get any sleep tonight pondering all this," I thought. I looked up as Swamiji picked up the phone, dialed, and instructed someone on the other line about meditation practice. When he replaced the receiver I asked how many

An evening with Swamiji in his cabin

students he checked up on each evening.

"More than two thousand," he answered quietly. "Personal contact is not necessary, but sometimes it helps the student."

"How's my game going?" Swamiji suddenly asked me, changing the subject. He picked up his tennis racket and bounced it on his hand. "Am I improving?"

I assured him that he was doing well with the sport. He had begun tennis by just hitting balls and not moving much, but grew better and better with legwork and powerful serves. I asked why he had taken up tennis after all these years.

"Let me tell you what happened, Justy," he said, leaning closer toward me. The story that emerged broke my heart. Some months back, in October of 1981, Swamiji had sat in the small back bedroom of his apartment doing a special advanced yoga practice of the subtle body in which he left his physical body. During that night a lamp was knocked off the table by the wind from the open window and hit the back of his head. His body was extremely sensitive due to the practice and should not have been disturbed in any way. With the hit of the lamp, the connection between his two bodies was broken, ending his life. "But my master pushed me back into my body," he said, "because I still had work to do." The event took a huge toll. There was a strain on the coordination of his brain and nervous system; his body began to bleed. He filled a bucket with blood that evening, and for many days ahead. The bleeding, diagnosed as "diffuse internal bleeding" by the medical community, went on for years, weakening the body, causing pain that could not be alleviated.

In order to keep Swamiji alive, his master ordered him to exercise vigorously three to four hours daily. "I don't care if you drop to the ground; just do it," the sage told his son.

So Swamiji chose to play tennis and it changed the Institute overnight. Students would hear that the teacher was on the court, and a crowd would suddenly appear on the sidelines, applauding every hit. Visitors were invited to play a set with the teacher, gifts of tennis rackets and designer tennis wear were brought by admirers and followers, students who taught tennis became valued residents. Half the campus took up the new sport, hoping to be challenged by the teacher.

"I'm worried because my master can call me back to the Himalayas at any time," Swamiji said to me. He warned me not to get attached to the Institute. "You have no idea what I'm doing for people here, but after I'm gone you will understand."

He hugged me warmly as I left his little house that evening, and I wandered down the hill to my room with a new sadness.

Swamiji's trips to the East were longer now; he spent less and less time in America. Theresa and I went to be with him nearly every evening he was in town, either in his apartment or his cabin. I did not find him recovering as well as I had hoped. As the weeks went on, his energy level varied. Some days he showed no sign of the toll that the internal hemorrhaging was having upon his body; other days he was ashen and weak. I couldn't believe my ears when he told me that he had been approached by some of the officers on the board who suggested that "it would look better" if he moved off campus during this period of illness.

From that point on I felt that our lives were lived on the fly. We would stay in neutral until he assigned us to some duty. In the meantime, my lectures picked up around the country so I was gone from the campus a bit, calling in every evening to see that all was well.

One late afternoon, after a trip to Texas, I finished a short run when Swamiji yelled from the court, "Don't you want to play?"

I thought it rather strange of him to invite me to play tennis since he had two players facing him on the court and at least three more on the sidelines waiting to join in, but I ran to my room for my racket. Swamiji signaled for me to be his practice partner. After waiting and waiting for a ball to be hit to me, I began to get quite impatient. I kept thinking "What good is it for me to hit one in ten shots? What kind of practice is this?"

At that exact moment, Swamiji, about fifteen feet away, turned to me and spoke aloud about learning to have reverence for the teacher, no matter who it was, even as he had had to learn. Answering my thoughts, he added, "Don't compete with me!" in no uncertain terms.

While I was mulling over those words, he stopped his play, told the student instructor to hit balls to me instead. Then he limped across the court, picked up all the stray balls and brought them to me. I had never seen him do that for anyone. I felt ashamed of my pride and realized that unless one commits wholeheartedly to the teacher, one cannot really learn, because part of the self is held back.

In those days I spent several hours a week teaching courses at two Eastern colleges and was frequently invited to speak at churches. In between, I joined Swamiji's roundup of volunteers to carry out his landscape design on the new, off-campus property of one of the board members. Swamiji guided us in clearing land, digging up rocks, planting trees and perennials and, in honor of his days in Japan, constructing a huge Japanese gate at the residence entrance. Afterwards, we would come back home, shower, and enjoy tilk with the spiritual teacher cum foreman into the late hours.

Wherever Swamiji went, Theresa and I went, unless told differently. Once we drove to Ramanamurti Mishra's Ananda Ashram in Monroe, New York, where Swamiji was an invited speaker. He taught about the need for discipline on the spiritual path. Afterwards we went to his room at New York's Grammercy Park Hotel with some of the Indian businessmen who had attended the talk. The evening was pleasant and relaxed, and Swamiji began to joke lightheartedly.

"We three have a pact," he said. "Whenever I need something and Theresa and Justin have it, they give it to me; whenever they need something, I give it to them. When we don't have anything, we sing the name of the Lord."

The guests liked the spirit and nodded their heads, smiling, so our teacher continued his train of thought.

"Theresa will do any work for you, provided you allow her the use of a bathtub; Justin will do any work for you, provided you give him a good meal. In his last life he was Ganesha."

The Indians roared their approval of the mention of a favored Hindu deity, the elephant-headed Ganesha. "If only," I mused, "I had Ganesha's power." Then turning to my teacher and watching him laugh along with us, I realized I had it.

A special mission was on Swamiji's mind during 1982. He wanted to prepare Mama for death. During that year, he visited her in Chicago many times, showering her with his love and care. She was ill with kidney failure and was put on a dialysis machine until Swamiji told her she needn't continue, much to the dismay of her doctor. Mama continued to live her life, gradually slowing down, spending day after day with the love of her life until he had to leave the country. Swamiji was in India, but he appeared at her bedside in Chicago as promised to assist her final crossover into the freedom of the spirit.

A few years later, Mama's brother Jack told me of her last days and invited me to collect her remembrances of Swamiji, now packed up in boxes. I went to her old apartment in Chicago, selected photos and tapes and letters, and said good-bye to Aunt Kitty, still sitting on guard, as usual.

One afternoon, Theresa and I were called down to have lunch with our teacher. A very different request awaited us this time. Swamiji had been spending much time in the Himalayan kingdom of Nepal these last few years and always visited with the royal family. The old king had been Swamiji's student for many years until his death. Now that his son had assumed the throne, Swamiji remained a revered guest in the family. As they discussed the history and future of the mountain country, Swamiji mentioned the royal children, including future offspring of the king's youngest sister, Princess Shobha. The princess was childless; she and her husband of ten years, Prince Mohan, desperately wanted children and had been treated by the best physicians in Europe and India to no avail. But Swamiji quietly insisted to the disbelieving group that she would bear a child. He requested a pen and paper, and writing a note, he folded it, handed it to the king, and told him to put it in a safe until further notice. All was done as requested. Swamiji then asked for Shobha to come to America where doctors in New York would help her. This last demand took some persuasion, even from a realized yogi, but reluctantly the king gave permission, and Her Royal Highness Princess Shobha Lakshmi Devi Shahi agreed to follow Swamiji to America.

We were fascinated with the story and asked if there really would be a child. "Of course!" Swamiji assured us. "Would you two help me? The princess is afraid to live here alone."

Of course we agreed to help in any way we could, honestly agreeing that the idea of meeting the Nepalese princess was rather intriguing.

A few months later, the entire Nepalese Mission to the United Nations drove up from New York City to the Institute to bring the princess and her husband to Swamiji. Theresa and I were introduced and spent a few days getting to know our new charges. They were charming and fun, curious about America and happy to learn whatever they could about their new home. Swamiji arranged medical care for Shobha with a highly successful fertility expert at New York Hospital. Assured that we would assist them whenever they needed us, the couple departed for the Big Apple to the upper east side apartment arranged by the Nepalese consulate.

So began a two year assignment wherein we drove one hundred thirty miles to New York City every ten days to take Shobha a half mile down the road to her doctor's appointment. We had a delightful time with the couple, becoming fast friends over tea, a few movies, many hours of the child's card game Uno, and stories of the world-famous Nepalese Gurka soldiers. Poor Shobha spent month after month of tedious and painful treatment followed by disappointment until one fine day the call we all awaited finally came: the princess was pregnant. With her husband traveling back and forth to Nepal for business, the princess asked Theresa to move in with her and the servants until the birth. Swamiji phoned often and sent notes to the women, encouraging Shobha in mothering and health, and Theresa in service to others. Together they walked the neighborhood for exercise, shared hours of stories, shopped the city's major stores and watched the soaps on TV.

During one of my weekly New York visits, I was invited by the ambassador to sit with the Nepalese delegation during a United Nations' session. It was a unique perspective on the relativity of political life. On another visit we all went to the home of Ambassador and Mrs. Bhatt for a formal dinner, after which we played numerous hands of Uno amidst gales of laughter and much royal intrigue.

On April 18th, the day before Theresa's birthday, the princess was delivered of two children, a girl named Manuja ("child of the Goddess") and a boy named Himavan ("son of the Himalayas"). They were beautiful babies, with big, dark eyes and rich, black hair. Prince Mohan called Swamiji and the family immediately. The king was told to open the safe and read the note written almost two years before. On it he found the words: "Shobha will have twins—a girl and a boy."

Members of the royal family flew to New York to see the children and Theresa brought them in, one by one, to lay in the lap of the Queen Mother. Theresa and I were asked to be godparents to the children, a task we happily accepted.

A few months later, we were guests of the Nepalese ambassador at the United Nations party in honor of the King of

Nepal. As we entered the grand hall, the ambassador stood in a circle of dignitaries from around the world, each clothed in rich, colorful, native dress. He welcomed us to the circle, raised a glass and announced, "To Dr. O'Brien, the man responsible for the Princess's children!" The stunned audience became silent, sipped their champagne, and then exploded in outrageous laughter as the ambassador realized his error and tried in vain to correct his statement.

Traveling back and forth from New York, where she played with the babies, and her room in Honesdale, where she did Institute work, Theresa began to look tired. Swamiji asked her to get a medical check up. She brought back from her doctor a questionable mammogram, necessitating a series of X-rays, heat tests, and more examinations. The doctors quietly diagnosed breast cancer.

I was stunned and frightened, not ready for this awful news, not knowing how to help my wife, realizing I had no money for any treatment. Our teacher called us into his office, initiated Theresa into the powerful healing mantra practice, *Maha Mrtyunjaya*, and said we should go to his 'very best' doctor, a friend of ours who had earlier taken training from Swamiji in homeopathy and now had an office in the Midwest. He wanted someone off campus to help her and thought she should have a good rest as well.

"Leave immediately. Don't tell anyone that you are going, and take your time coming back," he instructed.

We left a few hours later, making sure there was no unfinished work, and drove to the Midwest, telling our friend that we were coming for doctoring. We were warmly received by him and his family, but he looked confused. "Justin," he said as he called me aside, "you said to help Theresa, but what am I supposed to do?"

I was surprised, thinking he knew all about the case. Just as I was about to answer him, the phone rang. It was Swamiji on the line, explaining to the doctor the homeopathic ingredients and dosages that Theresa should be given. We stayed there overnight, took away a bag of remedies, and enjoyed ten days of traveling through the country visiting old friends all the way back home.

When we returned to Honesdale late at night, we found Swamiji gone and an envelope under the door of our room. It contained a sharp letter notifying us that we were to vacate the premises within twenty-four hours. We were told that since we had neglected to get the residential committee's permission to depart, we must face the penalty. It was signed by the new spiritual director in the name of the Institute.

Theresa was frightened; I was livid with anger. Swamiji's teachings flipped through my mind, but I could not find one to fit this situation. After a particularly rough night, I stomped off to see the spiritual director first thing the next morning. I carried the 1977 letter from Swamiji in which he stipulated that Theresa and I were to move to Pennsylvania to help form an Institute there, that we would not be held to any residential rules and regulations, that we were to answer only to him in all things. The eviction order was immediately rescinded. The surprised director apologized, and explained that the residential committee had compelled him to sign the letter in Swamiji's absence. Theresa felt relieved and quietly went back to her work; I knew the writing was on the wall.

The little town of Honesdale had a sign in the window of Art's Men's Store one day that summer. It announced its first Ugly Tie Contest. That sounded interesting, so I went home and began pulling ties out of my little closet. Theresa insisted that I enter the day-glo pink silk with green and yellow and purple paisley shapes scattered across its width. In the shop, Art winced when I entered my tie, a gift from Swamiji after one of his trips to India. When I won the contest a week later, I was thrilled with my prize of a new wool suit and went to tell my teacher about the news. At first he looked embarrassed when I explained which tie had won ("It couldn't have been from me, Justin!"), but then he decided that he had given it to me just so I could win a prize with it one day. We all laughed together over that one until we could laugh no more.

One evening in late July, Theresa and I were walking near the barn when Swamiji and his ever-vigilant dog, Raja, spied us from across the way. We all met at the crossroads and together continued up the path to the pine trees. He walked like the old Swamiji that night, firm of step, head held high. We reminisced about the growth of the twins, the successful summer Congress, the programs on the campus, the growth of students' families, the adjustment of new residents in their jobs. He told us that he had been calling students into his office and asking them what they wanted most for their futures. Then he tried to fulfill their dreams. I didn't know at the time, but this was part of his plan to get people settled before he moved on to his next major project outside America.

"The problems here slow me down," he said quietly.

Strolling by my favorite stand of trees as the stars blinked overhead, Swamiji caught us off guard. In the most casual voice, he asked, "What do you two want?"

Theresa told him that we had everything we needed, but he asked again, "What do you want?"

"What do you mean, Swamiji?" she asked.

He explained his final work on the campus to her. "This one wanted a wife, and now he has one. That one wanted property, and it was given. Another wanted authority, and I gave her that duty. One wanted money, and I made the proper arrangements." On and on he went, shocking us with the requests of those we knew, stunning us with the thought that he had fulfilled all their wishes.

His question could not have been clearer in the still night air, but he asked yet again. "What do you both want?"

I looked at Theresa, who was near tears, lifting her shoulders and shaking her head slowly from side to side. So turning directly to my teacher, I said for both of us, "Keep us always with you." Theresa found her voice and repeated the request.

Swamiji gazed at us for a moment, nodding yes again and again. "I asked my master who would be with me at the end," he said solemnly, "and he told me your names." We turned around and went back to the main building, a feeling of love and warmth surrounding us. I was pleased that I had asked for what was really in our hearts.

THE NEW YORK YOGI

A few days later we were in New York again as the expanded royal family was returning home to Nepal. We had helped shop for the dozens of gifts and mementos now packed and ready for shipping; we had played our last game of Uno the night before and promised to pull out the deck again in the future. Now we kissed the beautiful babies and said our good-byes to Shobha and Mohan as they flew off to Kathmandu.

The next day was spent back in Honesdale, getting Swamiji ready to leave for India. He spoke to the residents on campus, to the faculty, to the centers, and said he was leaving America now because his work was complete. He had established all the programs at all our centers, had made sure each had staff in leadership positions, had left a legacy of writings and tapes, and was ready to do the next work his master asked. Everyone was worried, unsure if they would ever see their teacher again. There were last-minute appointments, the phone rang continuously and a handful of us ran in and out of his apartment carrying out his requests. Theresa, Samskrti and Kamal packed three huge suitcases of clothing, vitamins, office needs, and items not readily available in India. Hefty resident men were requested to sit on the cases so the women could lock them shut.

Swamiji asked Theresa and me to drive him to New York on Friday to spend the days before his flight with him. The citizens of Manhattan were leaving the city that weekend to escape the heat, so the streets were less crowded than usual. We stopped first at East West Books on Fifth Avenue and made arrangements to sleep there. Next, we went to Raga's for a magnificent Indian lunch served amidst our gaiety and relaxation. Next, we went on a shopping tour through the imported fabric stores, watching the Scottish clerks blanch as Swamiji insisted on discounts for their fine woolens. For years Theresa had sewn Japanese kimonos by the dozens for her teacher in ochre cotton and wool. After each trip to India, they had been found to have mysteriously disappeared. It took only one story of probable loss during travel before she understood that Swamiji gave his clothes away to needy *sadhus* on every trip.

As we walked up Fifth Avenue, looking in shop windows and having fun, Swamiji said, "What about a sweater? Perhaps we should find a good sweater."

We were in the expensive designer area when we walked into one of the shops and found a long case near the wall filled with piles of sweaters. As soon as he put his hand on the glass top, Swamiji went somewhere else. He stared straight ahead with unblinking eyes, mouth partially open, not moving a muscle, barely breathing. Just then the salesman walked up to us to offer assistance. Trying to distract him from the yogi in trance, we sent him scurrying for one size and color after another, keeping one eye on Swamiji's condition. The poor man brought out most of his stock, telling us about the qualities of each sweater, sneaking glances at the strange, unmoving person next to us. Just as I was getting nervous, wondering what to do next, Swamiji opened his eyes wide, took a deep breath, and saw the big golden name Gucci on the wall in front of him. With a broad smile and a rather childlike voice, he stretched out his arm, pointed to the designer's name and said loudly, "That's my dog!" The clerk gasped, but Swamiji had already turned and began walking out the door. We ran after him, apologizing to the sales clerk as we tried to keep up with our teacher and protect him from harm.

We next went to Swamiji's room at the Mayflower hotel to have tea and allow him a little rest. "Will you get my mail for me?" he asked. It was waiting at our bookstore, so back we went again, Theresa warning her teacher not to open the suitcases for any reason or disaster would surely occur.

We retrieved the mail from Samskrti, who had driven it all the way to the city, collected the phone messages, noted who was waiting to see the teacher, and got back to Swamiji's room about an hour later. We knocked at the door but got no answer. We waited a bit and knocked again. Nothing. We rang the door bell with no response. We began to worry that something had happened to him and wondered whether to ask the front desk to open the room for us. Just then we heard the lock being released on the inside and the door opened a crack. "Tree," our teacher said quietly with his face smashed against the narrow opening, "Tree," he said again, in a pleading voice, "don't be angry with me, OK?"

The door was thrown open to a catastrophe. Clothes were everywhere—on the floor, on the furniture, on the desk and TV. It looked as if a typhoon had swept through the place. Theresa looked stunned. All her work for nothing. She looked around for Swamiji, now pretending to be scared, hiding behind the open door. "What could I do?" he asked. "I just needed to get a clean robe and the suitcase burst."

We also burst, into laughter. We made up stories of the suitcase bursting in the plane, in the airport, in the taxi in New Delhi. As Theresa knelt down to refold everything, Swamiji began throwing things at us. "Take this to Phil, give this to John, keep this for yourself, Justin." He handed me his watch, his jogging suit, two of his magnificent white meditation shawls. We spent the night in this gay mood, even turning on an old Western on the TV before it was time to meditate and say good night.

The next morning was for business. Swamiji dictated letters to Theresa, had me phone students and administrators, checked and re-checked his travel plans. By noon we were hungry, so we made our way by foot to another Indian restaurant. As we walked back to the hotel after lunch, Swamiji said to Theresa, "One good thing I have done, Tree. I served you once," he said.

We stepped off the curb to cross the busy avenue as Theresa said, rather confused, "But Swamiji, you have served me hundreds of times. You are always serving all of us."

"Yes, yes, I know. But once I really served you," he insisted.

Theresa asked what he meant and he simply said that he would tell her later.

Back in the hotel room, after tea was brought and Swamiji had settled on the sofa wearing his favorite kimono, Theresa asked if he would explain what he said to her.

Softly he spoke, looking deep into her eyes, "I took your cancer to myself."

Theresa looked stunned as the words took on a meaning; she then began to cry and shout at him. "Give it back! I don't want you to have it. Give it back!" she sobbed as she slapped his hands.

He pulled her close to him and wrapped his arms around her. He said softly, "Don't cry. It's all right. You won't have to worry anymore." He then took her hand in one of his and my hand in his other and brought our palms to his chest. I moved my fingers against several small, hard nodules.

Theresa was upset, insisting that he should not take her disease, asking him to undo what he had done.

"You are dear to me and I love you," he said. "Don't cry. When I go to India, I will transfer the cancer to a tree there. It's all arranged. I will not keep it. Don't worry, we will live in the Himalayas," he reminded us again.

After he repeated this promise again, he asked Theresa for more tea. Then he told us a story about his master advising a young couple to buy a particular house. They complied with their teacher's advice, bought the house and moved in. At night they heard sounds apparently emanating from the walls in their bedroom. They thought it might be the wind, but the sounds recurred night after night regardless of the weather. They finally decided to break open the place in the wall where the sound was the strongest. There, unbelievably, was a cache of jewels, precious gems hidden by a wealthy previous owner. The jewels allowed the husband to become a successful businessman and the couple then lived a fulfilled life.

As I pondered the meaning of that story, he added, "Money is for needs and helping others."

For some reason, my mind became distracted by the story and I entertained the legend of the gold that the outlaws Frank and Jesse James had buried somewhere in the South. The story says that after Frank got out of jail, he spent the last years of his life searching unsuccessfully for the pot of gold that they had hidden.

I gave Swamiji a brief synopsis of the legend and asked him if he would be able to locate the gold. He said he could.

"Do you want to find the James' gold?" he then asked me casually. "I can easily do it for you, and then my responsibility will be over."

Silence prevailed; none of us moved. I knew that he wasn't fooling. If he could find my ring in a sewer system, it was quite obvious to me that locating famous gold was a cinch. I just smiled, "No thanks, Swamiji, I'd rather stick around with you," I said, knowing that around him I always had to be on my toes.

He then proceeded to tell us more stories of his training with his master. He said that his teacher had extraordinary patience. He had wanted to catch up to the abilities of his master as quickly as he could and so he worked very hard and very stubbornly. If his master told him to do a practice fifty times, he would do it one hundred times. If he was told to meditate six hours, he would extend it to twelve. He pushed himself relentlessly, even hurting himself on more than one occasion. His master told him that the extreme practice had build so much energy in his body that if he did not do some extraordinary rebalancing, his skin would burst. Likewise, if he continued to stay in meditation for his usual eighteen hours a day, he would leave his body permanently. Consciousness would be accustomed to the deep meditative state and would give up its embodied state.

And so it went for the entire weekend as he rested, relaxed, played, ate and shared insights with us. As much as I could, I brought humor into our hours together, so pleased was I to give something to him who gave so much to us.

Unfortunately, the time to leave rolled around too soon and as we closed the door to the cozy hotel room, Swamiji handed us the electronic card to his suite, telling us to enjoy it for another day, since he had paid for it through Monday as a little gift. We drove our teacher to Kennedy Airport for his flight and walked him to the gate. "You know, Justy," he said almost impishly as we walked the corridors, "sometimes I create mischief at a place to turn people against me. Then I can leave freely."

"I'll have to be alert to those occasions," I promptly replied.

Charles, Phil and several other close students stood at the gate to see Swamiji off. He gave last minute instructions, hugged some and shook hands with others, gave directions for practice, thanked some for years of service.

Just before he stepped into the gangway, he called Theresa and me to himself, held us and said, "No matter where I go, Justin will always find me." He brushed Theresa's tears away with his hand and whispered, "Don't worry; we'll be together in Nepal and we'll all die together in India some day."

Amaldablam, a holy mountain in Nepal

Chapter 19
Up to the Mountains

I stood in a valley looking at the vast circle of mountains surrounding me. Fifty feet in front of me, huge elephants formed two long rows, one on my right and one on my left. Next to me, Swamiji told me to go meet the animals. As I approached them, they bowed their mammoth heads to me. I returned the greeting to the animals, surprised to feel comfortable before them. Off in the distance I saw a high snow-capped mountain with two peaks. From behind me, the master's words were clear: "You must climb the mountain."

THREE YEARS AFTER THAT POWERFUL DREAM Theresa and I landed in Nepal. We were asked by the royal family to come see our godchildren and could not refuse the invitation. Met at the plane by Prince Mohan in his bright red sports car, we were whisked past waiting lines of tourists, stern-faced officials, and security checks and driven into the city of Kathmandu, feeling a bit like Indiana Jones on a special mission.

The ancient capital of the Kingdom of Nepal is situated in a mountain valley, surrounded by awesome snow-capped peaks. The peaks, however, conspire to keep the exhausts of factory and airport hanging like an ominous dark cloud over the city. The smog seeped into my body, and within days of arrival, I went to bed with one of the few headaches of my life.

It was good to see Princess Shobha again. After greetings and embraces all around, she had nurses bring in the twins. Eight months old now, they seemed to be all eyes. Manuja was active and demanding, keenly interested in all her surroundings while her brother, Himavan, looked placid and controlled, calmly observing the two newcomers and just biding his time. These two little beings were unique in Nepal history. They were the first twins born in the royal household, the first children born out of the country, and the first born contrary to medical opinion.

We were placed in a fine suite on the ground floor of the home called 'Shobha Griha' and given a wonderful, intense schedule of sightseeing and entertaining that our hosts had devised for us. But first, we asked to see Swamiji.

In the fall of 1981, Swamiji had retreated to Nepal to help his body heal. He needed quiet and isolation so he could perform yogic practices to strengthen his nervous system and control the internal bleeding. One of his students owned the Yak and Yeti Hotel in Kathmandu and offered a room there. When Swamiji heard that the locals believed one floor of the hotel was haunted by terrible ghosts, he asked for that space. No one, not even the hotel staff, was brave enough to disturb the great yogi living on the haunted floor. Swamiji spent the days in rest and practice, writing, supervising the expansion of the hotel flower garden, and planning work on his next project, Hansda Ashram.

He had always loved challenges and here was another. The royal family had given him a piece of mountain land overrun with scraggly bushes and loose rocks, but 5600 feet high—the perfect height for healthy living. The property lay twelve miles east of the city, near the town of Banepa, and adjacent to the ancient and notorious Silk Road used for trade with the Far East. There was no road up the mountain, but only a foot path used by the small village nestled in its lower folds. Here he would build a new spiritual community.

Appraising the cone-shaped plot, Swamiji designed a series of ascending ridges, each with its distinctive collection of trees and shrubs to hold the soil, culminating in a plateau with brick sleeping rooms, a kitchen, a classroom, and a meditation room all built around two courtyards. A pageant of organically grown vegetables and flowers ringed its way around the whole. Almost like magic, a hidden well was found a few yards from the main buildings to produce channeled water for human consumption and plant irrigation. From the wide plateau one could enjoy breakfast while gazing upon the world's highest mountain range displayed before one's eyes or look down at the occasional traffic on the Silk Road far below.

Swamiji moved to the ashram as soon as the first rooms were complete and continued to supervise its expansion; he made bricks, dug in the soil to plant flowers, and cooked his special mountain bread for the workers. Chandon Swaroop, one of Swamiji's newer students, left her executive position in New Delhi as often as she could to bring a mother's touch and a hotel administrator's expertise to the practical running of the ashram. After awhile Swamiji invited international students to come for a retreat which involved plenty of manual labor as well. Charles and Phil and the Institute brought groups and much-needed goods, Samskriti and Gopala brought their new baby, Dr. Agnihotri and Virat came to help. Everyone wanted to be near Swamiji, now frequently called Baba, and enjoy the incredible beauty of the ashram. Dignitaries came for advice, climbing up the mountain to the sage and leaving with sure ideas and added blessings. Members of the Nepalese Parliament came often; principals of the Indian embassy were frequent guests; European politicians and Japanese businessmen flew in by jet. On several occasions Rajiv Gandhi drove quietly across the frontier to visit his mother's old friend and request counsel on affairs of state.

Swamiji came for Theresa and me two days after our arrival. Princess Shobha had the children propped up on a sofa to receive his blessing, and as the two of them watched the sage enter the room, they slowly, and in perfect unison, bowed their little heads before him, just as if they knew his prayers had brought them to this plane.

We were excited to be with Swamiji again, and we celebrated all day. We went to the Annapurna Restaurant for dinner, the Yak and Yeti Hotel for tea, the garden for rest, all the time listening to his wonderful stories about new adventures in the Himalayas and the hauntings of the hotel. He looked cheerful and strong, better than we had seen him in a long time. Only talk of the recent death of his beloved Master brought us to solemnity. "He dropped his body so he could give me part of his life," Swamiji said sadly. Remembrances of that great saint filled the next few minutes and I recalled that a few years ago our teacher had promised that we would meet his master. "Would we never have the grace of his presence now?" I wondered.

But soon it was off to the hotel jewelry store to buy Theresa earrings and necklaces, bracelets and rings, Swamiji insisting that she have all that she wanted. "Do you like this one? This? What about the turquoise?" Theresa was stunned, nodding her head, trying to decide what she should do about the strange behavior of her teacher. As the day ended, Swamiji left us to return to the ashram, promising we would be together again soon and asking us to thoroughly enjoy our royal vacation.

As the days passed, we explored the cobbled streets of the old city, the incredible temples and shops lining the roads, the neighboring ancient cities. We visited the Buddhist community in exile from Tibet, the medieval squares on market day, the native peoples wearing clothing styles hundreds of years old. We were interested in everything, intrigued by the simplicity and devotion of the people, angered by their poverty and exploitation.

One evening, the King and Queen came to Princess Shobha's estate to honor her birthday and to welcome us to their country. Protocol was followed, even though everyone in the room except us was family. No one sat until the king and queen did; when they stood up, everyone stood. No one spoke until their majesties broke the silence. When they did, we were asked our opinions of the country, our ideas about the twins, our personal backgrounds, and our history with our teacher. Warmth flowed as we reminisced over Princess Shobha's days in New York and the medical care she had received there. The topic of stress arose naturally, and naturally I mentioned the therapeutic benefits of yogic breathing for hypertension. Everyone's focus was immediately heightened, questions flowed, and teachings from the tradition filled the room. I was asked to instruct the king's older sister in breathing, and I promised to make a breath tape incorporating the yogic techniques for all the family to use.

Conversation turned to the beliefs regarding the sacred mountains well known in this region. The yogis had lived there for hundreds of years, seeking both the solitude and the long tradition of sanctity to be found within their caves. The old king and his wife had always protected the yogis, even keeping some mountains inaccessible to the public so that the yoga tradition could flourish there without interference. Now the king said that this kind of reverence had originated with poorly educated local inhabitants and was sustained merely for profit. From the tone of his voice, the Harvard-educated new king seemed to indicate that the beliefs of holiness were truly primitive and that he did not agree with them.

The fact that we were eating dinner with the heads of one of the few remaining theocracies in the world was not mentioned, but the subtle nuances were everywhere. The very religious (and sometimes very superstitious) people of Nepal regard their king as an incarnation of the God Vishnu and the Queen as an incarnation of the Goddess Lakshmi. The royal couple assured us that their citizens were happy and wholly committed to the monarchy. "This is what they desire to live by," they assured us.

The Queen then began a mini-sermon about real swamis as opposed to fake ones. "Genuine swamis live in huts," she said, "not five-star hotels. They wear old, torn robes, not suits. They wander about barefoot, begging for food from others; they do not wear leather shoes and eat in restaurants. Real swamis don't travel first class!" she emphasized disdainfully.

She sat on the plush sofa, wrapped in silk and bedecked with huge diamonds and emeralds at wrists, neck, ears, and hair, looking very satisfied with her just-delivered dissertation on the absolute criteria for genuine sainthood. Obviously, she disapproved of certain swamis, and it didn't take much imagination to figure out whom she wished to persecute that night. Her husband picked up his beer and nodded in approval.

I could feel my Irish starting to rise to the occasion. "Your Majesty," I said, "your interesting elaboration reminds me of a story.

"Once a stranger went walking through a small town," I began. "His upright bearing, clean attire, and cordial greeting to the villagers led the mayor to ascertain that the new arrival, resting in their best hotel, was indeed a wealthy and worthy gentleman. They eagerly approached him requesting that he make a contribution to the city council's favorite charity. Reading their hearts, the stranger politely declined, stating that he would help the poor in other ways. So the mayor and his council dismissed the stranger as a rogue and blocked all his efforts to assist the local poor, for that enterprise might embarrass the mayor. They closed the school he started for the children because surely someone better should do that. They denied permission to build a business for the unemployed. Soon the officials tired of his very presence and spread the rumor that the man was not all he appeared to be. They sought ways to hurry him out of town until they succeeded. The mayor and the council did not recognize the visitor for the great man he was. Like pickpockets looking at a saint, all they saw were pockets."

Silence ensued in the room. "We must be careful," the queen said after a few minutes, "not to see only saints."

When dessert was served, the king told us about some of his future plans for opening Nepal to the world. He thought more and more trekking areas should be preserved by the Park Authority and become one of the ways the country would be known.

Two days later Swamiji came by to collect us for a visit. We told him about the family dinner and listened while he spoke about the history of Nepal, from King Birendra's grandfather until the present. He said that a great yogi adept in our tradition, Goruknath, had predicted a thousand years ago that in the future Nepal would have a twelve-generation kingdom and that it would end soon after. Customarily, a yogi from our tradition had always blessed the next king in childhood, from the first coronation years ago, to the present king's son, assuring his succession to the throne.

The queen had been a great fan of our teacher until he had insisted on his own authority in spiritual matters. Swamiji would no longer visit the palace itself, despite invitations, he explained, because the teachings could not be interfered with in any way by mere secular authority. Since then, the royal helicopter no longer flew by the ashram in respect each time the royal pair left town.

"You both should understand the whole of the past few years as a divine unfolding. No royal money was involved at all. This drama is strictly a Himalayan game played by the sages and the civil powers. Everything here is a dream. Certain things are dialogues with the mind, not with God, just as one can't understand some scriptures unless one does the appropriate practices. The sages sent you to meet the king and queen, but this is not the first time you have helped me with such things. We have been together in many lives doing the work of the sages."

I could only guess at the multiple levels occurring simultaneously that he was talking about. I had only an inkling that we were playing some important part in an historical drama and was pleased to be working with my teacher again.

As royal house guests, our days were filled with one excursion after another. We flew around the top of Sargamartha, "The Brow of the Oceans," the world's highest peak (also known as Mount Everest) in a small plane, thrilled to see this special place; we entered ancient Hindu temples and clapped for the Child Goddess to come to her window and smile a blessing; we rode elephants through the jungle on safari and camped out in a treetop hut; we tiptoed through the midnight grasses to watch a wild Siberian tiger devour her evening dinner. With Shobha and Mohan we climbed to small mountain villages whose inhabitants came en masse to receive the princess's blessing, we explored foreign agricultural experiments, rode river boats and unusual ferries, and even went to the prince's Golden Eagle brewery, where I tasted the pure mountain water soon to be turned into beer. We walked in dry river beds and slept in the island hotel near Pokara; we camped at the snow line, playing Uno in the tent, and awoke in the early hours to find the full moon leaning on the twin peaks of Machhapuchhare, "The Fishtail," the forbidden holy mountain.

We were in the land of the Gurkhas now, those renowned soldiers who achieved such recognition for their bravery that they were known as "the bravest of the brave." Because of their fearless daring, Nepal has never succumbed to an enemy, not even to the large, powerful, British army.

The queen had recommended that we visit a "real" swami living in a small village close by, so we went with a guide by jeep, following the old dirt roads and walking through several dirty farm yards. In an old cement house surrounded by animals lived the swami—poor, simple, and sweet. He offered us boiled milk to drink with him and told us to say a mantra so the milk would not harm us. He used the mantra to make sure he never ate bad food, he told us. Seeing our camera, he asked if we would like his picture. He straightened his robe, patted his hair, and lifted his chin for the camera. We took a photo and left for the ashram. The next time we saw Swamiji, we told him about our visit with the old renunciate. "A sage would never use that mantra for himself; it is only for the good of others," he said quietly. When the roll of film was eventually developed, every picture on it was perfect but that one. In the middle of the roll, where the "real" swami should have been, was a blank piece of film.

One day a U.S. Marine delivered a small white envelope for us at Shoba Griha. It was an invitation to afternoon tea with the American Ambassador to Nepal, Carlton Coon, and his wife. We were delighted to walk through the little streets into the beautiful

Justin and Theresa with their godchildren

American compound. The ambassador brought us into a piece of our country, right in the midst of the strange, busy city. We drank tea from porcelain cups as we answered question after question about the royal family. Apparently it was unheard of for any foreigner to be invited to such intimacy in this monarchy, and Mr. Coon wondered why we were. Hearing of the children, he was pleased to learn that they were born in America and happy that we had such important friends in Nepal. Promising that we would meet again, the ambassador had us whisked back to our rooms in a big, black American limousine.

Finally, after several wonderful weeks, we packed up our clothes, kissed Shobha and Mohan and the babies, and rushed off to Hansda Ashram to live with a different sort of royalty.

Adventures at Hansda Ashram

Life at the new ashram was wonderful. One got out of one's taxi on the road below, lifted suitcases and bags to head and shoulders, crossed carefully and slowly over a large tree trunk thrown across the ravine, and began to climb. One passed the fields of vegetables climbing up the mountain, walked by the village houses with excited children running out to see someone new, and finally arrived at the wooden ashram gate painted with the rules of community life: hours of silence, meditation, meals, and appointments. Swamiji set us up in the newest completed brick building, with mortar not quite dry. In this cold weather, only the young American Charlie was there with a few village men and two village girls who came to cook each day. Swamiji had quiet time to spend with us until the weather changed and guests would arrive again, so we were especially blessed to have him all to ourselves. Some days we all went into town to buy provisions or meet various business people who asked for guidance or offered donations to the ashram; most days we just stayed at the ashram amidst those serene, ever-present snow-capped mountains.

Spending so much time with Swamiji, I was struck by his concern for people's bodily needs. We would be walking along, just chatting and window shopping, when suddenly he would say, "Let's have some chai." or "How about some food?" In a car, his face would beam suddenly, and we would stop for a picnic or pull over to the roadside for chai and pastries. After years with him, I knew it wasn't for him; he ate very little, especially for a man of his size. But he was very aware of our stomach growls or our thirst. Anyone who came to the ashram was immediately offered water and food or tea after their climb. The girls who worked at the ashram had the reputation of quickly becoming the fattest in the village. A remark Swamiji made the year before returned to mind: "Guru is more than father; once he accepts you, then he will do anything for you."

In the cold evenings, we would sit with him before the little log fire in his room and watch as he peered into the flames, poking at them before speaking.

"I used to heal people and tell them about it. Now I heal but remain quiet, working through others anonymously." He continued to stir the fire. "It is time now for you to speak from intuition."

Most of the time we would sit in silence, just enjoying the ambiance as time flew by. Naturally, he caught us off guard many times. "You have a complex: you measure yourself by brick and mortar. Why do you worry? You have been blessed and you don't know it."

Since that was my twelfth year with him, I had learned not to argue, but just to listen and learn what I could so I would not distract him or send him back into silence. "I am only an instrument of the sages," he said now, "a receiver and transmitter of their wisdom." After a brief spell looking at the fire he said, "Learn to enjoy everything in the world but don't establish proprietorship, otherwise it will bring disturbance. Justin, you are a king-maker, not a king. Be free."

Sometimes he asked rhetorical questions: "Why do people make sex an evil thing? It is one of God's joys, and should be used as an offering of love, a gift of being human." A little later he said, "People can't be talked out of their foolishness; they can only be trained out of it."

Once he came out of the quietness to say, "You should speak wisdom all the time and not only in your lectures."

One evening he spoke of a friend of his who had died in Europe, and he began to chant a little poem: "People die, people are reborn. For whom shall I rejoice? For whom shall I mourn?"

We always stayed in Swamiji's room until it was time for his meditation practice. Then he would say good-night or ask if we were sleepy and we'd regretfully leave his presence; sometimes he would walk us to our room so we could all enjoy the night around us in the open.

On one night we heard a wild animal roar nearby and Swamiji told us it was the female leopard. At first I thought he was joking, then I thought his words were an exaggeration, then I was not sure what to think as the sound grew clearer.

The next morning Swamiji came to our door early. "Be quiet," he said, "and come with me."

We walked slowly and carefully to the edge of the courtyard and followed his pointing finger. There, stretched out on a large tree branch, was a big, beautiful leopard. On the branch just below and in front of her lay three little leopard cubs.

The chief guard for the ashram was the elder from the little village halfway down the mountain. He was a good man, kind and gentle, yet strong and very honest. Swamiji loved him, and the feeling was mutual. When Swamiji first arrived to build the ashram, he was invited to the village where he taught the people, checked their health, and played with the children. Soon he could not walk down the mountain without shouts of "Baba, Baba!" from all directions. He sat down with the village chief and others to determine what he could do to help them best, and was requested to provide medical care, sorely lacking in most of the valley outside Kathmandu. Soon a small clinic was built by our teacher and staffed by his students. Medicine was sent from Swamiji's centers around the world and freely distributed by the doctors to whomever needed it.

Then Swamiji noticed that the children were cold, that the women did not have enough clothing to be comfortable as the weather grew chill. So again a notice went out across America to send used clothing and blankets, towels and shoes. Theresa witnessed those American castoffs become treasures during one distribution event. Our teacher, students from the ashram, and several Nepali women carried down the newly arrived boxes and suitcases of clothing. The villagers came out of their poor homes and stood in a large circle around Swamiji, who opened the first box, held up a shirt, and carried it over to the eldest person he thought could fit in it. He instructed the women to do the same, and went back to the box to find things for the little ones.

Everyone received at least one item and then the boxes were left for the villagers to find anything else they liked. In the end, a strange procession marched by the Americans: there were several children with mis-matched shoes prancing proudly home in their new clothes, women with men's shirts buttoned over their saris clutching blankets and towels, men with brightly-colored baseball caps added to their jeans tied with rope, toddlers carrying stuffed toys, women holding filmy nightgowns, not sure what to do with them, and one old man with a white bra tied firmly around his head. All smiled broadly and walked away happy that others had remembered them and sent gifts.

Next Swamiji studied what the villagers could do to help themselves. He found that the women climbed high into the mountains to get water for cooking and washing, sometimes carrying large oil cans of water on their heads for five miles. Swamiji collected donations from Indian and Nepali businessmen and bought pipe, constructing a water system from the source of the water up in the mountains to the little villages below. He provided water for bathing and cooking and cleaning to three villages, changing their lifestyle for the better.

Following that project was one to provide commodes to the villages so that people would not have to go out into the cold forest to relieve themselves. We were all surprised to learn that first he had to teach them how to use a toilet! "Priests preach to people about God, but yogis teach them about their bodies and minds as well" was a phrase often spoken and much practiced by our teacher.

It was then with much sorrow that he learned that the government had begun to tax all the incoming medicine for the free clinic, the donated office supplies, and the equipment for education. Duties were placed even on the used clothing. Requests for new roads were denied, and electricity began to turn on and off inexplicably on our mountain. That was the situation when Theresa and I arrived.

The new ashram in January and February was a cold place. High in the hills without heating as we were, our buckets of water froze overnight, making for an interesting morning shower. Occasionally Swamiji asked the staff to gather more wood in the forest so that water could be heated for a full bucket bath, but usually we said that everything was fine.

One morning as I shivered and dried myself off, my mind, going negative with cold, came up with an old, rankling grievance. For years I had taught most of the meditation classes at the Institute, but I was never made an initiator by my teacher. I believed I should have been offered the honor of giving mantra initiation to others. The thought popped up like it had before, only this time I chuckled to myself and dropped it. It didn't matter anymore, so I simply gave it up. My laugh barely faded when that familiar voice rang out loud and clear across the compound, "Justy!"

I quickly pulled my on pants and ran across the inner courtyard to Swamiji's room. I looked carefully at him wondering what to expect.

"Today, I'm making you an initiator," he said matter-of-factly. "See me about it tonight!"

"Hmmm," I thought to myself as I walked thoughtfully back to my room. "What else can I give up?"

UPANISHADIC EVENINGS

That night my life took another upturn. The sun vanished behind those magnificent giants and a familiar cold wave of evening darkened our region. Slowly, by the light of a single, huge burning log, Swamiji began his revelations.

"Mantras are sounds. Sounds are known, not by their meaning, but by their vibrations, for they are not words. The more you remember the sound quietly, silently, without moving the tongue, even without using breath, the more the sounds vibrate and transform the whole personality. Only a few sounds are meant to be coordinated with breath.

"The latter part of the *Vedas*, the most ancient scriptures of humankind, are known as the *Upanishads*. One of them, the *Swetasvatara*, declares that the sages of ancient lore received these sounds in profound meditation and contemplation. They imparted this knowledge to their disciples and thus it is passed on to the desirous and the deserving. When you remember your mantra continuously, your practice is called *japa*. When you continue assimilating it and make it a predominate part of your nature, it is then called *ajapa-japa*.

"The sounds are like seeds which contain all the potentials to become manifest. I sow the seed in the soil which you are; your job is to allow the seed to grow by nurturing it, that is, remembering it. Fifty percent of the work is the tradition's job, fifty percent is your job.

"Mantra is the representative of the ultimate reality. It introduces you, no, it leads you, to the soundless sound, the very foundation of love and life. For all things in the universe have come from sound, even light. To grow into this state, you also need to embrace two qualities described in the scriptures. First, develop devotion to practice itself, *abhaysa*. Second, foster the attitude of non-attachment, *vairagya*.

"Many things will come up in your mediation as they do in the world. Along the way, you will get hunches, ideas, symbols, fantasies often mixed together in your mind. Some may be pleasant, some not so. It doesn't matter. You must stay centered with your mantra and go beyond name and form to the silence."

All my university learning never even hinted at the realm of sound as an educational tool. There was so much material to explore already in his words that I wish there were two of me—one to continue listening while the other started pondering and experimenting with the topic. Obviously, sound affects the human organism. Music is an irrefutable example. Where in school did we learn that special sounds bear a vibratory power that could heal human tissue as well as directly affect the mind?

Swamiji then explained the various types of mantras and discoursed on the major ones—*Gayatri, Maha Mrtyunjaya* and *Ganapati*—along with their mythology. He taught about the various types of mala beads. He discussed and cautioned me about healing mantras, indicating their therapeutic power. Previous to this evening with him, he had introduced us to mantras corresponding to the divine feminine principle and now elaborated on devotion to the Divine Mother and the sacred sounds to honor her. Then he elaborated on the range of seed sound, *bija*, highlighting the various qualities of human manifestation that emerged from them. Finally he explained how certain mantras are especially deployed by our tradition.

"The sacred sounds of mantras are eternal; they are not invented and unless the initiator is truly linked with a living tradition, then any mantras dispersed are impotent."

The next day we three went into town to meet some of Swamiji's Indian friends at the Yak and Yeti Hotel. The owner, a close follower of my teacher, tried to convince me to stay on as hotel manager, but I knew the sages had other work for me to do.

We drove to the Indian Embassy where we met the ambassador and other dignitaries, many of them students also. We talked politics and peace, future plans and past problems. Sitting in the cool living room, I enjoyed the fact that I was with such important, world-changing people. But soon I began to feel a chill inside and shifted my attention from Swamiji to the thought that it would probably be poor manners if I got up to put my new jacket on. To the surprise of everyone in the room, Swamiji abruptly blurted out, "What are you thinking?"

Eyes darted around the room, bouncing off each person as the group tried to guess whom he was addressing. I was struck by his sudden intensity and a little embarrassed, because I knew he referred to me.

Barely finishing his sentence, Swamiji walked across the room and beckoned me over to him. He slipped the jacket on me and smiled. We sat a little while longer as the discussion continued, but I could only think of one thing. I kept returning in my mind to that 'shift' of thought. He had the ability to know the micro-second when we switch our train of thought in any direction. I realized anew that Swamiji was more aware of us than we are of ourselves.

I remembered an event that had taken place in front of me years earlier. My friend, Martin, had been waiting for weeks to ask our teacher a list of questions. He was finally called for an appointment, and he and his wife, Colleen, went to see their teacher. Swamiji proceeded to engage Colleen exclusively in a friendly conversation about the family and her other interests. Martin could not get even one of his questions in edgewise. Swamiji ended the appointment then, and Martin, with his list of questions burning a hole in his pocket, got up to leave. As they stood up, Swamiji called out, "Martin!" and then proceeded to utter seven statements—the answers, in the exact order, to the seven questions on the list in Martin's pocket. Both bewildered and grateful, Martin asked his teacher how he knew the questions. Swamiji smiled and replied, "The moment you think, I know."

Although I enjoyed the brief visits to Kathmandu with my

teacher, I preferred the days and nights at the ashram. Always there were stories.

"My master was very patient with me," Swamiji said one evening. "I wrote poetry, painted, studied music and sang, tried many instruments. He put up with these interests for awhile, but finally let me know I should stop them. 'Don't be a dilettante,' he shouted at me, 'you were born to be a meditator.' Actually, I was his worse student, for I practiced only when I was in the mood. But I always knew that he loved me. My master was pleased that I do what I say I'm going to do, but he always laughed and said that no one can make me do anything else. 'He is without lust for this world—he is my son' was something my master said frequently. He always insisted that I learn the ways of the world well so that I could be of best service to the world. My yoga training was thus unique and fitted for the world we live in now.

"Much as we all value Shankara's writings, they have an emphasis that does not suit our times. His commentaries are written strictly from a perspective of a renunciate. The object of life is not to renounce this world, as the great saint says; renunciation is only for a blessed few. Most people rather need to live fully in this world and yet remain above it. For most people integration, rather than renunciation, is the path."

When Swamiji paused, I found myself thinking that this was a corrective to much other-wordly spirituality. I found it very liberating, much as I loved the idea of renunciation. As I got to know various students in yoga over the years, I was amazed how many of them were closet Calvinists, knowingly or not. They were afraid of making too much money, of getting involved with society, of trusting their sensuality, appreciating beauty, enjoying their sexuality, or having ambitions. In a way, they tended to be more Buddhist than yogic, but I was pleased that at least they did not disdain the body like many of my intellectual Vedanta friends.

"Shankara wrote all his commentaries by the time he was eighteen," Swamiji continued. "His extra fifteen years of life were given to him by the sage Vyasa."

Suddenly he switched the topic. I loved being surprised by the twists and sudden turns in his conversation that led to different topics. "You know, I once turned down the Jewel of India Award, which is rarely given, to be able to work in silence. I withdraw myself from things to help you with your health and work and meditation. This is very exhausting to me, for you are hard people, more difficult than you think. There is too much individualism in America. It gives you difficulty in building something together."

Swamiji stared into the darkness outside, sitting very still. After some time he spoke again. "I have one mind here, another at work," he said. "One is in spiritual bliss, and one is at my master's feet." His beaming smile almost lit the room.

Lama Govinda and the plum tree

CHAPTER 20
WORKING WITH THE SAGES

As I walked with Swamiji in the beautiful mountains,
I burst into tears, bent over with emotion. I blurted out
how much I wished that I had concentrated even more
when he had spoken in the past. I felt I had not grown a
bit in all the decades I had spent with my great teacher.
"Don't weep," he told me. "We are not finished. I have
many interesting things for you to do yet."

ONE BEAUTIFUL DAY IN FEBRUARY, Swamiji, Theresa and I ate our ashram lunch together and then walked outdoors to enjoy the sunny weather. I told him about the dream. "Yes, you both have much work to do," he said seriously.

We sat down by a dead tree just past the garden wall. Swamiji had been cleaning his teeth after the meal and spat out his mouthwash on the dry twigs. "Now it will grow," he said softly. I remembered the violets in Honesdale years ago and knew that he spoke truth.

"Something important is coming," he told us. "You should prepare yourselves for Thursday." As usual, our teacher gave no clue as to what would transpire in a few days, but we were asked to fast in preparation. We also bathed in the cold morning water, donned clean clothes, and then walked up to the appointed place: a small plateau on the mountain near the ashram. Swamiji joined us and asked us to face north toward Gauri Shankar Mountain, the holy place where he and his master had spent many years doing practice. We bowed to the mountain, beseeching the master's blessing on all we did, and turned on our tape recorder.

Swamiji closed his eyes, lifted his head and spoke, but it was not his voice; it was a soft, light voice, heavily accented and full of warmth. Swamiji was in a deep trance and it was his master who addressed us. He gave his intuitive diagnosis of our health for the remainder of our lives. He told us things that happened to us as children which no one knew about, promises about our future, many other useful and wonderful things. He told us our work at the Institute in Honesdale was complete and that there was new work for us to do. "See this boy once a year," Swamiji's master said about his son, "and tell him that what I promise he must do for you." With a final blessing, the words stopped; only the wind whispered softly through the tall pine trees.

When Swamiji regained his consciousness a few minutes later, he asked to hear the tape. We all sat together, stunned and sad and full of joy all at the same time as we listened to Bengali Baba's kind and prophetic words.

Swamiji told us that the visit from his master was a promised gift and our completion of a level in the tradition. "Tomorrow there will be additional gifts for you, so prepare yourselves," he added.

It was shortly after 8:00 AM the next day when Swamiji joined us on the top of another small mountain above the ashram. Theresa and I had bathed again in the cold water and climbed the path with bundles of sticks as instructed, noting leopard scat along the way.

Beside a small fire, Swamiji conducted an ancient ceremony for us. As he chanted the sounds of a sacred mantra, the atmosphere around us was tangibly filled with energy. We threw our sticks, one by one, into the purifying fire. They represented all the actions of our lives. Our entire karmic history was burned to ashes and then transferred into the bowl of water next to the fire. During the ceremony I felt internal energy movements flowing between my heart and the space between my eyebrows. Up and down the energy flew as Theresa and I each threw one-hundred eight twigs into the fire.

"All your karmas are completely burned now," Swamiji said in a strange, solemn voice. "You have no past. Old memories may flair up in your mind, but they are now only an empty wisp with no power over you. Your past lives, including the seven times you were married to each other, are completely balanced, ended. At this point, you have no karma. Nothing can harm you, persuade you to act, or demand satisfaction. You will experience many things now so you should live by being selfless towards others."

We gathered the ashes from the burned sticks and put them in a jar. Swamiji told us they held powerful healing energy and should be used to help ourselves and others whenever we wished. He himself carried the bowl of water down the mountain to a plant growing against the ashram wall. We followed close behind, watching as he addressed the foot-high plant asking for its permission, and then poured the karmic fluid on it. Within three hours the plant had drooped down to the ground; it was dead the next morning. Swamiji made amends to Mother Nature, explaining why this event had taken place and thanking for the generosity of the plant.

The gifts flowed. Twice more the master spoke through his son to us. He enumerated the remedies for our physical well being, then made a psychological diagnosis, and finally proffered spiritual counsels for us both.

"You are to practice," he said, "a three-fold discipline for the rest of your lives. You are to follow the footprints of the sages." To me specifically he said, "You are not to sleep with any woman; you are on the path of self-surrender and conquest." The master concluded his visit with instructions for Swamiji, "Son, these are special people for you," he said, "they will carry out the mission."

Theresa and I pondered all the happenings that day and far into the night. They touched on the deepest fears and secret desires of our hearts, yet showed us the commitment of the sages to guide and protect us. Things I thought would happen in thirty years or so were pulled to the foreground; things I had not thought of for decades were displayed before my eyes. I was touched to hear that the sages had watched over me since childhood. The master had said, "When you fell down the stairs at three years of age, the sages protected you, promising to watch over you always." I knew that I had told no one, not even Theresa, about that serious accident and realized that many of the totally extraordinary happenings in my life must have happened because of the sages' grace.

The next day Chandon arrived from New Delhi, and Swami Ajaya and Dr. Arya returned to the ashram. We all went to Banepa, where Swamiji lectured to the town's people, urging them to do the ancient practice of meditation for their spiritual needs and take care of their physical needs as well. After the talk, as the crowds began to flock around him, Swamiji took off his own mala beads and placed them around my neck.

The people were frightened. They were concerned that our free clinic in the valley had been closed down by the government; they worried that the ashram staff would be leaving; they expressed gratitude for Swamiji's efforts on their behalf and asked what they should do next. The only university in Nepal had just been closed by order of the King after political lectures were held there. The evening before, one of the speakers had been found shot to death along the road.

Back in Swamiji's little room that evening, he spoke firmly to me. "I never curse, for my master said half of my curse would come back to me, but it is interesting that people won't accept my love unless it is on their own terms—money, health, political power, miracles, and so on. Watch what will happen and be careful of the occurrences.

"My mind is one quarter with students during the day and fully at night. Your minds come to me with questions, but you don't listen and hear only a little. How can I teach you when your mind blocks me? Come to me and sit in silence. I know your questions and will give you the answers. You and Dr. Arya show the religion of the sages—you in colleges and Arya among common people in India—so be careful with the sword of name and fame."

He told us a story of a time when he had gone to observe a famous adept who materialized gold rings and fine ash for his crowd of followers. Everyone was thrilled with the great miracles of the man, and his reputation grew day by day. When the adept walked up to Swamiji and asked what he wanted, our teacher replied that he wanted an old pair of sandals. The adept put his head down, smiled and said: 'Ah, you understand. I'm sorry.'

"No miracle or *siddhi* is ever done to attract the public," Swamiji said. "Why don't these men eliminate the impoverishment of the people they dazzle with their production of gold and ash? People are so gullible in thinking that these magicians are saints. Why could he not give me sandals? Because old sandals were not in his storeroom."

Swamiji explained that in the development of a special power, such as manifesting an item out of the air, the selected range is limited by one's training and spiritual progress. In this case, there were certain items previously placed in a warehouse—semi-precious stones, ash, and golden charms holding the yogi's picture—which could be retrieved on call, but nothing else. Saints have divine resources, however, which transcend these elementary states of competence. They can implore all of creation to respond to their unselfish requests and are usually answered.

"One afternoon my master called out for me but I replied that I was meditating. He came over and kicked me on my bottom and scolded me for faking meditation. Some of my student teachers are like that. They feel insecure and unconsciously need public acknowledgment that they are yogis. They assume an air that they think looks holy and hope it won't be missed by their students and the public.

"My master reminded me that I would have to go through fire. How can one grow otherwise? My whole life has been a series of helping others followed by persecutions, but I don't care—it keeps me free. Long ago, my master gave me a boon and a curse: 'You will succeed in what you do and then the people will turn against you.' I realize that he doesn't want me to become attached to anyone."

He turned his head to Theresa, knowing what concern was running through her mind at the moment. "You don't have to worry, you won't turn away, nor am I throwing you out of my life. You are with me on the path; the others weren't."

With that remark, my thoughts were transported to some scenes a few years earlier at Honesdale. I was jolted back when he said, "I remain civil to everyone but keep myself apart. I have never done anything I have regretted and am never in a state of anger. Righteous anger gives strength, but uncontrolled anger can lead to disaster.

"I once dropped in on a lawyer's home when I was very hungry. He was upstairs cleaning his shotgun while his wife was preparing *kheer*, an Indian pudding, in the kitchen. I came into the house and said I was hungry and asked for some of the pudding. The woman refused me so I raised my voice and insisted. She implored me to go away, but I felt insulted and reminded her that she must have forgotten her manners to a wandering *sadhu*. Then I went over to the pot to help myself to some of the food.

"Meanwhile, the husband heard the commotion downstairs and thought his wife was being molested behind locked doors. He blasted a warning shot through the floor, rushed downstairs, blasted the kitchen door off its hinges and ran into the room. He looked at me calmly praying over my bowl of *kheer*, saw his wife standing on the far side of the kitchen, and could not make sense out of the situation since it didn't match his emotional expectation. At the same time, I thought that it didn't matter to me if they wanted to kill each other, I was going to eat *kheer*. The frozen moment between the three of us was broken suddenly by the wife screaming to me not to eat the *kheer* for it was poisoned. She slapped it out of my hand and began to cry. The husband calmed down, apologized to me, and turned to his wife, weeping in the corner. It turned out that she and her lover had planned to poison the husband that day. I had spoiled it by wandering in and demanding food.

"My master scolded me for going into people's houses uninvited. He told me not to force my hunger on anyone and never to beg. That's why I rarely stay with people. Here in Nepal many influencial people criticize my lifestyle, but I follow the orders of my master. Others expect me to live in a hovel, wearing worn out shawls. It shocks their portrait of a holy man that I enjoy the things of the world, but I take whatever God gives me."

We then had chai, which on those winter nights was the best possible elixer.

"My master told me that snakes are the oldest creatures," Swamiji continued. "A snake can live in water, on the ground, or in a tree, and it never messes. It leaves off its skin each year and resides in a hole made by others. Its chief food—it can refrain from solid nourishment for six months—is *vayu*, air. A snake is like a yogi and a yogi should be like a snake.

"Why do I bother building things, if I'm leaving?" he asked rhetorically. "I know that my student, Dr. Sunanda Bai, understands me. She knows that my work is for humanity, regardless of the criticism, the time spent, or the results. I want to keep myself busy to the end."

It was hard for me to imagine any end at all. Wouldn't our teacher be with us forever?

POLITICS IN NEPAL

The next night, all the lights throughout the valley went off for four minutes in honor of the death of Yuri Andropov, General Secretary of the USSR. Swamiji, who had met the party head during his teaching days in Moscow, asked Theresa and me to offer his condolences at the Russian Embassy in Kathmandu. We entered the fortress-like building not knowing what to expect. Huge red banners hung across the walls, garlands of flowers encircled the painting of the deceased, and tall, armed stoldiers quietly and respectfully ushered us into the memorial room where a service was just about to begin. The Chinese delegation entered, bowing to all of us in the circle of mourners; the Koreans entered and saluted; the Afghanis marched in and eyed us curiously. After short remembrances by the Russians and a few guests, each visitor passed by the large portrait of Andropov, bowed to his memory, and left the room, signing the guest book on their way out. Theresa and I were nervous about signing, but we proudly left Swamiji's gift for the ambassador, his new book, *Enlightenment Without God.*

The next day the Indian ambassador called to say that the CIA wanted to know who the Americans were who had entered the Russian Embassy and why they had been there.

The moon was barely a sliver in the darkness of the star-filled sky. The ashram compound was fast asleep. Shots rang out in the stillness, followed by loud thumps on the metal roofs. Students woke up, confused and frightened. Without electricity in the late night hours, we all dressed rapidly and ran outside cautiously with our flashlights.

"Everyone come here into the patio," Swamiji ordered. When the local mountain men ran up from the village below to check on our safety, Swamiji asked them to scout about and search for the culprits. Rifles had been fired and rocks had been thrown on our tin roofs, but no damage was done to the compound and no one was hurt. Swamiji told us not to worry and tripled the guards for the remaining hours of the night, a practice which became the norm until we left Nepal.

We learned that the village guards had chased one of the attackers over the hills but he had escaped in the direction of the capital. It was obvious to us where the trouble had originated. I didn't care, to say the least, for the students being threatened this way and went to see Swamiji after supper. Well past midnight we talked, planning strategy. A mission was given to me and I felt honored to carry it out.

The next day the capital police arrived to collect information.

We sent them away, calmly replying that nothing was amiss. Swamiji sent all the guests out of the ashram and into city hotels for their safety, keeping with him only a handful of us. At the same time, I sent a pointed letter to the queen asking for a private audience.

The royal acceptance came a few days later when the queen flew in by helicopter and met with me in a large palace chamber. I walked in feeling such inner strength and clarity of mind that I was able to focus exclusively on the mission given to me. The articulation of the message came without hesitation, and as I spoke, my strength increased so that I realized that I dominated the entire engagement. I reviewed the content of my letter, citing more information about the workings of power. I reenforced the fact that I and my American colleagues were outraged and insulted that a craven attack could be directed at a holy ashram especially considering who lived there. We had been invited as guests to the country, had shared our knowledge, money, and skills with her countrymen and women, and had asked for nothing in return. I demanded to know why our charitable efforts on behalf of her people were constantly interfered with and suppressed. I asked why every improvement for the impoverished mountain people was sabotaged. I gave recommendations for honesty and generosity to the multitudes. The queen sat stiffly with her back to the brightly lit window wearing dark sunglasses. After a half hour, I ended the meeting, stood up, and walked out of the palace, fearing nothing.

Two days later I received a summons from the Head of the Royal Army to meet with him the next day. Again Swamiji and I planned my words carefully. Pandit Dr. Arya accompanied me as I went to meet the powerful Gurkha general on his grounds. We sat across from each other as he began politely softening the unfortunate event at our ashram. I bruskly interrupted him to repeat the same outrage displayed to the queen and added a few more inquiries about his own conduct. Every time he tried to answer, I interrupted again and gave him more private, intimate, uncomfortable information about himself and his maneuverings until he started smoking one cigarette after another. Finally I told my opponent that this meeting appeared to be a waste of time and walked out.

The next day, as a few of us sat on the mountain patio, we saw a large, black car stop on the Silk Road below. A man, dressed in a white shirt and dark pants began the climb up the mountain. We watched for twenty minutes as he climbed until he finally presented a letter addressed to me at the ashram gate. It was an embossed invitation, asking that Theresa and I attend a party in honor of the king and queen at the American Embassy. We stayed at Shobha Griha that day and left the house just before the princess. As we entered the magnificent party tent, the Marine band played, the glasses clinked, and the ambassador greeted us warmly, if nervously. "I will introduce you to the royal couple if you come near me when they enter," he told us, and we all laughed when he realized that we knew them quite well.

People were talking about the unfortunate attack on the ashram and repeating Swamiji's statement that it would soon be closed. Across the room I spied the general staring at me as he spoke with other guests until I was distracted by the formal arrival of Princess Shobha and Prince Mohan, representing the king and queen, who had mysteriously left town two days earlier.

As the party continued, an American worked his way over to me to ask why the Gurkha general had pointed to me and said, "I'm afraid of that man."

I half smiled and excused myself, thanking the sages for giving me courage under fire as the Himalayan drama played itself out once again.

SYMPOSIUM ON HOLISTIC HEALTH

Swamiji, Dr. Arya, Swami Ajaya, Theresa and I all sat together looking across at the mountains. Used to the years of conferences we had helped run in America, Theresa suggested that we should have a conference in Kathmandu. The patio became electrified; everyone offered suggestions and inspirations. We realized that this would be a first in the history of Nepal and decided to make it a rich educational experience for the triple-cities of the valley. We divided up assignments: Swamiji planned the guest list, Swami Ajaya and I began to write articles for the newspapers, Pandit Arya composed the schedule of lecture topics, Theresa worked out the design for the publicity. Doctors Rajinder Singh and A.P. Singh were asked to speak and demonstrate biofeedback; Barbara Bova was asked to leave her schooling in New Delhi to demonstrate hatha yoga. We all speeded up the normal three months of work to fill three very full weeks.

Swamiji had a strong reputation among the foreign governments in town, especially since he had patched up a few rough spots between India and Nepal, so Theresa and I went from one embassy to another throughout Kathmandu to personally invite the ambassadors and their staffs to attend Nepal's First International Symposium on Holistic Health. We were received with much respect and honor, bringing back promises of a fine foreign attendance. All attention was then focused on the conference: February 23 through 25 at the Everest Sheraton Hotel.

Some members of the royal family did not like our idea for educating the citizens in yoga and meditation and managed to stop our advertisements in the newspapers. After my article about holistic health was printed in the *Rising Nepal* newspaper, the publisher suddenly ran out of space for future articles. Nevertheless, we hand delivered flyers to all the foreign embassies, hotels, plazas, and offices throughout the cities. The villagers helped hang posters even if, not being able to read, some occasionally hung them upside down.

With all the restrictions, we still attracted nearly four hundred attendees who filled the ballroom of the hotel. I met dignitaries at the doorway and deliberately set the American and the Russian representatives next to each other so they could enjoy something together. We began by lighting the lamp of knowledge on the stage and continued with inspiration, humor, and wisdom as the flame burned throughout the three days.

One afternoon Swamiji sat with us in the middle of the hall as Dr. Arya ascended the podium to address the audience right after the lunch break. We turned to Swamiji when we noticed that the audience was beginning to fall asleep, due to the hour and their full stomachs. Swamiji nodded at us, closed his eyes and put his head down. Suddenly, Dr. Arya became much more animated. He took over the stage, moving arms and head emphatically, the strength of his zestful words taking on a magic sparkle. The audience leaned forward hanging on every word. It was a wonderful talk, bringing everyone to their feet in applause.

My turn to lecture came the next day. Swamiji again dropped his head to his chest to bless the work. All of a sudden, I felt a strong quickening of energy run through my body and focus at my throat and forehead. The next moment I began to quote in Sanskrit, a language I had not mastered, and connect my topic to the *Yoga Shastras,* which were unfamiliar to me.

The other speakers enjoyed their time at the podium with such an enthusiastic crowd, and the atmosphere in the hall was electric. Finally, Swamiji walked to the stage and spoke on yoga as the path of life. He then led a meditation and for the first time, Nepalese and foreigners, wealthy and poor, communists, royalists, and members of democracies closed their eyes and meditated together.

After the conference, Theresa and I stayed overnight in the hotel with Swamiji. We shared two small rooms with a connecting door. Early in the morning, Swamiji tapped on that door and asked Theresa to order tea. When the tea tray arrived, we decided to have a little fun. The big silver tea pot was covered in a bright Nepalese red, yellow, and orange tea cozy. Theresa handed me the cozy and carried the tea in to our teacher, solemnly declaring that a holy man, giving his name as Lama Govinda, had just arrived and was waiting for an audience with Swamiji. Theresa was told to admit the guest. When the door was opened, I came solemnly in wearing my bathrobe with the tea cozy perched on my head like a Tibetan monk's hat.

Swamiji broke into peals of laughter and when we could finally breathe again after all our laughter, insisted that I carry the tea cozy back to the ashram for future need. The hotel manager agreed, giving Theresa the unique large room key to take home as a souvenior as well.

The afternoon mail included an invitation to our teacher and us for afternoon tea with the Queen Mother, the beautiful, kind woman who had raised the king and his siblings, and now spent her days living quietly in a lovely section of the royal estate.

Swamiji did not go to tea, but sent us to the Queen Mother alone. Although disappointed by the respected yogi's absence, the Queen Mother warmly welcomed us, insisted that we sit next to her on the sofa, and entertained us with stories of her meetings with our teacher and the divine chants they used to sing together.

CLOSING AN ERA

Our days with Swamiji at the ashram were almost over. Each hour sitting with him before his fire was a treasure; each view off the mountain a scene to be remembered forever. One evening as we said good night, Swamiji asked me to roll up the small carpet on which we had all been sitting.

"I want you two to have this rug," he said. "Take it home with you. It has long been my meditation rug and now it should be yours." He handed us a letter assigning the rug to us for customs and then told us not to return to the Institute.

"Now you should live off campus. I want you to work in many places; you will see where I will send you! For now you should find an apartment that you like, but it should not have more than three rooms in it. I will be with you again."

With his hands on our heads, we felt his blessing as we carried off the beautiful meditation rug. "What will he sit on now?" I thought, but he insisted on everything, and the love surrounding us was so tangible that we could think of no words of protest.

The holiday of Shivaratri would soon be here, and many Indians were coming to join their Hindu cousins in Kathmandu for celebrations at the huge temple of Pashupatinath. Many would also visit the ashram to pay respects to Swamiji. It was too soon for the flowers to be in bloom so we collected some plants from the city to add color to our mountain top. Theresa worked on the planting with Swamiji sitting nearby.

"What's on your mind, Tree?" he asked. "Why are you sad?"

"Oh Swamiji, I was just thinking that I won't be here when the gardens blossom. We must depart in four days and it just isn't fair to have to leave so early."

I perked up my ears as our teacher replied, "What would you like to see blossom?"

Theresa sat back on her heels and smiled at her teacher. "My favorites are the daffodils."

"OK," he said. "What else? Do you like trees that flower?"

Theresa told him she loved flowering trees so Swamiji made a promise: "See the plum tree over there by the house? Before you leave, the tree will blossom just for you."

After working in the garden a little longer, I went up to the authorized tree to inspect its buds, which were about the size of a bead of water. It was Tuesday and we were set to leave on Friday morning. "This bears watching," I thought. So each day I diligently made my tree and bulb inspection. No discernible change by Thursday evening, and in the moonlight I went to do my scrutiny again. Still no alteration.

While eating breakfast early Friday morning, the sound "Treeee" rang out across the compound. Theresa flew out the dining room door, headed across the patio, and raced around the north building with me twenty yards behind. She ran faster that morning than I could ever recall her running before.

As I turned the corner, I found Swamiji and Theresa both beaming at a fully blossomed plum tree, while around their feet shone the bright yellow faces of fifteen daffodils.

The soaring mood suddenly inspired me. "Swamiji, isn't it time for Lama Govindaji to visit?"

"Yes!" he replied, "he should come on this auspicious day."

So Swamiji, Theresa, and myself planned a special treat. I was dressed in Swamiji's deep red kimono with his sandals on my feet. The tea cozy was perched on my head, shining in the bright sun. I stood by the flowering tree while Swamiji went to notify Swami Ajaya and the many guests from India.

"Hurry, hurry," called Swamij. "We have a holy lama from Tibet who came as a guest and wants to bless you." His voice rang through the ashram and twenty devoted Indians hurried to the front patio; Swami Ajaya led the way with his camera at the ready for pictures.

The group approached the patio reverentially, looking for the lama. There, with downcast eyes and hands folded in prayer stood the illustrious Lama Govindaji. For one brief, tantalizing moment, Ajaya acknowledged me as the visitor from Tibet with a bow, but as he walked closer he recognized his guru brother. He looked at Swamiji, standing next to me, with utter confusion.

"Go ahead, Ajaya," Swamiji said. "Touch the lama's feet!"

So the young swami performed the traditional acknowledgment and then laughed while he snapped photos. The Indian pilgrims approached in astonished bewilderment, respectfully bowing to the American with a tea cozy on his head standing next to the serious face and smiling eyes of the revered Master of the Himalayas.

Swamiji at Hansda Ashram

CHAPTER 21
CHRIST CONSCIOUSNESS

In the distance, I perceived Swamiji standing on a hill with something bright next to him. As I walked closer, I was enthralled by his appearance. He was attired in radiant white and his complexion glowed with vigor. I sensed enormous power in him. On his left was a luminous being, too radiant for me to look at closely. I tried to squint my eyes to discern who it was but the light shone so brightly that I was forced to look away. Then a shadow in the form of a cross appeared on the ground in front of them.

IT WAS A STRANGE DREAM; I could not connect the shadow with the bright being, the cross with the light. Over the months I thought of the dream, finally realizing that my teacher was linked in some way with Christianity. Years later, sitting with him in the mountains, I remembered the dream as his story continued.

"If we say God is good and the source of goodness, then why do we pray to God to get us out of our messes?" Swamiji asked one evening in his little ashram room. Outside, the February night was cold and damp; our mountain home turned in on itself trying to keep warm. I was happy to be with my teacher, sitting near the cozy fireplace. Theresa sat on the floor opposite, Swamiji between us. "People pray as though God got them into their mess in the first place," he said. "If God is good, then God has no intention of creating problems for us. Why then should we pray, 'Lord, do this,' 'Lord, do that.'? Prayer can inspire us, but the problems of our life are self-created and only we can remove them. The great ones never ask anything of God in a crisis."

That was a new and interesting idea. The great ones never ask anything in a crisis. My mind raced through past crises and evaluated what I did with them in reference to the divine. As Swamiji spoke, I realized that Western peoples' beliefs in God configure the divine into a sort of male hero.

Immediately Swamiji picked up my thought. "The worship of heroes can get in the way of ancient wisdom. Even Krishna in the *Bhagavad Gita* says he is modifying ancient wisdom for his times. It saddens me when I see how Christians have been taught to misrepresent Christ."

"In what way?" I asked.

"They have distanced themselves from Jesus to the point where they can no longer imitate his qualities."

"But Swamiji, there are many ordinary Christians living ethical lives and helping others."

Swamiji looked at me intensely, "Is that what Christianity is all about?"

I was taken aback by the question, but before I could think of a reply, he went on.

"Jesus, like Krishna and Buddha, symbolizes what human nature can become. Are we only to adore them? They are showing us what we can be. We are not to worship them; we are to become them, and then go farther. Christians are worn down by their sin consciousness; they forget the essentials."

"Which essentials do you mean?" I asked.

"Christians are confused in their thinking. Why should they think less of themselves while they revere Christ? That attitude forces them to be dependent upon others and neglect the God within themselves. Their fears often create a God that fits their desperate needs. Their faith gets caught within their deficient ideas about themselves. It is hard for me to understand how Christians, who insist that their God is all loving, assume that God creates problems for them. I don't find this kind of God when I read the scriptures. For me God is neither retaliatory nor a creator of problems. People create their own problems and search for ways to evade responsibility. It's so easy to put the blame on someone else, even God. Faith and reading the Bible can offer some consolation in daily life, but it can never liberate anyone. Only when one starts pondering the belief that God is within each person can the opportunity open to a personality transformation.

"We can't get along with our neighbors, yet we want to see and be with God!" the teacher continued. "We have no understanding of what that relationship actually means. Instead of using things of the world and then loving God, believers reverse it, doing neither themselves nor the w̶... path of a sage is very different from that of a relig̶... sage does not search for God but loves life itself e... Sages never talk of God; worried people speak of God."

Swamiji became pensive, took a sip of lemon tea, and aft... few moments continued his thoughts out loud. "I find it curious that religious people will kill for their religion, justifying the killing in the name of God. It's the same in the East. It's been there throughout history and continues today. Real strength comes from being serene. How strong one is when in an undisturbed state! That is why the first step in spirituality is not thoughts of God; the first step is controlling the mind so it does not create problems for itself."

My mind flashed back to the Crusades, the religious wars in Europe, the slaughter of women healers by the churches, the bishops blessing planes flying off to bomb Korea and Viet Nam. While I grew up I had noticed the fierce loyalty with which believers of each denomination defended their allegiance. It became obvious that the Calvinistic God did not match the Lutheran God, nor the Baptist God, nor the Catholic God, nor any other. The violence of the tribal God of Deuteronomy was in a class by itself. Believers, of course, had no sense of an ultimate divinity; they felt safer rallying around the tribal deity. Each group felt that their religion was the best and the only authentic one. They prayed, expecting God to rescue them from their perils, and, of course, banish their enemies. Religion seemed to me to be on the wrong track.

"What's missing in the churches?" I asked after a long pause.

"Where is the disciplined path that leads them to Christ consciousness?" Swamiji asked in reply.

"Why do they need one?" I said, hoping he would open up his mind further so I could grasp more wisdom.

"Show me any art, science, or philosophy," Swamiji began, "that can achieve without discipline. Thinking or living without discipline leads you to chaos. Christians are hungry for the spirit but they don't know what they are looking for; they have been conditioned to believe without verification. What good is belief in salvation when one is still suffering? Worry and suffering don't make one great; they make one stressful. Americans have an idea of 'no pain, no gain,' and they wrongfully attach it to religion."

...n back from getting involved ...asked.

...ostitute for real experience." he ...ns from trusting in their own life ...f the finest, most trustworthy ...et, but as regards their spirituality, ...at part. There have no systematic ...lives. They have their prayers and ...ents and taboos, but as far as ...ousness—experiencing their soul—it's a void ... ...ey try to fill with compliance of Church rules. How many ...are of the vast realm of consciousness? They are discouraged from trusting the urge to go within that can lead them to know themselves on the highest levels. How many of them search for the source of their own faith? Is God so limited that all he can do is give his followers faith?

"What can Christians do in this situation?" I asked.

"They could examine their beliefs calmly without throwing away their connection to Christ. Theologians propose that God created this world out of nothing. But you know that from nothing one gets nothing. If Christians accept the Genesis story of creation, they should take it fully to heart. In the opening story of the seven days, God endorses his work of art in the most sublime phrases; there is no room for pessimism about life. Right now, Christians have a weak affirmation of life—they live in fear. Everything is based on hell or heaven, reward or punishment. Yet death, the passageway, terrorizes the average Christian. How strange that is! Death is as harmful as casting away your breath in an exhalation. Since Christians are not taught to deal with fears, or understand from whence they arise, then death, the unknown, becomes their chief dread.

"Religions create fear and dependency, Justin. Without freedom from fear, no liberation is possible. The sages carry no self-condemnation. Their way is to be practical about living. Take a simple issue like 'I won't lie.' Then test your strength in it. Recognize the constant battle between your ideas and society's demands. When you are confused or you can't think how to explain what's happening to you, then you escape to God. This is weakness, for substituting God in this way won't bring lasting fulfillment."

"So what's really holding them back from getting involved with the Christ consciousness?" I asked.

"They have made faith a substitute for real experience." he said firmly. "Faith keeps Christians from trusting in their own life force. Christians are some of the finest, most trustworthy individuals that I have ever met, but as regards their spirituality, they miss the most important part. There have no systematic development in their inner lives. They have their prayers and rituals, their commandments and taboos, but as far as understanding their consciousness—experiencing their soul—it's a void in their lives that they try to fill with compliance of Church rules. How many are aware of the vast realm of consciousness? They are discouraged from trusting the urge to go within that can lead them to know themselves on the highest levels. How many of them search for the source of their own faith? Is God so limited that all he can do is give his followers faith?

"What can Christians do in this situation?" I asked.

"They could examine their beliefs calmly without throwing away their connection to Christ. Theologians propose that God created this world out of nothing. But you know that from nothing one gets nothing. If Christians accept the Genesis story of creation, they should take it fully to heart. In the opening story of the seven days, God endorses his work of art in the most sublime phrases; there is no room for pessimism about life. Right now, Christians have a weak affirmation of life—they live in fear. Everything is based on hell or heaven, reward or punishment. Yet death, the passageway, terrorizes the average Christian. How strange that is! Death is as harmful as casting away your breath in an exhalation. Since Christians are not taught to deal with fears, or understand from whence they arise, then death, the unknown, becomes their chief dread.

"Religions create fear and dependency, Justin. Without freedom from fear, no liberation is possible. The sages carry no self-condemnation. Their way is to be practical about living. Take a simple issue like 'I won't lie.' Then test your strength in it. Recognize the constant battle between your ideas and society's demands. When you are confused or you can't think how to explain what's happening to you, then you escape to God. This is weakness, for substituting God in this way won't bring lasting fulfillment."

reverse it, doing neither themselves nor the world a favor. The path of a sage is very different from that of a religious believer. A sage does not search for God but loves life itself everywhere. Sages never talk of God; worried people speak of God."

Swamiji became pensive, took a sip of lemon tea, and after a few moments continued his thoughts out loud. "I find it curious that religious people will kill for their religion, justifying the killing in the name of God. It's the same in the East. It's been there throughout history and continues today. Real strength comes from being serene. How strong one is when in an undisturbed state! That is why the first step in spirituality is not thoughts of God; the first step is controlling the mind so it does not create problems for itself."

My mind flashed back to the Crusades, the religious wars in Europe, the slaughter of women healers by the churches, the bishops blessing planes flying off to bomb Korea and Viet Nam. While I grew up I had noticed the fierce loyalty with which believers of each denomination defended their allegiance. It became obvious that the Calvinistic God did not match the Lutheran God, nor the Baptist God, nor the Catholic God, nor any other. The violence of the tribal God of Deuteronomy was in a class by itself. Believers, of course, had no sense of an ultimate divinity; they felt safer rallying around the tribal deity. Each group felt that their religion was the best and the only authentic one. They prayed, expecting God to rescue them from their perils, and, of course, banish their enemies. Religion seemed to me to be on the wrong track.

"What's missing in the churches?" I asked after a long pause.

"Where is the disciplined path that leads them to Christ consciousness?" Swamiji asked in reply.

"Why do they need one?" I said, hoping he would open up his mind further so I could grasp more wisdom.

"Show me any art, science, or philosophy," Swamiji began, "that can achieve without discipline. Thinking or living without discipline leads you to chaos. Christians are hungry for the spirit but they don't know what they are looking for; they have been conditioned to believe without verification. What good is belief in salvation when one is still suffering? Worry and suffering don't make one great; they make one stressful. Americans have an idea of 'no pain, no gain,' and they wrongfully attach it to religion."

More tea was poured and our teacher picked up a stick to stir the glowing coals in the fireplace. We listened to the wind whistling outside the door and wrapped our shawls a little tighter across our shoulders. After a little while Swamiji again began to speak.

"Many Westerners think that there is no description of Christ in Indian scriptures. If they would only familiarize themselves with the main scriptures, then they would discover that whenever God decides to incarnate into history, it occurs," he said with a tinge of sadness.

"Too many people approach religion like an antique shop, going from one old idea to another until they get confused. Others like to stick to the Bible, but they read it without comprehending that the writers composed it with three levels of discernment. There are many taboos and admonitions in the Bible, like the ten commandments. Rules are necessary for ordinary people in their search for security, but a much higher obligation is found in scriptures also. That message is found in the Sermon on the Mount. It is not for ordinary people, because it is much too stringent for their lives; it was for the disciples. But there is an even higher standard found in the Book of Revelations, where John is the instrument of Christ, who was doing for his time what Krishna and the Buddha did for theirs. How many Christians do you know that have a good understanding of the Book of Revelations?"

I was thinking that in all my theological courses, never was there any exposition of that scripture except in a very literal analysis, leading to bizarre interpretations. By most theologians, it was simply ignored.

"The writer of that book," Swamiji said as he leaned forward toward me, "is not the John of the fourth gospel. From a study of the language and symbols, you can easily discern the difference in authorship. If Christians stay only with their artistic impressions of Christ, like the paintings one sees in chapels and publications, then they won't understand what Christ consciousness means. Their interpretation is too personal and subjective to allow them to appreciate what John is disclosing in his narration."

He was moving in depth tonight. I grabbed my notebook and quickly glanced over at Theresa; she had the same recognition in her eyes.

Swamiji, Justin, and Dr. Arya walking in Banepa, Nepal

"Worry and meditation are very close. One is negative and leads to self-centerness, while the other is positive and leads to unselfish awareness. Worry makes you obsessive; meditation increases your freedom. John, the writer of the revelations, was concerned with the tyranny of his times. The world was suffering from the Roman notions of kingdom and the obliteration of any group, like the Christians, that thought differently.

"For the sake of the preservation of Christ' s message, John took these pressures to heart. What could he do to salvage the truth? So John entered into his spirit as the scripture states. His motivation was not for his own private safety, nor for the hierarchy's continuance, rather he had a much broader concern: the safety of all the Churches, the existence of Christianity itself. He disposed himself not for psychic channeling, but for a cosmic revelation, truths that were universal for all Christians and beyond. When you become a transmitter and receiver on those terms, then you are chosen as an instrument for the divine to speak through you. John's unselfish worry led him to a universal revelation for humankind."

Swamiji's words drew my attention with such a natural authenticity that I did not want this night to end. I was pleased that he continued after a few minutes.

"The Book of Revelation explains the book of life itself. It doesn't waste any time and gets right to the subject matter. But since people aren't used to meditation, John's progress in consciousness startles them. Without meditation practices for a long time, the symbols described by John seem too bizarre and foreign to our times. One can't grasp the meaning of this book though rational analysis, only through meditation.

"In meditation one waits, like John, and rejects all experiences for awhile, allowing them to pass, to exhaust themselves. You can't reach enlightenment by suppression of any of your thoughts, images, desires, or feelings. Your mind roams through three states of consciousness—everyday knowing, sleep, and dreaming—and has seven fields of awareness, as there are seven tones and seven major colors, each functioning differently.

"John is about to encounter the unknown part of his consciousness—the eternal—which stands before him and reveals the truth of life. But the treasures awaiting John are like diamonds embedded in the strata of a coal mine. First, one gets one's hands dirty, for that's all that rubs off. Don't stop at the dirt. In meditation, when sounds and images emerge don't try to imagine others or analyze them, for then they will vanish. Notice the sequence in John's progress. First, he hears a sound, then he sees a vision. Sound and light are closely connected in the make-up of your body. I'm not talking here about external sounds affecting your physical or gross body, as yoga anatomy refers to it, but your subtle body, which is the template of your biological body. In that body, John is witnessing how sound and light accompany each other. The sound leads you to the vision. The first vision is from the lowest energy center where John meets his everyday consciousness. There is also an ancient manuscript that describes the process whereby primal sound transmutes into light at a certain frequency."

I wrote as fast as I could while Swamiji paused. Suddenly I let out a sigh. It occurred to that I had been sitting utterly still and hardly breathing in my concentration on his words. Christians devotedly follow the Jesus of faith but have never understood the Christ consciousness, I thought, which is exactly what John narrates. No wonder he is so often misunderstood.

"The sounds and visions," Swamiji went on, "progress in their sequence because John's inner nature was unfolding. He was crossing the threshold between the rational mind and its unknown, unconscious domain. He was experiencing his astral body where he met the seven centers of differing awareness. Each center of awareness has its distinctive sound, color, shape, and odor. These centers are called chakras. There is, however, an association between these seven levels and the major endocrine glands of the gross body. John also had to go beyond this body and understand his innate subtlest body, the causal, which contains the seeds to the next world and retains all personal impressions, as well as motivations. By reading the scripture, one realizes that John's journey is still far from over, for he must cross beyond all the bodies to stand in silence before his divine self. For him to be successful, he must break the seven seals of ignorance. He must gain ascendancy over their energy to use and appreciate them for his spiritual growth. Breaking the seals means banishing the ignorance through expanding his awareness. John's inner description of his journey to arrive at the Christ consciousness is the same for everyone, since it is not a matter of his culture but a natural unfolding by anyone who has prepared himself.

"Compare this book to the writing of the sages in the *Chandogya Upanishad*," Swamiji said finally.

Placing the Book of Revelations within the context of yoga anatomy really galvanized our interest. A pressing question came to mind, so I asked it. "What makes the Tradition of the Sages so unique?"

"Our tradition makes you aware of the teacher within—your conscience. The sages' job is to slowly make you independent. What stands between you and reality is your mind. Most people's lives circumnavigate around the values and opinions of the external world. When you read the sages' texts, you see that their writings transcend the conventional rules of the material world. To show you how much wisdom you already have but aren't using, just privately record a dialogue with yourself about a problem which you attempt to resolve. Later listen to the recording and you'll be surprised at the truth in yourself. As you get accustomed to these experiments in truth, it will heal the division between your inner and your outer life.

Again Swamiji put his attention on the fire. He threw on a few more sticks of wood, played with the coals, and finally set down the poker. He drank some tea and said, "I will tell you something that happened to me long ago.

"My early training in Christianity came from a remarkable man named Sadhu Singh, who was a Muslim Christian. He told me to pay special attention to the Psalms, the Sermon on the Mount, and the Book of Revelations, but he emphasized that while the average person might derive some solace from these writings, their deeper truths only surfaced in meditation.

"At the same time that I met this man, I was very interested in the liberation of my country. I spoke out against Nehru and his party, proclaiming them false politicians. I encouraged the citizens to throw their votes into the ocean rather than vote for this group. Soon a warrant was issued for my arrest and I was taken to jail.

"I was dumbfounded. As I sat in my jail cell, I kept asking myself why this was happening, for I had spoken only the truth. I remembered that the truth will make me free, so I implored the Lord to help me. 'Lord, although I am being persecuted, I will continue to praise you.'

"I fell asleep. Suddenly I felt a hand on my shoulder and opened my eyes. There in front of me stood Christ. He said to me, 'Why do you worry? You will always belong to me. Be fearless and go out among the police surrounding the building. Test my power.' So I opened the doors and walked out. To my astonishment, I walked through the guards and talked to some of the police in the street. No one noticed me.

"The next day a message came down to the local authorities from the government to leave me alone and not bother me. That day the Commissioner of Police became my disciple along with several of his men."

We were thrilled with the story and asked dozens of questions about the experience, the politics of the day, the words of the vision. Finally I asked Swamiji what he thought was the biggest obstacle to truth.

"Justin, people say they want truth, but it is obvious that they aren't prepared for it by the way they live."

Intrigued, I zeroed in on the notion of 'preparation,' asking him to elaborate more.

"People fight change and thus stay afraid of it. Yogis don't deny the flux of things in the world but only that they are true; they admit the nature of things but deny that they are truth. They are apparent reality, the limited true. They can't be denied their existence, but they ceaselessly change. Destruction and death are in evidence everywhere. They are true but not truth. While they are not absolute reality, their existence shows that there is an absolute reality somewhere."

It took me awhile to grasp his subtle distinction which is never made in Western philosophy or, for that matter, theology. Swamiji divided truth into the everyday brand which changes, relative truth, and eternal truth, which never changes and is the basis for the relative world. Relative truth is the natural object for the discursive mind. The mind couldn't recognize absolute truth if it met it. Both physical sciences and Western philosophy accept the changeable character of nature and culture but the full implications leading to eternal truth are not inferred in them.

I found it consoling to look upon the world at large from this vantage point. This division served as the basis for respecting things in their limitations, without demanding more than their nature allows. I continued to ponder the implications of this marvelous distinction as it applied to so much of life and its problems. I also realized how terrifying life is when one's mind is convinced that the changeability of the world is all that exists. I could understand why some of the Existentialist philosophers committed suicide. With no real sense of the transcendent, what else is there to live for?

Swamiji looked at me briefly and then looked away saying carefully, "The sages have traveled the same obstacles as you. They have marked the stones for your progress. Eventually, you will see that there is nothing like obstacles at all. All adversities are here to help you. They can become instruments for your progress, but you don't understand this yet. Pain, suffering, disturbance amounts to the same thing—the most obvious obstacle. Yet here is the chance for self-study. Just note how your negative attitude toward others creates annoyance and conflict within and without.

"One learns to correct attitudes by doing spiritual practice, *sadhana*. Why not dialogue with the mind before meditation and talk out those things that bother you. Your mind can only give back what you present to it during the day. This is karma: you feed mind and it feeds you. All the mind can do is conceive name and form. People expect more from it than what it can give them. Study the limitations of your senses, mind, and actions—these are important—but know the force behind them.

"Yoga *sadhana* helps control all the fluctuations of your mind, the *vrittis*. When the first yoga-sutra speaks of 'now,' think that you are born fresh here and now, for now is part of eternity. When you live in the here and now, you will know the value of the past and future. Otherwise, if you misidentify with the things of the world, then you will never know who you are."

Coming back to my previous idea about the relationship between *sadhana* and attitude, I began to analyze how professional thinkers in any science often stay at only one level of understanding. By applying their specific methodology to a field of study, they acquire a certain competence, having gained over time the ideas and reflections that belong to that field. They are skilled intellectually in their science, but what about the rest of their lives? For many people philosophy has lost its connection to the formation of wisdom and become another abstract study of the history of ideas. Students are then left with the impression that philosophy is separate from science and just a bantering of ideas from different schools of thought, a strictly intellectual pastime. A similar tendency exists in theology which, in some instances, is a sophisticated form of catechism.

"Philosophizing with imagination won't get you through life," Swamiji remarked. "Your own life is the real study."

There. He said it. The field of study for yoga is the entire realm of living. Western science likes to divide things up, reducing them to their most minute parts, assuming that it then understands the reality at hand. It finds it hard to think in systemic and synergistic terms. Wholeness thinking is foreign to its analytical competence. Actually, corporate philosophy is getting closer to wholeness than science with its investigation of systems thinking.

The pieces shifted together with more coherence. The notion of samkhya, the philosophy of yoga, emphasizes discrimination in life. Its companion, the practices of yoga, energizes this power of discrimination itself.

"Swamiji pointed out that engaging the life force through mental concentration, focusing the imagination, pacing the breath rate, assuming a bodily posture, sharpens its utility and amplifies one's awareness. Discrimination dawns. Exactly the core insight in samkhya philosophy. Facing life with discrimination is what yoga practices induce—learning to discern the real from the fake, the true from the false, love from selfishness, mind from the body, control from suppression, relaxation from stress.

"When you learn to discriminate," Swamiji said, "then the mind gains a sense of balance and you aren't overwhelmed by the temptations of life, for you see them for what they are. When you operate your life with discrimination, then you view the world as it is, not expecting too much and enjoying what it offers."

He then leaned forward, lifting his finger to make the point. "Refrain from identifying with things of the world, but don't refrain from the world!"

We fell silent for awhile listening to the wind. I thought I heard the roar of the leopard outside the door, but said nothing. I felt safe.

"Peace and pain," Swamiji continued, "are never associated. Peace and happiness go together. Peace is possible only when the mind is calm. First, joy arises, and as it expands it becomes happiness. You don't find happiness by running from pain.

Freedom from pain results from facing it and understanding its causes. Samkhya philosophy doesn't start with a search for God; it first makes you critique suffering. It discriminates three levels of pain and then explores ways to get rid of them. Remember, the Buddha started out as a raja yogi."

Interestingly, I thought, Jesus never theorized about pain; he just got rid of it. I wondered if he, like the Buddha, had read the *Sankhya-Karikas?*

"Discern what is good from what is pleasant," Swamiji continued, "for both can be a source of pain or pleasure. I am not talking about objects here, but the lack of understanding that allows either pain or pleasure to dominate your life.

"People create their own problems and then blame others. Their minds are not calm because they simply react to their sense impressions. Someone says you look pretty, and you feel good about yourself; someone says the opposite, and you brood. Who is controlling whom? Body is easy to change but mind changes constantly: just examine your thoughts for awhile. You have to decide whether you want to direct your life or just be a conglomeration of sense impressions with an endless parade of thoughts. Go to chapter two in the *Yoga Sutras* and there you'll find out how to build an attitude to life."

I could hardly write fast enough as my mind wanted to explore the implications of his words. Swamiji saw me writing and waited until I caught up. Then he told a story.

"Walking along the river one day, a man acknowledged my master and myself respectfully. Then he asked what practice he could do to get closer to enlightenment. 'Don't lie for three months,' my master replied. Note that he wasn't told to tell the truth, but only not to lie. The man returned home and began his practice.

"At his government job, there was some smuggling going on. He knew about it but was not part of it. The following week there was a surprise investigation at his office and everyone was interviewed. When the inspectors asked about the smuggling, he remembered my master's words and told the inspectors everything. When the inspectors questioned the other men, they, in turn, put the blame on him as the chief instigator. The man was indicted.

"His wife was upset that he spoke as he did to the inspectors.

She reminded him that if he had kept his mouth shut none of this calamity would have occurred. He told her what had happened by the river with the great saint. 'Fine,' she remarked, 'since you have embarrassed me so much you can go join his holiness.' She filed for divorce.

"His friends thought he was a fool and laughed at his plight. Even his children said they preferred to live with their mother rather than with him. His wife withdrew all the money from their bank account and left him stranded in jail, unable to pay for a lawyer. Reflecting over his situation, he wondered what else could happen to him for not lying.

"Brought before the magistrate, the man was asked to explain his side of the story. He felt compelled to say how this whole business of non-lying began. His words intrigued the judge who took a recess and called the defendant to his chambers. There the judge interrogated him more fully about the two *sadhus*. Hearing the story, the magistrate realized that this man had met his personal guru. This caused him to probe deeper into the evidence and find contradictions. The case was thrown out of court.

"The man was now free but alone. He wondered what else could possibly occur. At the end of his three-month practice, he received a telegram informing him that he had inherited two million rupees. His wife quickly contacted him and admitted that she had misunderstood the entire situation. But the man politely declined his former lifestyle. So much had happened in three months that he wanted to embark on a new career to see what a lifetime of no lying would bring him."

My mind flew delightfully in all directions, interpolating Swamiji's words in my imagination. I proposed to myself that yoga is the alchemy of an embodied spirit. I started to redefine myself: I was not so much a human person searching for spiritual experiences, but rather a spiritual being evolving through human experiences. It wasn't over.

"In yoga," Swamiji then said, "knowledge is not the result of strain; it emerges from consistent practice. Practice promotes constant awareness. With attention you can enjoy the world. You are present to your work, to people, to life. Let your mind and body be attentive together, for that is the essence of practicality. How then can there be room in your awareness for turmoil? Don't intimidate your mind or people; purposeful interest should never be forced. Lead it. Create interest in its object. Especially resolve not to stay confused in your mind, for prolonged inner chaos eventually leads to bodily illness. In forty years, we will have hospitals of thinking."

"Practicing yoga organizes your energies on all levels of your nature. Without organization, your life force dissipates and your environment controls you. Books without practice don't help; they keep your mind in a theoretical state. Nice, correct thoughts by themselves don't do the trick. Nothing changes."

I couldn't have been more focused. All I was aware of were his words.

"The awareness of reality removes all pains. Eventually, the only pain left is that of others not being as aware as you are. Don't postpone or escape reality, regardless how painful it is when you begin."

It was now nearly 3 A.M. The energy in the room dropped in its intensity, becoming calm and light. It was time for my teacher's meditation. We stepped outside into the quiet, cool air of that moonless night and I looked up into a blazing dome of speckled lights. It reminded me that someone had just taken me on a tour, charting the stars within.

Justin meditating at Gomukh, the source of the Ganges

CHAPTER 22
WALKING WITH THE MASTER

I played a game of dominos very uncomfortably, feeling that I was losing badly. Swamiji appeared, smiling at me. I told him that I thought he was so successful with people because he touched their hearts. He agreed, telling me that he spoke more to their hearts than to their minds and added that I must do the same if I wanted to win my game.

AFTER OUR MONTHS IN NEPAL, Theresa and I went back to Pennsylvania and moved our belongings out of the Institute as instructed. We found an apartment on Church Street in the little town of Honesdale with exactly three rooms. I began again to lecture and teach around the country, and Theresa made a new home for us once more.

We had been in America for just three weeks when the call came from Nepal. "Justy, I want you and Theresa to come back to India," Swamiji's clear voice announced. "Come immediately, OK?"

We quickly made arrangements: Theresa would travel with the American group going on pilgrimage, but because I needed to fulfill a lecture contract first, I would meet the group in Delhi later. Swamiji approved the plan and then, unknown to me, telephoned Charles to drop everything and come to India.

In early April Theresa and a group from Honesdale flew to Nepal, meeting Swamiji in Kathmandu. She visited Princess Shobha, Prince Mohan and the children, and helped Swamiji pack up his belongings. The political situation in Nepal had worsened, so this was the last group to stay at Hansda Ashram, soon to be closed. Bed and blankets and sheets were given to the boys' academy near the town; furniture and food and cooking utensils were given to the nearby villages; trees were pruned, flower gardens weeded, vegetables harvested.

As Theresa packed Swamiji's papers one day, she asked about his ticket. He told her that he had no money to travel back into India, so they devised a plan. A little table was set up in the courtyard holding stacks of white Indian bath towels embroidered with 'Hansda Ashram' in blue letters. They had been a gift to the ashram from Kanpur students just months before. Theresa gave a short talk about how much Americans love souvenirs and sold the towels for $20.00 each, beginning with Charles and ending with two for me, sold at discount. She and Swamiji chortled over their idea later as they counted up the money, congratulating themselves on a good solution to the problem.

Everyone thought that Swamiji had much, but none of it was for himself; almost everything that he received, he gave away. Only a handful of students were ever asked for money for his personal needs; one was Charles, another was Roshan Lal. Our money always went to buy underwear and socks for him; the extra went to purchase cloth for his robes. Students and admirers sometimes brought gifts to the teacher, but these were always passed along to others.

I watched once when a very rich man, who had recently celebrated a birthday, came to visit Swamiji. He brought a large box wrapped with a bow, and ostentatiously offered it as a special holiday gift to his teacher. When the man left, Swamiji told me to open the box and just notice. Inside was a silk shirt in the color and style our teacher never wore and in a size much too small for him. It was, however, in the exact size that the giver wore.

Once when a group of Indians visited the Nepal ashram, they brought gifts of clothing, food and rupees. Dr. Agnihotri, one of the oldest disciples, was there those days and smiled as Swamiji began singing a happy little song in Hindi. "What is the song, uncle?" asked Charles, in Nepal on retreat.

"Ah!" answered the older man, "The words mean, 'I am being blessed today because I am given the opportunity to have the joy of giving.' Swamiji sings it whenever something is given to him, you know."

PILGRIMAGE TO THE MOUNTAINS

After a retreat at the mountain ashram, the American group

flew back to New Delhi, leaving Swamiji to close the ashram gate alone, return the property to the royal family, and fly back to India. I flew in that same night from New York, meeting everyone at the Akbar Hotel the next morning. We were all scheduled to bus to Rishikesh after breakfast, but Swamiji called me to his side just as we were boarding. "Justin," he said, "stay with me. You will join them later." I was puzzled, but pleased to be able to spend time with him again, so I said good-bye to Theresa and waved them all off. Swamiji was exuberant, full of energy, anxious to move along at his usual quick beat.

May is not the month to be in India's capital city. The air was dry and hot, the sun unrelenting. Students of Swamiji, the Sikh General Grewahl and his family, were always kind, taking care of anyone their teacher sent their way. Now they welcomed me into their home to rest and take lunch with them. It was like a little oasis in the burning desert, filled with cool drinks, wonderful food, a bath, and a fanned napping spot. Swamiji arrived near evening to claim me and spend time with our hosts. We stayed in the simple rooms of the International Center overnight and left at 4:30 A.M. for Rishikesh. We drove along the highway as the sun came up, witnessing village life churn itself into working mode for the day. We zipped along watching the carts bumping along to markets in larger towns, small farms being readied for the first meal of the day, animals being milked, or washed, or prodded to pasture. Swamiji was quiet, thoughtful, speaking little, but concerned for my needs as always.

I found my wife in the outskirts of Rishikesh, waiting for me in a small cement room with a wooden cot at the Government Tourist Bungalow. It was wonderful to see her again and swap stories of our days apart. I greeted old friends, then hailed an Indian three-wheeler open taxi and off we went to our ashram at Ram Nagar.

It always felt like coming home when I walked into the ashram compound. This time the government had made a change. We could no longer walk the few steps to the bank of the Ganges; now a huge dike separated the river from the ashram grounds, as the water was channeled to a dam to produce electric power for the growing city. The sleepy little village of Rishikesh had grown into a chaos of quickly-constructed buildings, small shacks of wood and straw, and commerce from carts, stalls, three-sided buildings, market squares. There were new hotels, restaurants, temples, and ashrams, and everywhere there was noise.

We all dropped off suitcases and packed the barest necessities for hiking in the mountains. We would be traveling by bus much of the way, by foot or mountain pony the other. Water was packed; blankets were rolled up, sleeping bags secured. We were ready for pilgrimage. Once more Swamiji told me to travel alone with him, so Theresa and I treated it as a special gift and hugged good-bye at the bus door.

The group departed for Barket; Swamiji and I left an hour later by car. We drove beside the Jamuna River, twisting upward to the north, past the hill town of Mussoorie, where we stopped. This beautiful town had been much used by the British as a summer home when the plains became too hot. It was still peppered with quaint Victorian homes and small restaurants. We enjoyed the view with a cup of tea and biscuits, then drove away just as the group bus slowly pulled into town.

The mountains unfolded their treasures: Swamiji showed me his little red writer's cottage where he had stayed years ago, meditating and writing journals; he pointed out a mountain temple that kept him warm one night while on pilgrimage; he showed me routes he used to walk as a wandering *sadhu*. He showed me the forest where he had lived, eating only leaves and tying himself into a tree at night for sleep as protection against predators. I was intrigued with everything.

We met the bus just as it began to rain. The little concrete rooms of the government inn were damp and dark; our belongings were wet from their space on top of the bus; everyone was hungry and tired. Tarps were pulled up on stakes over the little cooking area so the guides could prepare a hot meal. Some of us made our way to the open tea shop at the top of the road and sat around old wooden tables sipping chai in the steam of the tea shop and telling stories.

That night Swamiji called a few of us to his room where we all shared tea. We talked about his days as Shankaracharya, one of the five spiritual leaders of the Indian subcontinent, analogous to the position of the Catholic Pope. The sage, Shankara, had established spiritual centers in the four quadrants of India and a fifth in the place where he spent his last days. These centers have held their importance as spiritual seats through the centuries and their leaders are considered the spiritual authorities of India. We had heard the story of Swamiji's selection process before, but it was wonderful to hear it again in the land where everything had occurred.

"In the late 1940s," Swamiji began, "my master gave me a series of stringent spiritual practices which I was to do for six months. He told me to travel to the isolated forest outside Kherighat in central India and perform austerities on the sandy banks of the Narmada River. My only companions all those days were crocodiles. Many of them lived in the river and sunned themselves on the beach around me during the day. Some villagers brought me milk and bread once a day, but no one else bothered me, because the place was wild. It was one of the happiest times of my life.

"One day some big game hunters came through the forest and saw me sitting quietly in meditation. Several crocodiles sat in the sun around me, and because I was still, they were not afraid of me. Unknown to me, the hunters took photos of me sitting there in the midst of the wild animals and soon the photos appeared in the papers. Stories of an austere young swami, who ate only a meager meal once a day reached the ears of the residing Shankaracharya of Karivrpitham, Dr. Kurtkoti. He dispatched some trusted pandits to spy on my routine and report back. They collected information about my background, my knowledge of Indian philosophy, my master and reported back. Soon Dr. Kurtkoti himself came to see me. We both liked each other very much; I respected him as a spiritual man and a Sanskrit scholar. He asked me to consider taking his position as Shankaracharya so he could retire. I promised him I would ask my master."

Since Swamiji's credentials and training were impeccable, he was selected as one of three finalists for the revered position. It bore enormous responsibilities for the well-being of Indian society, but Swamiji's master, always ready to encourage him to find out first hand about life, let him accept the post.

The three eligible prospects were taken to a special lodge to spend the weekend. There they were ushered into separate, spacious rooms. Meal time came and a rich cuisine, as only Indians know how to make it, was spread before them. As his two educated peers graciously and amply helped themselves, Swamiji politely curtailed his meal to a size able to be served on a tea saucer. General conversation went on, and the host of the lodge lavished his guests with a broad tray of jewels, insisting that their choice would make outstanding rings befitting their exalted rank. While the other two humbly selected their jewels, Swamiji politely refused. As they headed for their rooms, the pundits admonished them to keep their doors locked throughout the night. Everyone retired.

"As I was preparing to meditate that night," Swamiji said as he picked up the story again, "I heard a soft knock at my door. I ignored it, continuing my practice of *nadi shodhanam*. The knock came again. I got up, unlocked and opened the door. There stood an alluring young woman, requesting that she would like to pay her respects to me for as long as I wished and saying that perhaps I could tutor her in the intricacies of philosophy. I was surprised to hear it, but I told her I only wanted to do my practice. I wished her well in the pursuit of her studies and closed the door, locking it once again.

"The next morning, the pundits called for the three of us to come to the dining room. I had been up for hours and did not want to eat but, out of politeness, I accepted a cup of tea. The pundits expressed their appreciation for the opportunity to welcome us on behalf of His Holiness and began asking questions. 'Did we sleep well? Were our rooms comfortable? Did we have enough to eat?' The other two young men volunteered that they felt refreshed from their undisturbed nocturnal hours. 'Ah!' said the pundits, 'Since you will be leaving shortly, may we have the keys to your rooms?'

"The two young men replied sheepishly that they must have misplaced them, so one of the pundits signaled with his hand and two smiling young women walked over and placed the two keys on the table. The two young men were thanked for coming, wished a blessed career of their choice, and told they should have kept their doors locked that night."

Swamiji took his key from his pocket, put it on the table, and opened a new chapter in his life. After an eighteen-day ceremony, he became His Holiness Jagadguru Shankaracharya Sada Shiva Bharati of Karvirpitham.

Countless telegrams, letters and wishes from heads of states, religious leaders, political leaders, and devotees arrived daily from all around the world for the newly-throned young man.

After his many years spent doing spiritual practice in his cave monastery, Swamiji assumed that along with his new duties he would have time for his daily *sadhana*. That was soon proved to be an incorrect assumption. The formalities of the office of Shankacharya with its traditional pomp and circumstance, unending appearances, daily audiences, travels for territorial celebrations, administration of hundreds of employees, and the ordination of countless young men into the order of swamis left little time for spiritual practices. "I felt like a swami factory," he told us.

Taking up where his predecessor left off, Swamiji continued the work of social reform. He raised the status of women, eliminating the custom of temple women as priests' servants; he opened the temples to the untouchables and insisted on their education; he called for the elimination of animal sacrifice in Hindu temples. The established upper classes who had benefited from these old customs were angered. Swamiji's efforts were so successful that four attempts were made on his life. Each time inner truth guided him to safety.

As the months wore on, he viewed the post less as an honor than as a punishment. He was bathed and massaged, brought the finest food, made to sit on a throne surrounded by flowers, and forced to allow others to worship him. One festival morning he was led by female attendants to an inner chamber holding a huge milk bath prepared for His Holiness. "How could I bathe in nutritious milk while impoverished families went hungry?" he asked. More and more, he began to see how this high office had accumulated superfluous privileges that glaringly contrasted with its spiritual duties. He wrote articles and a book under assumed names to advocate for change of these things; he instructed priests and swamis to educate the masses. Rituals and ceremonies did not hold much value for him unless they bore an intrinsic power pertinent to the benefit of the participant. Why complicate life with useless routine because the pandits said it was necessary?

He was living in a fishbowl, so at times he resorted to subterfuge in order to obtain a few moments to relax. Once, he told us, he borrowed a servant's clothes and a few coins and took a trip to the mountains of the Punjab. There he stopped to visit incognito with the caretaker pandit of the thousands-year-old astrology book, *Bhrigu Samhita*. Swamiji gave his birth date and asked for a reading. After consulting his valued manuscript, the pandit fell to the floor, touching his visitor's feet and crying, "Either you are the Shankaracharya of Karvirpitham or all the labors of my life have been in vain."

Swamiji's position demanded that he frequently attend ceremonies, blessing the community with his presence. Sometimes the music and chanting would continue for hours. Placed in front, he was seen by everyone, so he devised a clever way to get rest. He would place his shawl over his head while the music played on and go to sleep. "People thought I was in meditation, but it was the only time I could rest and get a break," he said and I could not help but laugh.

"I yearned for my freedom," he said to us. "I longed for the silence of my cave; I wanted to walk carefree in the mountains again." Swamiji admitted to us that a major factor in his decision to renounce the prestige of the office of Shankaracharya was his visit with the renowned yogic sage, Ramana Maharshi in Arunachala. So after almost three years in office he planned his escape, making sure his closest servants and their families were well taken care of.

"One night I managed to elude the pandits and colleagues and jumped in my car unnoticed. I drove to the railroad station and got on the very next train, even though I had no money or ticket. I attracted attention because I was still wearing my sandals and shawl of office, trimmed in gold. I convinced the conductor to allow me to travel to Allahabad where my journey would be fully paid. From there I made my way back to the place I longed to see. When I climbed to my Master's cave, he welcomed me and teased me. 'Have you satisfied your ego? Are you sure you want to leave all that attention? Well, at least here you won't have to wear your shawl over your head.'

"My escape was so effective that the officials searched for me for months," Swamiji told us. Since he was never officially removed from the office, he still bore the title and privileges of Shankaracharya, but he never returned to that part of India again.

JAMNOTRI AND GANGOTRI

We pilgrims next embarked for the Jamnotri Mountain

Range—the group by bus, my teacher and I by car. As the road became narrow and full of huge holes, I knew we could not continue, particularly as there were no rails along the edge of the mountain road as it climbed high above the river. We got out of the car and began to walk. We passed along the road, Swamiji stopping to point out healing plants, show me special pilgrimage sites, admire the incredibly beautiful view. We walked to within seven miles of the range.

"I have wanted to walk with you in the mountains," he said as we sauntered along. Then the trekking tips came: "Stay always inside when passing anyone, and especially an animal. Always avoid rest spots where an avalanche can strike you. Drink from moving water only."

As my mind was well alerted to trekking safety, he abruptly changed the subject in his next breath. "How much do you need to live? Would you meditate and write for six months and then roam for the other months if you had the money in the bank? Would you not touch your savings?"

I hesitated answering because I thought he must be teasing me. Who could say no to such a request? "Definitely," I answered, "that's my desire."

Now that I had bitten on that temptation, he changed the subject matter yet again.

"Theresa is like a German shepherd dog," he said slowly and thoughtfully. "One love. She serves me so much, I adore her."

He changed the topic again. "We should write a book using my English diaries. It would be extraordinary."

I agreed that it definitely would be wonderful, so many strange occurrences had he experienced, so much had he accomplished.

"Justy," he said after a pause, "will you do something for me? I want you to write a book about our life together."

Of course, my mind was overwhelmed by the implications of the request. Who was I to undertake so great a task? How could I possibly do justice to this phenomenal being? Realizing he was waiting for my answer, I promised that I would write, thinking that when I was very old, living up in a mountain cabin, I would begin the work and complete it when my master died. "What will we call it?" I asked. "How about *The Healing Yogi of the Himalayas?*"

But Swamiji looked at me and said "I think you should call it *Walking with a Himalayan Master.*" I tried a few other titles, and while he listened patiently, he came back to this one again, so I gave my promise once more.

For the last part of the trail we traveled on burros. They climbed slowly and securely, their hoofed feet clomping upwards just inches from the steep edge. There, high in the mountains at Janichatti, we enjoyed two nights. The view was exceptional; the evening lectures by Swamiji were revelations about practical spiritual life. He told us what we all already knew—that it did not matter how much one did practice or how high one advanced on the spiritual path if it was not reflected in the way one treated others. Like many other sages before him, he insisted on the practical aspect of love of others as the true measurement of higher consciousness.

After his talk, Swamiji called Charles, Theresa and myself to his room. It was delightful to sit in the wooden hut high in the mountains, candles lit, wrapped in shawls and blankets, enjoying a quiet evening with our teacher. He asked how we had enjoyed the day, what we had talked about, how we felt. He particularly watched Theresa as she made his lemon tea and pulled warm, dry clothes out of his suitcase. "Did Charles take good care of you?" he asked. "Did you get enough to eat? Shall I order hot water for you so you can take a bath?" This last question brought a huge smile to her face; she loved bathtubs and longed for a soak in the mountains. So our teacher had the staff bring three buckets of hot water to his room the next morning so she could bathe after he and I had departed.

THE MASTER'S LIFE

"Everyone has challenges awaiting them," Swamiji said as we gathered closer to him in his cold room. "My master was a man of austerities, yet he was more patient with me than I am with you. His own master had reminded him that he would have to go through a hard karma in this life, and he did. Before he went to the Himalayas, he was a judge in a district high court, the only Indian on the bench of British judges. This was decades before India had achieved independence from England. His son was involved with the underground resistance against the British and was caught in the assassination attempt of the British General Dyer.

"Dyer was a terrible man. He hated the Indian people and did everything to discredit them and further the British rule. Once when a British woman accused an Indian of accosting her in the street, all Indians were severely punished. General Dyer gave the command that Indians who passed along that busy thoroughfare had to do so crawling on their hands and knees. One brave woman refused to crawl. 'This is my country,' she said, 'the home of my parents and grandparents. I will not defame their honor in my own home.' To punish her, the general had her stripped naked and flogged in the public square. At a small window overlooking the square stood her young daughter who vowed, with tears flowing down her cheeks, that she would avenge her mother.

"Years later General Dyer had his soldiers open fire with automatic rifles on peaceful Indians in Amritsar who had gathered for a rally which the general declared unlawful. This incident was brought to world attention. The general was returned to England where he met a hero's welcome while the Indians buried the hundreds he had killed. Several years later, when it became known that General Dyer was returning to India for a celebration, the little girl who had watched her mother tortured declared that she was now an adult and ready to marry any man who killed the general.

"My master's son and four other men tried to kill him as he sat watching a race. The attempt was a failure; the young man managed only to shoot off the general's ear. Arrested, the men were sentenced to death by hanging.

"Because the other judges respected my master so much, they came to him and said that if he would write a public letter denouncing his son's terrorist behavior, they would change the verdict from death to life imprisonment.

"My master had the most difficult decision of his life to make. He told them that his son knew what he was doing and was well aware of the consequences of his action. If he did an unlawful act, then that was his responsibility. 'I cannot apologize for him. I am a judge. You British shouldn't be here in our country anyway.'

"The judges were angry at his remarks and retorted by forcing him to sign the death warrant. My master signed the paper, broke the pen in half, and walked out of the court. He disappeared, and while everyone searched for him, he was not to be found. His wife went mad with grief over her son and died a short time later. My master made his way to his penultimate abode in the Himalayas while the British were blamed for his disappearance."

I was deeply touched by this story. My heart went out to this man who had given his son for the world. His sacrifice helped to focus energy for the independence of his country and his decision to leave the world gave me my own teacher.

"My master taught by example," Swamiji continued. "Once we were walking near Mussoorie on the mountain trails and there loomed a cobra in front of us. We couldn't get around the snake. I immediately averted my eyes searching for a rock, the bigger the better. Meanwhile my master walked up to the cobra, bent down, and stroked its head three times. The snake slithered off the trail.

"He was always helping people, even at great distances from himself. He touched the lives of many famous leaders by his personal guidance. Politicians like Gandhi and J.P.Prakash, India's first president, as well as saints like Tagore, Ramakrishna, Aurobindo knew and respected him."

I found it heartening that Swamiji was sharing these precious memories with us as he himself was not feeling well and was beginning to speak about completing his work before he left the earth plane.

The next morning we started out on burros again and headed upward for a rocky climb, higher and higher, finally stopping for tea along a dirt road lined with rock. Swamiji had a gift for knowing when to attend to the stomach needs of others. We parked the animals and followed a trail the last half mile to the origin of Jamnotri. There, in the narrow valley between the high peaks, was an extraordinary pilgrimage site. A large pool held steaming 110 degree water which bubbled out of the side of the mountain and traveled westward down the rock and into the hot spring below. The water was so hot in the spring that here and there it was dotted with little cloth bags in which the local people were cooking their rice and lentils. Swamiji mentioned to me that certain stones oozed a fluid that was used as a health tonic.

As we slowly and carefully climbed into the pool of hot water he asked me, "Did you know that even the celestial beings take baths?"

"I have to think about that one," I decided as I held my breath and tried to submerge my achey body into the extremely hot water. Eventually I was able to sit in it without pain and actually enjoy the heat, but all too soon I was told that next we must jump into the cold water of the river crashing down from the mountains. So out we came, steam rising off our bodies in big, white clouds, and ran to the river, splashing in the cold, cold water there. Suddenly I felt completely energized, ready to take on anything. We dressed again, laughing at the incredible encounter and sauntered downhill to an old cave with a painted porch enclosing the entrance. Crossing the ravine, with pools of the mountain water for swimming on one side, we greeted the resident *sadhu*, a devotee of the deity Hanuman, and had lunch there at about 10,000 feet.

When I heard the yogi mention Hanuman, I recalled a clarification Swamiji had made earlier. "Most people think incorrectly that Hanuman was a monkey. He was a human being from a jungle tribe and his features were rather monkey-like. In his loyalty to Lord Rama and in his career as protector, he remained celibate, dedicating himself totally to service. He did not have a conflict with sexuality, but a conquest of self through service."

That was the last I remembered of his words. Some time later I found myself waking up from a deep sleep. Apparently I had napped in this cave with the yogis around me carrying on their happy visit. Now I heard the sounds of the group's arrival. The *sadhu* served them a welcome lunch for which he was generously repaid and they made a video of him and Swamiji walking along the mountain path. Swamiji enthusiastically told us that years ago he had walked five miles further up the mountain where the mythological seven sages once resided. The local belief was that they still lived there and would help anyone who requested their assistance.

Swamiji's eyes blazed with happiness as we travelled in these mountains; he clearly loved being there and sharing it with his students. When we had seen the group bus off and were back in our car again my teacher reminisced about his years in the monastery cave.

"You know, Justin," he then said quietly, "once I was married for a short time and had two children. It was a very difficult time of my life; I missed the peace and solitude of these mountains terribly. I realized that although I had done my karma, my life had to return to that of a renunciate. My master welcomed me back to the monastery with open arms and then prepared me for the rest of my mission in this body."

Immediately my mind went to the story of Gautama, the ancient prince of India, who felt the same irresistible call to renunciation and enlightenment. The prince left his wife and small child, his treasures and his palace in the dead of night to go to the forests to begin his deep spiritual pursuit. He also succeeded, and the entire world knows him now as the Buddha, The Enlightened One. The life of these great ones is not like ours, I mused. They have such determination to seek the ultimate end that nothing stands in their way; they are prepared to surrender everything for the truth they seek.

I was intrigued by my teacher's reference to "this body" as if it were not his. I was reminded of the many hints I came across over the years that he, like other great yogis, had dropped off one body and taken on another. Usually a body was found floating in the river, or killed by a snake in the forest, and the yogi put it on like a new suit of clothes. I wanted to ask Swamiji if he had ever done this, but did not want to disturb his quiet reverie as he looked out the window of our car climbing slowly and carefully up the steep mountain road.

After another day of travel, we finally entered the camp bungalows at the holy site of Gangotri. Here was the place many yogis had lived for thousands of years. Here the Ganges River, rushing from its source several miles up the mountains, began its powerful course down to the plains. The compound held several wooded buildings for pilgrims, a large temple, and a gathering of Indians who made their living each spring and summer by feeding those who came to the holy spot. In the winter, with the snow falling sometimes ten feet deep, the place emptied, and only the yogis stayed on in their caves doing practice.

Gangotri proved to be one of the most beautiful places on earth. All around one could see the snow-capped mountains, seemingly close enough to touch. The mountains around us were covered with trees and flowers. The river was a constant roar, calling one to the edge of incredibly shaped rocks, carved out by the pounding water.

I wandered about the pine trails, even trying to run, just to test my lungs, but at 10,000 feet I couldn't sustain the jog. Peering over the ledge of the ravine, I was fascinated by the shape of the bronze colored boulders in the rushing Ganges. From different angles, it appeared that the water had carved out contours of jungle animals over centuries. I traced the smooth outlines with my gaze until sight became a contemplation. But then the aroma of the pines swelled my sense of being alive and unsuspected reflections began filtering through my mind. "How strange," I mused, "that Swamiji separates me from everyone for most of this trip. Each day he calls me to his car and we chat as he points out familiar haunts from his younger years; each day he walks only with me through these trails, cheerfully reminiscing of similar times with his master." Often it was just the two of us that shared chai or a meal. I knew he had told Charles to look after Theresa on the bus, but no doubt some of the others were wondering what was going on. Then his words of some years back echoed abruptly before my mind:

"Careful, Justin, there is a sleeping renunciate in you."

Being married, I didn't know what he meant by that. But, of course, I did. In a flash, I knew with utter clarity what the future would bring. I didn't want to admit it to myself; it was all making sense, but I didn't want to encourage it further. As I turned, Swamiji was standing some yards away.

"Many people know my love for you; it's a special love, don't you feel it?"

I still couldn't or wouldn't put it all together. I held everything as separate parts, not knowing how they fit together. The first trip earlier this year amazingly wiped out my debts from the past. What did this new information mean for my career, my marriage, my future? Why the repeated public demonstration of separating me from my wife and my friends? While I never lost my disciple's respect for Swamiji, at times as we walked it seemed to me that we were like two independent, self-reliant buddies, enjoying each other's company in the forests, basking in the friendship, sharing stories, meals, and a mutual love for life. "Maybe one day I'll figure it out," I decided.

The next day was the long-awaited trek up the mountains to the source of the River Ganges. Swamiji would wait for us at the camp at Gangotri, so I was able to walk with Theresa and Charles and the others. We packed our sleeping bags, cameras, and our box lunches—boiled potatoes, boiled eggs, and cucumber sandwiches—and began the longest trek of our lives.

With the sky and our heads all clear, we walked for the next ten hours, uphill on meter-wide dirt and rock paths all the way. The higher we ascended the winding trail, the more the wind and the sun collaborated in burning their presences upon our bodies. Once after we turned a bend in the path, we crossed a narrow sandy edge that gave way as Theresa crossed. The sand, and Theresa with it, began a slide to the rocks a few thousand feet below, but at the exact right moment I turned and grabbed her extended hand as the trail, together with her lower body, slipped downward into space. We increased our attention to the firmness of the trail staying as close to the inner wall of the mountain as we could. After five hours, we felt we just had to rest. Lying down on the sharp rocks in a wide area off the side of the trail, we fell asleep. As we lay there on the rocks, the sun warming us, the talk of the Indian pilgrims passing next to us on the trail, we experienced one of the most comfortable sleeps of our lives. When we awoke a half-hour later, we were amazed at how restored and hungry we felt. We opened our lunch boxes and found that the three of us were given only two, so we shared the exquisite meal gratefully, thinking it was as good as the best French cuisine to our mountain appetites.

People who had passed us during our respite were slowing down and we soon regained our lead. By late afternoon, we finally hit the crest and looked down at the Bhojwasa camp, more appreciated than a five star hotel. We three entered the building of large wooden rooms and sat down on the floor. Theresa leaned against the wall, Charles and I lay down, our heads on her thighs, and we all fell asleep in that strange position until the group arrived twenty minutes later. We were awakened by shouts of food and followed the group a few hundred feet to our dinner at a special place. There, an elderly man sitting under a huge tarpaulin was cooking a vat of rice and lentils and vegetables. For him this was his principle sadhana: preparing meals for the pilgrims who visited this awesome region. We were hesitant at first, not knowing if the food was safe to eat, but the aroma drew us under the tent. We were offered tin plates filled with hot food by the old man who welcomed us with smiles and laughter. The food was exceedingly delicious; the atmosphere lifted our hearts after the long trek; the blessing of the server touched us.

After dinner we all gathered inside the room we had claimed

and, placing a lighted candle in the center of the wood floor, we all fanned out around it in our sleeping bags. We enjoyed the light and surprising warmth from the little candle until its flickering wick lulled us, one by one, to sleep.

We awoke to an inch of snow on the grounds around us, surprising us with its beauty. The July sun rapidly evaporated the snow and scorched us again as we ate our breakfast twelve thousand feet above sea level. But the trek wasn't over yet; we were only at the threshold of the holy place. Leaving our equipment at camp, we climbed upward another six kilometers, sometimes over huge boulders, four to six feet high. At midday, the first Western group ever allowed to visit this place stood before the ancient, mammoth glacier called Gomukh. It was two hundred yards wide with its jagged wall rising four to five stories high and its frigid depth wedged backwards for twenty miles. Like a frosted fortress, it defied the searing sun to melt its frozen surface if it dared. Standing a few yards before the awesome wall, I heard in the eerie silence the uneven dripping of the melting ice. Falling from the crevaced heights, splattering upon the barren, rock-strewn soil, these distilled splashings spread into multiple, silvery rivulets that zig-zagged along the ground searching to join together into a single, flowing mass of cascading energy. Here was the great source—Gomukh—The Mouth of the Cow, the sublime mother that continued to give birth to her child, the mighty Ganges River. Surrounded by this bleak, rock-hard emptiness, obscured at thousands of feet in high blue space, the irrepressible life-giving Ganges erupted downhill, bringing her fruits to the dry plains below, inspiring religious poets and yogis to record her mystery and thousands to bathe in her flowing assurance.

Having come this far, it would be remiss not to complete the traditional bath to the five limbs in this holy birthplace where adepts and sages have lived over the centuries. Just before the river surged downward, there was a fast-moving, broad stream that permitted human entry. Most of us stood in the icy waters that turned our ankles blue, quickly scooping up water to our faces, ears, and necks as we imitated the example of an old wandering *sadhu* across the river who had entered just before us. Charles wanted more; he disrobed and slid down into the shallow liquid for a few precious seconds, emerging fully bathed and wide awake from his cold encounter.

On the shores, refreshed, everyone became quiet, drawn to sit and meditate. In this barren and silent atmosphere, where no vegetation could be found, my thoughts centered around how overcrowded my lifestyle was and how little I really needed to live comfortably. I spied a flat rock and sat down to meditate in the blazing sun. As soon as I closed my eyes, I was startled by the vivid image of a grey shawled, elderly yogi standing before me. A wave of such complete peace filled me that I continued to stare at his image. After some time, the yogi departed, but his peace remained with me the rest of the pilgrimage.

That evening, back at Bhojwasa, we entertained each other in the cold room made cozy by those bringing up current interests and events, mixed with stories of the early founding days with Swamiji in Chicago and plenty of jokes. We had grown close through the common ordeal of the trek. A student from Chicago mentioned that she had almost turned back from the ascent two days earlier when the relentless heat, the steep climb, and the burning wind all taxed her endurance to the point where she had to take repeated rests to catch her breath. At one very tired juncture in her slow pilgrimage, the temptation to quietly turn around and return to Gangotri was interrupted by the sight of an old, thinly-clad village woman staggering upwards, very slowly, to the same destination. As she passed by, the panting student smiled at her and, bowing her head in the traditional greeting, noticed that the elder woman had no toes. The Chicagoan brushed aside her temptation and continued up the mountain.

The next morning we could hardly contain ourselves, so full of energy were we. Eating only a biscuit and tea, the three of us picked up three grapefruit from the offered fruit and bolted from camp heading downhill. Theresa took the lead as if she were qualifying for the Olympic walking marathon, easily catching and passing a student who had started an hour earlier. We charged downhill, feeling the sensation of runners' high. We stopped once to eat the fruit at a particularly beautiful sight, drank icy water cascading down a rock wall, and made it back to camp in the new record time of three and half hours. Swamiji was waiting for us, delighted at our speed, until we all noticed that Theresa's fingers were very swollen. Her gold-filigree wedding ring was cutting into her finger, turning it an ugly, deep blue. We were instantly concerned. Swamiji grabbed Charles' Swiss army knife and quickly cut the delicate wedding ring off my wife's finger.

We were invited into his room where he had tea ready for us and, like an excited child at Christmas time, wanted to know everything about our trip. We narrated our impressions almost as fast as we had walked.

"And then what happened?" his repeated question eagerly sought more.

We told him about the feel of the cold water, the awesome size of the glazier, the incredibly pure turquoise pools, the July snow. On and on we spoke, relaying our stories.

"What else happened?" he pushed us again. We paused, looked at each other and waited while he put his head down and closed his eyes for a few moments. His head sprang up with excitement on his face and he proceeded to remind us of every detail and incident that we had overlooked in our telling, about our parched, dry faces, our sleeping en route, the stories we told in the cabin, the devotee who cooked for us. We were delighted with his replay of our trip and wondered how he knew about it when he was hours away. Swamiji smiled and said, "Some day you will do it too."

The following morning Swamiji called the three of us. We went with him to explore some of his old caves farther north in the mountains where he had lived for three years. The sky was bluer than I could ever remember and crawling into the caves was fascinating. "Fast on Wednesday for Thursday morning," he said solemnly.

On Thursday at 7:05 A.M. with the wild river roaring and tumbling against the rocks to our right, our master touched us. He had us sit on the edge of the cliff while he chanted the initiation mantra. Theresa handed him the wild tulsi leaves and fresh water she had brought at his instruction, and he closed his eyes, gathering his energy. He then pressed his thumb on our foreheads, placed the bunches of tulsi upon our heads and sprinkled us with drops of the sacred water. We drank the rest of the water and were handed tufts of the ceremonial tulsi branches to take home with us.

"Each day the power given to you will grow," he told us. "I'm binding you three together; your future work is together." We followed him down the mountain path to the camp compound, not speaking, so filled with love and gratitude were we. He had passed on the energy and grace of the sages and blessed all our future life.

Later, as I was riding in the car again with Swamiji, he added another tidbit of information. "I'm not telling you everything," he chuckled.

I thought to myself, "What else is new?"

"My master will explain everything in time. You can talk to him and he will answer you," he said.

I replied, "I'll have to test that!"

Swamiji appeared startled by my remark and quickly chastened me aloud, "Don't say test; say wait!"

The next morning an interesting incident occurred as we prepared to board our chartered bus. A group of Indian pilgrims, led by a vociferous and rather aggressive pandit, decided that since there was room on our bus, the Indians had the right to climb aboard. So they did. When our group arrived, it was stunned to find the chartered bus filled with Indians. The Indians refused to leave, egged on by the pandit. Tempers began to flare; sides were drawn. A culture clash about space and travel ensued with the Americans sure that, because they had hired and paid for the bus, they had the sole right to it, and the Indians insisting that, since a bus was there and they needed one, they were not trespassing.

Swamiji and I were across the river but could see the entire affair. Soon Charles came to us with the Indian guide and asked Swamiji what to do. He told Charles to go over and settle things. Charles led them diplomatically to a compromise. If the Indians would get off and allow us to board our bus, then all the remaining seats could be utilized by them. The Americans sat two to a seat, filling more than half the bus; the Indians sat five to a seat, filled the floor and hung out the windows. A cultural difference in space. The angry, shouting pandit was not allowed to board. The group waved good-bye and headed westward to Uttarkashi.

As evening began, Swamiji and I caught up with the group at the old mountain town with an ancient, famous temple, beloved of many Himalayan yogis. Our group stayed at the government tourist center in green-painted, wooden rooms. Word had spread about the area that Swami Rama had arrived, so lines of people came for his blessing, filling the little compound. Several yogis and swamis entered the room and attempted to touch his feet in the traditional way of respect for an advanced adept; he pulled them up abruptly into an energetic bear hug.

That evening we convinced our teacher to talk to the crowd. He called Swami Ajaya, Charles and myself to sit near him on the dais together with the local pandits and swamis, who came bearing gifts of fruit and flowers. We all listened to him teach us how to become sensitive to the sages' messages and then chanted together into the evening hours. As our teacher stood up to leave, he gathered an armful of beautiful, white gardenias and walking toward the exit, dropped them into Theresa's lap.

The next morning he mentioned that we all might visit an old temple on the other side of the city. Off we strode looking for it down dusty streets until we found a dingy-looking, stone-layered edifice barely the size of a two-car garage. It was the antithesis of a spiritual temple to a Westerner. I was almost repelled by the ambiance—dirty and crumbling, with meandering cows mooing by the entrance, little kids playing in the mud near its steps, and older men relieving themselves next to its walls in the alleyway. Neither Charles nor I wanted to go inside. Theresa climbed the steps and entered the first temple chamber and quickly came to get us, insisting we must come. Reluctantly, Charles and I followed her up the steps to the small anteroom, ducking our heads as we passed into the inner chamber. In the center of the small room was an enormous sacred stone symbol of the divine male-female force of the universe. A priest chanted and poured oil over the top of the stone. A tiny candle burned at the center as the pilgrims entered and exited, receiving a blessing from the priest. I was impressed that so much light could radiate from a single candle. Theresa had gone over to one corner and sat down to meditate. Charles sat in the adjacent corner. I was in one of those "If you've seen one temple you've seen them all" moods so I nodded to Charles that I was stepping outside.

I waited and waited. We had agreed that ten minutes would be enough for the visit to this place so I wondered. What could possibly be holding them this long? I waited some more, impatiently. An hour later, Theresa staggered out of the temple, propped up by Charles, her eyes were half slits and she was unable to talk. The normal walk of five minutes back to our rooms took another half hour as she tried to walk. She wasn't ill; her condition resembled a semi-trance state. She was uncoordinated, unable to articulate her experience, yet seeming extremely happy and peaceful. An hour and half later, she began to come around and was able to speak. She was full of joy, calm and peaceful. She thought she had been in the temple for only ten minutes but when she had finally heard Charles calling her name, she opened her eyes and found her lap full of rice and flowers offered by the other worshippers in the temple.

Swamiji looked at Theresa, "You have had an experience!"

"Yes," she answered slowly, smiling.

"This was not your first visit there. You have done many days of *sadhana* at that temple. It was one of your favorite places. That's where Ramakrishna had his early experiences of the Divine Mother. When his pupil, Swami Vivekananda preferred philosophy to meditation and complained that meditation was just an empty experience, Ramakrishna sent him to the same temple and there he was transformed by his visions. Many saints have meditated there over its two thousand year history."

Sitting on my bed that night I reviewed the day. "So much for odors and appearances," I thought. Once again my limiting expectations had gotten in the way. Due to my own arrogance, I had placed myself above this ancient ruin and missed a wonderful opportunity. Obviously, the grace was there, the whole place was charged with blessings, but I couldn't receive them. Over the next week, I pondered much about how to dispose myself for receiving truth.

The next morning we all departed farther south for Rishikesh. In spite of my best efforts, I fell asleep in the front seat of Swamiji's taxi. Upon awakening, I was a little embarrassed.

"You had a good sleep?" asked my teacher. It was less a question then an appraisal. I felt exceptionally clear and balanced and thanked Swamiji for these trips to his home territory.

"You know I love you and Theresa unreservedly; now you will shine."

I asked him if he knew what he would do in the next two years. He smiled and nodded affirmatively, but quickly called my attention to a spot out the window. "Rama Tirtha entered the water here at the end of his life," he exclaimed as we passed by a bend in the road near the river.

The last days in Rishikesh and New Delhi were spent ruminating over the meaning of the last two trips and deciding to go on another. There was something I must learn; I just knew it.

THIRD TRIP

A few months later I left Theresa in our little apartment in Honesdale working on a new book assignment from Swamiji and I traveled to the Valley of the Flowers, a favorite spot of my teacher, with another group that included my dear friend and brother, Ladd Koresch.

This trip was different. It took us to incredible mountain vistas, with Ladd and I leading the group most of the way. We slept in the open, in the usual cement blocks for pilgrims set up by the government, and in the quiet rooms of our Rishikesh ashram. There were a few private moments with Swamiji, but never again like on the previous tour.

One evening Swamiji told us about his days with some of the great ones. He spoke about his days with Mahatma Gandhi and told us that during his stay at Gandhi's ashram he noted that this saint didn't play favorites. Gandhi's son had wanted to purchase a train ticket once when the excursion was sold out, so he made a ruckus, insisting on special treatment because he was the Mahatma'a son. No ticket was given. His father had called the depot in advance and insisted that there be no exceptions for any of his people, including relatives. In fact, if his son caused trouble, the station master was to call the police.

Picking up on this quality from the Mahatma, Swamiji did the same when he was assigned to schedule appointments at Gandhi's ashram. When anyone requested an audience with the Mahatma he was listed in a book and given an audience in exactly the same sequence. In spite of the rank or self-importance of the visitor, Swamiji kept the sequence intact. Some complained to Gandhi about the stubborn guy who scheduled them, but to no avail. Gandhi sent word that he knew he could trust Swamiji's objectivity.

My teacher also lived for a while with the sages Sri Aurobindo and Ramana Maharshi, among many other saints. The telling of the stories struck a nerve in Swamiji, for he immediately warmed up to the topic and continued on into the night. "Ramakrishna was a moon" he said to us, "and Ramana was a sun."

After several weeks in the Himalayas, our group returned to Rishikesh. After dinner, all the students went to the main building for Swamiji's evening lecture. Sitting there pensively as we waited for our teacher to arrive, I started to deliberate my next sojourn to India. Questions about where I would visit, how long I would stay, whom I would meet marched before my attention. Suddenly my mind became crystal clear: I didn't need to come back! "What I want in India is already inside me," I realized. "When I return to America, I carry the Himalayas with me." The mountains brought me to that self-awareness. Visiting temples and collecting photos of ruins would never give me what I was looking for, because they only pointed to the ancient structures of consciousness. Whether I was in the States or in Rishikesh, meditation would be the same. What difference did it really make where I sat since I always had to cross the threshold to the unknown within myself?

At that moment, Swamiji marched into the room and started out his lecture in full swing. "Why do you people come to India? What are you looking for? What you are seeking you already have within yourself! Visiting temples and saying mantras in some old temple won't get you what you want. You spend your time traveling around, wearing yourself out. You must go within and that journey can be done in your home."

I was flabbergasted. I looked up and just smiled at him as he winked quickly at me and continued his talk.

"Don't come to India thinking you are going to get enlightened; it doesn't happen that way. If you do come here, then have a daily schedule for yourself. Stay put in the ashram, follow your schedule, do your practice. It's quiet here, no one will bother you. If you want to visit a place, then set a time, visit, and return to your schedule. Don't make yourself weary going from place to place thinking that visiting shrines will get you what you want."

I knew then that when I went home I would be richer than ever before; I would take India and the teachings of my Gurudev with me.

But first there was a final surprise awaiting me. In New Delhi Swamiji took me to a bank and opened a safe deposit box. Inside the box was the ten-pound emerald, the sacred stone that I had heard about years before.

When Swamiji was a young monk, he was inspired with an

idea for a project that would require a great deal of money. By this time he knew that if he planned unselfishly for the good of others, circumstances would work out to ensure its success. This time, however, he decided to play it safe. So he went to his master and asked for financial assistance. The master took him to the cave of jewels and presented him with a pure ten-pound emerald. Swamiji accepted the gift and was reminded that he would have to take care of the jewel. A few days later, sufficient money unexpectedly came to Swamiji for the charitable project. Now he had a priceless jewel on his hands and did not know what to do with it. He wanted to give it back, but knew that would be impolite. One day his master asked about the project, so Swamiji explained that he had received all the money he had needed and now did not know what to do with the jewel. His master nodded and said, "That gift is your responsibility. If you had waited and trusted, you would not have had this burden."

Swamiji later told me that he had to pay yearly insurance on the emerald to insure its safety; it had become an albatross around his neck. "I learned a lesson in both trust and freedom," he said.

At the bank he placed the precious jewel in my hands. It was a beautiful green, about a foot long and five inches in diameter. For some reason, I decided not to ask questions but just appreciate the event. The bank manager, a student of my teacher, then helped us lock up the treasure.

Back on the sidewalk, we turned the corner and walked past a men's clothing store. "What would you like?" he casually asked me as he noticed me looking in the window.

I couldn't resist the temptation. "That beige safari suit looks sharp," I answered. Immediately he led me into the store, and in spite of my embarrassment, ordered the suit to be custom made and delivered before I left the country.

We left the store, focusing on the next event, but my mind reeled with his love. Swamiji just put his hand on my shoulder and said quietly, "Justin, you have all you need—you have me!"

Exploring Japan in 1985

CHAPTER 23
LIFE IN JAPAN

The day was warm and sunny. I walked down the busy Tokyo street and entered a tea shop. Dozens of Japanese, dressed in colorful kimonos, knelt around low tables sipping green tea. Someone brushed by me as he went out the door. I looked up and recognized the back of my teacher's head. He wore a white kimono crossed with thick, blue lines and seemed to head toward the nearby Shinto temple. I dashed after him. When I caught him on the temple steps, he turned to me and said, "You are going to Japan sooner than you think."

HE DREAM ENDED AT THE GOOD PART, as usual. I had always wanted to live in Japan, finding the idea thrilling since childhood. Four years after the dream, Theresa and I landed in Tokyo.

Swamiji had telephoned our little apartment in Honesdale, a few months after my last trip to India, to tell us that we should prepare to come to Japan. He was staying at the Atami headquarters of the spiritual organization called Sukyo Mahikari. This group was founded by Okada San, the first person Swamiji had met when he was sent on his world mission. At that time there were many religious groups arising among the Japanese as part of their recovery from the trauma of the war. With the Emperor no longer officially viewed as a divine incarnation, the restless people searched for religious guidance. Many new theologies mixed with traditional religions and formed new life philosophies. One of these, Omoto, influenced the founder of the martial art of Aikido and became known to Okada San. Okada San gradually added his own theological concepts to the ideas of Omoto and centered his new organization around redemptive and healing dimensions, emphasizing a virtuous life and devotion to the community.

In 1969 Swamiji had brought a message and some teachings from his master to the Japanese spiritual leader and had spent six months living in Japan before coming to the United States. Since then he visited the Japanese group once a year or so, loving their enthusiasm and generosity, the beauty of the mountains, and the graciousness of the founder's daughter and successor, Keiju Sama. He had insisted that the organization develop an international conference on spirituality, health, and science, an idea he had long-ago discussed with the founder, but when the present spiritual head voiced concern that it was a very great task, Swamiji had told her not to worry; he would send two of his disciples to help her.

As he explained all this on the phone, we were overwhelmed by his trust and wondered if he had not exaggerated our abilities just a bit, but we promised to give up our apartment and go to our next adventure.

The week before we left Pennsylvania for the Far East, we were surprised to find Swamiji and Phil ringing our doorbell on Saturday afternoon. While Theresa made tea for our guests, Swamiji sat down on our deep rust sofa which matched the color of his robe. I was amused as he smilingly eyed it and felt the contours. "Why do you have a sofa in my color?" he shouted over the whistling of the kettle.

"Oh, Swamiji," Theresa said, "I love that sofa. I made it from scrap material from all the robes I've sewed for you."

That threw the gauntlet down directly, I thought. Swamiji laughed and accepted his tea, but I could not let the joke drop. Theresa and I both knew that he needed a couch for his cabin on the Institute grounds, but I also knew Theresa wanted to keep it. "Swamiji," I said, "you no doubt recognize the superior quality of that sofa. We selected it especially for its color and are thinking of storing it while overseas."

"It would be more properly cared for in the living room of my cabin than in a damp, dusty storage bin," he answered, sounding so logical. Swamiji winked at Phil as he turned his head away.

"I agree, Swamiji," I added, "it definitely would add sophistication to your living room." For a moment, he lifted his chin and inhaled with surprise; then we all broke out in laughter.

So once again our meager belongings were divided up. A few things were sent into storage; several boxes of books and papers were stacked in a friend's attic; some pieces were given to the Institute. Swamiji sent the big, blue truck, this time to pick up the sofa and install it in his cabin. He sent a note with the truck stating that he would "hold it without charge for awhile!"

Tokyo in early August of 1985 was hot and humid. The Sukyo Mahikari officials who met our plane smiled as they wiped their brows, apologizing for the weather. We were driven into the city to be left for recuperation at the Hyatt Century Hotel while our apartment was readied. The next day one of the religion's teachers, Mrs. Senshu, bubbled over with a contagious enthusiasm as she told us about Swamiji's last visit. She sped us on a delightful journey from Shinjuku ward through the Ginza strip and concluded our wandering at the Ashoka restaurant. As we ate our first Japanese tempura, she told us that we had just retraced Swamiji's last tour exactly.

After a few days we were escorted to the spiritual group's headquarters, a newly constructed, gleaming white building, where we met the smiling staff that carried on all the work of the world-wide organization. The office work, the publications, the youth organizations, and the ceremonies were all cared for by volunteers who lived in group homes nearby. We were guided on a fifteen minute walk through the busy streets to our own three-room, traditional apartment on the tenth, the uppermost floor, of a building in the Suginama ward. Our delightful interpreter, Kim, showed us how to care for the tatami mats, how to use the knee-high refrigerator, where to shop for groceries, how to do laundry at the neighborhood washer, where to set out trash, and where to catch the trains.

During the next months I felt like I was on a different, almost mysterious planet, a feeling that never left me during my stay. I found a strange mixture of history and modernity, even stranger than that in Europe. We watched the cornerstone of a new building being blessed in an ancient Shinto ritual; we listened to the gender-different, new tones of the unfamiliar language shouted around us; we noted the office workers rushing down the streets in blue suits, carrying briefcases, and sometimes wearing face masks; we observed as mothers on trains removed the shoes of their offspring so the upholstered seats would not be soiled by little feet; we watched as everyone else pulled books out of their pockets to spend travel time reading. Anywhere we went, except at the impossible train stations, at least three attendants materialized from nowhere bowing and smiling their willingness to accommodate us. I thought that shopping in a Tokyo department store was a wonderful brief therapy for depression: there elevator attendants and stairway guards in uniforms and white gloves bowed as a customer entered and departed, at least two attendants stood by each counter ready to serve, door guides provided long plastic sheaths for wet umbrellas on rainy days. One need just walk casually in the door and experience all the attention one could ever want.

Mahikari surrounded us with courtesy, making sure that our wishes were always fulfilled. Theresa and I were installed as consultants to assist the organization with its conference on peace and the future of humanity. We were also idea people on the executive committee, suggesting and inviting international speakers; we acted as liaisons between East and West; we taught practical English to the staff; we edited the translations of the spiritual head's teachings.

Swamiji wrote to us, encouraging us to take advantage of our time in Japan. He insisted to Theresa that his dog was sleeping on her sofa in the cabin so she probably would not want it back anymore. He also told us to enjoy the culture and have fun, so we decided to throw ourselves into as many arts and cultural opportunities as time allowed. Theresa learned the art of wearing kimono, performing the tea ceremony, doing Japanese flower arranging. I enrolled in Tai Chi and took a semester on the history of Buddhism. Together we took private lessons in sumie painting and celebrated the special, seasonal five-hour tea ceremony at the beautiful private residence of the tea sensei's .

Tucked away behind some enormous trees in the heart of Tokyo, we found a Buddhist monastery that offered meals as an expression of spirituality. The monastery's head, Abbess Koei Hoshino, taught the centuries-old Japanese temple cooking and served as chief chef. Every lunch was a seven course meal, delicately served with an emphasis on the placement and design of the food, its color and its flavor, always according to season. Theresa was so impressed by the woman and her understanding of the profound importance of food as a path of spirituality that she interviewed the abbess for her book and attended her classes in this special cooking art.

We loved walking through the city and suburbs. Every few blocks we would find something wonderful: a small Shinto shrine with some fruit or flowers or coins laid before the enthroned deity; artisans weaving tatami mats and baskets, blowing glass, arranging flowers, trimming bonsai trees, sewing futons. We celebrated a springtime picnic under the flowering cherry trees; we wandered boldly into the cacophony of the Shinjuku night life and the explosions of sound from the pachinko gaming parlors.

With our interpreter, we traveled to the ancient city of Kyoto, staying in traditional inns, visiting the vast temples, and meditating in the rock and moss gardens of the Zen monasteries. We explored the Imperial Palace grounds, the old city of Kamakura, the kabuki theater, World Expo '85.

We rode on the Bullet Train to the Japan Alps, staying in its heart—Takayama—in Hida prefecture. In Japanese mythology the place is known as the soul of mankind, and there Sukyo Mahikari built its Main World Shrine, a huge golden ark, floating amongst the clouds of the mountains. We were pleased to attend monthly ceremonies of the group, meditating in its vast prayer hall and greeting thousands of followers. Each month, after the ceremony, we met with Keiju Sama, who always asked about our teacher and was especially pleased when we had a message to deliver from him.

Japanese TV was highly entertaining; the game shows were as zany and rowdy as those in England. An American film was shown one night of each week and we often used the opportunity to welcome our American friend, Cha Thorpe, as a guest for dinner and a movie. One evening, as we watched Indiana Jones flee before the mammoth boulder rolling perilously after him through the cave, my cup of tea slid from the right side of the table three feet to the left and back again. Just as I made a surprised comment about the incredible Japanese special effects, the pictures and mirrors began to fall off our walls and smash on the floor. For almost a minute we experienced a 6.2 Richter-scale earthquake that swayed the building and shattered thousands of windows in the area, but left the city free of serious damage.

We found earthquakes in Japan like snow in Minnesota: they come with the territory. After fifty quakes, I stopped counting them. Most were slight tremors that we felt as we walked down the street or sat at our desk; no one paid much attention to them unless they increased in strength, which happened about once a month.

One day in Tokyo I met William Johnston, an Irish Jesuit who taught theology at the prestigious Sophia University. He had a wonderful, worldly acceptance of the many traditions of spirituality and a profound respect for the importance of meditation. He invited me to attend his class as his guest. It became a delightful rendezvous as, not infrequently, two Buddhist nuns and I would debate the merits of Buddhism versus Yoga. Father Johnston would sit back, chuckle, and let the three of us go at it. One of my chief objections to the Buddhist philosophy was its emphatic extinction of all desires. I viewed man as a teleological animal. Wasn't nirvana itself a desire? I understood nirvana as the fulfillment of life in which all other desires are extinguished. Our discussions heated up one day over whether the Buddha had an ego or not. The nun defiantly insisted that the Buddha was egoless; I held the opposite view.

"Really?" I finally asked her, my own ego burning, "then why did he run around claiming he knew the way? It took a colossal ego to foster the ambition to liberate every creature in the world."

That did it. My words were sacrilegious. The poor nun glared at me, struggled with her composure and then, surprising all the students, picked up her books and stomped to the classroom exit. Before she slammed the door, never to return for the rest of the course, I said good-bye by adding, "It's all a mirage anyway."

An invitation to speak as usual at the Himalayan Institute's Congress arrived in the mail toward the end of our first year in Japan. It provided the opportunity to speak privately with my teacher that I had wanted all year. Since 1984 my mind had been sporadically wrestling with notions of renunciation for myself and I wanted to clarify the issue with him. While I loved my wife dearly, I was beset with strong urges to end the state of marriage and take up one of monasticism or renunciation. So I left the heat of Tokyo and flew to the heat of New York, bussing into Honesdale once again.

It felt good to be in Swamiji's presence, even though my private time with him was very short. He presented me his new book *The Perennial Psychology of the Bhagavad Gita,* and I spoke to him about my growing desire to take vows of renunciation. I was surprised by his brusque reply, "You're two years late."

As I reeled from the sharpness of his words, people suddenly descended into his room and I knew that at the moment I could not get the kind of attention I felt I needed. We did not see each other again, for I had to return to Japan the following day. His words alone did not help me shed light on the matter so I put the idea aside for awhile.

During one of my stays at Sophia University I heard about another Jesuit, H.M. Enomiya-Lassalle, who had attained the status of roshi and led Zen retreats at his mountain monastery. He had come from Germany many years ago, studied Zen Buddhism, and established the monastery in 1980. His stated goal was to follow the recommendations of the Catholic Church's Second Vatican Council and investigate other religions for possible integration into the Christian faith.

A young priest, Father Lassalle's student, traveled with me sixty miles into the mountains for my first Zen retreat while Theresa and Cha climbed to the top of Mount Fuji. I wanted to witness Buddhist monks at close range thinking that perhaps the experience would help me decide about becoming a monk again myself. Many years ago I had learned that being a Catholic monk was not right for me, but perhaps, because of their emphasis on meditation, becoming a Zen monk would be. On the train ride into the mountains, we talked about the impact of meditation in our lives.

"I have been certified," the priest proudly remarked to me. Since I had never heard that expression before, I was curious and asked him to explain.

"One goes before the roshi who determines whether or not one has arrived at *kensho,* and if one has, one is certified as having reached it," he said.

"Do you mean enlightenment?" I asked, surprised.

"Yes, *kensho* is also called *satori*" he assured me.

"You have reached enlightenment?" I was truly curious now.

"Yes," he smiled, proud of his achievement.

Rumbling through my mind was his need to be confirmed or "certified" in enlightenment and my own suspicions about it. Why would one have to go outside oneself to get proof of personal experience? I asked him if I could inquire more about his attainment. He readily welcomed all questions, so I decided to probe in a more objective way, rather than make him feel like I was putting him on the spot.

"When the mind attains *kensho*, does that mean one has transcended the mind and body? That one knows in a self-evident immediacy all questions about life and the cosmos?"

"No," came his honest reply.

I pressed on. "Does *kensho* mean that you have expanded your consciousness to an awareness of reality in which you can inspect the past, present, or future of anyone?"

He shook his head sadly, "No."

"Have you conquered your fears and the dread of death through your *kensho*?" I eagerly asked.

"No." His voice became quieter.

Obviously, his idea of enlightenment was different from mine. I tried a new tact. "Have you ever read the *Upanishads* or any of the works of Shankara?" I asked. He was unfamiliar with both.

"Well, in the yoga tradition, there is a little different spin on enlightenment," I began and stopped there. His certification was very important to him. He was kind enough to befriend me and I didn't want to hurt him. I wasn't interested in debating our differences, merely reaching clarification, so I suggested that he might be interested some time in discussing the yogis' idea of enlightenment.

The five days of retreat with the monks at the Zen monastery were intensely packed, with every minute accounted for in a precise schedule. Everything—from eating in common, to cleaning the rooms, to walking and sitting and folding cloth, to holding cups and arms and legs precisely, to meditating nine times a day in short sittings—was done collectively under careful watch. Quite different from any other retreats I had ever attended, this one, particularly in the interface between the participants and the roshi and his assistants, seemed to me more like boot camp. I wondered how much of this anxious striving was cultural and how much was integral to the Buddhist approach? I could not help but get the feeling that my sincere, panicky comrades on the path were convinced that the week would be an utter failure if they didn't get "certified" at completion. Not surprising during these days, my assessment of Buddhist monkhood convinced me that the Buddhist path was not for me. While I was grateful for the experience, I departed knowing that in this life my path was the self-reliance and independence of yoga. The pull toward renunciation and my feelings about marriage were conflicted in my mind; the issue needed resolution but I wasn't sure how to accomplish it.

Meanwhile, the Mahikari people were so solicitous for our welfare that they kept providing us with unusual events and places to explore. When they heard of my keen interest in Sumo wrestling, a delightful senior member of the Mahikari staff, Bucho San, took us to the exciting last day of the sumo tournament to watch our favorite wrestlers. We applauded loudly as Konishiki, the only American high-ranked wrestler, easily won his bout and then watched as Japan's most prominent wrestler, Chionofuji, "The Wolf," a combination Arnold Schwartzennegger-Michael Jordan-Wayne Gretzky, performed magnificently and won the tournament.

I was pleased to be able to pay a visit to Professor Motoyama, a renowned scientist who experimented with the yoga concept of chakras. He studied Swamiji's work and had developed an AMI machine to test the electrical power of chakra energy. At that time he was investigating meditative states of consciousness with electronic measurements to analyze the type and change of energy as the mind focused at the various chakra centers. Among the many topics we shared, I will never forget his predictions.

"The more civilization learns to control matter," Dr. Motoyama said, "the less religion will exist." As we talked, I saw that he was not underestimating religion's value to inspire people but emphasizing that our growth in understanding and controlling the relationship between consciousness and matter would advance us beyond our reliance on Church organizations to achieve our destiny. He believed that our hopes would continue to be more directly experienced.

Theresa and I were asked to stay on in Japan past our promised year to assist with the conference itself, held October 30 through November 1, 1986. Meticulously prepared and efficiently delivered, it successfully presented over fifty-one speakers and accommodated two thousand participants from twenty-one countries. The presenters shared topics on religion, education, science, and medicine, all with a view to the future of humanity. One of my favorite speakers was Dr. Robert Mendelsohn of Chicago, a famous family physician. He startled the audience with "The Malignant Effect of Modern Medicine on World Peace."

With relentless wit and indisputable evidence, he slowly dismantled modern medicine to its core essence, namely, that it was not a science but a belief system, with all the trappings of a modern religion. For him, the posing of medicine with science was as much an oxymoron as plastic glasses, civil war, or military intelligence.

"Ninety percent of medicine, even according to the reports of Congress," he wryly pointed out, "consists of unproved remedies, the polite term for medical quackery. The other ten percent that have been subjected to controlled studies are, for the most part, disproved by those same studies and abandoned." He energetically wove startling facts with his own medical experience, cited journal articles with incisive comments that exposed how dangerous medicine had become, and proposed common sense changes with humor, compassion and courage. We shared many fulfilling hours together over the conference days and for years afterwards.

Perhaps the individual who stands out most in memory by his life and voice is that incomparable Dutchman, Frederick Frank. We instantly liked each other and shared a love of humor. His incorrigible sense of what is real and what is pretense never abated when I conversed with him, and his critical articulation was so spiced with humor that my merriment left me reeling as he dismantled society's latest Emperor's robe with gleeful perception.

He took on the theme, "On Criteria of the Human," and insisted that he positioned himself, at the august affair, as the representative of the enormous number of human beings, the untitled non experts, whom, like the present speakers, are equally passionate about the meaning of existence, both personal and cosmic. In developing his theme, he underscored an "undervalued consensus" between world religions regarding the endorsement of the full potential of humanness. He saw in the heroic efforts of Amnesty International, Greenpeace, and other such organizations, a vanguard of awareness for the sacredness of life and the irrefutable interdependence of "all earthly phenomena, without claiming religious labels."

My own paper, "The Formation of Religious Consciousness in the Twenty-first Century," derived its context from my experiences of yoga and meditation with their emphasis on the practical steps to achieving an integrated lifestyle aimed at transcendence. I showed how mainline religions were meagerly engaging the modern world because they dodged a holistic engagement with life, kept their theology so abstract and distant from the marvelous cultural diversity of human experiences, and yet authoritatively imposed their ecclesiastic structures and policies on new generations of believers, often with punitive denunciations of those who resisted.

"Religions today," I claimed, "are evading their primal responsibility to bring forward the evidence that awakens the human spirit to its inherent wisdom.

They lack a testable criteria for measuring the practical validity of their belief system."

I was invited by one of the conference presenters, Dr. Patrick Pietroni, president of the British Holistic Medical Association, to join the faculty of the University of London Medical School and teach wellness to physicians and nurses. He had also received the support of the government and private funding to start a holistic clinic as well as offer a series of courses for the medical and nursing schools of the city. Would I be Director of Education at Marylebone clinic, teach courses in stress management and wellness, and be part of a team of doctors to care for patients? It was an opportunity to apply the techniques I had been learning for the last fifteen years. I was ready to swim to the United Kingdom for the job! I immediately made arrangements to begin work the following January.

The lingering images of swamihood, renunciation, and marriage swirled more intensely than ever in my mind. The more I tried to distract myself, the more my mind returned to thinking about them. Theresa and I talked and talked. She already knew the direction my life was heading well before I would definitively acknowledge its new direction.

The day after the conference, as we were packed and ready to leave Japan, Swamiji phoned us to announce that he had just cut the legs off the sofa! He then insisted that we come to India briefly before returning to the States. It was a poorly-timed request, since tickets were purchased, our apartment was given up, and good-byes were said, but we packed an overnight bag, left our suitcases in the Tokyo airport, and hopped on the next plane to New Delhi. We would stay the weekend in India. Little did we know the events that would unfold, not altogether painless.

INTERLUDE IN INDIA

When one is around Swamiji, anything can happen, and more than likely it does. The unexpected for our next visit began as soon as we arrived in New Delhi at 3:30 A.M. Although Swamiji's staff was informed of our coming, no Indian taxi was there to meet us. No room was available at the hotel, in spite of our reservation. We were tired and annoyed and wondered what to do next. When we spied a large sofa in the lobby of the Hyatt, we plopped down to sleep until 6:30 when we called an old friend who lived in the city. She managed to get through the incredible phone system to our teacher who assured her there was a room waiting for us. At that moment, and quite unexpectedly the receptionist said, a room opened up. We found our way up to the room and slept until noon.

Refreshed by a wonderful Indian fruit breakfast, we headed across town to Swamiji's apartment. I was pleasantly shocked during the ride, for the roads appeared less dirty then I last remembered them; the buildings were better made. "Maybe it's just this route," I thought.

When we greeted our teacher at last, he opened with the inquiry, "Did you notice that the streets are cleaner then before?" With innocent, wide eyes he continued right on to ask how we were and how we enjoyed our stay in Japan.

It always left a good feeling in me to have him hint about my thoughts. I never felt, as some people did, that it was an invasion of privacy; to the contrary, I was charmed that my teacher thought enough of me to insinuate that I was on his mind.

This time I got right down to business. It was time for me to embrace the next step on my journey, to take vows of renunciation. I had decided to became a swami like my teacher. My memory frequently recalled his startling words of several years ago, "There's a sleeping renunciate in you," and at last I was ready to do something about them. I poured out my heart to my teacher, telling him of my desires, the worries I had overcome, the decisions Theresa and I had made.

Swamiji looked piercingly at me. "It can't be done till March," he firmly and coldly replied. I immediately suspected something not quite right, but the suspicion vanished when I told him I couldn't possibly return in March because of my new work in

London. "Ah, yes!" he said slowly, pleased with the idea, and then suddenly instructed me to go to Dr. Arya, now living in India, to select a date and make all the necessary arrangements for me to take vows as soon as possible.

The next day we arrived at noon, as invited, for a lunch with Swamiji. Anticipating a sumptuous meal, we had skipped breakfast. Just as we were about to sit down at the table, our teacher hurriedly informed us that we should depart immediately. "Go now! My student, Anil, will take you to the deluxe bus for Rishikesh."

"There's no rush, Swamiji," I said, eyeing the wonderful bowls of food being brought to the table, "we can stay overnight and catch the short flight instead."

But he would not hear of it. He insisted we leave immediately; I tried to persuade again, but it was no use. He was adamant in a very business-like tone. It didn't make sense to me why we had to rush up there and wait, and the feeling of something being amiss tugged at my mind again.

"You have to take the bus and get there today; it's only a five-hour ride. *Chello, chello!*" he demanded again, "don't miss it."

Slightly perplexed, I grabbed four apples, Theresa hugged him good-bye and off we went.

We took a taxi to the bus depot and I discovered that it wasn't a real bus that was about to pull out; it was, as far as I was concerned, a cattle car. This contraption hadn't seen a washcloth since India's independence. I turned to Theresa, "Hey, let's not get on this refuse truck; let's go to a hotel and fly out tomorrow instead. What Swamiji doesn't know won't hurt him."

It must have been the hunger speaking, because even I could not believe that I said he wouldn't know.

Theresa wouldn't hear of it; she wanted to do what her teacher said. We argued. Anil waved the bus tickets at us passionately, yelling that we must run after him. I visualized a deluxe horror story for the next five hours. Theresa was obstinate, I was fuming, but we dashed for the bus, just hopping on as it pulled out of the station.

The bus interior resembled a hot, dusty recycling center that had partially imploded. Items of all sizes—gadgets, pieces of rusted metal and bue plastic, old tires, wooden crates, even children in assorted sizes—filled every space. My attire was superbly fitting for this excursion: my best navy blazer, gleaming white shirt, Italian tie, freshly pressed gray pants, and polished shoes. Stares greeted us from the packed occupants, who weren't exactly in their power suits and cocktail dresses. They wondered why these strange Westerners would travel third class.

The bus gathered speed and we chugged along the highway, getting hungrier and dirtier with each mile. My worst nightmare unfolded as we went; it was not five so-called "deluxe" hours, but many more. If we were to take Chicago's Dan Ryan Expressway at rush hour and squeeze it onto New York's JFK Expressway, adding a few animals for color, then we would be approaching New Delhi traffic. It wasn't the crowds, which were exceedingly polite as always, nor was it the first four hours sitting on an iron bar followed by a turn on a tread-worn Michelin tire; no, it was the infernal stopping, which allowed the interior to heat up to boiling point at every hamlet, roadside shack, and chai shop along the only major highway, using the latter term loosely. Once outside Delhi, the bus driver communicated his intentions to the oncoming traffic by horn, since there was no separating center line on the road. Brakes, I decided, were mostly obsolete.

Midway to our destination, the bus paused for a longer rest so I decided to get some food. Theresa was so hot she wasn't hungry, but I was famished. I jumped off the bus and headed down to the outdoor fast food pans and bought something that looked safe. As I stood there eating, I noticed a bus similar to ours slowly turn the corner at the end of the block. Someone in it was waving wildly at the rear window. In a flash I realized that it was Theresa. I ran my heart out trying to catch the thing, jumping over dogs and carts. Theresa had just threatened the bus driver's life amidst shouting and tears, and as he finally slowed down, I leapt aboard. Naturally, I got severe indigestion. Exasperating words arose incessantly in my imagination against my teacher, holy man or not. Hadn't he said this was the only way to go? If I reviewed our plight once, I rehearsed it like it was headed for Broadway, adding nuances each time that egged me on stronger. "Surely this is just a mad dream that will end soon," I decided so I could calm down.

The bus finally pulled into the center of Rishikesh at midnight. We achingly stepped off and laughed at each other in the light of the station. My shirt now matched my oil-speckled pants; my sleek blazer gave off a muted blue cast under a protective film of dirt. My tie remained on the long gone bus, used to hold a broken window in its frame. Theresa looked like 'before' in a before/after commercial.

Being the reasonable yogis that we were, we made an exception in our diet and ushered in the morning with French fries and chai at the only open restaurant, busy serving truck drivers. Then peering all around us in the brisk night air, we woke a sleeping taxi driver to take us to the ashram at Ram Nagar.

Once the driver was paid off and had gone, we reached the locked ashram gate. The guard kept right in script; he refused entry to us. "No one informed me that two Americans were coming tonight," he said as he calmly fingered his rifle.

I looked over at Theresa; she wasn't smiling. It was now 1:15 A.M. We had begun our trip thirteen hours earlier. "At least he's consistent," I sagely observed, trying once again to persuade the field marshal to let us in. Fifteen minutes later, when he realized we would not leave, he reluctantly permitted us to cross the barrier. I can't remember for sure, but I may have promised him my first born.

It was true; the ashram had not been informed of our coming. "The plot is thickening," I surmised, as a sleepy member of the staff brought us to an empty room and tried to find sheets. One dominant thought haunted me the rest of the early hours: "Why are we here?"

Dr. and Mrs. Arya invited us to their home the next day to prepare us for the ages-old ceremony of renunciation in which I was to perform my own funeral rites. It had long been Dr. Arya's wish to take the same vows when his children were grown, and he kindly gave me everything he desired for himself: the ochre dye, the traditional clothing, a translation of the Sanskrit ritual. We had rest and wonderful food in his home for two days before leaving again for the ashram.

I tried in vain to reach the airlines in the hope that something could be done about our non-refundable tickets to the States. I needed to call Japan also so that our possessions might be rescued from the Tokyo Airport, but all the phone lines were down. The telex, my next attempt, was found to be malfunctioning also. We managed to send a message to Swamiji with a driver going to Delhi. Within a few hours, a doctor told the airlines that I had contracted a severe jungle ailment and would need at least another three weeks in recovery, I was able to get through to New Delhi airline operators as if nothing had been a problem at all, the air lines immediately revised our tickets and issued new dates, and Sukyo Mahikari sent a staff member to retrieve our bags in Japan. It all made me suspicious; it was now too easy.

These necessities handled, Swamiji then telephoned to say that Theresa and I should go on a retreat. It was a welcome instruction after all the chaos. The ashram was empty except for the staff and us, the weather was beautiful, the days long and quiet.

With only a single change of clothes in our overnight bags, we were forced to buy local clothes. Theresa was fitted out with saris and Punjabi suits and I went about in custom-made traditional white pajamas. We met Ashok, a long-time friend of Shivnath, a dear student of our teacher, who took us to nearby temples and led us on explorations of the fields and forests along both sides of the Ganges. One day Ashok pointed out what looked like a small hut in the middle of a farmer's field. As we wedged our way carefully through the growing grain, we found the ancient shrine to the God Shiva where sages had performed millions and millions of *Maha Mritunjaya* mantras over the centuries.

Ashok told us that a few months earlier he had been motorcyling along the road when the wind blew apart the tall grass and he saw a slight piece of white stone about four feet above ground. He went back to explore the spot with some friends, and after cutting back yards of thick brush, grass, and tree limbs, they had found the shrine. The farmer remembered that his father had said something about it, but he did not find it important. Ashok's party cleaned the shrine well, gave it a fresh coat of white paint, and washed the sacred stone side with milk. From the first time we saw it, Theresa and I were drawn to that place. We paid a daily visit there, bringing wild flowers as offerings and sitting in meditation before the sacred stone in the middle of the wheat field.

Each day we also walked along the river's edge, turned through the village to the temple complex and crossed the little stream, nodding to the women on the steps. Sometimes, on special days, we purchased little bags of coconut, puffed rice and colored sugar bits which we offered before the sacred images at the temple. The priest would accept the offering, mark our foreheads with red powder as a blessing, and return a bag of treats to us to take away as a gift from the divine.

After our first week of walking to the temple, the villagers seemed to count on our presence. They smiled to us along the road, some bowed the traditional greeting, others admired our Indian clothing. One day we spied a snake charmer on the grass path back to the ashram. When he saw us coming, he immediately stomped his old cobra to attention. Although he had a rapport with his snake, the poor animal looked weather-beaten and weary. As it stood up three feet tall and tilted from side to side, it seemed more like the snake was trying to catch its balance than respond to the rhythm of the flute, but we threw our rupees in the little basket, accepted the charmer's polite bows, and walked on. There was a mother cow feeding her calf; there was a group of pigs rooting in a pile of trash; there was a system of intricately connected vines with incredibly beautiful purple and white flowers climbing over the straw huts of the villagers and turning the place into paradise.

One evening Swamiji telephoned from New Delhi, asking us to travel to the hill town of Mussoori to visit with the headmaster of an elite, all-girls prep school. An Aide de Camp to the Nepalese royal family was anxious to place his daughters in the school and asked Swamiji to help him. Always willing to do anything for others, he asked if we would assist. We were pleased to aid the man we had met in Nepal, and also to enjoy the wonderful trip up the mountains, exceptionally beautiful in their autumn color. We remembered our last pilgrimage through these mountains, and I pointed out the places which were particularly important to our teacher when he lived there. The British educators at the prep school were most hospitable, walking us through the entire facility high above the town and promising us that they would consider the applications carefully. A few weeks later the girls began studies in the school.

Swamiji telephoned another day to talk with Theresa; after awhile I was called to the phone. "Justin," he said, "if you have time, you should visit the old Siva temple." His suggestion felt like more than a hint so while Theresa worked with the ashram gardener the next day, I went out the gate along the Ganges, following the familiar track and wondering what awaited me. I walked up the long stairs and stood in front of the temple structure, but after a few minutes I knew instinctively that this

Swamiji in his bedsheet welcoming Justin

temple wasn't the goal. An old Indian walked over to me and asked if I needed help. I asked about old temples in the area and he told me that there were ruins about a hundred meters around the village corner. I knew that was it. Rounding the corner, I peered to my left and saw, about the size of a tennis court, a set of crumbling walls rising a few feet above the ground. Inside them I could see the remains of three partitioned rooms. As I walked slowly toward this two-thousand-year-old place of worship, my eyes gazed at a *Siva lingam,* the sacred stone, jutting out of the ground in the far corner. From that point on, my mind was pulled into an intensive, tranquil reverie. My eyes closed involuntarily and I just stood there, not able to move. No thoughts rambled through my mind, no worries came forward, no images, no words, no feelings but only a conscious expansion of awareness filled with sheer peace mixed with perfect joy.

I wanted to remain at the spot forever, but gradually I heard faint voices filter into my mind as if from miles away. Some village women were coming along the path. A slow tug of war started in my mind; I wanted to persist in my contemplation, yet I didn't want to draw attention to myself standing there in the way. Reluctantly, I pulled myself from the space where my awareness abided and back down to the pedestrian level sufficiently so that as the group walked by me I was able to shuffle slowly away and head for the ashram along a quiet route. The lingering peace stayed with me for most of my return trip, finally dissolving into memory. I went right in to telephone Swamiji and told him what occurred.

" You did your *sadhana* there in your last life," he said bluntly.

The quiet weeks flew by too quickly, and my ceremony was only a day away. A local Pandit had been found to perform the service on the banks of the Ganges, Swamiji had driven in from the capital, and all was in readiness. A group of American students, who had been on tour in the north, arrived on the weekend, filling the ashram and a nearby hotel and discussing what they thought was startling news: Justin was to become a swami. In the group was my friend, Mike, who asked if I would walk with him along the Ganges shore. He was curious to know if the incredible rumors floating through the group and across the country were true, that Theresa had thrown me out and so I was taking vows.

"Mike, you know me and you know Theresa. Do I look like a thrown-out man?" I asked him. "People and their rumors!" I told him that this decision was my choice and that Theresa supported it, that it didn't change my love for her, but only my marital status. Actually, we both plan to have separate rooms in the same building and to continue to work together as we always had.

Back at the ashram I found my wife upset by many of the rumors that the new arrivals were heaping on her. It was a blessing that the evening silence time came soon after and we could get some respite.

The next morning Swamiji called us to his room. He began lightheartedly engaging us in conversation. "How was your retreat? What did you do? Is everything ready for the ceremony?"

But then his questions took a pointed turn. "Justin, are you sure you want to go through with this?" He seemed so innocent in his question, but I felt the strong meaning behind it.

"Yes, Swamiji, without a doubt." I answered, but that 'Delhi Airport feeling' twinged again.

"You know you'll have to wear ochre clothes, and I know you don't like to wear anything that looks like a uniform," he went on solicitously, with a little concerned look on his face.

"That's true, Swamiji, I hate uniforms. But perhaps I could wear only ochre underwear, since that would keep the symbol intact," I eagerly replied.

"Hmmm, I don't know if that's possible; I don't really think that's possible," he said as he shook his head slowly.

"I'm sure we can work something out," I answered, sort of holding my breath.

"Aren't you going to England shortly to be on the medical faculty?" he leaned forward with a very serious look on his face.

"Yes, I begin in January. I'll work in London for three years," I replied, starting to get a little bewildered since I couldn't follow his train of thought. "Is there something wrong?"

"Not at all, Justin, but you know, of course, that the British don't care for swamis. They don't like anything Indian, and since you have been accepted on the medical faculty and will be dealing with professionals, as well as the public in the clinic, being a swami may cause problems for you. You'll have to give up your name and title."

Before I could reply, he quickly turned his head to a visiting businessman from Delhi who sat quietly in the corner. In a solicitous voice he asked the man while raising his eyebrows, "Isn't that so?"

Without hesitation, the gentleman confirmed Swamiji's entire paragraph.

My mind raced. "What's going on here? Is this a test? Am I missing something that's obvious to everyone else?" While I surveyed these questions, I also felt the pressure to answer him but I didn't know quite what to say.

"You know we have a barber here to shave your head," he spoke now with a less demanding tone.

I realized that I had forgotten that traditionally one's head was shaved for the ceremony of renunciation.

"Of course," Swamiji continued, "you will have to keep your head shaved for twelve years. You know, I suppose, that the British don't like bald heads."

The Indian in the corner solemnly nodded his head in agreement.

"You and Theresa, of course, won't be able to see each other or talk to each other for twelve years either," Swamiji added with a calm assurance as he finally sat back in his chair.

Stunned silence followed his words. This last requirement stoked my full attention. I knew that traditionally swamis avoided home, friends, and relatives for at least twelve years, but the rule was frequently modified, especially for non-Indians. I felt that Swamiji had just shot his last volley and was satisfied with its delivery. The ball landed clearly in the center of my court.

My relationship with Swamiji had always involved the freedom to candidly explore all his statements. I questioned whenever I needed to. I was disinterested in competing with him at any level, not because I feared losing, but because I had too much respect for him. I had always enjoyed working with him on projects, often acting as his liaison in the West, his reporter in the East, his researcher in philosophy and theology, his practical man on the street. Once he called me his 'universal bolt' because I could fit in anywhere. I relished doing tasks that he would not entrust to others. From the beginning of our days together, I felt I could always approach him in a combination of teacher to student, man to man, friend to friend. He had actually verbalized those terms to me when I first met him at the farmhouse in 1972.

I firmly believed that there was nothing I could reveal to him that he wouldn't listen to and advise on for my best interests, no matter the cost to himself. I always strove to preserve that sense of homage for him. I could get frustrated and mad and swear at him under my breath, but he was still the only mentor in my life and the man I most cared about. Now I did not know what to say.

As all these thoughts ran through my mind, Theresa, who had been sitting quietly all this time, jumped vigorously into the conversation. "What do you mean that Justin can't see me for twelve years? That's ridiculous! I have never heard that mandate for any renunciate you blessed."

Swamiji stayed matter-of-fact in his tone, calmly pointing out the traditional requirements. Suddenly I felt a barrage of emotions flood through me, from exasperation to frustrated anger to sheer embarrassment. The arrangements had been made already, the Americans were waiting out on the beach for the ceremony to begin, and the whole situation was unraveling. I even thought that perhaps Swamiji was making it easy on himself by getting rid of us.

Theresa was not finished with her harangue. She was furiously angry at the half-truths, the jibes of our so-called friends outside, the fear of the future. Just then an Indian woman entered the room carrying Swamiji's lunch and bent to set the tray of food before him.

"And who started all those terrible rumors," she shouted at her teacher, "since no one knew about the ceremony except you?"

The serving woman dropped the silverware to the floor and stood there in shock. I was surprised to see the corners of Swamiji's mouth twitch with a repressed smile. He said, "How would I know about rumors? I merely mentioned it to a few people."

"Who did you talk to?" Theresa demanded again.

This time he could not stop the smile, "Only a few who would never say anything," he said, naming the two instant telegraphs of the Institute. He lifted his tea cup to his lips.

"Oh!" yelled my wife in anger, "Aren't you afraid you'll choke on your food with all those lies!"

That did it. The woman ran out of the room, Swamiji dropped his tea cup on the tray and began to laugh uproariously. My emotions jumped around like mice in a tight cage.

After his laughter died down, Swamiji asked to speak with us alone, and the other guest departed. Looking at us both fondly he said, "You came together and now your paths are moving in different directions. Justin should now not be married and Theresa should be with someone else. Don't you already know that deep within? This is the new path to be taken, otherwise you two won't grow. I only want you to make your life decisions wisely. Don't be afraid; go boldly ahead with what you already know within."

Silence again. We looked at each other as the entire concatenation of events since Nepal flashed before me with all its enrichment, its well-intentioned mis-cues, detours, inexplicable barriers. My anguish over whether or not to stay married came together with all the rest all at once. I heaved a sigh as painful clarity finally emerged. I no longer found marriage to be my spiritual path, but Hindu swamihood was not it either. My renunciation must take a different direction.

I lived through the growing rumors; I lived through the confused tears of my wife; I lived through the embarrassment of telling my friends that my vows were off. Then I began to feel sure and right within.

Swamiji sent us away for two days to relax at a student's elegant home and then flew with us in a small plane to New Delhi. He kept us near him for two more days, letting me speak with him whenever I wanted, feeding Theresa with his own hand when she was too upset to eat, taking us with him to the wedding of a close student. In the midst of the celebrations, we three stole away. Back at Swamiji's apartment, we packed our bags, received his blessing, worked out our next plans, and kissed our teacher good-bye.

We were off on another adventure.

The Music Man singing in the Himalayas

CHAPTER 24
LIFE IN LONDON

*Swamiji stood powerfully before me. "I have the book
from the cave," he said solemnly. I replied that I really
wanted to learn because so many people in London need
the wisdom of those pages.*

IT WAS A STRANGE DREAM. I did not know the book I dreamt
about even though I knew I would be going to London soon.
Theresa and I had arrived back in Pennsylvania in December,
gathered our belongings in a Ryder rent-a-truck, and headed
westward. Rumors followed us. Some people thought we had left
the Institute due to our disappointment about some unspecified
topic; others thought we were kicked out, if not in '85 when we
left the country, certainly now, when everyone knew we had been
told to leave Ram Nagar the week before. We heard the rumors
over the months and were surprised that no one telephoned to
talk to us directly. Rumors were more fun, we decided, but we had
our work from the Master and nothing else was important.

A snow storm had paid its dues to the Twin Cities of
Minneapolis and Saint Paul when we arrived. We slept on a
friend's office floor that night and drove around in the truck
during the day until we found a small, affordable apartment. The
two of us unloaded the truck during the next whitened afternoon.
Theresa went to work part time and spent the rest of her day
organizing a publishing house—Yes International Publishers—as
Swamiji had instructed, and getting the first books ready for
production. I prepared to immigrate to the United Kingdom.

My position on the London University medical faculty as a
Research and Education Fellow in Holistic Medicine began in
January of 1987. My contract placed me in Dr. Patrick Petroni's
dream of an integrated holistic health clinic and medical training
facility based on the fairly new concept of wellness. It was a first

for England.

Patrick and I had met when he had come to the Himalayan Institute in the early '80s. He took my classes in Superconscious Meditation and became my jogging partner. He keenly observed how our Combined Therapy Program functioned in a country setting where patients could utilize the extensive grounds as part of their healing, and once back in London he adapted our program to the needs of his city population. To complete his professional team, he needed someone with credentials, experience, and skill in teaching holistic self-care practices. I was asked to join the team as Director of Education.

The Marylebone Holistic Health Centre was below ground in the former crypt of the Marylebone Church. The program—covered by National Health Insurance—emphasized healing rather than treatment, and thus caught the attention of the public. The caskets in the Church crypt had been carefully transferred to the city graveyards and the underground space had been refurbished to suit our needs. At the celebration open house Prince Charles endorsed the project and stopped by for some quick tips on proper breathing. I was pleased to be invited to speak to the Marylebone Church community and for the occasion was asked to sit at the cherished antique of this parish, the writing desk of Elizabeth Barrett Browning.

I fell in love with London, basking in the many atmospheres of history and always finding audiences who enthusiastically wanted me to share ideas for the future. Teaching medical professionals and interfacing with the public in the clinic gave me an opportunity to use my years of experience in wellness and yoga. The unique core of our holistic engagement with the patients was education. Instead of simply writing prescriptions, we went one major step beyond prevention: we taught people how to manage and enhance their vitality through self-care practices. Evenings and weekends, we offered workshops in stress management, breathing, diet, hatha yoga, and massage.

Opening protocol with a client usually involved three staff members—a general practitioner, an acupuncturist, and myself, the self-care teacher. After taking the person's history, we discussed procedures. Whenever stress factors were obvious, the patient saw me first since stress always interferes so seriously with the possibility of healing.

With me, time was never rationed. I allowed patients to tell their stories, thus letting the healing commence. When appropriate, I taught a self-care technique on the spot and gave them a practice as "home work" to report on during the next visit. Whenever I had a patient I felt I could not help, I telephoned Swamiji and got the assistance I needed.

One morning a discouraged-looking gentleman came to me accompanied by his anxious wife. He had recently retired to spend his last years in the leisurely pursuit of oil painting. Two months earlier he had collapsed; brain scans revealed that his brain tissues were rapidly dying. Two additional examinations confirmed the same prognosis—less than six months to live. The man and I spent nearly two hours talking together. His breathing was acutely irregular and he had lost his sensitivity for the voluntary use of his diaphragm. After putting a small sand bag on his abdominal area, I coached him in breathing practices until he could resumed slight voluntary control over his diaphragmatic motion. He practiced the sand bag procedure three times a day at home with the help and encouragement of his wife. His diet was boosted with vitamins and carefully selected food. Two months later, a new examination indicated that the brain cells had stopped dying. His hope rose; he now made breath practice a component of his lifestyle. At the end of the year, I received a gift of one of his paintings and a Christmas card telling of his wonderful health.

Invitations to lecture poured in together with media interviews. I was busy teaching and healing, the things I loved doing most. Evening classes were expanded and weekend workshops were begun in all phases of holistic health.

After a few months Theresa arrived from the States and made my cold London apartment a warm, livable place. Together we explored the English countryside, the city museums and churches, the homes of friends. She volunteered at the center and carried on her publishing work via phone and telegraphs.

SWAMI SANTA

One winter evening the phone rang as we sat in our snug reading room with the rain coming down outside. The beloved voice said, "Hi, Justy! Hi, Tree! May I come to visit you?" We were excited and full of joy at the thought and began to search for a place to keep him because our own apartment in Kensington was too small. We asked friends who owned a large house outside the city if they would like to have a saint stay with them, and they welcomed the three of us into both their house and their hearts.

On Christmas afternoon, after two weeks of preparation, we received the best present ever: Swami Rama stepped off the plane at Heathrow Airport to stay with us for four weeks. With his presence, Yuletide took on a new meaning. English winter had come down hard on my feelings, for the sun there takes a vacation and rain and dampness abounds, but now we sat with our teacher by the small fireplace, or lay on the bedroom floor with him telling stories, or walked with him through the city, feeling sunshine everywhere.

Without any pressing tasks to do, Swamiji practiced his singing. Since his work in America was finished, he went there for only a few months each year to check on students, earn money for his new project in India, and to complete books. Now he had permission to take up his music again and did so with enthusiasm. Everyone around him either sang or played an instrument or listened to hours of practice scales and Indian ragas. In between singing he worked on his new book, *Indian Music*.

As we sat listening to Swamiji sing a chant one evening, I was reminded of the time in Glenview years ago when the intellectual professor had his heart opened. I had always detested the idea of chanting ancient rhythms, thinking it was a meaningless waste of time, so when it was announced that Swamiji would lead chanting before an evening lecture, I purposefully came late. Opening the auditorium door, I saw my teacher on the stage playing a sitar and singing. He looked radiant. He turned his head toward me and smiled, touching my heart with energy. I was caught off guard by the beauty of the music, his look, and the intense energy in the room. I stood there transfixed, not able even to sit down. Something changed in me at that moment; I now looked upon singing as another spiritual path.

We knew it was a privilege to hang out with our teacher whatever he was doing, and spent every minute with him when he wasn't sleeping or meditating. Theresa presented him with a copy of her first book, *The Spiral Path*. He smiled broadly, closed his eyes and held the book up in both hands, offering it to his master. "Make many more books," he told her, laying his hands on her head, "you must teach and write this life, so I am pleased that you have begun."

One afternoon, one of the medical directors called to enlist Swamiji's advice. His wife, a few months pregnant, was hemorrhaging heavily. The attending physicians were seriously concerned since they could not stem the bleeding nor find its cause. The woman's blood count had dropped dangerously low when the call came and the physicians feared for her life. I relayed the phone message to Swamiji who listened, put his head down and said solemnly, "I will pray for her." The doctor seemed dissatisfied with the yogi's response. "If he has those magical powers," the doctor demanded, "couldn't he do something more definitive?" A few hours later when I called the doctor, I learned that the bleeding had spontaneously stopped. The hospital presumed it was their victory and the woman, now on her way to healing, dismissed the yogi's intervention as irrelevant. This reaction, I knew, was not the first of its kind, nor would it be the last.

The Marylebone clinic asked Swamiji to teach and immediately sponsored him for a three-lecture series. On short notice more than three hundred people attended the series at the Regent Park Auditorium. Swamiji spoke on the significance of yoga philosophy for modern stress-filled lives. During the second lecture he asked me to demonstrate and engage the audience in breathing practices, thus pointing out my usual work to them. Many people were intrigued with the vision that Swamiji presented and signed up for clinic classes as a result.

One of the most important parts of the visit happened during an intense series of tutorials that Swamiji set up for Theresa, the clinic director and myself. We sat with him every day as he used an ancient manuscript from his monastery as our textbook. The unique pages contained the distillation of hundreds of experiments that the monks had carried on over the centuries, as they explored the human potential for health and well-being. He always first made an invocation to the Tradition of the Himalayan Sages with closed eyes and softly chanted sounds.

"There are two important systems in your body," he began, "nourishing and cleansing. In the West a great emphasis is placed on the first. Yogis place more emphasis on the second, for they know that the finest cuisine won't nourish as it should unless the body is prepared by cleansing. Junk food, overly roasted dishes, eating too fast or too much—all disturb the body's ability to absorb the nutrients of the meal. If the proper saliva is not mixed with your food, then digestion is impaired. Avoid stress while you eat; seriousness has no business during meals. If you eat while you are upset, you can poison yourself. The best appetizer is laughter. There are two levels of enjoyment in eating. One is from tasting the spices, the other is from the flavor of the well-masticated food, but the latter is only possible when you chew and chew and chew.

"The most important organ for nourishment, as well as for overall health, is not the heart but the liver. The liver also governs longevity. This organ is very sensitive to your thoughts. Your mind directly impacts the liver, which in turn influences your saliva."

This was a new approach that I had never heard before from him. I was struck with the importance the monks gave to the liver for generating health and preventing degenerative illnesses. My mind connected Swamiji's words about the importance of the liver to a workshop I had recently attended on the Gerson approach to degenerative illness. Dr. Gerson was a German physician who demonstrated that the crucial organ involved in cancer was the liver. Unfortunately, funding for his totally natural approach for cancer cure was voted down for further research by the U.S. Senate due to the pressure of the medical lobby that supported surgery, radiation, and the poisons known as chemotherapy.

Swamiji had stopped speaking when our hostess brought in a tray of tea. It led to another discussion of food and drink. "Those who like to eat heavy and late in the evening," Swamiji said, "are inviting Yama to dinner," he remarked in all seriousness.

I found the reference fascinating. Yama is the King of Death mentioned in the *Kathopanishad*. To eat late at night, as far as the monastery text was concerned, was inviting an early death because of the burden it put on the liver.

Swamiji then discussed the importance of keeping one's mouth clean, and said that rubbing the gums stimulated the roots for healthy teeth. He talked about the important of resting for a few minutes after each meal, making sure that the right nostril flowed freely, for this assisted in digestion.

After explaining the tradition's viewpoint on health maintenance, Swamiji then gave us an exercise to enhance the functioning of the liver. With both seriousness and humor, he also showed us how to grow taller—Theresa was especially interested in that procedure—as well as how to slow the heart rate for profound relaxation.

The following week Swamiji spent some days deepening my knowledge of the mantra tradition and teaching me how to perform intuitive diagnosis.

THERAPIST YOGI

To advance the clinic work, Swamiji accepted the invitation to speak to the clinic medical personnel and invited outside therapists. Homeopaths, nurses, counselors, administrative staff, and conventional physicians from various hospitals attended. A wide range of health practitioners, most of them allopathic trained, came to hear the unusual man who, according to their own prestigious encyclopedia, could control his entire autonomic system.

Swamiji spoke in the crypt's lecture hall and chose as his theme the practical question: What is the essence of therapy? While he pointed out the necessity of technical competency, he said that the most important ingredient in therapy was their own skill as human beings. "Your presence affects your patient. How much you have developed within yourself affects the healing process. Unless you are living a life consistent with the meaning of healing, then your efforts will not be as effective as they could be," he said. "Technique is not enough. You don't have to know all the technical answers before healing can occur. The essence of healing is your love for the patients. Listening to your patients is extremely important, otherwise they won't feel your love for them. You must arouse hope in the patient, otherwise the healing process is impeded. They must feel that love, then they can hope."

Swamiji continued to insist upon the importance of self-training for the healer. Without it there is a tendency for physicians to rush people in and out of their offices. One could have heard a pin drop in the hall as the audience assimilated his message.

One physician raised a crucial, practical question. "On the basis of your understanding of therapy, how many patients would someone see in a day?"

"Three or four," Swamiji replied. Many in the audience shook their heads at this reply, dismissing this yogi as a dreamer. Although he made sense, he seemed to be unrealistic in today's world where one had to earn a living. I saw two different mind sets at odds. One viewed healing as a privileged art; the other viewed it as a necessity of business. My mind flashed to the recollection of a physician whom I held in the highest regard, Milton H. Erikson, a genius in counseling, who charged only forty dollars per patient, regardless of the number of hours his therapy sessions took.

After the lecture Swamiji asked to go to a quiet area to rest. Theresa took him to one of the consulting rooms. When I walked in a few minutes later, he had a mischievous smile on his face.

"What's up, Swamiji?" I inquired.

He turned his head and cast a glance to the center of the floor while saying, "Did you know that there's someone else in this room?"

Before my puzzled look rendered a reply, he continued, "There's a corpse beneath this floor."

We couldn't help but laugh at his surety and surprise. Apparently, the excavating crew had missed at least one coffin.

After we explained why the body existed, he looked at me and asked, "What did they think of my talk?"

"You certainly brought a different approach to therapy," I answered, "one that contrasts with their training. As far as I can tell, therapy is a business for most of them. When you mentioned seeing only a few patients a day many could not accept that recommendation. Since they have to make money, I think they then dismissed you as being impractical."

He listened and slightly shook his head up and down.

"What do you think?" He caught me by surprise.

"Your words on the importance of preparing oneself in order to deal with patients made the most sense to me and . . . "

Swamiji suddenly interrupted me. "Without self-understanding, how can doctors possibly understand the patients? They go to two extremes. Either they identify with the patient's illness and get ill themselves or else they stay aloof from the patient as a person and give no help. It's important that they have the intention to help the patient, but they also need inner will power to avoid identifying with the disease. At the same time they need to demonstrate compassion and close the distance to the patient."

It seemed to me that the afternoon lecture was just the warm-up for this post critique.

"Medical books," Swamiji continued, "don't tell the students about their natural powers nor about that of their patients. To do therapy well, you must develop sensitivity toward the patient. First, you need to observe whether the patients truly want to get well; you have to note their capacity. Not all patients want to be healed. Then you must convince them of their own power within. Healing comes from the inside; it is not found in externals. You need to stir up hope. Finally, you must train yourself to be with the patient with full attention. In this way, you do justice to your actions. If you can't love your patients, then don't do therapy."

I asked him, "What do you do when you fail?"

"Whenever I failed, I sat down and prayed for the patient with intensity. Whatever happens, go to your center, otherwise you get lost in thoughts and emotions. Unless you touch your center, you won't be able to handle the barrage of patients and their cries."

As we drove home together, we watched the darkness settle over the city. "Should we go shopping?" Swamiji asked.

The next morning we headed for Oxford Street. Swamiji visited an eye doctor and told us to meet him in an hour. When we returned to the office he was not there. "Perhaps he went outside," we thought, so we ran outside into the drizzle and peered up and down the street. There, across the street beneath a red awning, was His Holiness, the Himalayan yogi, waving his arms to get our attention like he was sending a semaphore signal, while unknown to him the legs of a dozen dancing mechanical showgirls were high-stepping in bright striped leggings above his head, looking like the Rockets line in Rockefeller Center. There are a few sacred moments when a camera is appropriate. We missed this one.

A few days later I met a friend, a prominent physician who told me that years ago he had wanted to meet a real *sadhu* who could lead him to enlightenment. He had just come out of an appointment with Swami Rama.

"Have you fulfilled your wish?" I asked him as he walked out of the room.

"By all means," he assured me, "and now I'm way ahead on the path. In fact, he promised to come to lunch with me next week. Will you and your wife join us?"

His car arrived to take the three of us to a regal Indian restaurant at noon. As we entered the doorway, Swamiji looked around and announced that he didn't want to eat there. The doctor, a little embarrassed, politely explained that the chef was prepared to accommodate his wishes in a wide range of cuisine. Swamiji shook his head and walked out the door. After apologizing to the maitre d' the doctor came out and recommended an equally exclusive restaurant farther down the street. We all walked into another fashionable restaurant and the doctor made sure it could prepare Eastern cuisine. Again Swamiji looked around and said "Not here." The doctor, now impatient, remembered another restaurant and we walked around the corner to its entrance. Starting to show his frustration, he assured Swamiji that it would serve fine Indian dishes. Swamiji calmly said he didn't want to eat at that place either. The more flustered the physician got, the more curious I became at what was on Swamiji's mind. Twice more the rejection scene was repeated. It wasn't hard to tell that the doctor was at his wits end. Suddenly Swamiji turned the corner and spied a sign reading "Kebobs" in makeshift lettering.

"You want to eat there?" the doctor emphatically questioned as we followed our teacher across the cobblestone street into the little cafe. It was a dinky, run-down place sandwiched between an alley and a laundromat. Fast food emporiums, in comparison, would be superior. There were six rickety tables crowded on the broken tile floor. The menu specialized in lamb.

"Yes, of course, we'll eat here," Swamiji enthusiastically answered. Then he casually walked into the kitchen, spoke in a foreign language to the gratified cook for a few minutes and walked triumphally back to us.

"Relax, this is a nice, quiet place; they will make a wonderful lunch for us." He looked contented. The doctor slowly scanned the smoke-filled atmosphere, noted the peeling wall paper and sat down with a forlorn look on his face. He may have been on the brink of tears. Theresa bit her lip to prevent laughter. I couldn't tell whether her suppressed laughter was due to Swamiji's exaggerated admiration for this bistro or the doctor's forsaken look. What must this man be thinking when his holy teacher, brought up in a totally vegetarian tradition, preferred to indulge his hunger in a barbecue diner?

The waiter came out of the kitchen and set salads before us with great aplomb: sliced raw onions and tomatoes with basil sprinkled on top. The doctor watched Swamiji enjoy the onions, which we knew he didn't usually eat. The rest of our utterly simple vegetarian meal was soon served while our teacher kept up a stream of lively conversation, entertaining us with stories of his travels through Europe, occasionally casting a glance at the doctor and offering a tribute to this fine eatery. While the doctor tried to look charming and attentive, I realized that he had no clue as to what was happening.

Over the years, in more than fifty countries, Swamiji had dined with royalty, presidents, governors, ecclesiastics, CEOs, saints and tribal leaders. Superb and exotic cuisine was hardly new to him, so for him to rave about this struggling, neighborhood family diner on a shambling side street in the heart of London had nothing to do with the menu. This meal was not about food; it was about motivation. Where was the doctor's heart when he had made the invitation?

Swamiji respected but didn't always play by the rules of polite society. He was one shrewd holy man who wouldn't be used by others to impress themselves. If one came to him for knowledge, one had better be prepared to get shaken out of assumptions. If this prestigious physician had merely wanted to take the Eastern visitor to dinner rather than show him off, nothing out of the ordinary would have transpired. But he had asked as a student, thus giving permission to the teacher to teach. Teachers don't impose; they need the student's permission. Then different rules governed the relationship. It was a slow learner who didn't realize that this spiritual teacher endangered self-deception.

STRANGE EVENTS

Since Theresa and I were staying at our friends' home to be near our teacher, we slept each night on the floor of an empty room. Theresa challenged the dampness of the winter by making sure Swamiji had warm long underwear and wore a woolen cap. She countered her own shivering by sleeping with a hot water bottle and snuggling close to the radiator on the wall. One night she turned over in her sleep and pressed the water bottle against the heater. The rubber melted and sent out a stream of water to completely drench her and all her bedding. She spent the rest of the night in a pair of my underwear, covered with our day clothes and bathroom towels. The telling of the story the next morning was a delight. Swamiji asked to hear it again and again, saying that he thought a special edition of *The Times* with a full page picture of her in the water-logged attire should be issued immediately.

One day a strange event happened in the kitchen. Swamiji and the women were making a special dinner that included his famous mountain bread, this time baked in a large cast-iron pan. The pan was placed in the oven at 425 degrees. When it was ready to be removed, Swamiji opened the oven door and reached in, grasping the hot, heavy pan in his hand. He stood in the middle of the kitchen holding the pan as it burned him saying, "Oh! This is hot, very hot!" After several seconds he finally dropped the pan down on the top of the stove and blew across his hand. It was bright red. "Swamiji, you've burned your hand!" exclaimed Theresa.

"Yes," he said. "It hurts."

Everyone wanted to do something, to put something on his hand, to call someone for help, but he would only sit down on a chair, holding his right wrist with the painful hand extended out in front of him. Theresa quietly asked if we could get him a homeopathic remedy for burns. "How long will it take you to bring it?" he asked. When we explained that we would have to go by bus to the train station, then take a train into town, and then walk to the pharmacy, he agreed that we should go. Two hours later we returned with a cantharis remedy and administered it to our teacher who was singing in the living room. He thanked us warmly, but acted as if nothing had happened. The burn was not mentioned again.

It was obvious to us that he had grabbed the pan on purpose and held it much longer than anyone else could have, but I did not know why. It looked as if he had wanted to be burned. I have often been puzzled by some of his actions, wondering what he was doing, why he did things in unusual ways. Sometimes he would tell me, other times he kept silent. I did learn through years of observation and discussion that he was always working for his mission and his students, often in the face of hardship, pain or ridicule. Once when I questioned his action he told me that he was balancing the karma for someone. It seemed to me that whatever he did was to bring his students to the major obstacle that was keeping them from self-enlightenment, and then to take on the karma of pushing them past it. He would gladly suffer for others when the possibility existed that they might be free.

Late that evening he called Theresa and me to his room. We massaged his feet as he told us stories.

"Once I got restless in our monastery and began to think about living in the world rather than roaming in the mountains. My master walked in and told me to follow him. He led me to a deep cave in the mountain where donations over the centuries had piled up. I saw a huge, twelve-foot mount of gold, silver, and jewels. I was transfixed by their allurement. My master, of course, knew well my liking for fine jewels.

"Suddenly, I noticed that he was gone. I turned to the side of the cave and saw my master standing alone, completely enveloped in flames. I was overwhelmed by the contrasting sights between the flames and the riches. 'Make your choice,' my master called to me. 'Either enter the world and take all those treasures, or else follow me into the fire!'

"I stepped into the flames with my master. All my desires for the world and its allurements were burned to ashes that day."

The days went by too fast, each one bringing fresh joy and knowledge. By this time in my life, I had sustained a double awareness whenever I was with my teacher. He had the knack of turning nearly any occasion into a tutelage as well as an opportunity for delight.

With only a few days left before Swamiji returned to India, we took him to visit the Russian mystic, Irina Tweedie, a dear friend of Theresa and myself. A few years earlier, on a visit to London, I had walked into her open *satsang*, held four days a week, for those interested few seeking the path of the heart. I had been ushered into her living room where about thirty people were meditating. She, nonetheless, nodded with a welcoming smile to me and

Swamiji singing for Irina Tweedie in London

pointed to the tea and cookies in the kitchen. A few minutes later, she closed the meditation, found me a seat, and with a vibrant voice and the self-assurance of a woman of the world, greeted everyone and asked those present for the first time to introduce themselves. In mentioning my background I added that my teacher knew her revered guru, Bhai Sahib. If smiles bequeath money, she would have made me the richest man in London that day. Later I had a more personal visit and was greeted with such a huge hug by this little woman in her late 70s that it almost took me off my feet. Two hours flew by with stories, scones and tea with the most energetic Sufi saint that I have ever had the good fortune to meet. The following year she accepted my invitation to speak at our Congress in the States.

When we brought Swamiji to Irina Tweedie's home one cold afternoon, the living room, kitchen, and corridors were brimming over with people whom she had notified about the great yogi's visit. Swamiji greeted the crowd, told of his acquaintance with her master, and asked the group if they wanted to chant. Mrs. Tweedie implored Swamiji to sing a solo first and he did. There was a double surprise as Swamiji charmingly brought her into the singing with a chanting duet. Both of them then fascinated us with stories of yogis in the high Himalayas. The energy in the room was tangible, full of love and peace and joy. No one wanted to leave and so we all closed our eyes and meditated with the saints while the night folded us in its arms and the city lights twinkled outside the window.

That night as Theresa and I massaged his legs in his little room, Swamiji looked at us with love and said, "You two are no longer attached to each other. That's good! Now you will advance. But don't stall anymore; it's time for you both to end your marriage so you can go on to higher things." He asked us to bathe and fast for another initiation. The next day we were given a new mantra, instruction in an advanced practice of our tradition, and new names. Theresa was named Devi, meaning "Goddess," and I was named Jaidev, "God's victory."

Swamiji wore my new Irish hat to the airport, teasing us as we drank tea and waited for his plane. "I will wear this to India and never take it off," he said. "It's a wonderful hat and just fits our personality, right Justin?" But all too soon his plane was called and we walked together to the gate. He gave last minute instruction on the manuscript that he had left with Theresa to edit, on the work he wanted me to do in his name, on the clinic patients I had asked him about. He asked if we needed anything and gave us warm embraces, and then, just as he turned to enter the gangway, he took off the hat and with a quick flick of the wrist sent it sailing into my hands.

BACK TO WORK

The months of my final year in London brought a host of surprises. After counseling an Irish nun, an invitation came from her superiors asking if Theresa and I would lead the entire order of her Benedictine sisters in a five-day retreat. We spent a delightful time at the convent, teaching the sisters, from ages 40 through 92, how to claim their own wellness, how to meditate, and how to use breathing as a tool for spiritual growth.

For months I had been working on a revision of my book, *Yoga and Christianity*, that the Institute had published in 1978. When the new edition was complete, I offered it again to the Institute, but the president turned it down, thinking it did not fit the focus of their press. I was disappointed at what I thought was a narrow view, and sent the manuscript to Penguin Books instead. They published it to great acclaim and excellent reviews.

In roving about the British countryside, I was stirred by an uncanny feeling associated with Oxford University. Since I was a teenager I had felt that I would love to visit the school and perhaps even teach there. One day an invitation arrived to speak at a medical conference at Oxford University. Entering the seven-hundred-year-old dinning hall, I felt goose pimples rise on my arms as an overwhelming sense of *deja vu* filled me. As I addressed the conference, I could not help but feel that this was not my first time teaching on the campus.

It was almost eerie how my last months had played themselves out. "How nice it would be," I would ponder, "to speak before that particular audience or visit that historical area." Within a matter of days or weeks, my wishes would become reality.

Work at the clinic went on as before, only more intensified and interesting in the challenges that people brought through the door. The healing techniques I had learned from Swamiji amazed me in their effectiveness with the most recalcitrant of cases, and once patients became well, they came to learn meditation, hatha yoga and yoga philosophy. The classes began to overflow the rooms.

As my work in England came to a close, my guru brother, Charles, visited us in late summer and helped us move our possessions and our work back home to America.

Swamiji relaxing at the medical city in India

CHAPTER 25
THE LAST PILGRIMAGE

I looked up into the sky and there peering over a large, billowing, white cloud in his chariot was Lord Krishna. He rode chest high above the cloud's edge, one hand holding the reigns of the team of horses he drove. His head was bent to one side as he smiled down at me. I looked for the archer, Arjuna, who should have been in the chariot behind his driver, but he was not there.

THE DREAM SHOOK ME AWAKE. "Time for meditation," I thought, getting out of bed. As I settled into the stillness, the entire scene of my dream flashed crisply across my mind in vivid color. Continuing to look at Krishna's charming smile made me realize that I myself was Arjuna, the archer, the aspiring one.

The classic tale of the *Bhagavad Gita* involving Krishna and Arjuna had captured my attention over the years. Its mythical dramatization outlines the struggle of the aspirant to know ultimate truth. The story takes place on the battlefield of life, the Kurushetra, as opposite camps clash for the rule of the kingdom, the rule of the human soul. The forces of dark chose to enhance their armies, while Arjuna, the warrior of the light, chose a single charioteer, Krishna, the divine inner dweller of all, who leads his rider to victory. Arjuna must fight his own battles, but he has the divine adviser. In applying the symbolism to myself, I thought, "Who needs armies for my life battles? I want only the chariot driver." I knew who my Krishna was.

Finally, after spending many unsure years in marriage, feeling like Arjuna afraid to hurt someone I loved, I realized that I could no longer resist the wisdom of my teacher. The longing in my heart for the freedom of the sages had led me to explore Christian, Buddhist, and Hindu monastic lifestyles, letting me know that my way was different.

Following a civil divorce, Theresa and I gathered with a few friends in a small chapel one sunny afternoon and I renounced all acts of hatred, all acts committed through ignorance, confusion, fear and sloth. I renounced the harm I had given to anyone here or elsewhere and asked forgiveness. Finally, I renounced all conjugal relations and benefits, individual and family, to follow a path of celibate love, making Theresa my sister. From that day I promised to use my energies in living a humane and wise life, to preserve my friendships always, and to love boldly without attachment, pursuing the truth wherever it led me and sharing it with all who would receive it. Swamiji sent a warm greeting from India with the envelope addressed to "Theresa the Pure and Justin the Wanderer." All was well.

We now continued Swamiji's work from our base in Minnesota. Charles, Theresa and myself shared a common household; we expanded the Twin Cities Yoga Center that Swamiji had begun in 1972, teaching numerous classes and renaming it The Alpha Institute of Learning and Research.

The momentum of our training expressed itself in ever-widening ventures. I returned to graduate teaching at several universities and continued my work in healing and wellness. For three years I organized Wellness 2000, a city-wide conference that shared ancient traditions of healthcare with the public. My research in body/mind communication led me to connect it with tantra yoga. I studied Ericksonian hypnotherapy and Neuro-lingusitic Programming, receiving certification in each, as had my brother Charles, years earlier. On a cold, blustery autumn day in the open air with only the initiator and the sacred fire as witnesses, I was ordained as a pandit in the Himalayan Tradition, using the name Swamiji had given me, Pandit Jaidev. The ceremony's bleak simplicity, carried out by my dear guru brother, Pandit Rajmani, stirred images of my days at Gomukh.

Theresa focused on the publishing house that her teacher asked her to run, receiving advice from him on topics, titles, and covers, and winning seven national awards. Each year she brought him the latest books just off the press and received his smiling blessing on each, after which he gave her the latest report on the state of her useless sofa. At his insistence she began to teach yoga spirituality and lead retreats around the country.

Charles expanded his work in yoga philosophy and

psychology to include the corporate world. His skills brought him into membership in the National Training Laboratories and the professional staff of the Gestalt Institute of Cleveland. He became a much sought-after consultant in leadership and systems theory using Swamiji's teachings as the core.

During those years our teacher had spent much of his time writing books. He published small parts of his twenty-five diaries and poetry; he wrote on Indian music; he wrote on techniques of spiritual practice; he wrote on the spirituality of Sikhism. He left his students, present and future, a rich legacy of wisdom and inspiration. The rest of the time he was totally absorbed by his new project of building a medical city in India.

Our teacher now came to America infrequently and only for brief visits. We spent time with him each year, sometimes when he came to the Twin Cities, sometimes when we drove to Chicago or Honesdale to see him. Always he told us the next steps in our work, gave instruction in the way we should focus our lives, gave practical advice and suggestions, asked our advice on his projects, and blessed us with affection. "Pursue meditation," he told us on one visit, "so that you learn not to desire. Instead you will deserve." Once we had a complaint to voice, but did not receive sympathy. "The world is for work, use, and enjoyment. Don't expect anything else," he told us in reply. On another trip, after listening to what we had accomplished during the months since we had last seen him he said, "Yes, keep living in a way that you catch the eye of the sages."

In 1993 Swamiji visited America for the last time. He took a few weeks away from the project in India to speak at the Yoga Congress and collect funds from all the centers for the hospital. But he always had time for us, even if it was limited. I realized that his time on this plane was truly short. "Always keep a joyous mind; then there is no space for distractions," he reminded us. "Your work is blessed by the sages; keep it going. You will get all the help you need."

Swamiji wrapped up all his own work at the Institute, confirming Pandit Rajmani as spiritual director of the American Institute. Dr. Arya had recently embraced his long-held dream of becoming a swami in the Bharati order and was given the name Swami Veda together with the added responsibility of spiritual director of the ashram in Rishikesh and the new hospital complex.

Swami Rama then departed from the Institute for the last time, traveled to Russia to speak at a conference and returned to his homeland again.

One morning during her meditation practice, Theresa was told by Swamiji that we should come to India soon. She dropped all her work and prepared to join a tour leaving on pilgrimage with Pandit Rajmani. Charles and I had contracts to complete before we could join her five weeks later. With the group, she went to the pilgrimage sites in the mountains of Simla and Dharamsala, the holy places in and around Benaras, and finally made her way to the ashram in Rishikesh for a retreat. The evening the group arrived at Ram Nagar, Theresa received a message from Swamiji to come at once.

"Where are my two gunks?" he asked her with a laugh after they had embraced in his little apartment in the medical city. "I miss you all and have something for you."

So she completed the retreat, the next pilgrimage, the city tours, and stood waiting for us in a blue silk sari with an attendant and a taxi driver when we arrived at Indira Gandhi Airport at 2:00 A.M. on November 1. After a short rest, we were whisked off to see our teacher in the Himalayan foothills.

We pulled into the familiar driveway at Ram Nagar to the high walls of the ashram. A guard saluted us and swung open the gate. The ashram manager, Prem, greeted us warmly in his crisp British accent and offered us fresh fruit for our late breakfast. Sweet and juicy, the tropical treat revived us from the long trip and welcomed us back to our second home. There were only a handful of people in the ashram and the atmosphere had a bright quietness. Masses of flowers grew along the paths tended by a shy but smiling gardener. We walked through the new sections of the ashram in the noonday sun, finding our guru sister, Kamal, standing amidst five sleeping dogs. They were the ashram guard dogs, who slept during the day and prowled on the alert at night. We unfolded exotic gifts for her: peanut butter and jam, chocolate and strong thread, candles and stationery and books. We were invited to tea by our guru brother, Swami Veda, and enjoyed an afternoon with him, learning of his work to save ancient yoga manuscripts from extinction.

Near evening we taxied through the wooded countryside to

the hospital grounds to see the master, entering his small bungalow where all the planning work of the hospital complex was carried out. Swamiji came to see us there. Dressed in maroon jogging attire, he looked ready to run a 5-K race. He greeted us warmly with hugs all around and immediately recommended a walk. "You haven't seen the place; let's go!" and we were off with him just like old times.

Swamiji was the thinnest that I could remember him and all his hair had turned white. His body had aged faster than it should have in my estimation. I knew he was dealing with illness, but he did not want us to worry about it. He was in his glory, showing off the hospital, the medical college, the staff housing inside and out. Under the light of the moon and his flashlight we walked the grounds, Swamiji telling us the intricacies of the architecture, the farm, the water system, and seeking our approval on how fast and well everything was erected. He walked more slowly than my remembrance of his stride, but his energy reminded me of a boy delightfully showing off all his new toys, wanting his friends to admire them. When we walked to the center entrance of the main building, I could not help but feel something like a dense, pleasantly energetic force in the air, invisibly permeating the round vestibule. I mentioned the experience to Swamiji and his eyes widened in delight. "Yes, you can feel it; there is something special there."

He wouldn't elaborate, but since he spoke with such exuberance it was obvious that he had much more to share with us. I was so glad just to be there that I decided my probing questions could wait. After he told us more about the construction history we returned slowly to his little house. Workmen entered with construction reports, the director wanted to check in with this main foreman, the bursar came with financial needs. Our donation was counted and immediately handed over to the director. Swamiji shrugged his shoulders, opened his palms wide and laughed. "In and out, in and out!" After awhile we realized it was time for his practice and stood up to leave. As we touched his feet, we were asked to return for lunch the next day. We climbed into our waiting taxi noting that something was different about him, but he wasn't talking about it.

When I woke up the next morning, I couldn't help but notice that more city noises now crowded around the ashram. Without the surrounding walls, there would have been little peace. The ashram, like Rishikesh, had expanded into a marvelous complex of rooms on two floors with a connecting corridor leading directly to the top of the dam on the Ganges River. School children, cows and goats, and strolling pilgrims on their way to the river walked along the wide dam and looked down into the ashram. Some waved, some bowed, some pretended they were not interested in the Americans sitting there so quietly and peacefully. Most of the advanced *sadhus,* of course, had moved north years before the city's expansion had disturbed their solitude.

When we arrived the next day for lunch, Swamiji stood in the midst of carpenters and delivery men who were carrying in a huge painting given as a gift by an admirer. Charles and I were asked to move the old painting off the living room wall to make room for the new one. It was just like we still lived down the hallway and had been called to help ponder where to place the furniture or help plan the day-to-day running of the place.

"What do you think, Tree? Is that the right spot for it?" Swamiji queried, "At least my two gunks haven't lost too much of their strength." We both stood there holding the heavy painting against the wall while the two artists decided exactly where it should be placed.

When we dislodged the old art piece, a small lizard ran from behind it, across the wall, and to a new hiding place in a plant. "Is that a pet, Swamiji?" Theresa asked, surprised at the creature.

"Yes! It's my pet!" answered the guru.

"What's his name?" Theresa wanted to know.

"Ah! I call him Tree," Swamiji answered looking at her and laughing. She found out later that while it was a small, quick lizard, its bite was poisonous.

We were served a delicious meal made by Maithili and Barb in the tiny kitchen, and afterwards sat in the living room with Swamiji. He wanted to know all about our activities, our teaching, our practice. He told us about the staff who traveled in a van to the poor mountain people to give them education and health care. They taught sellable crafts to the women so that they could earn their own money when the items were sold in the hospital shop. They taught birth hygiene and distributed small packets of soap, razor blades and clean strips of cloth for use in safe births. They helped start a small business of bee-keeping, selling honey from pure mountain flowers. Hospital staff had designed a sturdy, portable clay cooking stove to help prevent eye disease from smoking fires and was teaching its use.

The newest project was the raising of nearly-extinct plants from which Ayurvedic remedies had traditionally been extracted. Generous and creative support was provided by our longtime guru brother, Horst Rechelbacher, and his company, Aveda. Soon there would be a laboratory to prepare and distribute Ayurvedic remedies as well.

These vast efforts were a challenge, for the Garhwal mountain people, neglected for centuries, were suspicious of the new ways. Some politicians had recently been demanding separation from the state of Uttar Pradesh. The poor district believed that they would become wealthy if only they could win independence. They wanted Swamiji's backing, and when he refused it, they decided to attack the medical complex. Guerrillas blew up the hospital helicopter at the nearby airfield, they caused a ruckus at the dedication of the medical college, they wrote scathing articles in the newspaper. Swamiji quietly and wisely continued his work, offering free medical care and education for all.

Now he leaned back on his small sofa and smiled at us. "What did you see on your trip, Tree?" he asked.

She told him of her visit around Benaras, the area where Swamiji used to live, of the aghora yogis she had met, and of the small shrine to the memory of Bholi Baba who had dropped his body in the place where she had prayed.

Swamiji took on an strange look. "Did they know me?" he asked carefully as he casually picked up the newspaper and seemed suddenly and unusually interested in it.

"Yes, Swamiji. They knew you quite well."

The paper rattled a bit as he looked over the top edge at her. "What did they say?"

Theresa answered that they had spoken of him as a great being, that they wanted to know about Swamiji's students, that they had been surprised that some of the Americans could chant with them the Sanskrit verses of the *Sundarya Lahari* that he had taught us many years ago, that they had asked if we wanted to see Bholi Baba's place of death.

All this time Swamiji pretended to read the paper. "Hmmp" he said as he listened carefully to everything Theresa told him. He looked over the paper's edge again. "Did you see it?"

"Yes, Swamiji, I did. Many of the students did not know what it was, but Panditji kindly told a few of us where we were."

"Hmmp," he said again. "What did you think?"

"Well, Swamiji, I wanted to know why you dropped your body when you were Bholi Baba. You were so young. Why did you take another body?"

Swamiji squirmed on the sofa. He cleared his throat and said, "Oh, Tree, you know. You know me."

"Please tell me, Swamiji, because I really want to know."

Finally he put the paper down on the table and looked at her. "Tree, I was doing experiments, many experiments. I wanted to know if I could drop my body and take on another."

"And you did," said Theresa.

"Yes," answered Swamiji slowly.

"Will you do that again this time?" Theresa demanded again.

"No, not again. It is not so easy to take a body from the river any more. The government has regulations around death these days and bodies are hard to come by."

Theresa told him that she liked his present body and thought he should keep it a while longer. "If you do change to a new one," she asked him, "would you please keep your beautiful eyes?"

"OK," he said, laughing at her. "Hey, Tree," he said, drastically changing the subject, "your sofa is getting old now. Maybe I should throw it out!"

Theresa went right into her role in the on-going sofa drama, insisting that Swamiji return her sofa because she could not live without it. When the banter between them ended, one of Swamiji's secretaries entered the room and was asked to read him the latest press release on the new medical college. We all worked on the writing a bit, took some photos, and then quietly left, allowing Swamiji some rest.

Back at the ashram, we got into the rhythm of the retreat our teacher had requested we undertake amidst the uninterrupted tranquil atmosphere. The rainy season was over and it was surprisingly cooler than we had anticipated, perfect for rest and practice. We spent our days reading, pulling weeds in the flower beds, walking along the river, doing our meditation practice, and, of course, spending time with our beloved teacher.

Swamiji, who had insisted that she was a natural, had told Kamal to raise pigeons after several were given as a gift to the ashram. Since then a small flock of them had roosted happily on the second floor rooftop outside Swamiji's room. They danced their strange dances, cooed and fluttered as Kamal took care of them. She seemed to know exactly what each bird wanted. We were enchanted by her stories of the harrowing escapes of her winged trust from the omnivorous evil hawks that circled overhead dreaming of pigeon lunches, and we finally decided that Kamal herself had begun to resemble a pigeon. Swamiji loved the idea, and Kamal happily entertained all of us with her rendition of pigeon behavior.

One afternoon Swamiji told us that he wanted to give us a new initiation into the higher practice of our tradition. We were instructed to fast in preparation and Theresa was told that she had a special requirement.

"Before I can initiate you, you have to finally sign over your sofa to me! I don't want any karma hanging over me because of it." Then, with his tongue firmly in cheek he walked past her saying, "If you don't sign it over, you don't get higher initiation."

Early on Thursday morning, in the midst of the solemnity of our next spiritual step, Theresa signed a small sheet of paper giving up her rust sofa to her teacher to do with whatever he wished. He nodded, accepted the paper, and walked with us along the Ganges, about a quarter mile west of the ashram. There, at the water's edge, he chanted the blessing, whispering instructions for a new practice, and laid his hands on our heads. "Return to me in six months," he said, and we vowed that nothing would keep us away.

The next day it was time to leave India again. We drove to the medical city and found Swamiji sitting outside in the sun wearing red robe, sunglasses, and a big, wide-brimmed straw hat. When he saw us, he immediately called us over. "Hey kids, are you leaving now?" We sat down at his feet, basking in his attention, his incredible smile. "Keep teaching," he said solemnly. "Teach at your center, at the Institute, at the universities, at the corporations. Keep teaching. You have my blessing."

He reached over to a bowl of fruit on a little wooden table near his chair and selected a red apple for each of us. "Remember that I love you very much!" We could not speak, our hearts were heavy as we reluctantly left him, waving from the window of our taxi as we drove off to our plane.

Justin and Charles with Swamiji in Rishikesh in 1996

SECOND TRIP

The months in America sped by. In the midst of my teaching and writing and lecturing, thoughts of returning to our teacher filled my mind. It was never easy for all of us to leave our many projects at once, but by the end of March we could wait no longer. We ended classes, suspended appointments, put contracts on hold, left the office in the hands of a secretary. At last we were on our way to India again. We immediately found a cab at landing and drove through the long night to the ashram as the sun rose red and hot over the farmland and villages.

Prem thoughtfully gave us our same room and we immediately began our retreat. When we saw Swamiji this time, he looked extremely ill. He was weak and looked as if he were full of pain. His body looked like a shadow of the intensely strong physique he had always carried, and now all his power was focused in his intense eyes.

We were given the last steps of our practice by our master and told to continue all the work we had been doing. The doctors at the hospital insisted that Swamiji be flown to Delhi for more tests. "If you wish," he told them, allowing his students to do whatever they wanted with his weak body. One test after another revealed nothing; the doctors could not understand why his entire body was shutting down. Still, we had all seen the incredible power of this man to bring himself back into vibrant health. We wanted it to happen again and so we believed it would.

The police had closed all the highways in the area because of a general strike by the rebels demanding statehood. Guerrilla activity erupted here and there as shops closed, busses ceased running, and armed guards multiplied overnight. We continued our practice, praying for Swamiji's safety whenever we could not use the roads to reach him.

The evening before we had to leave India again, Swamiji came by car to the ashram to see us. "I came just for you," he said, looking terribly weak. We wanted to do something for him who had done so much for us, but he only smiled at us. "Everything is all right. Don't worry. Everything is right."

He called us up to his rooftop patio and we sat with him as the sun rose up over the river, the pigeons cooed in the background, and the dogs guarded the entrance below. Speaking seemed difficult for him, but his eyes were full of love. We gently massaged his hands as he whispered to us not to worry. Before we could ask the questions we needed to know, he answered them carefully, one by one. "You are doing the work the sages want you to do. Keep doing it. You are being guided by me and the others. Do not be afraid. We will be together again, don't worry."

We sat with him as long as we could, damning our plane schedule and not caring if we missed our flight. Finally he smiled at us and whispered, "You go now. I love you." One at a time we knelt to touch his feet as he laid his hands on our heads and said, "God bless you."

On the stairway Theresa burst into tears and could not be comforted.

On Wednesday, November 13, 1996, our entire world was shaken to its foundations. The call from India came in the morning. I stood at my desk not believing the words. Slowly, carefully, I laid the receiver into its cradle and turned to Theresa. "You need to sit down. I have sad news."

But she looked at me intently and said, "I know already. Swamiji has left his body." She had had a powerful dream that morning in which Swamiji had said good-bye to her.

We cried together for a few minutes and then tried to contact Charles, working in Washington. He had telephoned a few hours earlier convinced that something had happened and that Theresa would need him, but he had been assured that all was well.

When we finally reached Charles and shared our sad announcement, we all immediately decided that we would fly to India once more. Swamiji had "dropped his body," as the yogis say, near midnight. The news was incomprehensible at first, portions of our mind saying it could not have happened. He could not have died with us not there. In the midst of our sadness, however, we realized that this was the way Swamiji had wanted to leave: simply, quietly, and without fanfare. Our students joined us for a memorial at the Alpha Institute, and then, because we needed to be in the place he loved so much, we made plans to fly to India. We wanted to personally bring our respect to the one who had changed our lives forever.

Once again appointments were postponed, work canceled, tickets purchased. But now, as if to test our determination, adversity waited around the corner. We found we could not get a visa in time to arrive for Swamiji's cremation. It was too late for mailing visas; they could only be issued that quickly in person. So I flew to Chicago with our passports and awoke the Indian consulate while Charles and Theresa packed my bag and theirs and taxied to the airport. I landed in the Minneapolis airport two hours before our takeoff for India, just as they did due to a faulty cab driver. Boarding the plane for our direct flight to Germany to connect for India, we were informed that instead we were going to Detroit. After a four-hour layover, we flew not to Germany, but to Amsterdam. Our meals were not put on the flight; the attendants had no record of my ticket so I had to sit in the extra seat in back. After another layover in Holland we flew to Germany, assured that we would still make out connections for India. In Frankfurt, two airlines pulled us up on the computer as arranged, but Air India declared that we were not in their computer and gave our seats to Indians instead. We were assured we would get on their next plane. Hours passed. When we lined up to board the last plane to Delhi, once again we were mysteriously not in the computer and our places were given to others.

This was evolving into a classic pilgrimage—full of unforeseen obstacles, delays, extra costs, and illogical events. We were committed to our goal in spite of it all, so I thought, "Whatever merit can be found in this ordeal I offer to the sages; I'm not going to worry, I'm just going to plow on and stay alert."

Since the airline would not compensate us for meals or a hotel room, we were on our own. We went to get our bags and found they were lost. An hour and a half later, the handlers found them and we checked into an airport hotel. "Swamiji, this trip is yours; do what you will with all that's going on," we prayed.

The only room available in the hotel had a broken air system, making sleep difficult. The next morning, we boarded a Lufthansa plane for India, arriving at 3:30 AM in New Delhi. Our confirmed taxi had already returned to Rishikesh since we were a day late, so we had to bargain for another one, finally traveling northward into the early morning sunrise with a bill for both taxis. The entire ordeal distracted us from the anguish we felt about Swamiji's departure; we were too exhausted to think about anything.

A somber mood filled the air at the ashram. Prem tearfully embraced us, Kamal hugged us, looking more pale than usual. We listened to the events of Swamiji's passing. Since March he had been officially diagnosed with cancer. The doctors were baffled, however, by the way his affliction was rampant throughout the entire body; they could not diagnose the kind of cancer he was suffering with. I remembered Swamiji's question years before asking why ordinary people were getting cancer when it was the yogis' chosen disease.

The night passed and I arose upset. A rumble of inexplicably mixed emotions—sadness, anger, frustration, and who knows what, filled my person. I jumped into a conversation with Theresa and Charles while waves of anger burst the words out of my mouth. An emotional pressure heaved through my chest for several minutes producing endless tears as I spoke. "I didn't want him to die, not that way. It was unfair to go through all that excruciating suffering. If only I had known! But there was nothing I could do." Slowly, the sobbing ebbed. I didn't want to hold him by my weeping. Thoughts of his freedom from pain finally softened my sense of loss. His body was gone, but that was not the end of Swami Rama. He lived on; we weren't abandoned. My mind kept returning to that conviction. I apologized to my colleagues, knowing that they were equally suffering.

Charles read to us a passage that had caught his attention the night before. The scholarly author stated that when a great yogi requests cremation rather than burial, as Swamiji did, it means that he will reincarnate in three months' time. We sat silently, looking at each other and wondering if our teacher would follow that prescription.

After lunch, Kamal came to our room. She did not waver, but gave us instruction in a voice more like Swamiji's than we had ever heard. "You must go to Tarkeshwar," she said firmly. "Go now, while you are here."

Swamiji had always spoken with a fervent reverence for that area, emphasizing how he and his master had spent time there. The last time we saw our master he had told us, "I will take you to Tarkeshwar. I want to go there with you."

We all picked up on the urgency of Kamal's voice and immediately packed some clothes, grabbed sleeping bags, and called a taxi. We drove for the next five hours, rising and curving higher and higher into the beautiful mountains. The bright, clear day sparkled. Butterflies, singularly and in pairs, crisscrossed over our taxi. I felt a fresh, energetic joy, knowing that we were heading for an area dear to Swamiji's heart. The pilgrimage was not over; perhaps it was just beginning.

We visited Landsdowne, where Swamiji had established a college, and bought vegetables and rice before continuing up the mountain. For the next two hours, we wove back and forth on dusty roads through the magnificent scenery, peering down at the verdant valleys, following the distant river tributaries that snaked their way southward from their Himalayan source.

Within a half hour of our destination, I wanted to repeat a favorite mantra, but as I began internally uttering the initial syllables, a different mantra emerged in my mind and would not leave. Surprised, I dismissed the mistake and began more deliberately. Again, the intruding mantra came forth in my mind so I decided to continue with the persistent arrival. When I finished a mala, I turned to Theresa commenting on what had happened. Before I could tell her which mantra was in my mind, she already knew it because she had the same experience. Was this a portent of surprises?

The taxi curved into a small hollow and pulled to a stop. The weather was cool and the sky was gray. We walked downhill through a forest trail until we came to a small clearing where the open arms of smiling Swami Hariharananda surrounded us with hugs. Bearded, nearly six feet tall, his slender body belied his age. Somehow he had known we were coming. He was the keeper of this sanctuary, assigned ten years ago by our teacher to this work. Quite focused, cheerful, with an irrepressible sense of humor, he was utterly devoted to the master. I instantly liked the man and felt at ease with him. He took us up a small cement stairway and showed us into the little room that Swamiji always used.

We walked down the hill from the ashram and were immediately encircled by gigantic pine trees, some soaring eight stories high, spreading from us in a ripple-like pattern into the forest. Awed by their appearance, I realized, surprised, that I was totally devoid of sorrow. In the strangely wonderful atmosphere of Tarkeshwar, I felt the presence of my teacher and knew that he lived.

Charles led us around the ancient temple, ringing the bells as we walked the traditional three times around. The six-hundred-year-old Shiva temple's circular structure was small, ten feet in diameter. We sat facing the burning flame before an old crumbling stature of Shiva, closing our eyes for meditation.

As I sat in the dark temple, three bright, circular radiances lined up vertically before me. I felt their presence in the center of my forehead. The intensity filled my entire person with such lightness and vigor that I did not want to leave the place. Gradually, as the intense power dimmed, I followed Theresa and Charles to the adjacent temple dedicated to the Divine Feminine. As I sat down in this sacred space, I thought I would say a healing mantra. Instead a mantra to the Divine Mother spontaneously came forth from my memory and repeated in my mind one hundred and eight times.

I reflected later that the temples represented a sacramental presence of the two esoteric principles of reality—male and female, the central symbolism of the entire universe. In a way, these sacred grounds comprised a sense of wholeness. It was filled with a profound peace that we could not evade, and a charged feeling of joyful lightness permeated everywhere.

The next day we climbed a large hill and perched on top, viewing the valleys below and the snow-capped range away to the north. I spied two reddish-black hawks circling on the rising air currents above the valley floor. I acknowledged them and invited them over, and they gradually widened their patterns and veered toward us, one flying directly over me and the other angling off to watch his partner. Huge bees and butterflies frolicked near us as we sat for meditation. Flowers bowed their heads in the mountain breeze.

Our few days passed too quickly. Swami Hariharananda escorted us through the upper valley path, stopping before the Shiva trident-shaped tree, the oldest in the area, and on to a plateau which jutted out above the north valleys. Here our teacher had sat years ago, composing his diaries with the breathless range of the Himalayas calling to him.

As we retreated along the path toward the ashram, green parrots and small birds darted across the crevasse. The renunciate smoothly led us off to the right and down into the gorge and then climbed steeply back up to an opening in the mountainside. We entered the cave of our teacher. This was where Swamiji had lived for many months at a time, where he had performed *sadhana*, where the spirits had brought him food and grace. In its special beauty we closed our eyes and meditated while the sun began its slow descent.

We sat on the edge of the pool next to the ashram and exchanged stories with our host. He told us of the ashram's history, of *sadhus* who had come here for centuries to perform their austerities, of the mysterious chanting and music that one could hear radiating from the temple in the quiet of the night, of the five-headed serpent who lived in the water where we sat. One day, he told us, as he was washing his clothes, that incredible eighteen-foot creature suddenly sprang above the water and undulated up and down, dancing upon the surface. In the most beaming of smiles, the swami offered us his summary observation of these grounds, "Here, two plus two equals five."

The energy of the place was so intense that we could barely sleep. We lay in the pitch black of the room doing practice; we walked under the intensity of stars to the temple to sit in meditation. We felt Swamiji and his master everywhere.

My sorrow was gone. I was healed, feeling aligned with life. Coming to this place had filled me with blessings. Our energy sought the future anew, for the master had encouraged us to continue in our multiple careers, telling us that they would be the vehicles for the sages' intentions for humanity.

We traveled back to Rishikesh and visited the room in which Swamiji had given up his body. We greeted our guru brothers and sisters who had joined the work over the years. We watched the procession of holy ones who came to the formal memorial service fifteen days after the death. We threw our offerings in the huge fire pit with the other mourners. We sat again by our initiation spot at the Ganges.

Then we returned to America and named our property Ram Nagar, the home of The Alpha Institute of Learning and Spirituality. At our teacher's request, we continued the work of the tradition of the Himalayan Sages, knowing that we were blessed indeed. Our pilgrimage was complete; the new one had just begun.

The Immortal Master

I stood in front of a large room teaching yoga philosophy to the students who filled every seat. Swamiji, wearing his ochre robe, entered the room, checked that the teachings were going on, and then walked out. When I turned back to my work, there was a large, blue egg before me. It glittered in the light, as if it were something very precious. I knew it was mine.

I AWOKE WITH A START, realizing that it was the ninth day of the ninth month, exactly twenty-five years since the day I met my teacher. I had just completed the book he had asked me to write many years ago, the first major piece of work I had completed since his death

The dream stayed on my mind all day. I liked the idea of my year of work being symbolized by an egg, something that holds life, something that will grow into something else, much larger and more important than the effort that went into it. I was satisfied with the work I had done and mentally offered this blue egg to my teacher on the anniversary of our meeting.

Later that day, a friend and colleague who admired Swami Rama for his spiritual writings and demonstrations at the scientific level, spoke about how instrumental my teacher had been in making yoga less of a suspicious anomaly to American culture and institutional religion. Listening to his praises of Swamiji's contributions in changing American thinking, I realized that he appraised Swami Rama as a raja yogi *par excellence*. He was undeniably that. But my professor friend did not know about the full magnitude of Swamiji's world career.

"Tom, let me tell you a few activities that depict more about the kind of individual Swami Rama was." I told him then about the man I knew, one of the most important yogis of the century.

"In the early '90s, while quite ill, he erected a medical city for the mountain people near Dehradun, India, which combined newly accredited schools in medicine, pharmacy, and nursing, along with research laboratories and herbal experimentation.

"Starting from scratch, in 1989, he took about 280 barren acres and in less than four years—which is impossible by Indian construction standards alone—erected a modern 500 bed hospital with apartments for the nursing and maintenance staff and houses for the doctors.

"He also healed. He was a homeopathic physician who had delivered more than two hundred babies, had studied India's indigenous medicine called ayurveda, and trained with yogis who were adepts in the ancient healing methods. The countless number of people he healed would fill volumes; hospital doctors sought his adivce before major operations. He inspired Western medical personnel to contribute their expertise to the medical city. While he was fulfilling this dream for the Indian people, he constantly dealt with opposition and sabotage. Over the years, I always noted enormous opposition to his efforts.

"That accomplishment was only his most recent public one. A study of his philanthropy would include establishing Liberal Arts colleges and eye clinics, organizing ecological pledges for preserving the Himalayan forests, along with endowing dozens and dozens of higher education scholarships for students all over the world. Most of that charity never will get publicity; probably it shouldn't. I know personally of six American students for whom he picked up the monthly tuition and housing charges for four years and more. He knew how to organize and delegate, inspire trust and create new civil enterprises. Conflict management skills were as natural for him as attracting the affection of children. He sponsored artists, (being an oil painter himself), made loans to people without demanding return payment, and was sought after by bankers, entrepreneurs, inventors, and politicians, not necessarily for his spiritual acumen, but for his uncanny business sense. His government awarded him the country's highest award, The *Bharat Ratna* (The Jewel of India) for his extraordinary scientific and humanitarian contributions, but he humbly refused to accept it so as not to draw attention to himself."

"He studied in the West at Oxford and in Germany, visited and lectured in more than fifty-six countries, possessed a road engineering certificate, was a superb chef, loved to play polo, trekked all his life through the high mountains, was at home with horticulture, and raised show-class roses and cacti. He assisted people to immigrate to other countries, finding sponsors and employment for them. He enjoyed sports, composed and published poetry, sang professionally, and wrote dozens of books on yoga philosophy, psychology, spiritual practice, and music. He was a connoisseur of jewels, rugs, fine teas, and fabrics.

"My apologies, Tom, but at the moment these are some of his contributions to humanity that I can recall. I am aware that I know only some of his interests," I said, looking keenly into his eyes, "but I am aware that there are many more."

He started to shake his head slowly back and forth, "I had no idea of the caliber of this man," He said, thinking carefully. Then he almost shouted with delight. "He was really into matter!" Then he smiled and energetically pumped his fist as if to make a point for his audience of one.

"Many spiritual masters inspire great undertakings in their students without themselves necessarily getting their hands 'dirty,' if you know what I mean," Tom said. "That's all right, I suppose. But your master seemed to get right down at street level and move the dirt around. You know, Justin, he's truly special for our times. Forgive me, I don't mean to tell you, but Swami Rama's life says something that I have never heard before."

"Absolutely!" I exploded, not being able to wait any longer as I picked up his energy. I could have hugged him then, for I saw real understanding in his face and heard it in his words. Tom had long been fully dedicated to his own path and often shared with me the inspirations he received through dreams. I highly respected his opinions.

"For me, Tom, Swami Rama embodied the philosophy of life he spoke about. It was a philosophy that ennobled humanity. I tried for years to fault him, to find some drastic flaw of inconsistency, but to no avail. What made his activities ring true for me was his blazing passion for life. In the last few years before he left for India in the '90s, he said to me, 'Love without an object, Justin. Love life.'

"I thought I had heard many radical statements by this man, but this one struck me the most. My reaction to his words told me that there was something there that I needed especially to learn.

But I pondered how one could transcend loving specific objects and simply love. It didn't seem to make sense to me, so I tried to rationalize his words as nice poetry. That was wrong. One night during my practice, my mind went off on a tangent and I was back with the question again. I scanned the various episodes of my teacher's life and I saw clearly that he had embraced whatever life presented, not in a naive sense, but as honestly and shrewdly as he could. He embraced life with all its setbacks and problems and loved it without question, the way a mother unconditionally loves her children. I realized that one cannot live that way unless one is completely fearless."

"Your teacher was a tantra master," Tom said, surprised by his insight.

"What else, my friend?" I answered. "Swamiji was equally at home in the realms of matter and spirit while acknowledging their subtle differences. Since he honored them, they whispered their ancient secrets to him. Because his inner devotion celebrated the universe as essentially sacred, he was entrusted to play with nature's energies. Mother Nature gave him her entire playground for the multiple missions and epochal activities he was sent to accomplish. I recall that around the buildings at his new medical complex, an enormous variety of flowers and shrubs from gardening zones three through eleven were impossibly thriving. His secret resource must have been his devotion to the sacred matrix of the universe, the Divine Mother. His personal experiences of her as Durga, Saraswati, Tara, and many other forms quickened her own qualities in him. He acknowledged that the glories he had tasted in his life were hers. With her abiding presence, life and love, knowing and being, action and silence all came together, manifesting in him through his creative endeavors. How could the Mother refuse her son anything?"

The energy between us quieted down and we both looked at each other knowingly. "You know, Tom, through Swamiji's teachings and influence upon my life and studies, one could say that I profess a holistic theology based on a tantric methodology. As a result, I read both Christian and world scriptures differently, using the paradigm of a sage to interpret the meaning.

We said good-bye and walked thoughtfully away.

REFLECTIONS

My story is nearing its closure, but only on one level. I want to share some reflections upon my teacher's life and scientific contributions, both the formal ones registered under laboratory conditions as well as the spontaneous ones, equally amazing, equally valid.

Unless we pierce through the data to the cause behind these new landmarks in human excellence, its subject will remain simply a glittering episode for the archives of biofeedback. One has to look beyond what scientists label the hard core physical data of Swami Rama's experiments—the thermistor readings, the printed brain wave patterns, the blood pressure calculations, heart rate recordings, the x-rays of rooms through waxed eyes—amazing as they are. The data, including undisclosed experiments that Menninger will hopefully reveal one day, is indisputable. My point is that the profundity of Swami Rama erodes if we only admire his past presence by these recorded measurements.

This saint walked among us as a consummate human being, a rare virtuoso working in the holy medium of the life force. His mission was utterly unique. To put his life into context, we have to search out those fabulous mythologies that speak of heroes and heroines emerging throughout history as a challenge to adversarial forces that would restrain humankind's advancement. An impresario of life enhancing capacities, he appealed to the destitute as well as the wealthy. His words chimed in our hearts, recalling the forgotten music of our true nature. He sang about the stars, the ocean, the woods in his poetry, beckoning them to resound with their healing tunes of enchantment to call us beyond the clatter of our stress-filled world. He listened to the ancient sounds of the sages and joined with them in a chorus that blesses our existence. Coming from his lectures, we found ourselves octaves above the noise of the streets, hearing perhaps for the first time the eternal music of our true homeland.

Swamiji's sole endeavor was to awaken us to what we could be, not to comfort us as we were. He redefined the somber tones of holiness and freshened them with a panache that defied categorization. He wanted his students to be decisive about life and not resort to sanctimonious excuses whenever struggles became apparent. Over the years I have found that we don't need dark reminders of our plight; we need the scintillating vigor and beauty of our unimagined destiny which that sage made so palpable in his own person. The charm, the joy, the wisdom that thousands saw in his freedom mirrored our own, even when we were too dim to recognize it.

When first hearing his awesome statement—"The entire body is within the mind, but the mind is not completely within the body"—I felt cheered in my own speculation about the colossal frontiers of human consciousness in contrast to the orthodox limitations of the human mind that I had learned in modern philosophical and theological writings. The statement flashed in my mind as a summary principle that illuminated much more than his scientific career. It was a postulate of awareness that formed the basis for all the other experiments of his life. This radical clarification of the relationship between human consciousness and its body provoked fruitful inquiries that scientific research until now has neglected to pursue. Swamiji's declaration echoed the perennial truths that he experienced, not without struggle, in his training.

As he often said, "After learning comes practice, then assimilation, then direct experience." It is an utterly simple methodology that rings evidently true as we learn first-hand by placing ourselves in the dynamics of living. It became patent to me that the ancient practice of uniting oneself to life in body, mind, and spirit promoted an expansion of self-awareness that redefined one in the eternal terms that characterized so much of Swamiji's encouragement to us. "I've done it," he would exclaim, "and you can too."

In commenting on life in all its wonder, which was his chief topic of conversation, Swami Rama elaborated to us an understanding of everyday human nature that had its roots in the sacred utterances of the sages, those fabulous men and women who had traveled in the inner space where few had gone before. Their words, which exceed the grandeur of most bibles I have perused, did not entice him as much, however, as the truth of their worth, which he had accepted not because of their authority, but by the experience of his life force. He tested their veracity in his own experience. His body, mind, spirit became the three-fold proving ground of eternal truth. He could then live and speak from the authority of experience, as truth should always be presented. For him these ancient statements were not taken on faith, but pulsated from his heart as emissions of reality. To Swamiji, life itself had opened its fountainhead of truth, *paravidya*, the transcendental knowledge that enlivens one's entire being. He winked at us with its message, beckoning us to follow. Not everybody winked back.

"People try to measure the universe with the foot rule of reason," he often lamented. Swamiji accepted the fact that we ordinarily live in a three-dimensional world. He knew that as a culture we had a healthy appreciation for empirical verification. He found Westerners to be down-to-earth people with a strong work ethic, but learned that when we put reason and sense verification together we believe that we have the best of both worlds. Swamiji once asked a Russian audience, "After you successfully complete your five year plan, will all your questions about the meaning of life be fulfilled?" The officials cut short the remainder of his scheduled lectures.

Swamiji never downgraded the rational side of the mind; he wanted us to probe continuously with it until we bumped into its borders and realized that our genuine questions about life were still unanswered. He hoped that we would contend with the paradox that reason raised questions that it could not answer. "Perhaps," he would tease, "your reasonable questions have originated from another unknown portion of your mind. What's that all about?"

He had shown that yoga and some of the Himalayan tradition could be examined and vindicated within the domain of scientific rationalism. He had indicated with familiar empirical terms how he was working with his mind and body up to a point. The laboratory technology could substantiate his empirical claims for yoga, and the accumulation of his laboratory experiments demonstrated its scientific verification. The challenge loomed, however, since the conventional medical/physical model of scientific reasoning can't explain most of the data he presented. The reason for this incapacity is that rationality, by its very nature, utilizes only a tiny portion of the field of consciousness. His performance in the laboratory derived from a broader spectrum of consciousness than reason could affect. He redefined human nature before the eyes of the researchers, but they refused to run with it. Although it flies in the face of our democratic education,

Swamiji proved that the cosmos has intelligible dimensions that are off limits to unaided reason. That made him suspect among many scientists.

The full explanation for the experiments performed by Swami Rama won't ever show up within the borders of any scientific model derived exclusively from sense-based reason, yet there is enough consistent empirical data in his demonstrations to force reason to respect it and analyze it as far as it is capable. Up until the '70s, medicine did not believe that most of the systems of the body communicated with each other. With the startling advances in the field of mind/body medicine, it became apparent that mind and metabolism are not strangers but intimate companions. Current science is starting to catch up with a tiny bit of ancient wisdom.

The inherent limitations of material-based science aren't the only source of resistance to the understanding of reality. There is a quaint maneuvering side to the mind that can operate independently of sensory data. Some people, I found, judged Armstrong's landing on the moon in 1969 as an entertainment hoax conjured by the media. Traveling that far in space was not within their rational framework of human endeavor. Space travel was unbelievable. Some physicists still hold Newton on a pedestal that has no room for Einstein.

In deliberations about the data of its experiences, one's ego can deliberately refuse to consider evidence. For all its accomplishments, the mind has an exasperating capacity to protect its outlook in the face of contravening facts. Deletion, distortion, and astounding generalizations are a few of the ways we tamper with evidence so that it suits our preferred outcomes. The mind, at times, has an attitude problem which it doesn't like to admit. When Jacques Monod, the Nobel laureate in biology, was asked how he could have arrived at the startling conviction that the universe and humankind were ultimately the products of chance, he told his interviewers that in his research and method-ology he had avoided any evidence that indicated the presence of order, design, or purpose!

Swamiji found out the hard way that these attitudinal impedances existed among many educated adults who refused to acknowledge the truth of his activities, even when they witnessed them. The self-regulated control of his person, his seeming ability to bypass the prevailing universal laws of physics, could not happen in their world view. The root issue there was neither objectivity nor truth, I believe, but the contravention of personal ego. Rather than broaden, adjust, or amend its way of viewing life, the ego prefers to outlaw the messenger.

"You can't persuade people to stop being foolish; you can only train them out of it," he cautioned me. Yet he brought this magnitude of awareness into play in the most hospitable opportunities. He would get so excited in assisting someone to explore their nature that he could not help but extend his encouragement in delightfully unorthodox displays. One afternoon, an enthusiastic physician met his appointment with the master at the Minneapolis Holiday Inn. As Swamiji helped him off with his winter coat, the visitor suddenly stopped his motion and a frustrated look appeared on his face.

"Is there a difficulty?" Swamiji looked puzzled.

"I have forgotten the microphone for my recorder and now I'll have to drive back home to retrieve it," the physician replied, annoyed at his foolishness.

Concerned for the man's time and his willingness to drive across the city on a snowy afternoon, Swamiji asked him to wait a moment.

"Where did you leave the speaker, exactly? the saint asked.

"In my bedroom," answered the physician.

"Where is your bedroom located?" Swamiji pressed him.

"On the second floor next to the stairs," he answered wondering at the questioning.

"Exactly where is the microphone in your bedroom?" Swamiji asked again.

The physician paused to remember and then replied, "It's on the top of the dresser next to the south window."

He was just about to ask about his host's interest when Swamiji smoothly moved his right hand from behind his back and asked with a slight triumphal smile, "Is this it?"

The physician stared wildly at the small microphone held out to him, looked up at Swamiji, then back down at his speaker. With a sigh, he slowly put on his coat, while weakly uttering, "I can't take this," and departed.

Accepting Swami Rama's gift proved too much reality for the physician's world view. Swamiji's concern cost him the man's presence, but that man will never forget the incident. We, too, are challenged by this shattering episode in an otherwise rational world. If we can't resort to reason for an explanation of his thoughtfulness for the plight of this physician, or anyone else he helped over the years, then where do we search?

The reluctance of intelligent people to stay intrigued with the saint's message has puzzled me for years. Some couldn't deny the data of their experience but they walked elsewhere. Others were reluctant to accept the experiments at face value. "Human beings can't produce these results," they insisted. What upset me even more was when good-hearted people abandoned him after reaping his love. Years later I had to admit that many aren't interested in enjoying the unknown bounty of life; they would rather play it safe by living within their own limits and their immediate agendas. They only trust the truth that supports their egos.

As I realized how difficult it is to stand before a revelation of reality that neither occurs nor is comprehensible within one's personal world view, my sympathies broadened over the years. I discovered that training people to enlarge their world view takes incredibly patient resources. "You can't force people to awaken," Swamiji would insist. "They must desire it."

How can we begin to fathom the exquisite sensitivity that allows someone to invite nature to do his bidding? How many people does the average person know that can literally withdraw terminal illness from someone and take it upon himself to expiate? Would someone not want this model of humaneness for the conflictual world? No doubt we imagine that we would embrace that superlative energy, but the hard reality is that few of us can handle that much reality when it greets us. Only tiny doses seem to be effectual. Yet without room in our world for the magical and mystical, we will continue to do what we have always done and remain with the same expectations, doubts and outcomes.

Swami Rama's mind was essentially no different from yours or mine, except that his thoughts and actions arose from a transcendental magnitude of awareness, a mega-breadth and depth of enlivening power that transfused every level of his being. There was nothing timid about his demeanor. He drew upon his immortality, not by belief as we would, but through the experience of its energy. He was privy to the universal life force that supports every being in the cosmos. This radical amplitude of self-consciousness differs from a mere change in brilliant ideas or attitude. I do not speak of an alteration in attitude. Changing one's viewpoint on life won't change one's viewpoint on life. Unless we access the princely power from which ideas, images, attitudes, and everything under the sun derives, than we have merely moved the furniture of our minds around. That task gets weary. If we want to immigrate to the celestial spaces to enjoy the liberties where sages roam, then rational endeavors are not short cuts.

"We doubt because we don't see the whole," Swamiji once emphasized. "Our rational mind does not have the capacity to see things as they are. Seeing the whole is only possible with direct experience."

It became evident, sooner or later, that "direct experience" meant surpassing reason with its discursive outlook on life. Throughout his life, Swamiji was the living evidence that reason utilizes only a portion of the field of consciousness. The discursive mind, however, has a hard time admitting its limitations. It gets dazzled by its own success or distrustful by its failures. Being astute often brings admiration and financial rewards; careers and civil enterprises rely upon the execution of shrewd decisions; society prizes its reasoned plans and smart policies. But with all the notoriety, there is a vested interest for one's ego to assume itself to be the exclusive guide to life. The archetypal myth of Narcissus lurks in the ego's shadow. The rational mind easily falls in love with itself.

In this century alone the rational West has produced, among other items, the greatest abundance of material goods, the bloodiest wars of history, the most destructive weapons imaginable, and a rapacious disregard for nature. The technological prowess of our era surpasses the dreams of the industrial revolution, and yet there is more degenerative disease than ever before in medical history. Billions and billions of dollars, for example, have been spent vainly for a material cure for cancer. The sheer barbarism of chemotherapy is proposed as the best treatment, while other natural non-invasive interventions are banished because they fall outside scientific reason's conventional paradigm.

"Research in cancer is going in the wrong direction." Swamiji mentioned one evening. "They are ignoring the mind." This was said by the only individual who proved under scientific conditions that he could generate and dispel cancer cells at will anywhere in his body.

Side by side with the mechanical advances of modern existence is a profound skepticism. Confusion and anxiety about the world's future leave people questioning the ultimate coherence of existence. A sense of the transience of life dominates more strongly and easily today than in the past. That is why the implications of the life and experiments of this saint open hints, powerful clues, and encouraging data that foretell incredible possibilities for our freedom and peace of mind.

People sometimes ask me why nothing has been done to explore further what Swami Rama proved to us. I have thought about that question for years. My replies seem incomplete, so let me recall what the master once said: "No one wants to learn. I'm here and no one comes. People respect and admire me, they come with their worldly problems expecting me to assist them. Some want a spouse. Others want blessings for their children. I do for them as well as I can, but few want to follow the path of wisdom."

Many know this man beyond his scientific prowess. Some keep the secrets of his friendship tucked away in their hearts from the rest of the world. Some know him with an intimacy of feeling that exceeds the astute boundaries of any science. They are the wiser ones. I know one cozy, warm-hearted lady in the Midwest who was asked by the saint to act as treasurer of an organization year after year for decades. No fanfare on her part; just quiet dedication. He knew she could be trusted; she knew her love for him made it all worthwhile. They had an understanding. He honored the saint in her; she saw the genius of his holy heart.

This man from the world's highest mountains was an ambassador of the human spirit, a delegate from realms of awareness that angels envied, a troubadour who wrote poetry to the universe and chanted the name of the divine until he forgot his surroundings. He was a visionary with a message to mend the wounds of humankind. A traveler of his times, he overcame the struggles in his path and vindicated for us all the universal quest for the ultimate meaning of life.

I feel that he delighted in the role of Krishna, the declared foe of selfishness and ignorance. He sought after his students with a liberating agenda for their well-being. By hook or by crook, vigorously and deftly, he sought to remove a host of impediments from people caught and dragged down by their follies. He constantly cast us into circumstances where we could meet those sides of ourselves that evaded detection. I was reminded recently by a friend that Swamiji's prodding, rambunctious manner with some people, his scathing castigations of an innocent student in front of the person for whom it was really meant, his repeated impassioned efforts to retrieve someone from making a disastrous decision, always included a silent service to each and every individual that crossed his path desiring help. He resolved upon himself, in mysterious ways that escape my comprehension, the chores of their karmic debt. He could not help himself; he could only love people. Is this not the enlivening compassion of the true Bodhisattva?

Some months after Swamiji dropped his body, a strange dream occurred that made me ponder again the wonder of my teacher.

> *I was in a large full classroom, hurring to the rear of the room to see two women who wanted to ask me a question. As I spoke with them, an elderly sadhu with a small boy passed me and slipped into seats on the aisle. Both were dressed in white clothes and gray shawls. Someone then handed me my basket of seven large, multicolored eggs.*
>
> *As I walked down the aisle on my way to my seat, the familiar voice of my teacher called out, "Hey, Justy, what's up? Where are you going?"*
>
> *I turned with surprise to find that Swamiji's voice had come from the smiling face of the little boy with shining black hair and big brown eyes. Spontaneously I knelt down on one knee before the sage and the boy and handed over my eggs to them. The boy smiled his acceptance.*
>
> *Then I stood up, peered over the crowd, and joined Charles and Theresa for the evening lecture.*

GLOSSARY

ABHYASA *Systematic spiritual practice.*

AGNI *Fire.*

AJAPA JAPA *Repetition of the mantra done spontaneously without effort.* AMRITA *Ambrosia; nectar*

BIJA *Seed; indicator; root of knowledge.*

CHAKRAS *Spiritual centers separating one level of consciousness from another.*

CHANDOGYA UPANISHAD *A major Upanishad forming the last eight chapters of the Sama-Veda.*

CHITTA *The store house of memory; the unconscious mind.*

DARSAN *Being in the presence of a holy person or deity to have a glimpse; a way of looking at reality.*

DEVATMA SHAKTI *The power of individual divine consciousness.*

DEVAS *Bright beings; celestial beings; shining ones.*

DIVINE MOTHER *The absolute power of the universe.*

DIVYA CHAKSU *The third eye.*

GANAPATI MANTRA *A mantra to propitiate the deity Ganesh.*

GAYATRI MANTRA *A mantra of purification and protection, considered by many to be the most sacred verse of the Vedas.*

GURU *One who dispels the darkness of ignorance; a spiritual guide.*

HATHA YOGA *The yoga comprising the first five rungs of Raja Yoga: Yama, Niyama, Asana, Pranayama, Pratyahara*

IDA *One of the three nadis or energy currents, corresponding to lunar energy and situated on the left side of the spinal column.*

JAPA *Repetition of the mantra.*

KAPALBHATI *A type of pranayama in which one exhales forcefully and inhales normally.*

KARMA *Action.*

KUNDALINI *Primal force latent at the base of the spinal column.*

MAHA SHAKTI *The kundalini.*

MALA *A string of 108 beads.*

MANTRA *A sacred sound.*

MAYA *The force through which the infinite is experienced as being finite.*

MRTYUNJAYA MANTRA *The conqueror of death mantra*

NADI SHODANAM *Alternate nostril breathing.*

Pandit *A wise or highly respected scholar.*

PINGALA *One of the three major energy channels, situated along the right side of the spinal column, corresponding to the solar energy in the body.*

PRANA The life force.

PRANA VIDYA Knowledge of prana.

PRANAYAMA Expansion of or voluntary control over the pranic force.

PRASAD A gift, usually food, that has been offered and blessed.

RAJA YOGA The royal path. The eightfold path as described by Patanjali in the Yoga Sutras.

SADHANA Spiritual practice.

SADHU One who has chosen to devote his life to spiritual practices.

SAMADHI Spiritual absorption; the eighth rung of raja yoga.

SAMKHYA The most ancient system of Indian philosophy.

SAMKHYA KARIKAS Textbook on Samkhya philosophy.

SAMSKARAS Subtle impressions of past actions.

SANYASIN A renunciate.

SATSANG Company of the saints.

SHAVA A corpse.

SHIVA The Supreme Reality. Pure consciousness, existence, and bliss.

SHAKTI The dynamic power of The Supreme Reality.

SIDDHI A power or accomplishment that is achieved through yogic practices that usually accompanies inner development.

SMRTI Memory.

SRI VIDYA A treatise that establishes the relationship of microcosm with macrocosm.

SRI YANTRA A symbolic diagram of the human structure and the cosmos both manifested and unmanifested.

SUTRA A unifying thread, a set of aphorisms or rules that comprise many of the traditional spiritual texts.

SVETASVATARA UPANISHAD Part of the Yajur-Veda.

SWARA SWARODHYAM The science of prana.

TANTRA Method. The transformation of obstacles into means.

UPANISHAD The end of the Vedas. Texts that should be studied at the feet of the teacher.

VAIRAGYA Dispassion or non-attachment.

VAYU Literally the air element, that which flows.

VEDAS The source book of revealed wisdom, experienced by the great sages in deep meditation.

VIDYA Knowledge.

VRITTIS Modifications of mind; thought constructs.

YOGA The practical system of Indian philosophy systematized and codified by the sage Patanjali.

YOGA NIDRA Yogic sleep. Remaining awake while the body sleeps.

YOGA SHASTRAS Collection of stories about yogis.

BOOKS FROM YES INTERNATIONAL PUBLISHERS

Yoga and Spirituality:
>
> Walking with a Himalayan Master: An American's Odyssey
> Justin O'Brien
> A Meeting of Mystic Paths: Christianity and Yoga
> Justin O'Brien
> The Living Goddess
> Linda Johnsen
> The Yogi: Portraits of Swami Vishnu-devananda
> Gopala Krishna

Self-Transformation:
>
> Pigs Eat Wolves: Going into Partnership with Your Dark Side
> Charles Bates
> The Wellness Tree: Six Step Program for Optimal Health
> Justin O'Brien
> Ransoming the Mind: Yoga and Modern Therapy
> Charles Bates

Women's Spirituality:
>
> The Spiral Path: Explorations in Women's Spirituality
> Theresa King
> The Divine Mosaic: Women's Images of the Sacred Other
> Theresa King
> Daughters of the Goddess: The Women Saints of India
> Linda Johnsen
> Circle of Mysteries: The Women's Rosary Book
> Christin Lore Weber

Inspiration and Poetry:
>
> The Light of Ten Thousand Suns
> Swami Veda Bharati
> Soulfire: Love Poems in Black and Gold
> Alla Renée Bozarth